Denmark is a small country composed of the peninsula of "Jylland" (Jutland) on the top of the European continent between the North Sea and the Kattegat, and more than 200 islands, the largest of which is Sjælland (Zealand) in the east separated from Sweden by Øresund (the Sound) and Fyn (Funen) in the center of the country separated from Sjælland by Storebælt (the Great Belt) and from Jutland by Lillebælt (Little Belt). The major towns mentioned in this book are the following:

SJÆLLAND (Zealand):
København (Copenhagen): The capital of the Kingdom of Denmark on the east coast of Sjælland (Zealand), separated from Sweden by Øresund (the Sound). The author's engagement in the Resistance movement started here with contributions to the underground press and the rescue of the Jews, who were sent to Barsebäck in Sweden. After the rescue operations the group joined the sabotage organization Holger Danske as group no. 2 (HD2), which worked primarily in Copenhagen, but eventually also in Jylland (Jutland).

FYN (Funen):
Odense: The third largest town in Denmark, where the August Uprising in 1943 reached its climax. Three members of the author's group came from Odense.

JYLLAND (Jutland):
Horsens: The author's native town, where he made his first and three more attempts of sabotage.

Ålborg: The main city in Northern Jutland, of primary importance for the German-Norway contact and where the organized sabotage started.

Århus: The largest town in Jutland. A university city with close ⌐   ⌐on with the underground press and the author's group.

Kolding: Gestapo headquarters in South Jutla⌐ ˙

Esbjerg: Gestapo headquarters in West Jutla

Varde: The locals had close collaboration with   ⌐urtant operation was the sabotage of the Varde Steelworks.

Padborg: German-Danish frontier where repatriated Danes were received only a few miles from the prisoners' camp at Frøslev.

Åbenrå: Town of mixed Danish-German population, where the author's group was finally dissolved.

To the south of the Danish-German border the map shows the Bay of Lübeck, where numerous KZ prisoners were killed at the end of the war.

RESISTANCE FIGHTER
JØRGEN KIELER

RESISTANCE FIGHTER

A Personal History of the
Danish Resistance Movement
1940–1945

Translated from the Danish
by Eric Dickens

JØRGEN KIELER

gefen
publishing house בית הוצאה לאור
JERUSALEM ◆ NEW YORK

Typesetting: Jerusalem Typesetting, Jerusalem
Cover Design: S. Kim Glassman

ISBN 978-965-229-397-8

Edition   1   3   5   7   9   8   6   4   2

Gefen Publishing House   Gefen Books
6 Hatzvi Street, Jerusalem 94386, Israel   600 Broadway, Lynbrook, NY 11563, USA
972-2-538-0247 • orders@gefenpublishing.com   1-800-477-5257 • orders@gefenpublishing.com

www.israelbooks.com

Printed in Israel   *Send for our free catalogue*

With thanks to Julie Prag Grandjean for her good advice and critical appraisal of the manuscript and to the Lundbeck Fund for its generous economic support to cover the translation and publication of the book.

To my brother Flemming, in deep gratitude. Without our mutual assistance neither of us would have survived the war.

CONTENTS

PART IV: PRISONERS

INTRODUCTION

For me September 25, 1937, was an epoch-making day. I had just turned eighteen, and was living in Munich. Three months earlier I had begun a sabbatical year studying languages and literature in Munich, Paris and Cambridge. But that particular day, my mind was occupied by problems quite different from those of philology. The city was in a festive mood. Hitler and his guest Benito Mussolini were being honored on his first visit to Germany, where the two leaders would be discussing the foreign policy of the Axis powers.

Along with thousands of others, I was on Königsplatz where the two dictators were being fêted by the mesmerized crowds. I had climbed up onto some grating, which held the onlookers from the exercise yard where an ss company were going to parade before the Führer and Il Duce. From there I had a marvelous view of the balcony where the two heads of state were to appear; I was only some ten or twenty yards away.

Hitler had previously visited Mussolini in Italy. There was no doubt that he was much inspired by Il Duce who had, as early as March 1919, organized his *Fascio di Combattimento* (Combat Group) to fight Communism, and had marched on Rome at the head of his followers and subsequently seized power.

In November 1923, Hitler had tried to emulate Mussolini with the Beer Hall Putsch in Munich and he too had planned to march on the capital,

Berlin in his case. But the revolt was suppressed, several people were killed, and Hitler was sentenced to five years imprisonment. As it happened, he only served one year of his sentence, which he used to start writing his book *Mein Kampf.*

Munich was the cradle of the National Socialist German Workers' Party (NSDAP, *Nationalsozialistische Deutsche Arbeiterpartei*). It was there that Hitler staged his failed coup d'état, supported by the paramilitary organization the SA (*Sturmabteilung*) with their dreary brown uniforms, and it was there that the NSDAP had its headquarters in a classical style building, built roughly a century before. This building was dubbed *Das Braune Haus* (the brown house), and Munich was called *Die Braune Stadt* (the brown city).

As I sat there, clinging pretty uncomfortably to the grating, it was not all the works of art on the Königsplatz that occupied my mind, but the host of positive and negative impressions that I had gained during my many holiday visits to Germany during my childhood and teens and now that I had become a student. I had read *Mein Kampf,* and would now see Hitler in full dress in his brown uniform, accompanied by Mussolini. The time had come for me to compare the democratic, divided and indecisive Danish society in which I had grown up and the dynamic, self-assured and seemingly unified Germany, where rearmament was in full swing, which both solved the problem of employment and gave Germany the status of a superpower, albeit one that did not tolerate any form of democracy.

The conclusions I drew from the comparison would be of seminal importance for me and my family, which comprised my father, the doctor Ernst von Führen Kieler, my mother, Margrethe, my three sisters, Elsebet, Bente and Lida, and my brother, Flemming. That is what this book is about.

I have discussed the historical background to all of this in another book, *Hvorfor gjorde I det* (Why Did You Do It? [Copenhagen: Gyldendal, 2001]) where those interested in history can read a more thorough appraisal of that aspect, including source material.

Hørsholm, April 9, 2007

Jørgen Kieler

PART I: THE STAGE IS SET

Hitler and Mussolini when they met in Munich, September 1937

CHAPTER **1**

Between Two World Wars

Peace without Danger: The Aftermath of the First World War

I was born on August 23, 1919, in the small provincial Danish town of Horsens, where my father practiced as a doctor. This was a good time to be born, only a few months after the Treaty of Versailles (on January 18 of that year), which rounded off the First World War and marked the founding of the League of Nations (February 1). There were hopes of peace and the Western powers had begun to disarm.

But peace was not absolutely guaranteed. There was still unrest in Russia, where the Communists wanted to spread their Marxist message throughout the world. On June 1, 1920, it was announced in Moscow that the aim of the Third International (the Communist régime of the time) was, by way of armed revolt, to stage a social revolution and thus establish the dictatorship of the proletariat. This background made the creation of Mussolini's *Fascio di Combattimento* more understandable.

The unrest in Eastern Europe continued with the war between Poland and the Soviet Union and the war between Greece and Turkey; things were not improved by the fact that Stalin had taken over from Lenin in January 1924. Communist infiltration was a fact in many countries and led to, for

3

instance, Great Britain breaking off diplomatic relations with the Soviet Union in 1927.

But it was especially in Germany that the Communists were out fishing in troubled waters. Social needs were great and Germany was not able to pay war reparations to the victors. This led to a temporary occupation of the Ruhr by France. Even though Hitler was pardoned and released from prison in December 1924, Communism was regarded as a much more dangerous threat to peace than Nazism. It would be necessary to normalize relations between Germany and other countries, in order to prevent the Communists seizing power.

When Hindenburg became president in 1925, fears of a Communist coup in Germany diminished and the peace process was able to continue. The occupation of the Ruhr was lifted and, in October 1925, leading politicians from France, Britain, Italy, Germany, Poland, Czechoslovakia and Belgium met in Locarno, where they agreed to respect the existing national borders in Europe. The next year, this gesture of reconciliation was ratified when on September 8, Germany was accepted as a member of the League of Nations. In 1927, the USA helped by extending a large loan to Germany, which stabilized the German economy, and in August 1928, a general peace treaty could be signed in Paris. This meant that, at last, after four years of bloody conflict, plus a decade of truce and difficult negotiations, the combatants could put the First World War behind them. I was, of course, too young to understand anything of what was going on; but it was a reality that my parents experienced and set its stamp on the upbringing I received.

The optimism that the peace treaty generated was of short duration. The Wall Street Crash of October 1929 led to an economic crisis which rapidly spread throughout Europe. We felt this also in Denmark. It is there that my personal memories begin.

The rapid rise in unemployment not only created problems for working-class families, but also for many members of the middle class. The wives of directors were obliged to start trading in tea, selling lottery tickets, and so on, in order to pay for the bread on their tables. The crisis meant that political differences were exacerbated, which was especially evident when elections were held. Torvet – the town square – in Horsens where I lived was filled with red banners. The excited speakers with balled fists let there be no doubt that the "class enemy" was the Conservative newspaper, housed right next to us, and its readership, i.e., us.

I had spent the first ten years of my life mixing with all the young boys in the area around the square. My parents were neither particularly rich nor poor, and social class differences had been an unknown concept to me. I knew that my father was much loved by his patients, mostly workers and farmers for whom he had been the family doctor for two or three generations. This social hatred that we now experienced took me completely by surprise. My parents were Conservative, but their conservatism lay, for the most part, in their attitudes to the hotly debated defense question. In contrast to the Socialists, who tended to have defeatist views with regard to the defense of Denmark, my parents were very much in favor of a strong defense policy, something which did not, however, become an issue until later.

Peace and New Dangers: *Das Dritte Reich*

Our school education included instruction in English, German, French and Latin. This opened up opportunities for contacts with the larger countries in Europe and, at a later stage, with America. This opportunity was used with gusto by my parents who, inspired by the Scout movement, would take their five children on long holidays, traveling by car around Europe. If the destination was not Scandinavia or Britain, but the European mainland, we would inevitably have to travel through Germany, which I visited for the first time as an eight-year-old, then on countless occasions afterwards, both before and after Hitler had come to power. In those days, camping was not yet a large-scale activity and organized campsites did not exist. When we wanted to pitch our tent, or obtain water, we automatically came into contact with the local population, both in the countryside and suburbs of the larger towns. We were always received very amicably and with curiosity. Germans could not afford to travel abroad and were therefore keen on fostering contacts with tourists in order to hear the news from other countries. A doctor's family with five children that traveled around Europe like gypsies was something of a rarity. We overcame the language difficulties involved, and therefore obtained a good insight into the living conditions of the average German as the banking crisis took hold of their country.

When personal information had been exchanged, the topic of conversation would move on to social and political matters. Inflation, unemployment and the inadequacies of welfare for war veterans and old people were some of the first impressions I received, and poverty was clearly reflected in the Germans' housing, clothing and food. You would often notice the tensions between workers and farmers and between young and old. In actuality, these tensions were little different from the ones we knew in Denmark; but they were that much more magnified. One thing was clear: the Communists had a substantially larger following in Germany than in Denmark. But differences were somewhat smoothed over, owing to a universal love of singing and music, and amidst all the misery you did detect a national awakening which was expressed in, for example, hiking and a love of nature. During my literary studies at the University of Munich, later on, I would have plenty of opportunity to make my acquaintance with the inspiration Germans derived from their poetry.

Against this background, it was not entirely incomprehensible that a growing number of Germans saw Hitler as the savior of the German people, someone promising a new Germany – the "Third Reich." The first German Reich had fallen apart as Napoleon took Berlin; this rose again and its revenge was to reinvent itself as the German Empire, following the Franco-Prussian War in 1871. Frederick the Great of Prussia and Bismarck became great ideals, admired both by Hitler and the German people as a whole. But now they had lost for a second time to their archenemy, France, and needed political leaders who could free Germany of her inferiority complex and poverty, which were the results of the First World War and the Versailles Treaty.

Even with my very limited overview of what was occurring in Germany in the 1930s, I did understand that a large majority of German voters brought Hitler to power in 1933. But it was equally evident to me that the German emperor and not least Bismarck were regarded, from a Danish historical perspective, as enemies, something of which huge monuments were an everyday reminder later, during my time in the concentration camp Porta Westphalica.

During our subsequent trips to Germany, we could follow the progress being made. Inflation and unemployment were brought under control and the construction of enormous stretches of motorway were proof, kilometer by kilometer, of the upswing in German fortunes. The population were again filled with renewed hope, which was understandable. Only later did people realize that behind the motorway construction and the struggle against unemployment lay a conscious policy of rearmament.

Warning lights began to flicker for me in 1934 when we traveled to

Prague. We visited Berlin and Dresden where we noticed, to our alarm, the many SA men in their brown uniforms dominating the street scene. We passed through Theresienstadt without realizing the significance that name would have in future years. It was on this trip that we saw, for the first time, that people were busy, even in the smallest town, hanging up banners with the inscription:

Juden sind hier nicht erwünscht!
("Jews are not wanted here!")

The mysterious Reichstag blaze in Berlin in February 1933 was followed by a propaganda offensive that entailed a hatred of Communists and Jews. This culminated in April of that same year in Hitler's call for a general boycott of Jewish businesses. For us, there was no clear connection between anti-Communism and anti-Semitism. Things did not become any easier when in October 1933, Hitler took Germany out of the League of Nations. At the same time as this happened, we could see placards in other cities which read:

Gemeinnutz vor Eigennutz
("Common use rather than private use")

Despite the fight against Communism, which soon broadened out to embrace the persecution of Social Democrats as well, there was no doubt that the NSDAP was also a Socialist party which, for instance, started the powerful *Kraft durch Freude* (Strength through Joy) organization, which sent many Germans to popular holiday destinations.

Total confusion ensued after the "Night of the Long Knives" on June 30, 1934, when Hitler had Ernst Röhm and his close associates murdered. We did not immediately understand that this was a quarrel between the two wings of the NSDAP: a Socialist wing, backed by the SA and strong in Berlin and northwestern Germany, and a nationalist wing, which dominated in Bavaria. It was the nationalists, with Hitler at their head, who triggered the internal revolt. The concentration camps, which were already being constructed in 1933, were soon filled with German Communists, Social Democrats, socialist-inclined Nazis and Jews.

The existence of the concentration camps became general knowledge after the purge of Röhm and his men. This was not the first political murder that the Nazis would have on their conscience, but as Hitler wished to set an example to others, censorship was eased.

These impressions, both positive and negative, that I received during our 1934 trip were confirmed the following year when we traveled to Vienna. The Austrian chancellor, Engelbert Dollfuss, had foreseen German aggression and had, to the chagrin of Hitler, banned the Austrian Nazi Party in 1933. This cost him his life. In July 1934 he was murdered, but the unrest that followed the murder was crushed, so that Hitler's dream of *Anschluss* – the annexation of Austria by Germany in order to create a Greater Germany – would have to wait. The walls of buildings in Vienna bore the scars of this revolt and were an early warning sign that Hitler's ambitions involved more than merely getting Germany back on its feet after the humiliation at Versailles.

Prelude to the Second World War

In August 1934, Hitler followed Hindenburg as head of state, and it was not long before all parties but the NSDAP were forbidden. At this point, things gathered pace. Hitler managed to make his peace with major capital interests and the Jews became the hate objects of the socialists, instead of the capitalists. At the same time, they were also blamed for Communist infiltration and Germany's defeat in the First World War.

Hitler, now backed by major capital interests, began to look at what the nation needed to do. In January 1935, Saarland voted to return to the Reich. Two months later, the German air force was recreated and Hitler proclaimed the introduction of conscription for all males. France was busy constructing the Maginot Line, but Britain was not yet ready to counter Hitler's undermining of the Versailles Treaty. In June, Britain signed a naval agreement with Germany which in effect meant that the *Kriegsmarine*, the German navy, had been reborn.

The year 1936 was no less eventful. Like a bolt from the blue, Hitler sent his troops into the demilitarized zone of the Rhineland. Britain and France could not agree whether to intervene, and their weakness was unmasked when they accepted, without protest, the capitulation of Abyssinia on May 1. In July, the Spanish Civil War broke out. British and French attempts to adopt a policy of nonintervention failed, and Hitler and Mussolini swiftly went to the aid of their new ally, Franco. The Spanish government received help from the Soviet Union, and Communists from many countries, including Denmark, volunteered.

For many Danes, however, it was difficult to choose sides in the Spanish Civil War. The triumvirate Hitler, Mussolini and Franco were not popular in Denmark, but nor were Danes enthused by the extreme left-wing groups in Spain. It was nonetheless clear that the government had been elected legitimately and that Franco was a usurper. When the Italian foreign minister, Count Ciano, visited Berlin in October, cooperation began, and this soon became known as the Berlin-Rome Axis. This cooperation was ratified and expanded, so that by November 1936, Germany, Italy and Japan had signed what was termed the "Anti-Comintern Pact" in order to counter large-scale Communist infiltration.

The dark clouds that had already been gathering since Mussolini's invasion of Abyssinia had already spread out over Africa; now they would also be seen in the Far East. Japan, which, like Germany, had left the League of Nations in 1933, now felt free to attack China and was given help by the Soviet Union, and economic aid from the USA. This was the prelude to a new world war.

As a reaction to this development, Britain and France began to cooperate in military matters. In May 1937, Neville Chamberlain succeeded Stanley Baldwin as prime minister of Great Britain, and that country began eventually to rearm. No one could know how long Hitler would continue his policies of blackmail; but there was no doubt as to his militaristic intentions. On the National Socialist party day at Nuremberg in September 1936, the agenda included Germany's right to have colonies in order to guarantee her raw materials, so that she could remain self-sufficient, but Hitler's initial aim was to unify the German people. The murder of the Austrian chancellor, Dollfuss, in 1934 already made clear that Austria would be his next target; but here he crossed paths with Mussolini. This was what their meeting in Munich in 1937 was all about, and I had the opportunity to see this event with my own eyes, hanging uncomfortably from the grating in September of that year.

Munich

After a happy childhood and a stormy youth, I left my birthplace, Horsens, in June 1937 and started my studies in Munich, living with the family of one Director Boeck, who lived with his wife and thirty-year-old son, Hermann, in Friedrichstrasse in an elegant apartment. Director Boeck was a lawyer and had also had a less successful career as a civil servant. He was a member of the NSDAP, which only emerged some while after my arrival. I do not think he was a full-blooded Nazi, but party membership was a must if he were to keep his job. Frau Boeck was a small, rotund and jovial *Hausmutter* with no opinions of her own. Their son was an eternal student of medicine, and was bitter about the fact that he had not been allowed to study as an architect. He had, however, won back an element of his self-esteem by enrolling with the SS.

I followed a series of language and literature courses at the University of Munich. The instruction was of a high quality and without any propagandistic dimension; and there was enough time to study and discuss politics in a private capacity along with other foreigners, whose views of Germany and Hitler's intentions were as vague as were my own. Reading Hitler's *Mein Kampf* did give me cold shivers down my spine, but as with so many others, I found it difficult to take it seriously. It was as absurd as Karl Marx's *Das Kapital* was long.

Alongside my studies at the university, I also studied art history privately and enjoyed the rich collections of the museums, plus the many architectural pearls of Munich. In the autumn of 1937, I witnessed the opening of the anti-Semitic exhibition *Entartete Kunst* (Decadent Art) and the opening of the new art museum, the Haus der deutschen Kunst, only a stone's throw away. At the first of these, I made my acquaintance with Emil Nolde's art and that of artists such as Barlach, Marc, Kokoschka and Kubin, all of whom displeased Hitler. It was Emil Nolde who was perhaps the main butt of his hatred.[1] A total of 1,052 of his works were confiscated, and now I was able to see some of these exhibited at the *Entartete Kunst* exhibition. In among the works of art, caricatures had been placed, as well as life-size freestanding wax figures, making fun of Jews. The Jews were held responsible for the "cultural degeneration" that the exhibition was meant to illustrate.

At the other exhibition, you could see, over the large staircase in the entrance hall, a huge portrait of Hitler on horseback in full armor with his characteristic toothbrush moustache and carrying a lance. There followed the rest of this exhibition of Aryanism. I turned around and went back to the *Entartete Kunst* exhibition. I think it was the attitude of Nazi Germany with regard to experimental and innovative art that awoke in me an interest for modern art, which at the same time immunized me against the positive and seductive impressions I had gained from Hitler's dynamic society.

The propaganda in the largest daily newspaper, the *Völkischer Beobachter*, gave rise to many discussions with my host family. *Lebensraum, Realpolitik* and *geopolitics* were the most common expressions to be found in the headlines of articles in this, the main organ of the Nazi Party, which had been chemically cleansed of concepts such as morality, justice or even decency. It took no genius to understand that these slogans covered up a growing aggression on the part of the German people. In his official capacity, Director Boeck had access to weekly press commentaries in the foreign press covering the events unfolding in Germany and Spain, and even though they were confidential, I was allowed to see them in exchange for playing rummy with my host. In 1935, the Danish press had been convinced of Hitler's peaceful intentions; but by now, Danes had grown more skeptical about developments in Germany.

The lack of correspondence between the contents of the German and foreign press was the topic of many discussions. I was made aware, for instance, of the existence of Dachau, the first concentration camp, built in 1933 near Munich. I knew virtually nothing about concentration camps. The Danish press was rather reticent with regard to explanations and was sometimes even misleading. The Berlin correspondent of *Berlingske Tidende*, a leading Danish daily, had visited a concentration camp and on April 29, 1936, he wrote a long article, setting minds at rest, stating that the camps would soon be shut down. There were not many prisoners left, and those who remained were living in good conditions.

I received no different information from Director Boeck, apart from the fact that it was there that the followers of Ernst Röhm and other political opponents were incarcerated for an indefinite period of time. Boeck did not wish to talk about the details and given the fact that most of those interned were Socialists and Jews, this whole matter was not a topic for polite conversation. There was no doubt about the fact that he feared Dachau.

On the other hand, the Spanish Civil War was something that could be talked about openly. The *Völkischer Beobachter* published scare stories and details of Communist atrocities. The news aroused feelings, especially in Catholic Bavaria, when it was told how Catholic priests were buried alive, so that their heads stuck out above the soil, after which a road roller was driven over the heads of these unfortunate victims of such torture.

I did not believe a word of these stories, and even Director Boeck doubted their veracity, but his son Hermann, who was one of the ss faithful, did credit them with an element of truth. Seven years later, I was to learn that there are no limits to human bestiality, whether it be of Communist, Nazi or religious origin.

Hitler's meeting with Mussolini in Munich on September 25, 1937, was at the height of Germany's period of revival. The aim was to make their joint foreign policies look like a triumph for Hitler. Mussolini had in fact supported the Austrian chancellor, Dollfuss, and resisted Hitler's plans for Austria. But now the time had come for a change of tack. This was a victory for Hitler which would naturally be used in the propaganda campaign. The idea was for the two dictators to give speeches to the people on Königsplatz.

Königsplatz

Hermann Boeck, who had still not graduated, wore a loyal Hitler moustache and *"die schöne schwarze ss-Uniform die die Mädchen so gerne haben* (the beautiful black ss uniform that the girls like so much)." He was to take part in the parade.

As bells were rung, the two demigods appeared out on the balcony. Hitler was wearing his usual straightforward sa brown shirt, while Mussolini was dressed up in his pale blue uniform with many medals. An expectant hush fell over the huge throngs of people; but a few minutes later, my eardrums were nearly burst by a cacophony of shouts of *"Sieg Heil!"* while thousands of arms were stretched forward to salute the Führer. Hitler "heiled" back in gratitude for the no doubt entirely anticipated applause.

I had plenty of opportunity to watch him from close up. His face was quite uninteresting, crudely chiseled, brutal and not particularly expressive when he was not speaking. His power over the masses was something you first understood when you heard him speak. Technically, he was an expert speaker who mastered variations of vocal expression, mimicry and gesture, and he was a master at planting leading questions with his audience and making dramatic pauses until he gained the answer he wanted. There was no doubt that he was blessed with demagogy, and he effectively staged ss parades and other mass demonstrations with banners, orchestras and lighting effects.

While the Führer was approaching his hysterical climax, the slogans, the unproved facts, the hate and self-glorification showered down on the thousands of people on the Konigsplatz in whom they provoked a national orgasm, and the orgasm rose in the soul of the Germans present, until neither trousers nor teeth could resist the thunderous shouts of *Sieg Heil*, which marked the end of that and many similar meetings in the German Fatherland. One huge act of intercourse. Community in the *Gemeinnutz* sense so it creaked. Oh, how good it felt!

Hitler looked a little contemptuously down on Mussolini, as if wishing to say, "So let's see what you are good for." Mussolini was not very tall. His pale blue uniform was far more stylish than Hitler's primitive sa one, but he was a small round blob of a man and stood on his toes and lifted his chin high, in order to disguise his short stature. The only thing that was big about him was his mouth, and this would have graced a hippopotamus. In a word, he was simply ludicrous, and over the next few days, I heard several Germans, including the young ss man Hermann Boeck, express his doubts whether they had found a worthy ally in Mussolini. Their doubts proved justified over time.

During the parade on the Königsplatz these doubts were, however, in no way expressed. It was now Mussolini's turn to speak, and he shouted at least as loudly as Hitler had done. But he did so in Italian, so no one understood him. It must have been the yelling that did it, because the crowd yelled *Sieg Heil* and cried out like madmen, while the ss soldiers presented arms. Then the catastrophe happened.

When the shouting had receded the ss general asked the men to stand at ease. These mechanical dolls worked perfectly, with one exception. One miserable sinner – may God have mercy on his soul – had the misfortune to get his rifle tangled in its shoulder strap and the rifle therefore came down to the ground a split second after the rest. This could be heard all over the square, as the rifle butt hit the ground and a sigh of despair was heard regarding this national outrage. Only I was amused – and maybe Mussolini whose gaze I caught at the moment of the catastrophe; but we both kept our masks and so did not end up in a concentration camp on that occasion.

The international and local press commentaries on the occasion left no doubt that Hitler had invited Mussolini to Munich in order to persuade him to accept the merging of Germany and Austria (*Anschluss*). What was perhaps less clear was the fact that, in recompense, Hitler was to give

Mussolini a free rein in the Balkans. I only had the opportunity of following the rest of the developments in Germany at the time for a further couple of months. On December 1, 1937, my studies in Munich came to an end, and with echoes of the cries on the Königsplatz ringing in my ears, I went off to Paris, where I soon found out what the French thought about the cordial relations between Germany and Italy. And in general, quite different experiences lay in store for me.

Paris

In Paris I lived in a *pension* on the rue des Arènes in the Fifth Arrondissement right in the middle of the Latin Quarter. I could not have found a better place to live. I was received very cordially by the two older ladies with a slight moustache who ran the *pension*, where three other students were living. The ladies gave me a little tuition in the French language; but I also attended an excellent language course run by the *Alliance Française*. In this course I did not meet many of my own age, and felt much more isolated here than in Munich. The *pension* on the rue des Arènes was hardly what you would call a university, but the building across the road was the remains of an ancient Roman arena, and it was five minutes' walk from the Boulevard Saint Michelle, the rue Mouffetard, the Sorbonne, the Panthéon, the Luxembourg Gardens and the Arab mosque. This was all rather fine, and I soon became acquainted with that district of Paris.

At first, my circle of friends was limited to my fellow lodgers, and it was there I made the acquaintance of Yvonne. She was a German, an Aryan and a Nazi sympathizer to her very fingertips. Her parents were Sudeten Germans, and had lived in South America. But she was now on a study trip to France. I was glad I had met her, for she could help me out as an interpreter. She spoke excellent French, and my German was not so bad either. Later on, she became something of a central figure in our political discussions in the small *pension*. She had never actually lived in Germany, and yet was an uncritical admirer of Hitler. She gave me a good idea of what Sudeten German fanaticism looked like.

Although my French at the time was only good enough for the simplest of conversations, I nevertheless received an impression of how worried the French were about developments in Germany. People already foresaw the occupation of Austria and were worried about Czechoslovakia.

On February 20, 1938, Hitler gave a major speech at the Kroll Opera, in which he boasted about Germany's rearmament and, to Yvonne's delight, promised to support all Germans living abroad. There was a cartoon in the French press at the time, depicting Germany as a wolf's head with Austria as the lower jaw, and Silesia as the upper one, ready to gobble up Czechoslovakia. Now the wolf had shown its teeth. The French had understood this, but soon I would travel to Cambridge to continue my studies, where I realized that not only was the English Channel an obstacle to traffic between the British Isles and the continent of Europe, but also a barrier for ideas.

Cambridge

The six months I spent in Cambridge were some of the happiest in my life. I was studying English Language and Literature and would take my finals at St. John's College. It can be seen from my finals papers that I wrote, among other things, on the subject of: *"A just war is better than an unjust peace."* There could hardly be a topic more relevant to the problems with which I was wrestling as a seventeen-to-eighteen-year-old. I made many friends, including three students from St. John's College: Tom, Arthur and Frank. Tom was studying French and German. As far as I know, the Secret Service made use of his linguistic talents during the war. Arthur studied political science. He became an RAF pilot. He was one of the few who, according to Churchill, will be remembered with eternal gratitude, as he helped save London.

Of the three, I was probably closest to Frank Glassow. He studied medicine. His parents were of Russian-Jewish provenance, but he himself was born and grew up in Newcastle. The previous year he had met my sister Elsebet, when she was studying in Cambridge, so I too now enjoyed his company. It became friendship for life. Frank was one of the young surgeons who gave first aid to the wounded on the beaches of Normandy during the invasion. Frank was also the first Englishman I met when I returned home to Denmark from the German concentration camp. I later learned that solid friendships are a characteristic of Jews. Now in my eighty-eight year, I still regularly correspond with Frank.

The days flew by in Cambridge on account of the hard work I was putting into my study of language and literature, my great times on the river and the tennis courts, and the architectural discoveries I made in Cambridge and Ely. In general, most Cambridge students had no interest in politics. They collected money eagerly for the Socialists in Spain, but Germany and Hitler were of secondary interest; and the anxiety I had encountered in Paris was lacking. Cambridge was, and still is, one of the great cultural centers of the world; but Cambridge was also a fine playground for intelligent young Britons. Student fun flourished and students, much to the chagrin of the city's decorous middle class, managed to hoist a naked wax dummy up the spire of one of the most beautiful buildings in England, King's College Chapel, which event was afforded as much attention as when they beat Oxford at rowing, or made outstanding scientific achievements.

One of my most pleasant memories is of the frequent and inspiring get-togethers organized by the director of the botanical gardens. He spoke Danish and in the spring and summer of 1938, he brought together students of many nationalities in weekly meetings, where I also met several German emigrants. I think it was then that I had the first opportunity to realize that Germany still enjoyed an opposition, and it was the first time in my life that I was confronted with the problems faced by political emigrés. These thoughts were in stark contrast to Yvonne's worldview and her fascination with Nazism.

On March 12, 1938, it was announced in the press that Hitler had marched into Austria and that *Anschluss* was a fact, which was no surprise either to myself or to the French nation, but certainly was to the students of Cambridge. People waited tensely for what Mussolini's reaction would be; but the whole matter had already been sewn up back in Munich. By now, the Berlin-Rome Axis had been a reality for a good while.

The international group of friends who met at the botanical gardens were for the most part well-read intellectuals of a left-wing tendency who had the deepest distrust of Franco, Hitler and Mussolini, but also of the international armaments industry and the Western democracies. Their sympathy for the German emigrants was genuine, and their support of the Spanish government was well meant. On the whole they were rather idealistic people, which was something I liked; but they were no advocates of Western democracy.

What made me most uncomfortable was the boundlessly theoretical view that left-wing academics had of reality. The individual human being vanished amongst dreams of equality and the great promises and quite naïve ideas about the moral superiority of the common man. On the Königsplatz in Munich, I had received a clear impression of how equality smothered every form of individualism, and the German concepts of *Gemeinnutz vor Eigennutz* ("common use for individual use") could not conceal the fact that the common man was easy prey to demagogy. Was this the same with the young intellectuals I met at the botanical gardens in Cambridge? I strongly suspected this to be the case, and the balled fist struck me as being at least as threatening a greeting as was the outstretched arm. *Heil Stalin!*

I benefited from my experiences at Cambridge some four years later when I began working with Danish Communists in the cross-party atmosphere of the Resistance. For the most part, it was that same type of academic Marxists that I met here, and their arguments were exactly the same. Stalin's invasion of Finland in 1939 made permanent our differences of opinion.

I never did become a Socialist, neither a National Socialist nor an International Socialist. The denial of many facets of existence, and of the differences between people, were things I regarded then, and have ever since, as an expression of a fear of life, from which people sought collective sanctuary under a cloak of uninspiring uniformity and tedium. The antidote to this were scenes of mass action, as I had witnessed in Munich, but such scenes only constituted a short-term solution. I would soon be given proof of just how dangerous such uniformity was.

Home Again

The atmosphere I encountered on my return to Horsens was primarily one of uncertainty and anxiety. The Danish government had urged the press to observe a measure of self-restraint when describing events in Germany, and so the general public found it difficult to obtain a true picture of what was happening south of the border. But there was nevertheless widespread skepticism about the truth value of German propaganda, and the Danish Nazi Party had few adherents. But things in Germany remained worrying. On September 12, 1938, Hitler suggested that the Sudeten Germans should have the right to self-determination, and this triggered an international crisis. Chamberlain had to travel three times to Germany to try to appease Hitler, but in vain. On September 30 he returned from a meeting in Munich, in which Mussolini and Daladier also took part, with the famous message *"This piece of paper means peace in our time."* But Czechoslovakia had become the victim and Churchill commented: *"They had to choose between war and dishonour. They chose dishonour. They will get war."*

Not only the Czechs suffered. An attack on a diplomat at the German Embassy in Paris on November 9, 1938, led to *Kristallnacht*, which was the worst anti-Jewish pogrom up to then, and now the aims of the Nazis had been revealed for all to see. Fear spread throughout Europe.

When Franco held his triumphant march into Madrid in May 1939, the Danish government was so worried that, unlike the other Nordic countries, it signed a nonaggression pact with Germany on the last day of that month, on terms dictated by Germany. This was in line with Danish neutrality and in itself a logical consequence of defense policy at the time.

I matriculated in the summer of 1939, and used the summer holidays to drive my brother Flemming down to Leipzig, where he was about to begin his sabbatical year, and from there over to Paris where I would be picking up Bente, who had just ended her stay abroad. We attended Bastille Day in Paris. As usual, the climax was an impressive military parade, which gave a false impression of security. There were a lot of horses, but few tanks. Otherwise, it felt strange to be driving through Europe. The atmosphere was tense. Everyone feared and expected war; but the tension was greater than the fear.

I celebrated my twentieth birthday in Horsens, and heard that day of the arrival of Ribbentrop to Moscow. On the following day, August 24, 1939, at two o'clock in the morning, he signed, along with Molotov, the Russo-German nonaggression pact, to which was appended a secret agreement to divide up Eastern Europe into a German and a Russian sphere of influence.

Unconscious of the catastrophe which was so rapidly approaching, I moved to Copenhagen in August 1939, where Elsebet and I, after a considerable search, finally found student accommodation in a two-room attic flat in the rear part of a house, at Klosterstræde 5. Our landlord was a jovial picture-framer, and the location in central Copenhagen was both romantic and practical. We had running cold water and a wood stove, but modern conveniences were totally lacking. The kitchen was little but a pantry at the top of the stairs, and the toilet was five floors down, by the yard. Our nearest neighbors were the pigeons on the roofs of Copenhagen.

War Breaks Out

My parents were so worried about political developments that they telegraphed Flemming in Leipzig, telling him he should come home right away. His professor at the university there tried unsuccessfully to convince him that war would not break out. When the ticket had been bought, all he could afford was a soda water and he had to spend the night sleeping on a bench in Potsdam. But he managed to go and see the Sansouci palace again before starting his trip back to Denmark. This occurred on September 1, 1939, the day that Hitler attacked Poland and therefore began the Second World War.

Britain and France sent Hitler their ultimata, which he ignored. In Denmark, the reaction was as it had been during the First World War. A security force of thirty-five thousand men was mobilized. But to the bewilderment of the nation, they were sent home again a few weeks later.

On September 28 the Molotov-Ribbentrop Pact was signed by Germany and the Soviet Union, and this gave Stalin free rein in the Baltic countries and Finland. After having made a number of unacceptable demands on the Finnish government with regard to border adjustments, Stalin attacked Finland on November 30, 1939. He was met with unexpected and heroic resistance, which raised a good deal of sympathy for Finland in the free world. The performance of the Russian army was not impressive, but Stalin could count on military and especially political support from his new friend Adolf Hitler. Around twelve hundred Danes volunteered to fight in Finland. I was one of these, but I was rejected as I had not yet done my military service and had therefore not received the necessary military training.

Sending the Danish security force home created uncertainty as to the aims of the Danish government. But to our relief, the *Folketinget* (parliament) declared on January 19, 1940, that "any means at our disposal shall be used as necessary to guarantee the freedom and independence of the realm." I was one of those who was naïve enough to believe this promise, and I can well understand that the parliament was not shouting about which specific means were at our disposal. In all our naïveté, we simply believed what the government told us. But at the same time we were beginning to fear that Hitler wished to break the nonaggression pact, if it suited him to do so. We could even, perhaps, imagine a German occupation of key positions in Denmark. But then, on April 9, 1940, came the revelation that I witnessed from our corner of Klosterstræde street in Copenhagen.

The Day of Reckoning: April 9, 1940

Elsebet and I were woken that morning in our little flat in the Klosterstræde by the sound of the aircraft engines overhead. We were completely disoriented and wondered whether these could be Danish, German or Allied planes. It turned out to be German bombers. We got dressed hurriedly and walked out onto the street. At the corner of Kronprinsessegade and Gothersgade near the Royal Gardens, I saw my first German soldier, who was standing right in the middle of the thoroughfare with fixed bayonet, and hand grenades hanging from his belt. He was surrounded by a group of inquisitive cyclists.

Elsebet went down to see the German army at the port. When we met up again, we had also managed to get hold of a circular that announced that Denmark was now under German protection against British attack. We knew we had now been invaded. We felt boundless shame and sadness when we realized that Denmark had, in effect, capitulated without resistance, despite the assurances of politicians that they were going to defend us. Parts of Denmark had previously been occupied or leased out, but at no time in its thousand-year history had our nation lost its liberty so totally. Given my pro-defense attitudes, which were part and parcel of my political views, I felt very bitter about the government. Like many others, I was clear about the fact that there would have to be not only a political struggle, but also a struggle for our Danish language and culture.

The events of April 9 not only exposed the politicians for what they were, but also the army and the navy, whose leaders seemed not to have been following events. In southern Jutland, things went according to the traditional pattern of occupation, but the fact that the Germans could manage to take over the airport at Ålborg was incomprehensible, and events in Copenhagen, where everyone had been caught napping, were outrageous. I was not yet particularly negative about the Danish army and navy at the time, but I was filled with anger that thirteen Danish soldiers' lives had been sacrificed for nothing, and my anger increased when I later found out that three Danish border guards had been shot by plainclothes Germans.

CHAPTER **2**

Occupation

The occupation of Denmark was a disaster that was not made any better by the announcement that the Anglo-French declaration of war on Hitler had not been followed up by any kind of military offensive. The Western Allies were not prepared for war, and on the Western Front, nothing happened for some nine months. This was the period of the Phony War.

It was Hitler once again who took the initiative when he attacked Western Europe one month after the occupation of Denmark. The Netherlands capitulated on May 14 and on the twenty-eighth of that month, Belgium was obliged to follow suit. On June 10 it was the Norwegian armed forces' turn, and that same day, Mussolini sent his declaration of war to France and Great Britain. "I need a few thousand deaths to justify my presence at the peace table" was the shameless justification for his action. Then France's turn had come. On June 14, Hitler entered Paris. And on the twenty-second, the French had to sign the armistice agreement under humiliating circumstances in the forest at Compiègne, upon which Hitler declared that the war in the west was over.

Hitler appeared to be invincible but not infallible. He had already avenged previous German defeats, but in the moment of victory, under pressure from Göring, he ordered his armored troops to rest for three days after their occupation of northern France. This allowed the evacuation of some 350,000 British, French and Polish troops from Dunkirk to England on June 4. The description of this amazing rescue action has gone down in history as the "Miracle of Dunkirk."[2]

The National Coalition and Divisions

By no means did we understand at the time what crucial significance the Miracle of Dunkirk was going to have. Prospects of a swift German victory were shocking and both the German and the Danish National Coalition's plans for the future were unknown. When the country was occupied, the German ambassador, Cecil von Renthe-Fink, had sworn a solemn oath that Germany did not wish to interfere in Denmark's internal affairs and would respect her integrity and independence after the war was over. There were not many who believed these promises.

Dissatisfaction also affected the Danish government and the resentment against the politicians who had brought this national disaster upon us clearly made itself felt in the opposition parties, especially the Conservatives. But their hopes were frustrated as it was essential to undertake some form of political cooperation, and this prevented us from reaching a political settlement. One day after occupation, we already had an eighteen-member coalition government in which six ministers without portfolio sat, from the liberal Venstre party and the Konservative Folkeparti.

Cooperation became the watchword of this coalition. The word soon took on a double significance as cooperation was not only between the democratic Danish parties but also, to an increasing extent, between the government and the occupying forces.

I spent the summer of 1940 in Horsens, and conversations with my parents contributed to my understanding of these cataclysmic events and what our attitude towards them should be. I knew that on April 9 my father suddenly became very busy burning a number of secret documents. He said nothing more about them, but I did have my suspicions that he had been working for Danish intelligence. But what was now important was to find out more about the aims of the coalition government.

We had no doubts about the fact that the reason to invite the opposition to join the government was to emasculate any criticism of the defeatist defense policies that had culminated in the capitulation of April 9. Prime Minister Thorvald Stauning and Foreign Minister Peter Munch were chiefly responsible for these policies, and it was therefore necessary for them to silence the opposition in this area. Von Renthe-Fink was quite clear about this, which can be seen from his reports to Berlin. At the same time, the opposition were being made jointly responsible for the coalition policies that were to be implemented in the future, and were therefore confronted with the dual nature of the coalition.

There were principally four political parties that wished at this stage to protect parliamentary democracy and strive to counter the efforts of the right and left wings, especially the Danish Nazis (DNSAP) and the Communists (DKP), plus the party that criticized the system but was not anti-democratic, the Dansk Samling, and various other right-wing parties with a background in commerce.

The biggest threat came from the DNSAP, which dreamed of taking over power after the German occupation. But in the long run, the DKP could become the greater threat. At the start of the occupation, Hitler and Stalin were still good friends. They both regarded the Western democracies as their greatest enemies; but no one knew how long this friendship would last.

Popular support rose and fell, however, with the cooperation between the government and the occupying forces. Great emphasis was placed on attempts to retain Denmark's neutrality, but it was clear that an occupied country could not remain neutral. Either you had to fulfill the wishes of the occupier, i.e., collaborate, or you could resist. Foreign Minister Munch tried to maintain an illusion of neutrality through a policy of passivity of implementation, as he knew that we did not wish to ally ourselves with Germany. No reaction would be given to German demands until they were actually spelled out; and thereafter there would be an effort to limit these demands by negotiation.

It took several months for us to realize that von Renthe-Fink had, right from the start, been adamant about pursuing peacetime occupation policies in order to exploit Denmark with the least cost for Germany and the occupying forces. This policy, which was later continued by Werner Best, made us become a little suspicious when the occupier did not, against all expectations, start the persecution of the Jews. The anti-Semitic campaign, which would come sooner or later, was left for the time being to the Danish Nazis to carry out. What was also unexpected was that the Danish army was not demobilized, but received permission to continue functioning under supervision until further notice. The army did have to give up some of its artillery pieces and other weapons, but it was not disarmed. The navy was allowed to carry out some maneuvers and mine-sweeping activities, and had later on to give up six torpedo boats. But the training of naval officers continued.

The German "willingness to cooperate" was also manifested by an effort to counter the effects of large-scale unemployment. Their contribution was to set up, on May 24, 1940, a German employment bureau in Copenhagen. A total of 128,000 Danish workers went to Germany to look for work and 14,000 went to Norway. This was a shameful business.[3]

Despite an element of bitterness and mistrust on the part of the population at large, the coalition government nevertheless managed to rule the country with broad national support, and initially it lived up to expectations. It attacked the Nazis' anti-Semitic propaganda hard and made great efforts to keep jurisdiction in Danish hands. Obviously, the Gestapo had already been in place in Denmark even before the invasion and a limited number of Danish anti-Nazis were arrested and sent to Germany shortly after the start of the occupation. But after this, the Gestapo seemingly had no further executive powers. Police work was subsequently left to the Danish police, who were however kept under strict German control.[4]

The policy of passive implementation ended with the change of government that took place on July 8, 1940. Peter Munch resigned from the post of foreign minister and was replaced by Erik Scavenius. My parents were outraged. They had experienced Scavenius as foreign minister during the First World War and knew of his extremely positive attitudes towards Germany; in his opinion, Denmark should never come into conflict with that country. Now he took up his post and gave a speech that supplied us with evidence of his admiration of the great German victory, and promised that Denmark would cooperate with Greater Germany.

Passive implementation of policy had now been replaced by active implementation, so that the Germans would receive concessions they had lacked before. Scavenius believed in a German victory, and hoped that Denmark as a Nordic nation, willing to cooperate, would thus receive special treatment once Hitler had achieved total victory.

I was glad that we had gotten rid of Peter Munch, but Scavenius made no bones about the fact that we had now come out of the frying pan and landed in the fire. On July 18, he took us out of the League of Nations, and soon rumors began to circulate about negotiations that had been instituted when a Danish delegation traveled to Berlin on July 30 to discuss a currency and customs union with Germany. If the plan, supported by Scavenius, had gone through, Denmark would have become a German colony. But luckily, the politicians did not go along with the plan. Resistance began gradually to make itself felt, now after four months of occupation. We could already see that Scavenius was hovering on the brink of treason, and today I cannot understand how Danish historians can present him as a great statesman. He was deeply compromised.

The collapse of the talks about the currency and customs union were a serious blow for Scavenius who knew he ran the risk of being regarded as a traitor and he was unsure of the support of either his minister colleagues or of the *Rigsdag* (the Danish parliament). With his defeat the German foreign ministry began to take a greater interest in the activities of the leader of the Danish Nazis, Fritz Clausen. In a report from October 22, 1940, von Renthe-Fink writes:[5]

> The Danes are not willing to draw the consequences of where the power lies with regard to political relations within Europe. Evidence of this is the failed attempt by Scavenius to push through a currency and customs union. At the start, the climate of public opinion was reasonably friendly towards Germany, but over the past few months, things have deteriorated…. So long as the present government is in power, there is no chance of Denmark wishing to genuinely have closer ties with Germany.

Von Renthe-Fink blamed, among others, the Conservative politician Christmas Møller for this. Removing him from political life was one of the most urgent tasks that the German ambassador wanted to carry out and on October 3, 1940, Christmas Møller was forced to resign, leaving the Rigsdag as well some three months later. In April 1942, he managed to escape to England.

In several speeches, Danish Prime Minister Stauning made attempts to flatter Germany by, for instance, praising their planned economy and promising them loyal cooperation when the war was over. *Neuropa* – New Europe – was not something people should be afraid of. However, Stauning's speeches did not impress von Renthe-Fink who, at Christmas 1940, tried to get a change of government. His attempts failed, but his efforts made it clear to all that German promises not to interfere in the internal affairs of Denmark were totally lacking in credibility. What Germany was after was the dismantling of the parliamentary democracy; Hitler had no respect for the Danish constitution.

All this was taking place while I was on holiday, living with my parents in Horsens, which offered me the opportunity not only to discuss developments with them, but also to hear, via their radio set, the commentaries made by the BBC and Swedish Radio. In our student flat, we could neither afford a telephone nor a radio set. Jamming broadcasts often made it difficult to hear what was said on the radio. But we were in no doubt that there was condemnation of Scavenius and his actions even far beyond Denmark itself.

My stay in Horsens also gave me the opportunity to test the water in other circles, with people I met daily. The king had asked the people to behave with dignity. Not everyone followed his advice. On the morning of April 9, I myself was shocked at the number of residents of Copenhagen who clustered around the heavily armed German soldiers. They were treated like tourists. It was the same story in Horsens. During my many cycle tours that summer through the countryside in central Jutland, I noticed that in rural districts there was an especially pro-German attitude. We received the impression that cracks were appearing in the unity of the occupied Danes, and that these cracks did not necessarily follow traditional party lines. My national inferiority complex grew and grew.

There was plenty to talk about during the holidays in Horsens. One expression of national unity was song festivals (*Alsang*) where national songs were sung. Thousands of participants would meet. There were also hiking trips (*Algang*), which were to demonstrate an element of national unity. I took part in a number of these festivals and was pleased to see that social divisions were being eroded. The class struggle was entering its terminal phase, but I soon came to the conclusion that these initiatives would hardly lead to any form of active resistance to the occupation.

The same can be said for the comfort I derived from the idea of a Nordic identity, which was one way of resisting the erosion of a national identity. We now dreamed more than ever of Nordic unity, which would be able to counter the cultural and political pressures to which we would be subjected, should Germany win the war. But I realized that more was needed.

Student Lodgings in Copenhagen

The summer of 1940 is engraved in my memory as a grim period of my life. We had soon become used to the blackout and to rationing, and bombing raids were an experience that only a few Danes suffered at the time. What was much worse was living with a bad conscience. In 1940, my brother, sisters and I had no way of escaping our feeling of paralysis other than by immersing ourselves in our work. My sister Bente and brother Flemming were in the unfortunate situation that they had to make decisions about how to continue their education. With a German victory the likely outcome of the war, this was not easy. But it was decided that Bente would study at the Suhr School of Domestic Science and Flemming would study medicine in Copenhagen.

After the summer holidays in 1940, the four of us cycled from Horsens to Copenhagen. The place on Klosterstræde was too small for all of us to live in and to the disappointment of our kind landlord, we moved at the end of August to a three-room apartment on the fourth floor of a building at Raadhusstræde 2A on the corner of that street and the Nytorv square. We used a tricycle to carry our belongings.

The flat consisted of a small entrance hall, with a door through to a small kitchen and a coal place. My sisters shared the large living room, which looked out over Raadhusstræde; they had their own entrance. Flemming and I took the two smaller rooms, which looked out over the corner of Nytorv and from where you could see the cathedral, the main thoroughfare Strøget and the fountain on Gammeltorv Square and, a little further off, the Church of Our Lady, the university and the student refectory, nicknamed the "Cannibals' Kitchen." When we went down onto Raadhusstræde, it was only a few minutes' walk to the canals and Christiansborg, the seat of government and parliament. We could not have lived more centrally. "On the corner of where it all happens, just like back home" is how Elsebet described it when she sent greetings to our parents on their wedding anniversary; in Horsens, we also lived on the corner of the main street and the town square.

We heated the flat using stoves, when there was fuel to be had. There was cold running water, but if we wanted to have a bath, we had to go to the Copenhagen Public Baths. So this was no wildly luxurious existence, but very pleasant for all that. The building was owned by the book dealer Wroblewski who had his business two doors away next to the police station on Nytorv. Wroblewski was of Jewish-Polish origin. He turned out to be a very brave man and shielded us as much as he could when the Gestapo began to take an interest in our nest of illegality. He showed solidarity to all, something I remember with gratitude.

I attended lectures at the university, although I had difficulty concentrating. The major hurdle to be gotten over in the primary examinations was anatomy. This was a question of learning by rote so that you nearly went crazy. But we had a very good teacher, Professor Hou-Jensen, who was living at the Medical Anatomical Institute. It was through my studies that I met two students of medicine, a little older than myself: Cato Bakman and Holger Larsen, who assisted on the dissection course that I was attending. It was they, plus one of their teammates, Niels Hjorth, who later established contacts with the Resistance, and while at the Anatomical Institute, I decided to get through the first part of my studies as quickly as possible and then leave my books on the shelf. I was directly inspired to do this on account of Professor Hou-Jensen's tragic death. On October 16, 1940, the rumor spread through the institute that Hou-Jensen had been killed by a German soldier who was visiting his housemaid in his home. Hou-Jensen wanted to throw him out, but the German started a fight, which meant that Hou-Jensen fell down the stairs and died. Our anger knew no bounds.

Economy of a stricter kind was part and parcel of our everyday life. Rationing did not affect us particularly much, and hoarding was simply beyond our means. We could only rarely afford new clothes, which was a bigger problem for my sisters than for Flemming and me, who were not particularly interested in the fashions of the time. We lived very simply. Many of our meals were taken in the student food kitchen on Nørregade, but we also made our own food. Carrots and stews were our answer to our limited budget and rationing. We ran a joint household, taking account of the gender roles of the time. Elsebet was the boss, which made me a spoiled and ungrateful wretch who, after two weeks of carrots, pointed out to my elder sister that I was suffering from carotene poisoning.

Our financial problems were also those of most students from the provinces. Those who came from Copenhagen had the advantage of being able to live at home, while students from elsewhere had to either find a charitable trust to support them, or live on the money they received from their parents. It was rare for students to look for paid work during the course of their studies. The chief aim was to graduate on time. But despite every effort, it was hard to concentrate on studying, since our thoughts were constantly wandering away to the tragedy being fought out over England at the time. After France had capitulated, the defeat of Britain by Hitler seemed only to be a matter of time. But assessments proved wrong. The invasion kept being postponed.

After the Miracle of Dunkirk, Hitler's plans for a swift invasion of Britain and therefore an end to the war against the Western Allies came unstuck. From that point onwards it became the task of the Luftwaffe to combat Britain, while Hitler turned his attention to southern Europe. The year 1940 came to an end with the situation in the world quite unpredictable, making any rational planning on the part of the Danish Resistance almost impossible. There were the energetic dictators who had come to the gaming table. Hitler was at the center of events and had become the great victor; but Britain had not given up yet.

The grim summer of 1940 was followed by a severe winter with temperatures dropping to minus twenty-five (–32° C). We froze. Sometimes there was even ice on our bedsheets when we woke up in the morning. We could hardly ever get hold of coal, and the coke we did get soon had to be supplemented with peat and other emergency fuel. We read for our studies in the university library, where they managed to keep a temperature up to fifty degrees (10° C). We acquired bast shoes (made from plant fiber).

In order to save money, we cycled home that Christmas, all 155 miles (250 km) of the journey. This took two days. I stayed the night in the youth hostel in Odense. It was a chilly trip, but I cycled back nevertheless. I made this journey several times. If I went via Aarhus, I could do it in a day, as this was a mere ninety miles (150 km). But this included having to pay an expensive ferry ticket at Kalundborg. Bente cycled with me on a couple of occasions and proved to be a tough young woman. Once we stood under a tree and saw how lightning struck a farm, which burned to the ground. One bolt struck near Bente's front wheel, but did not seem to affect her and we cycled on in the rain to Copenhagen and an uncertain future.

Contacts with Britain

The first decisions to start resisting the invader were made against a background of significant risk, as Hitler was adamantly determined to win the war. Ethical considerations, rather than *Realpolitik*, motivated Danes both

at home and abroad as they tried to create an alternative to the collaboration policies of the government.

Among those who, during the first year of the occupation, began Resistance activities were our sailors who joined up with the Allies, plus a number of diplomats, led by our ambassador in Washington, Henrik Kaufmann.
These were people who no longer felt bound by the Danish government
policy of the day. And many Danes who lived in London showed solidarity
with the British people during the bombings there. On September 30, 1940,
the "Danish Council" was set up, which was a big boost for those of us who
were hoping for a British victory, even if things at the time looked grim.

On the home front, several army and naval officers took the initiative
and performed intelligence activities. Under the code name of *Ligaen* (the
League) they carried out espionage work, and this would soon prove to be
of significance for the British effort.[6] The information they provided es-
sentially involved the movements of shipping through the Great Belt, German troop movements and military installations. The greatest problem the
League encountered was a lack of contact with the Western Allies.

After France had capitulated, Britain stood alone, and few imagined
that she could survive the vicious air raids which then followed. It was in
this desperate situation that Churchill gave the order "Set Europe ablaze!"
In order to execute this order, the "Special Operations Executive" (SOE) was
set up in 1940 by the Ministry of Economic Warfare, an organization that
aimed at supporting sabotage carried out in the occupied countries.[7] The
minister of economic warfare, Hugh Dalton, was enthusiastic about the
plan, while the foreign minister, Anthony Eden, and British intelligence
were skeptical. This would have consequences for the somewhat vacillat-
ing course that the SOE followed in the years to come.

One of the leaders of the SOE was the banker Sir Charles Hambro,
who was a good friend of the Danish nation. A special Danish Department
was set up in October, run by Lieutenant-Commander R.C. Hollingworth,
who had earlier served at the British Embassy in Copenhagen. Hambro
traveled to Stockholm to negotiate closer cooperation with the League's
contact there, Ebbe Munck, who was sent in October 1940 as foreign correspondent of the Danish daily *Berlinske Tidende*. The aim was to start a
Danish Resistance movement which, with British help, would carry out acts
of sabotage. According to Munck, Sir Charles justified the significance of
sabotage with the following words: "As there will not be aircraft for quite

some while to bomb targets in Denmark, destruction from within will be of much greater use and will, at the same time, prevent unnecessary loss of life and damage to property."

Initially, the League was against sabotage, as it feared that this would lead to the demobilization of the Danish army and therefore hamper intelligence-gathering activities. Since the British had no opportunity at the time to supply Danish saboteurs with instructors, weapons, explosives, and so on, the following priorities were listed:

1) Intelligence activities.
2) Expansion of news services and the BBC.
3) Sabotage.

For the civil population, and therefore for my family, too, the situation was unpredictable. A direct revolt against the occupying forces was pointless; but German propaganda, press censorship and the Nazi Party's anti-Semitic campaigns and calls for a political takeover were challenges the people, the government and the authorities had to meet. There was universal condemnation of the anti-Semitic propaganda of the Danish Nazis; but what had to be faced up to was that right from the start, the fight against German propaganda politicians had been given up, and they took part in the struggle against a free press and the zealous implementation of censorship. How far the Danish government was prepared to collaborate with the occupier remained unclear for quite some while, which naturally made it difficult to formulate any form of legal and illegal politics of resistance.

The Moment of Truth

Here at home, the year 1941 began depressingly. The limits of the powers of resistance of both government and parliament to German demands were soon revealed. On February 20, 1941, the government disassociated itself from the Danish Council in London, and on April 16 Ambassador Kaufmann was dismissed and was charged with treason when he refused to return to Denmark after having signed the Treaty of Greenland with the USA on April 9. We soon realized how far our government was prepared to go in its policies of appeasement. The dream of neutrality had already received a fatal blow on February 5, when the six torpedo boats had been handed over to the Germans.

It was a cold and depressing spring that ended in June of that year, which I spent studying hard for my summer examination. In early June, I was even caught in a snowstorm as I was on my way to the Rockefeller Institute. The summer had had a tough time trying to break through that year, but when it came, it did so with all the drama you could wish for. On June 22, Hitler started "Operation Barbarossa," that is to say, the attack on the Soviet Union. Ignoring the advice of his generals he waged war on two fronts, one of which he reckoned he would win by the end of the year. He had presumably allowed himself to be misled by the poor performance of the Russians during the Winter War with Finland. Meanwhile, Germany had lost valuable time by coming to the aid of Mussolini in the Balkans, and by the time that was over, the Russian winter had set in.

The Communists: Friends or Foes?

Inevitably, Hitler's attack on the Soviet Union became a topic of conversation above all else. The attack took us – and Stalin – by surprise. The Soviet Union had been supplying the Germans with export articles, necessary for the war effort, right up until the last minute. I, like many others, thought that the two sides on this conflict were like two peas in a pod; every shot that went home would be a hit. "Now we can't lose," was the cynical commentary on events, and this was not only our spontaneous reaction, but that of many others. But this feeling diminished as it became clear that the Soviet Union was now an ally of Britain.

The attack on the Soviet Union put a severe strain on the Danish policy of neutrality. It was obvious that diplomatic relations with the Soviet Union could no longer be maintained; but this did not necessarily mean active participation in the war in the East. Since October 1940, it had been permissible for the Waffen-ss to cooperate with the Danish Nazis and the German-speaking minority in the southern part of Jutland to recruit for the ss regiment "Nordland," which consisted of volunteers from Germany, Norway and Denmark. There was a fear that otherwise the Germans would start full-scale conscription of Danes in southern Jutland, making them join the German forces. The recruitment was illegal and against the purported policy of neutrality by the government, and it left the population at large with grave doubts as to where the line was being drawn by our politicians.

With the attack on the Soviet Union, this recruitment had to be seen in a new perspective. Germany wanted a definite contribution by Denmark in the war effort against the Russians. Scavenius had already said earlier that the German occupation of Denmark was the only protection possible against Soviet aggression. So more active engagement was now expected of the Danish government. Out of fear that the Germans would start conscripting Danes for the campaign on the *Ostfront*, the government accepted, on July 28, that Danish volunteers could form a purely Danish ss corps, *Frikorps Danmark*, which would, under the Danish flag, take part in the war against the Soviet Union. The volunteers swore allegiance to Hitler on August 5 in Hamburg. We now had to ask ourselves whether we were on our way to entering the war on the side of Germany.

Summer drew to a close without our finding out where the DKP stood. We had not really been able to understand what the contribution of our Danish Communists in fighting against the policy of collaboration was going to turn out to be. But with the attack on the Soviet Union on June 22, 1941, the situation changed totally. That very day, as Hitler was attacking the Soviet Union, the Danish police carried out a large-scale *razzia* (raid) of Danish Communists. The Germans had wanted the arrest of leading Communists; but in the end far more than the leaders were rounded up. With the approbation of Stauning and subsequent approval by the government, a total of 336 people were arrested by the Danish police without any court appearance, and house searches took place, plus the confiscation of documents. This campaign was carried out with unnecessary zeal and with no warning.[8]

Later on, some of those arrested were again released, but on August 21, the remaining 120 were transferred to the Horserød internment camp. In order for there to be room for these new prisoners, between forty-five and seventy German internees had to be shipped off to Germany where they suffered a grim fate, as became clear after the war.

On July 8, the Danish minister of justice, Harald Petersen, was by German demand replaced by the police chief Thune Jacobsen. On August 20, the latter presented the draft of Law 349 to the parliament: "The Prohibition of Communist Activities and Communist Organizations." This unconstitutional law was passed two days later.

Within the space of a few months, the deepest mistrust in politicians, the police and the legal system had thus arisen, and events had now turned the Communists into martyrs – an act that rather exaggerated the true nature of their role in Danish society, since by that time people were beginning to realize that the Soviet dictator was no Sunday school teacher either. The persecution of the Communists had the unintentional effect that the finishing off of the Danish Communist Party at a political and moral level was overshadowed by the mistrust people now had in politicians in general. There was now room to build up cross-party cooperation, which became the basis of the development of an effective Resistance. The demonstrations that middle-class students organized in protest against the signing by Foreign Minister Scavenius of the Anti-Comintern Pact towards the end of November 1941 represented one important step in this direction.

The Demonstration against the Anti-Comintern Pact

By the time we had returned to our studies in Copenhagen after the summer holidays in 1941, the situation had changed totally, both at home and abroad. The German army was pushing forward over the Russian steppe and on October 10 the final defeat of Russia was proclaimed. "Only local battles remain to be won and now the German army is free to return to other tasks" is what was written in the press; but the credibility of this announcement was dealt a blow when, three days later, we read: "Berlin is asking: has not the Soviet Union understood that it is now defeated?" The next day, heavy snowstorms on the Moscow front were reported. The ambiguity was heaven-sent.

The issue became very topical when at the end of November, Denmark joined the Anti-Comintern Pact.[9] Like many others, I was suspicious that Scavenius had been taken to Berlin to sign the Three-Power Pact and rumor was rife that a large stock of German uniforms was ready for Danish troops out in the Free Port at Copenhagen. This proved not to be the case; but such things could happen in the future.

On November 24, rumors were already circulating that a demonstration was going to be staged at the university. The next day, I read in the *Nationaltidende* that according to German sources, the pact was tantamount to engagement on the military front. Not only the Bolsheviks, but also their allies would be hit. The Anti-Comintern Pact was therefore also aimed at Britain, on which the whole resistance effort of the free world rested. It was against this background that on November 25, I took part, along with my sisters and brother, in the student demonstration against Denmark joining the Anti-Comintern Pact.

The initiative for this action was taken by students belonging to the non-Communist parties (the KU and Dansk Samling) and not by the Communists. It was in "Cannibals' Kitchen," where we went almost daily, that we were drawn into preparations for the demonstration. We were nearly all wearing our student caps, and there were many at the meeting. There was a mood of revolt and people were enthusiastic as we marched along Strøget. "Sing on, students!" was what people were calling to us. We tried, but were not particularly good at singing. And we were also busy looking out in case we spotted any Germans, whose interference we expected. But we were only confronted by the Danish police. They swung their truncheons without, however, doing much damage.

One can wonder about the decision to lead the demonstration up to Amalienborg, the Royal Castle, as it was chiefly against Scavenius; but the king was regarded as the hidden ally of the protesting opposition. The declaration, which was delivered to the king at Amalienborg, despite the police presence, has been preserved. It is remarkable that it includes the following words:[10]

> Your Majesty should know that we would rather share the living conditions of the Norwegian people than to allow, without resistance, the name of Denmark to be used in utter contradiction to our will to live in a free Denmark, governed by the people.

It was expected that the demonstration would provoke a reaction from the university authorities, and it therefore came as no surprise that the vice-chancellor warned that participation in demonstrations would lead to our being expelled from the university. The vice-chancellor's threat did not, however, have the intended result, partly because of a far more important announcement that was made a few days later: the USA was going to enter the war.

I was to take the first part of my medical exams in December and January. This was six months before the set time, and a year before people would normally be going through this purgatory. I thought about dropping out. It was still cold, about minus four (–30° C). With the aftereffects of the student demonstration against the Anti-Comintern Pact and the expansion of the war now becoming a global struggle, it was almost impossible to concentrate on reviewing my textbooks and notes, but under the pressure of my study partner I carried on, and so I went to take my examinations in physiology and biochemistry, and straight after Christmas, also in anatomy. I was relieved to be able to leave the examination table with top grades and leave my tough studies behind me. "You have me to thank for it," said my study partner. So I did, and broke off my studies, hoping to resume them at a more suitable date.

The Revolt Is Organized

Despite the developments at a military level, 1942 became the year when the Resistance began to get seriously organized. There was no question of opportunism. Hitler and his allies seemed invincible. Everything pointed to this fact. Both in Southeast Asia and in North Africa, things were going badly for Britain and America, nor were things shaping up well on the *Ostfront* – the front in Eastern Europe. In April, Hitler set in motion his spring offensive along the southern part of the front, where the German army had nearly reached Stalingrad and the northerly oil wells in the Caucasus. But both Moscow and Leningrad were still holding out. Nevertheless, the belief in a victory for the democratic powers and the Soviet Union often hung by a thin thread.

The Anti-Comintern protest demonstration marked the start of co-operation by a number of students in organized resistance against occupation and collaboration, and the beginning of a movement whose chief weapon at the time was the illegal press. As a direct consequence of the demonstration, two student organizations were founded: the *Studenternes Efterretningstjeneste* (SE; the Student Intelligence Service) and *De Danske Studenter* (DDS; the Danish Students). The SE was started by a group of Conservative students, and the DDS by more left-wing ones.

In early spring 1942, the cross-party resistance organization *Frit Danmark* (Free Denmark) came into being, to which the DDS affiliated itself.[11] Both right- and left-wing opponents of Nazism and Danish collaboration met here. On April 9, 1942, the organization produced its first issue of the illegal publication *Frit Danmark*, which was to become the most important of the Resistance publications that began to appear as the Danish government gave in to German pressure to an increasing extent. The print run increased from 1,200 copies in 1940 to 301,000 copies in 1942. My contribution to this explosive growth was modest. I was a paper boy with no personal contact with those who had started the newspaper, which was to be blamed on the fact that I had volunteered in the spring of that year to work at the Sundby hospital far away from the academic district of the city, which meant that I lost contact with my colleagues at the university and the university hospital, from where the impulse to start the paper had come.

One of the founders of Frit Danmark had been the Conservative Party leader Christmas Møller, who fled to England with his family in April 1942. Over BBC radio, he urged people to take part in more effective forms of resistance, which made the Germans begin to doubt the soundness of Danish collaboration politics, and as early as May, the usual diplomatic channels were indicating great German dissatisfaction with developments in Denmark. Strong hints were dropped that it could not be taken as a given that Denmark would regain her sovereignty after the war was over. More positive support for German policies was required.

On May 3, 1942, Prime Minister Stauning died. His funeral became the last great Social Democratic demonstration, and was attended by Swedish Prime Minister Per Albin Hansson. To my disappointment, I found no protest against what had been Stauning's defense policy in the underground press. Apart from the king, no one was more sacrosanct than Stauning; but Per Albin Hansson did use the opportunity to call for more Nordic cooperation in the future.

This was clearly encouraging for us, but not for the German Embassy who let themselves be soothed by the way that Foreign Minister Scavenius assured the German ambassador that Stauning's successor, Vilhelm Buhl, wanted to continue the pro-German policy that Scavenius called the only realistic way of defense against the Soviet Union.

Buhl was greeted with considerable skepticism by the Germans, partly because he was a Socialist, and partly because he had argued against the Anti-Comintern Pact. Von Renthe-Fink thus told him what Germany expected to hear in his inaugural speech. He would have to promise good behavior and to fight against Danish anti-German sentiments.[12]

Christmas Møller's broadcasts on BBC radio were not the only information we received from Britain. On February 12, 1942, we could read the following in the legal daily newspapers:[13]

At around three o'clock on the morning of December 28, 1941, two people parachuted from a low-flying plane near Haslev (south of Copenhagen). One vanished, leaving behind his parachute, and has not been seen since. For any information leading to the arrest of the man in question, a reward of 5,000 kroner will be given.... The other man was killed as he landed and has not yet been identified.

No one was in any doubt that these were English secret agents; but what we did not of course know at the time was that these were the future SOE leader in Denmark, Doctor Carl Johan Bruhn and his assistant the telegraphic Mogens Hammer who had been sent to establish contacts with the growing Resistance movement. Carl Johan Bruhn's parachute failed to open and therefore became the first SOE member to die in combat. Mogens Hammer, who did not know Bruhn's instructions, had on his own initiative to make contact with the Resistance movement.

The illegal press were the first to benefit from his operations, especially the organization *De Frie Danske* (The Free Danes); but Hammer also established contact with Frit Danmark. He was welcomed with open arms and could show that Ebbe Munck and others had been too pessimistic when they suggested that the Danish Resistance would never spontaneously get off the ground. It had in fact gotten off the ground, once the SOE arrived. But up to that time it was still the illegal press that was ahead of the game. Sabotage was more difficult to get going. What was of crucial importance to the preparation of sabotage operations was the fact that Mogens Hammer and the Danish radio engineer L.A. Duus Hansen managed to establish regular radio contact between the Danish Resistance and the SOE in London.

Another area of progress was the organization of places where the RAF could drop weapons, explosives and other equipment that would be needed if sabotage was to prove effective. The landowner Flemming Juncker and the editor Stig Jensen took the initiative here for Jutland and Sjælland. They soon began to cooperate well with the SOE when Christian Michael Rottbøll, the newly appointed chief of the SOE in Denmark, and two telegraphists were dropped in western Sjælland in 1942. On July 31 three sabotage instructors came, too, dropped over the heath at Trend in northern Jutland. These were all expatriate Danes who had volunteered, after long and thorough training, to be sent to Denmark. At that point, Mogens Hammer was called back to London and the SOE kept a total of six officers in Denmark. These moves did not, however, have any immediate effect on sabotage operations. The Danish intelligence officers in the League were still very much opposed to sabotage, and Rottbøll did not obtain the necessary backing from London to start a sabotage offensive in the spring of 1942. The initiative had therefore to come from elsewhere.

The Start of Sabotage Operations

The "Churchill Club" in Aalborg was the first organized sabotage group that could be read about in the underground press. It consisted of eight young people, of whom six were still schoolboys, who said openly after their arrest that they wanted to create Norwegian conditions in Denmark. What made a deep impression on us was that three of them continued with sabotage operations even after their arrest; they first escaped and after carrying out an act of sabotage returned to their cells, using their arrest as an alibi.

The boost in morale that the Churchill Club gave was great; but in terms of practical results, their effect was limited. Matches and gasoline were all that the saboteurs had at their disposal, and the effect was proportional; but a beginning had to be made somewhere. This was also the case with regard to those Communists who had not yet been arrested by the police. They began to study explosive techniques and collect explosives, but hesitated when it came to using them for fear that their actions would be regarded as a Communist revolt and therefore not get the necessary support from Danish people at large.

The situation changed, however, when the ship's carpenter Eigil Larsen, who had been taken prisoner, escaped by way of a tunnel on June 10, 1942, from the Horserød camp, where he had been interned with several other Communists. He began building up an organization of Communist partisans called KOPA, which consisted of volunteers who had fought in the Spanish Civil War.[15] On July 26, they carried out an act of sabotage against the Nordbjerg and Wedell shipping wharf in Copenhagen. This led the German admiral in Denmark to demand that action be taken and so von Renthe-Fink turned to the director of the foreign ministry, Nils Svenningsen, demanding the institution of the death penalty for spies, saboteurs and parachutists, either by changing Danish criminal law or by allowing the Germans to take over jurisdiction in this field.

Von Renthe-Fink's threats may not have been sanctioned by Berlin, but Scavenius, to whom von Renthe-Fink presented his threats a few days later, could not do anything. The government allowed itself to be bullied and decided that the prime minister, Buhl, should give the Danish people a warning over the radio. This broadcast was made on September 2, when he held a notorious anti-sabotage speech, in which he condemned sabotage and encouraged informers. Buhl's speech received, as could be expected, a good deal of support from the censored legal press, but on September 6, he received a reply from Christmas Møller who spoke on BBC radio and encouraged acts of sabotage.[16]

Christmas Møller had a mixed reception in Denmark. The Germans were, of course, furious, but many Danish politicians as well, who had previously admired him and his flight to England, turned their backs on him, even some colleagues in the Conservative Party. The legal press distanced themselves from any form of sabotage, while the underground press was in favor. *Frit Danmark*'s answer to Christmas's encouragement was given in October under the headline "Yes, Christmas! Our Nation Is Ready!"

I more or less agreed with Christmas Møller, and was more than willing to take part in active resistance, especially in sabotage. But I was not yet ready for action, and lacked all chances of taking the initiative in any way. I had no idea about sabotage techniques, knew nothing about weapons, or about objects to be targeted. I do not regard this as an excuse, because neither did the Churchill Club have any basis on which to start operations, which can only increase my respect for them and KOPA, who actually managed to carry out the majority of acts of sabotage that autumn.

As autumn wore on, we were informed by several sources that the Danish police, in conjunction with the German police, were on their way to becoming the most dangerous enemy of the burgeoning Resistance. The organization of the German police force was so complicated, in that they had units such as *Wehrmacht Abwehrstelle* and *Geheime Feldpolizei*, which were answerable to the German army, and units such as *Sicherheitsdienst* (SD) and *Geheime Staatspolizei* (Gestapo) under the SS. The Gestapo became the greatest threat to the Resistance movement. Officially the German police had no executive power over Danish citizens before August 29, 1943, but they had been keeping the Danish police under strict control all the time.

It would soon become evident that both the German and Danish police used paid informers and with their help the Danish police, over the course of 1942, managed to arrest more than thirty members of the two Resistance organizations De Frie Danske and Frit Danmark.

Apparently Buhl's anti-sabotage speech had had some effect. In my family, we regarded telling the police about saboteurs as treason; but we could not anticipate that the Resistance movement itself would be forced to resort to liquidations in self-defense, or that this would one day become a personal problem for us ourselves.

On September 5, it was the SOE that became the target of their actions. The Germans had found out where the telegraphist Paul Johannesen was sending from and the Danish police went into action, with the result that one of the Danish policemen was killed and Johannesen himself committed suicide. Three weeks later, on September 26, Christian Michael Rottbøll was killed by Danish police, and on December 2 another telegraphist and two SOE instructors were arrested by the Danish police and handed over to the Germans. They all ended up in prison or in a concentration camp. Finally, on November 5, 1942, the Danish police had succeeded in arresting the wanted Communist leader Aksel Larsen, in connection with the arrival of Werner Best to Denmark, and he was handed over two days later to the Germans and deported to the Sachsenhausen concentration camp.

Sabotage unleashed a debate in our Raadhusstræde flat, which by that time had developed into a rendezvous for my brother, sisters and fellow students. The newspapers featured many notices about major German advances in other occupied countries. No one could be in any doubt that they were out to ruthlessly crush all forms of resistance. But at the same time, there was an increase in unrest. Despite Buhl's speech and warnings from Christmas Møller's political colleagues, sabotage was on the increase.

The Telegram Crisis

September 26 marked not only Rottbøll's death but also the birthday of the king. His Majesty received birthday greetings from Hitler, to which he replied, via telegram, "*Spreche meinen besten Dank aus. Christian Rex.* (My best thanks. King Christian.)"[17]

This led to what was termed the "telegram crisis," apparently triggered by the brevity of the telegram, which had angered Hitler.[18] On orders from Ribbentrop, von Renthe-Fink sent the Danish foreign ministry a note that was reproduced soon afterwards in the newspaper *Frit Danmark*:[19]

The Führer has sent the king of Denmark amicable greetings on the occasion of his birthday. The king has merely sent what amounts to a brief acknowledgement of the receipt of these greetings. It therefore looks as if the king of Denmark has misunderstood entirely that greetings from the Führer of Greater Germany are to be interpreted as a special honor.... *All ways and means possible will be employed to prevent a recurrence of such behavior.*

The emphasis is my own, but we were left in no doubt that the monarchy was now under threat. The telegram crisis resulted in von Renthe-Fink's being recalled to Berlin and in the return to Denmark on October 2 of the Danish ambassador to Germany, Mohr.

There was hardly any information about this crisis in the legal press, which initially limited its reports to a number of elaborate German commentaries on "foreign rumors that a tense situation has arisen in Denmark." The king tried in vain to smooth over the cracks by offering to send the crown prince on a courtesy visit to Hitler. This proposal remained unanswered. We had the suspicion that a war of nerves against Denmark had begun, and that the thunderstorm could break at any moment.

On October 6, the Rigsdag met, and in his opening speech Buhl declared that Danish policy remained the same and that Denmark continued to be a noncombatant nation. The next day, we could read Buhl's speech in the press, plus a long Ritzau News Agency note from Berlin, which gave the following explanation of the telegram crisis:[20]

With regard to rumors that have been circulating abroad, and which we wish to counter, that there is increased tension in Denmark, the competent authorities in Germany have been exhibiting the greatest reserve. However, it has been hinted at that not everything in Denmark has been occurring as would have been expected, given the very correct behavior of German institutions in Denmark.... Certain Danish institutions have misunderstood this relationship and have thought that they could permit themselves rather a lot.... One matter which has given a particularly bad impression is the fact that those Danes who have risked their lives fighting on the *Ostfront* as volunteers have, on their arrival home, been treated with disrespect, contempt and even with mockery. Such actions have led to a deterioration of relations between the two countries and have had a number of consequences.

Precisely which consequences was something that the press did not wish to go into. Von Renthe-Fink was aware of the ideas of the ss ideologues concerning the Nazification of Denmark with a view to ultimately incorporating the country into a greater Germanic Reich, as the "Nordmark" Gau (county). But he was not himself a proponent of this policy. He had never at any point in time believed that Germany wished to hold to its solemn vow to respect Denmark's sovereignty, even after a German victory. But he did see that it was in Germany's short-term strategic and supply interests that Denmark were, for the time being, to be subjected to no more than "peaceful occupation." Von Renthe-Fink, therefore, wanted to adopt a "wait and see" policy, termed "attentism" by his successor, Werner Best.

The king's telegram, Hitler's wrath and the internal German struggle with regard to the policy to be adopted by the occupying power are indeed important elements in the telegram crisis. But in reality, the biggest problem for the Germans was the thought of an invasion by the Western Allies, between the Nordkapp up in Norway and the tip of Brittany in the south, the weakest point in the defenses being along the Danish west coast, where the Germans were building up defenses against British and American landings. As early as August 1942, it was decided to replace the German General Lüdke by General von Hanneken, whose main assignment was to fortify the Danish west coast and protect German forces from a rear attack by the Danish army, the Danish police and Danish Resistance. From May 1, 1942, Denmark was deemed to have become an "operational zone."[21]

On October 12, von Hanneken arrived in Denmark with instructions that included the information that in a New Europe under German leadership there would be no place for any constitution that included a democratically elected government. On account of Denmark's strategic importance, the country was to be turned into a province of Germany, and the monarchy and the present form of government were to be abolished. Denmark was to be regarded as an enemy nation and the aim was now to install a puppet government, led by Danish National Socialists and with a prime minister who was under no illusions about the fact that in case of the withdrawal of German troops from Denmark, he would be strung up from the nearest lamppost.

Von Hanneken was no Nazi, and was therefore not qualified to lead political developments in Denmark. So partly at the behest of Ribbentrop, Hitler had appointed the director of the German foreign ministry, ss-Gruppenführer Werner Best, to become the supreme authority in Denmark. Best was one of the pioneers of the NSDAP, a founder of the Gestapo, an officer in the ss and a former department head in occupied France. No one could seemingly be better fitted, in the eyes of Ribbentrop and Himmler, to fill the post – but not in the eyes of von Hanneken.

The decision was announced around October 1, while the telegram crisis was still brewing, and it is quite likely that it had been made some time earlier. Both von Hanneken and Best's appointments were likely to-kens of a long-term plan, merely expedited by the telegram crisis, but it is reasonable to assume that the original decision had been made as early as the late spring of 1942. In any event, the result was that power became divided between von Hanneken and Best; a balance was struck between the risk of a Western invasion of Jutland, which was the headache of the Wehrmacht (and therefore of von Hanneken) and the planning for a New Europe, which was of importance principally for the ss and the German foreign ministry.

Best's primary task was to have a new government elected with Scav-enius as prime minister. This gave the collaboration politicians a better chance of saying no, and several politicians were keen at the time to make the break that would lead Denmark into a "Norwegian situation." Form-ing a government without consulting the Rigsdag was something every-one wanted to avoid; but the politicians tried to avoid allowing personal antipathies towards Scavenius from being the determining factor. So the politicians gave in immediately and allowed Scavenius to become the new prime minister on November 9. This added to the illusion that Denmark was neutral and to the further illusion that policy of concessions and ac-tive collaboration would do the trick, and would ensure Denmark's inde-pendence after a German victory.

When the list of ministers was made public, we could see that to our pleasant surprise, no National Socialist had taken office as a member of the government. To the surprise of many, the list was even accepted by Berlin; this may have been connected with the American invasion of northwest Africa (Operation Torch), which occurred at about the time Scavenius was appointed.

Negotiations at Christianborg were, of course, confidential, and the general public was kept in the dark as to where politicians wanted to set the limit. But when Scavenius's appointment was announced, it was stated, among other things:[22]

Outwardly, the government regards it as one of its principal tasks to work for the strengthening and consolidation of good and neighborly relations between Denmark and Germany and to promote mutual trust and cooperation which will help continue the fruitful work the two countries have done with each other over time and which has had such great significance.

The result of the telegram crisis was a humiliating one; but nothing is so bad that no good comes from it. The crisis had perhaps brought about a postponement of the planned persecution of the Jews. No one knew that at the time, although later on it was to be very important for the salvation of many. In 1942, Sweden was not yet prepared to accept a stream of Jewish refugees, and it is doubtful if the Wehrmacht would have reacted as passively regarding the Jews as they did one year later. On the other hand, there can hardly be any doubt about the fact that the persecution of the Jews was going to follow, sooner or later, as had already happened in, for instance, Hungary.

It was not particularly surprising, therefore, that this was all discussed eagerly on Raadhusstræde. We were living under daily moral pressure, and a solution had to be found. We could now wait no longer. It was simply not sufficient to distribute a few underground newssheets now and again. More had to happen. I received the opportunity when a student of medicine told me, "We've heard you could well do something for us." This was neither a Tarzan nor a spy with blue-tinted spectacles, but a small, rotund and nearsighted student who hardly looked like a combatant. I knew that his name was Niels Hjorth, and that he was in the year above me; otherwise, I knew nothing about him. It wasn't his appearance or his name to which I paid much attention, but the assured tone of his voice, which sounded like an echo of firm conviction.

Niels Hjorth wanted me, my brother and my sisters to help distribute a letter written by Professor Mogens Fog to Danish students, when we went home on our Christmas holidays. Mogens Fog was a professor of neurology and, as he was a Communist and one of the founders of the Free Denmark movement, he had gone underground. When all four of us said without any hesitation that we would, he returned with a bundle of Mogens Fog's letters, which we read with great emotion and excitement. In his letter to students, Fog called upon us all to take our personal responsibility for the outcome of the war. And to those who were uncertain as to the use of Danish resistance, he wrote: "Only a drop in the ocean, that's what they say. Well now, the ocean consists of drops."

Niels used the opportunity to ask us if we would in any case keep in our flat a duplicator and start helping to print *Frit Danmark*. We were also glad to do this and it was soon after revealed that he was a member of the DDS, where he worked together with Cato Bakman and Holger Larsen, whom I knew already from the Anatomical Institute, plus three students of law. So we could then travel off home at Christmas with the student train as active members of *Frit Danmarks Studentergruppe* (the Free Denmark Student Group). Two and a half years wandering in the wilderness were over.

The four Kieler students: Flemming, Elsebet, Jørgen and Bente on their way to Copenhagen

PART II: GETTING INVOLVED

Our home, illegal meeting place and printing office on the
4th floor at the corner of Raadhusstræde and Nytorv

Our fight with the police in the main street (Strøget) in Copenhagen
during the Anti-Comintern demonstration, November 1941

Newly appointed Danish prime minister Erik Scavenius and German
pluripotential ss-Obergruppenführer Wemer Best, November 1942

CHAPTER 3

Free Denmark

There has hardly been any period of Danish history that has attracted the attention of so many historians as the occupation of 1940 to 1945. Many books written about the period suffer from rather muddled concepts and lack any description of circumstances during the time just before, and also fail to learn lessons from then regarding what is happening today. Nor does it make it any easier for historians that there are still eyewitnesses around from the times involved who can look over their shoulders as they write.

The confusion of concepts comes most clearly to the fore when historians start considering the term "Resistance." When using this term, it is sensible to ask yourself: resistance against whom and what? Against Hitler, against Nazism and the occupation, that for certain. But this is but a part of the answer. During the course of the first three years of the occupation, it gradually dawned upon a growing number of people that there must also be resistance against the Danish policy of cooperation with the occupying forces – i.e., collaboration.

Ius Resistendi

As far as I am aware, the concept of resistance can be traced back to 1215, when King John of England was obliged to sign the Magna Charta Libertatum – commonly known as the Magna Carta – which defined the limits of the powers of the sovereign and also set out a number of rights that

citizens enjoyed. This great charter of freedom consisted of sixty-three articles, written in Latin. One of these articles, "*Ius Resistendi*," outlines the
rights of citizens to revolt, should the monarch exceed his powers. The
revolt did not necessarily involve the use of violence but would inevitably
bring the person in revolt into conflict with those in power.

In Denmark, the use of the concept *Ius Resistendi* during the German
occupation suffered from the fact that it was not absolutely clear who those
in power actually were. *De jure*, these were the king, the government and
the Rigsdag, or parliament. The politicians had been elected legally and the
government had received its mandate as recently as March 1943. It is true
that the country had been occupied by Germany, but Denmark was not at
war with Germany, and the government maintained the convenient fiction of
neutrality and cooperation with the occupying power, based on a memorandum that guaranteed Denmark's integrity and independence in the future.

However, *de facto* there was no doubt that the Germans had usurped
power and now controlled the country, something which the population
were made aware of time and time again whenever the government was
forced to go against the constitution. The *right* the population enjoyed to
revolt was something that people hardly doubted; but this did not necessarily mean that this right was also a *duty*. Only those who viewed it thus
were prepared to join the Resistance movement. This is something that
historians who have wished to defend the policy of collaboration with the
occupying power have not always been clear about in their own minds.

It is not only the concept of *resistance* that causes historians problems,
but also that of *movement*. What is to be understood by this term? People
naturally think about organization and politics, which leads to the conclusion that there is a certain amount of popular support, a joint aim and
leadership. This is then a *resistance movement*. However, a resistance movement can also be seen as a grassroots movement, developing as a type of
popular revolt.

Many Danish historians have wished to distance themselves from such
conclusions, and wish to claim that illegal activities were orchestrated from
above and kept going with a political leadership, especially with regard to
the Danish Communist Party (DKP) or the Danish Unity Party.

My most decisive argument to reject such conclusions is that it does
not take into account the fact that *everyone* who took part in the Resistance,

irrespective of political affiliations or lack thereof, did so voluntarily. No one could force them to risk their lives, and no one could prevent them from dropping out, should things get too hot for comfort. Participation in the struggle was primarily a matter of private initiative, which can only be understood if it is clear in the mind of the observer that the Resistance was first and foremost an ethical revolt, one which did not respect the usual social and political divisions, except in that traitors to their country were set apart from the rest of the population. Nor was there anyone who harbored any illusions regarding the neutrality of Denmark, a policy in which national politicians were finding themselves more and more entangled.

Such private initiatives led to the formation of many different groups, and a whole variety of strategies and aims. What they did have in common was the struggle against Hitler and collaboration with Germany. The most important concentrations of effort can briefly be named here: the League (intelligence), the Ring (education and information), the Free Danes (the underground press and armed resistance), Free Denmark (the underground press), the Danish Unity Party (underground press and sabotage) and DKP (underground press and sabotage). Fate would have it that my brother, sisters and myself joined Free Denmark.

The Free Denmark Student Group

After the Christmas holidays, I returned to Copenhagen in January 1943 and soon made contact with Niels Hjorth, who had given us to understand that our role would be the printing of the *Frit Danmark* newssheet. We were all prepared to do so and were soon assisted by old and new friends. We all met at Raadhusstræde 2A. And so an illegal group had now been formed, consisting of the following students from provincial towns and cities, plus their colleagues from Copenhagen:

Students from Horsens
The four brothers and sisters:
    Student of literature Elsebet Kieler (born August 4, 1918)
    Student at teacher training college Bente Kieler (born September 21, 1920)
    Student of medicine Flemming Kieler (born June 22, 1922)
    Student of medicine Jørgen Kieler (born August 23, 1919)

Another brother and sister:

 Polytechnical student Hanne Møller, known as "Nan" (born October
  18, 1922)

 Polytechnical student Hans Tellus Møller, known as "Tellus" (born
  December 25, 1923)

Students from Odense

 Student of medicine Niels Hjorth (born August 4, 1919)

The brother and sister:

 Law student Jette Stampe Jensen, known as "Trunte" (born December 8, 1921)

 Law student Helge Jensen (born May 2, 1919)

Students from Copenhagen

 Law student Jørgen Jacobsen, known as "Tromle" (born April 11,
1919)

 Student of medicine Holger Larsen (born April 11, 1920)

The two sisters:

 Polytechnical student Ebba Lund (born September 22, 1923)

 Polytechnical student Ulla Lund (born November 15, 1924)

Other students from outside Copenhagen

 Student of medicine Cato Bakman (born March 15, 1918)

 Polytechnical student Klaus Rønholt (born April 10, 1923)

The group was very heterogeneous with regard to political convictions.
The students from Horsens were clearly conservative. At the other end of
the spectrum were Jørgen Jacobsen and Niels Hjorth, who were avowed
Communists. The rest of the group were somewhere in between. But we
all agreed on cross-party cooperation, something which was the basis for
the fight against Nazism and collaboration.

 The nearest Free Denmark ever got to a political program was the following declaration, which we could all accept: "National unity without can
never be achieved without social unity within." I would personally have
preferred the opposite formulation, i.e., "Social unity within can never be
achieved without national unity," but this is but a quibble. It was national
unity that was our greatest problem at the time.

Raadhusstræde 2A

Niels and his colleagues had already started printing work, but activities were soon transferred to Raadhusstræde 2A where we started off with great enthusiasm, banging away on an old typewriter, making stencils, using masses of ink and a good duplicator. We started by producing and distributing the newssheet *Frit Danmark*. But, owing to the increased censorship of the student press, we also decided to spread an underground student newssheet, which was entitled *De Danske Studenter* and first appeared on April 1, 1943. We also produced a substantial edition of Steinbeck's *The Moon Is Down*.

For safety reasons, we moved the duplicator around from one address to another. But Raadhusstræde remained the place where we met, and where many long political, philosophical, moral and practical discussions took place.

Producing illegal newspapers and books was not easy. Professional printers were only used at a later stage. We accepted the manuscripts of things to be published from an anonymous editorial committee and then wrote them up on the rather brittle stencils using old-fashioned manual typewriters. None of us could touch-type, so we typed away with one finger. We would write until late into the night and would despair if a stencil fell to pieces when it was nearly ready. This had to be repaired with nail varnish, or be rewritten; the newssheet *had* to be published. Then the stencil would be duplicated. This was also a manual activity, and again, there was a great risk that the stencil would disintegrate, which would mean starting from scratch.

Our fancy title page with the words *Frit Danmark* had to be printed with an engraving needle and this made the stencil even more likely to fall to pieces. Nail varnish was useful, but once the ink had seeped through the perforations in the stencil, no amount of the most fancy red nail varnish could help anymore, so you either had to rewrite everything, or send out the newssheet with embarrassingly large blots.

A stencil would hold out for the production of around two hundred sheets, made by rotating the handle of the duplicator. After that, copies became illegible. So this became our initial print run for quite some time. Later on, we obtained an electric duplicator that worked somewhat more smoothly. With this machine, we could produce five hundred copies per stencil.

I did not know who edited the two underground newssheets that we produced. Contacts were maintained via Niels and Tromle. I had my suspicions that Tromle himself helped edit the student newssheet *De Danske Studenter*. This later turned out to be true. His most important contribution was an article in that newssheet in June 1943, where he exposed Werner Best's dubious past, belonging to the group that had planned a violent Nazi coup d'état, and as a founding member of the Gestapo.

It was the resistance against Nazism, the critical attitude towards the opportunism of the government and the struggle for freedom for Denmark, which bound the people who produced *Frit Danmark* together. Political and ideological differences were not expressed in the columns of the newspaper, despite the fact that they existed; but political discussions within the group were naturally inevitable.

The elections to the *Folketing* (the Lower House of the parliament) in March 1943 gave rise to a lively discussion that focused especially on the cooperation between Best and Scavenius. The election came as a surprise; but we could not avoid regarding it as part of the collaboration policy, whose aims were clearly set out in the government declaration of November 10, 1942.

We were not sure how to vote. There were four possibilities. We could follow calls by the Ring and Christmas Møller to vote for those people within the various parties who, in our opinion, were offering most resistance to the Germans. We could also vote for the Danish Unity Party, or vote blank as Free Denmark and the Communists advised. Finally, we could abstain from voting altogether out of protest against the fact that the elections were not free. We were forced to adopt the last of these alternatives, as we had no right to vote. But we could not avoid having opinions on the matter, as we were involved in election propaganda. This meant that we decided that the best thing to do was to vote blank. For me, a vote for the Danish Unity Party was a possible alternative as we could not vote for Christmas Møller. We helped distribute electoral voting forms, which had no effect. The ideas adopted by Christmas Møller and the Ring won the day.

The result of the election was satisfactory in that it was clearly inspired by democratic voting patterns and clearly rejected the DNSAP. Scavenius and Best, on the other hand, also claimed that the result was an indication that voters supported Danish-German collaboration, which was shown to be false by developments in Denmark over the next six months.

The political differences between the right-wing and left-wing members of our group made themselves felt when, on April 12, a public announcement was made about how, in the Katyn Forest near Smolensk, the corpses of some eight thousand missing Polish officers had been found; they had been executed by shots in the back of the head. Who were the guilty ones? There was no reason to believe Hitler, who claimed that Stalin was the murderer; but there was equally little reason to believe Stalin, who blamed the Germans. The Polish Government-in-Exile in London were more inclined to believe Hitler than Stalin in this matter, and so did I and many others outside of left-wing circles in the Resistance here at home. The suspicions against Stalin proved later on to be justified. This was probably the only occasion on which Hitler was suspected of telling the truth. And on April 26, 1943, the Soviet Union broke off diplomatic relations with the Sikorski Government-in-Exile in London.

There was also a clash of opinions in the group when the Danish Students group began to express anti-Finnish sentiments and protest against the collection of clothes and foodstuffs for the Finnish population. This led to more discussions on the anniversary of the Soviet attack on Finland in November 1939. The Communist members of the group defended this action as strategically necessary in order to defend Leningrad for the German attack that was expected to follow. This opinion was not supported by later developments on the Finno-Russian front.

Before disagreement about Finland had reached a critical point, the issue was overshadowed by the question of whether we should take part in sabotage. In the spring of 1943 we were not yet ready to take the definitive step, even though we knew we would soon have to do so, one way or the other. German reprisals pointed us clearly in that direction; but we had no idea to whom we should turn, should we want to start working as saboteurs.

Thanks to Elsebet, our discussions on the Raadhusstræde often took on a philosophical and religious guise. One source of inspiration was the poet Kaj Munk, whose play *Niels Ebbesen* had been banned by the Germans in 1942. He participated fearlessly in the debate and encouraged open revolt. Pacifists did, however, find it difficult to reconcile their Christian belief with the revolt that Munk was fostering. Elsebet acknowledged his dramatic talent, but he was not the prophet she was searching for. She was a convinced pacifist and refused to bear arms.

Elsebet and I could still debate with one another, but we nearly always arrived at the opposite conclusions. "It was not the war that brought awareness to me," she writes, "I was always well aware what was going on. That is the reason that I kept my distance with regard to the resistance struggle, and believed in my own internal development. I wanted to be open to events, but I wanted to weigh up carefully any steps I would have to take – and in tune with that, I wanted to justify myself as human being." She received the opportunity to do so when, in October 1943, the onset of the persecution of the Jews put the debate into the proper perspective.

While Elsebet was busy searching for a "prophet," I was mostly working for the underground press. But I also made the attempt to pass my exams. Both things were on my mind during the spring of 1943. I found that our situation was a most unsatisfactory one, in that the environment we lived in was very much a student existence, as compared with what was happening abroad and here at home in the Resistance movement which, despite a degree of organization, partly lacked proper leadership, but as a movement or a popular uprising was on its way to snatch power from the politicians.

Splits in the Student Group

As mentioned above, the Finland question did not lead to a schism in our group, since the question whether the struggle should take on a more militant form had arisen. Here, opinions were divided. I argued for action that Elsebet regarded as violence, and other members of the group wanted to continue unarmed resistance and the underground press for a variety of reasons. Taking part in sabotage meant taking personal risks, but also grappling with whether it was appropriate and responsible. These were tough questions and we argued them from all sides in our many conversations.

In support of the use of militancy, I pointed to the limited success of the Royal Air Force bombing raid on the Burmeister & Wain (B&W) wharf in January 1943. We would be able to carry out such a raid more effectively, and with less of a risk for both the local population and for the Britons involved, and we also wished to make a greater contribution to giving Denmark her place amongst the Allied nations. This argument had the support of Flemming, Nan, Tellus and Klaus.

To my disappointment, I could not convince Cato and Holger Larsen. They were not against sabotage; but as the two law students, Tromle and Helge maintained that we students were the wrong people to carry out acts of sabotage. They supported their argument with an article in the second issue of the newspaper *De Danske Studenter* (The Danish Students), where it was stated:

> Sabotage is one of those means that Denmark has been employing and over the past few months has taken on such proportions that Denmark is on its way to becoming a model for others. By propaganda in the newspapers, the Germans have sought to isolate these heroes, and for a time it looked as if they would succeed. But it has now become clear that the Danish nation has recognized the validity of sabotage as a legitimate weapon against the Germans. *But*, and this cannot be over-emphasized, sabotage is only one of the means at our disposal against Nazism. If it were the only one, we would soon risk defeat. Saboteurs are recruited, in the main, amongst workers who have the appropriate physique and knowledge about factories, also contacts with other workers in factories, without which sabotage could never take place. The other layers of society, including students, must fight on other fronts, where their specialized knowledge can be useful. The struggle against Nazism must therefore be seen as one whole. We shall each make our contribution and do so effectively, and this does not require students to carry out acts of sabotage. This should only occur under exceptional circumstances. Sabotage is an excellent means for the struggle, *but our means are equally important, and in the same way as we recognize the importance of and admire what saboteurs do, so they recognize our contribution as well.*

I wished in no way to belittle the contribution made by the rapidly expanding underground press for the Resistance. I had, of course, no idea at the time of the dimensions of this activity. We only saw the whole picture after the war. But the underground press did play a significant role, and that I was aware of, even at the time. But for me personally, there remained one unsolved private ethical problem. Could I be encouraging others to become saboteurs if I myself were not prepared to run the risk involved? Elsebet remained firm in her convictions. She and Bente stood by the Fifth Commandment: "Thou shalt not kill."

We were confronted with a crisis of conscience, one which we all took very seriously. As Elsebet had no one to consult about Christian principles, she wrote to Kaj Munk who was both a member of the Resistance and a clergyman. He would, no doubt, understand her dilemma. She received the following reply:

June 3, 1943, Vedersø

Dear Miss Elsebet,

Burn all your literature on this topic – at the present moment it is not relevant, or is simply a millstone round your neck – and learn how to use a machine gun. It is the will of Christ that we should help widows and orphans, and this can be, among other things, by shooting robbers if they want to attack them. It is, on the other hand, not a Christian act to allow others to take part in the resistance struggle and the pain involved upon your shoulders, while yourself living in Nirvana. That is an opiate and depravity. Remain a Christian and learn how to kill in the name of Jesus.

– Yours sincerely,
Kaj Munk

That was what he had written. But they were not words she could do anything with. She did not allow herself to be won over. She and Bente still stood firm by the Fifth Commandment: "Thou shalt not kill." She has said the following about her convictions:

I could not see it any other way than that a pacifism governed by principles could be anything other than the result of the commandment which says: thou shalt not kill. And Bente thought the same…. There we were; but it was painful and as we wrestled with the basic problems of existence, our pleasant student flat was changed, little by little, into a general headquarters and a trench. We had two doors to the flat: one with a knocker, leading to Bente's and my room, and one at the joint entrance and leading to the boys' rooms. I always referred "violent" people to the boys' door – even though within the walls we were all friends and were a family together. One for the muck, the other for the cinnamon, so to speak. It was a hard thing to do; but it was a question of life and death – also that of the spirit, the integrity of our conscience.

At that point in time, we could not come to any agreement. I did not share her religious convictions and her pangs of conscience. Denmark's ever-increasing contribution to the German war machine, which took on the form of food, industrial products, repair work and transport, were all helping to sustain a criminal war. This contribution had to be stopped and when it was announced on May 7, 1943, that the saboteur Hans Petersen had been sentenced to death on April 12 by a German martial court, it became clear to me that the ethical problems that had been drawn to my attention by the article in *De Danske Studenter* could no longer be ignored. Life had to be equally valuable for both a worker and for a middle-class student. And so I made my decision.

The August Uprising

If 1942 had been the year during which the underground press had made its breakthrough, 1943 became the year when sabotage took on serious forms. Compared with 1941, there was six to seven times as much sabotage taking place in 1942 and this tendency continued in 1943. In the first three months of 1943 alone, over a hundred acts of sabotage were carried out – in other words, as many as in the whole of the previous year. Developments sped up as the SOE developed.

At the start, the SOE had been dogged by bad luck, culminating in the death of Rottbøll. But in December 1942 and February 1943, Flemming Juncker traveled to Stockholm in order to negotiate with the former press attaché in Denmark, Ronald Turnbull, who mentioned that a new head of the SOE had been appointed. The new head turned out to be Flemming Muus who was then dropped, along with three other parachutists, over Støvring in Jutland on March 11, 1943, shortly before the elections to the Lower House. About three weeks previously, his second-in-command, Ole Geisler, had landed at Furesøen, to the north of Copenhagen, along with three other parachutists. Geisler was stationed in Aarhus, while Flemming Muus went to Copenhagen. The SOE was back on track, as would soon be evident from sabotage statistics.

Crucial to the success of SOE activities were the many parachute drops, first in Jutland and later also on the island of Funen. The pioneers were the Hvidsten Group, under the leadership of the publican Marius Fiil. As things developed, later in 1944, we ended up having common links and destiny with the Hvidsten Group. Elsebet first made contact with Marius Fiil's daughter, Tulle Fiil, in the Western Prison; I was able to maintain the friendship that arose there right up to Tulle Fiil's death in 1983.

The increase in acts of sabotage in Copenhagen can be attributed to the reorganization of KOPA, which now became BOPA (Bourgeois Partisans),[23] plus the founding of the first Holger Danske organization[24] in March April of that year. But it was outside of Copenhagen that sabotage was most on the increase. It was still difficult to transport English sabotage equipment from the drop points in Jutland and Funen to the capital. The Germans had tight control of the Great Belt between the Danish islands and this presented a major problem. It therefore became sabotage and strikes in the provinces that showed most clearly the attitudes towards Scavenius's policy of collaboration.

The frequency of acts of sabotage achieved by March continued for several months to come. In June there was a slight decrease, but in July and August there was an explosive increase. This began in Aarhus, Esbjerg and Aalborg in Jutland and culminated in Odense on the island of Funen. But activities also spread to many other provincial towns such as Horsens, where it nonetheless was difficult to get things going.

Once I had decided to take part in sabotage, I cycled home to Horsens in June, in order to make contact with a younger former schoolmate, Peer Borup. I was also visited by Niels who was at the time working at the hospital in Varde in southwestern Jutland, where he followed sabotage activities in neighboring Esbjerg. We discussed the topic: what was it that they could manage to do in Odense and Esbjerg that we could not in Horsens? We were in no doubt. We were by now completely involved in the struggle against the Germans and their Danish collaborators. The course of events tended to be: 1) sabotage, 2) German reprisals, 3) strikes, 4) street disturbances, 5) state of emergency, and 6) the expected breakdown of Danish-German relations in the hope the Allies would recognize Denmark as one of them in the struggle against Hitler. In this way, the ethical revolt had found a well-defined aim and strategy. All that was lacking in Horsens was sabotage and support from the workers there.

In Aalborg, the situation was almost tantamount to full-scale war. A Resistance group, which had received a stock of weapons and explosives dropped by the RAF to the south of the town, was caught by surprise by a German patrol, which killed one of the Resistance members, Niels Erik

Vangsted, and took prisoner another, Poul Kjær Sørensen. A general strike broke out in Aalborg and the surrounding towns, and this spread to Aarhus, where rumors circulated that Poul Kjær Sørensen had been condemned to death.

We in Horsens had to do something. I talked with Peer about the opportunities that Free Denmark had to organize a sympathy strike in Horsens. Peer was always a very enthusiastic person. A number of handbills were written in all haste, and we dealt them out to shopkeepers who were impatiently standing in front of their shops, waiting for the signal to shut them. Unfortunately, we had far too few handbills and although there was certainly a willingness to shut shop, all that we achieved was a partial shop strike. There were no strikes in the factories. The Conservatives were in revolt, but not the Social-Democratic workers, who hated the Communists more than they did the Nazis. Peer and I realized that more had to be done, and taking into account Niels's experiences from Esbjerg and Varde, this would mean sabotage.

Stensballe Sound

After a not particularly successful attempt at sabotaging an electricity substation, Peer was keen on trying again, this time against a larger target. It was not megalomania but simply a combination of reasoning and a lack of knowledge that made us decide on the bridge spanning the Stensballe Sound.

In its own way, the target had been well chosen. When the Swedes revoked their transit agreement with Germany, this turned the railway in eastern Jutland into the most important route to occupied Norway. Given the many acts of sabotage that had been carried out on the stretch of line between Aarhus and Horsens, the Odder line became important as a parallel route for trains between various towns via Odder. One of the weakest links in this route was the railway bridge over the Stensballe Sound. If we could manage to blow up that bridge, connections between Horsens and Aarhus would be disrupted. This was certainly not a bad idea. There were, however, three things that narrowed down our chances of success. The first was a lack of explosives; the second was the total lack of knowledge as to how to go about blowing up a railway bridge and the third was an imperfect idea of how long it would take to repair the bridge. We had to take the difficulties in the order that they arose.

Our first problem was getting hold of explosives. Peer knew that the Communists had a store of explosives in a shoemaker's shop, so we would have to turn to them for help. Who among them actually put together the bomb is something about which I have no idea, and I know equally little about whether the shoemaker gave Peer any instructions as to how to handle such a bomb. He had nevertheless received some instruction from some Communist or other, someone who himself wanted to avoid taking part in the action. There was no SOE agent in Horsens to advise us.

Peer made sure that the bombs had been collected from the shoemaker's. There were two of them – one an explosive device, the other a firebomb. What was actually inside them was something we did not know; but the effect of the explosive device gave us an idea that it could have been the British plastic explosive P808, and the investigations carried out by the police afterwards showed that the firebomb was a British termite bomb. The two bombs were equipped with fuses that were linked to what were termed detonator pencils, which meant that the bomb could be lit one hour or more before the intended explosion. This gave us a feeling of security; by the time the bomb went off, we would be back home in bed.

The cycle trip out to the Sound was a strenuous one. It was raining and we cycled very carefully out of the fear that the bomb could explode at the slightest jolt. But we arrived at Stensballe Sound without incident and could attach our bombs to the bridge without being disturbed. This was an iron construction carrying railway sleepers. The explosive device was attached to an iron plate between two load-bearing girders, while the firebomb was placed on one of the sleepers. Then we lit the fuse, and cycled back home. I went to bed immediately, but could not get to sleep. I was listening anxiously for the explosion and was worrying about all those windows that would be shattered in the villas around. I think that I did hear an explosion – but a very small one, so I was not sure. Then I fell asleep.

The next morning, I rose early and cycled with Peer out to the bridge. There were few people around, and everything was very quiet. To my great joy, I saw that there were no broken windows anywhere, and to my great disappointment, I also saw that the bridge was virtually undamaged. A hole some ten inches (25 cm) in diameter had been blown in the middle of the bridge, one single sleeper had been damaged by fire, and a few nails had been forced out. That was all.

The police, who had been summoned shortly after the explosion, found near one of the rails a large metal box, three by five inches (7.5 × 13 cm) in size, which weighed 2.75 pounds (1.25 kg). This was filled with a yellow substance and equipped with two fuses, each about an inch and a half (4 cm) long. Closer inspection revealed that the detonator pencils of the firebomb had been ripped off in the first explosion.

For many years after the war, I was left in uncertainty as to when exactly my first act of sabotage had taken place. It was not until I later had access to police reports that I found out that the attempt to sabotage the Stensballe bridge occurred between August 28 and 29, 1943, when a state of emergency had been declared for Denmark.

The conclusion of the police report was as follows:[25]

Bomb explosion on the Horsens-Odder Bridge over the Stensballe Sound, dated 28.8.43, around 24:00 hours. Only minor damage. An undetonated British firebomb has been found. The investigation has been closed. The case remains unsolved.

When we stood there on the bridge on Sunday morning, August 29, we did not yet know that "Operation Safari" had already been set in motion. The last thing we had heard from the government was a broadcast on August 28 of its declaration, dating back one week, consisting of the usual call for law and order to be maintained. We knew nothing about the fact that the Danish government had, that Saturday afternoon, refused to give in to a German ultimatum and then handed in its resignation. Nor did we know that the Germans were busy disarming the Danish army and navy. German operations began in Horsens at 03:45 hours, when twelve to sixteen German soldiers stormed the P24 marine cutter, arrested the captain and confiscated the ship.

More dramatic than this was what the police commissioner Borchorst underwent. At four o'clock in the morning, he was fetched by car by the German city commandant, Oberleutnant Tettling, and taken to the German headquarters in the town. On the way through the town, they were intercepted by a German patrol who opened fire, as the chauffeur had not stopped quickly enough. Tettling was hit and died on the spot. Most of the Germans panicked and fled. Borchorst nevertheless managed to persuade one of them to drive the car to the German HQ in the Allégade school, where the police commissioner could deliver the dead commandant and express his thanks for the ride.

Peer and I agreed to work together in the future. We understood that our fiasco was due to various factors. We had started from scratch without any contact with the SOE, without any knowledge of previous or new instructions coming from Britain, with no knowledge of explosives, nor any assistance from any experts, be it Communists, Danish sappers or the navy. What we would now have to do is establish contact with someone who knew what sabotage was all about, because we certainly did not. We agreed that Peer would continue to work in Horsens, while I would go off to Copenhagen to establish links there.

I said goodbye to Peer and my parents, and traveled with my younger sister on the last train going to Copenhagen, before railway traffic was temporarily stopped. It took quite some while to get to Raadhusstræde 2A, but I was still completely unaware of what was taking place throughout the country at the time. I had nonetheless managed to see posters with von Hanneken's proclamation, which read:[26]

PROCLAMATION

Recent events have shown that the Danish Government is no longer in a position to maintain Law and Order in the country. Unrest caused by the agents of enemy powers has been directed against the German Wehrmacht. I hereby declare, according to Articles 42–56 of the Hague Convention of Land Warfare, a state of emergency. I am ordering the following, to take place with immediate effect:

1) Civil servants and government officials and institutions shall continue to loyally fulfill their professional duties. They shall follow instructions given to them by the German supervisors.

2) Crowds and meetings involving more than 5 persons on the street or in a public place are prohibited, as are all assemblies, even in private.

3) Closing time is decreed to occur at sundown. From this point onwards, traffic on the streets will also cease.

4) All use of the Post, Telegraph and Telephone is prohibited until further notice.

5) All strikes are prohibited. Fomenting strike action which causes damage to the German Wehrmacht assists the enemy and will normally be punished by death.

Any encroachment of the above edicts will be punished according to standard German law. Any acts of violence, assembly of crowds, etc., will be ruthlessly suppressed by force of arms. Every citizen of Denmark who adheres to the above rules will be guaranteed the inviolability of person and property in accordance with martial law as based on common law.

    – The Commander-in-Chief of the German Forces in Denmark

AT LAST – Denmark had finally said NO.

Stensballe Sound, where my first unsuccessful sabotage of the railway
bridge was carried out August 28–29, 1943. The rails were removed after
the war, and the bridge is now used by pedestrians and cyclists only.

CHAPTER 4

State of Emergency

The train journey to Copenhagen lasted nearly all day. What was special about it was the total lack of dramatic episodes, not to speak of anything resembling war. Even at the Great Belt, German passport control on the ferry occurred without any signs of crisis. It was Sunday, and a strange silence had settled over the land, a silence more oppressive than that which is usually occasioned by the observance of the Third Commandment: "Thou shalt hold holy the Sabbath." So I arrived in Copenhagen late in the afternoon without the slightest inkling of the fact that injustice against the Danish army, navy and population as a whole had taken place that same day, August 29, 1943.

On returning to Raadhusstræde, I met not only my brother and sisters, but also several people from the Free Denmark group. We exchanged rumors, which soon proved to be very unreliable ones. We had not much to go on. We had to make do with the German announcements and the many rumors broadcast on Swedish Radio. Von Hanneken's proclamation was made public in an extra edition of the Copenhagen morning newspapers for Sunday, August 29. The next day, there were no newspapers; but the underground press had obviously been on a high state of alert. We distributed circulars announcing the ultimatum the Danish government had been issued and how this was countered with "a resolute *no*." We also produced a supplement to the monthly newssheet *Frit Danmark*, which consisted of a sheet with the rubric *Frit Danmarks Nyhedstjeneste* (The Free Denmark News Service), which initially appeared several times a week and later on, regularly three times a month.

On August 29, we published a number of short notices about military and other matters; in retrospect, these can be seen as a desperate attempt to understand and explain a complex of problems, including acute ones, which had arisen on account of the state of emergency, plus longer-term issues which this new situation could give rise to. Only after the war did we find out exactly what had happened. But as this all greatly affected what we actually did at the time, I will give a short summary of our attitudes.

The German Change of Tack

There was no doubt that the fact that the Danish government had stopped collaborating with the Germans was a major victory for the Resistance and therefore also a victory for us, although our contribution had been a modest one.

The question as to who was responsible for this change of tack triggered fierce debate at the time and this still rages, many years after the end of the war. It is not easy to avoid being confronted with the ethical issues involved. What was disputed was whether the rejection of the German ultimatum was an aim that the Danish government long had in mind, or whether it was a defeat of their policy of collaboration, which should be blamed on the Resistance – or indeed credited to them. Many column inches of newsprint have been devoted to the question. But one thing that those debating the issue always tend to forget is to look at the answers given by the government itself. The answer can be found in the official reply to the German ultimatum:[27]

> The implementation of those measures demanded by Germany would destroy the ability of the government to maintain order amongst the population at large, and the government therefore regrets that it is unable to regard it as right to cooperate in carrying out these measures.

In other words, it was the August Uprising that forced the government to say no. But we were obviously also aware of the fact that the fear of an Allied invasion of Jutland played a crucial role in the German reaction.

What we were, however, not so clear about was that the immediate reason for the Germans' presenting Denmark with the ultimatum was Hitler's rage when he was shown, at his Wolfschantz headquarters in East Prussia on August 20, pictures by the military photographer Walther Frentz. Apart from the pictures he had taken of the German fortifications along the western coast of Jutland, he also showed several photographs of sabotage including a Wehrmacht hotel and the barracks for the German lady switchboard operators. Hitler was enraged and the reports submitted by von Hanneken on a daily basis did nothing to improve matters. Best was duly summoned to the Führer's headquarters on August 24 to be lectured on the matter.

He left Copenhagen to the accompaniment of the thunder of a massive explosion at the Forum, which had been requisitioned by the Wehrmacht on August 20. It was to be used to house the two thousand men who had been called up as reinforcements. At around midday on August 24, the Forum was sabotaged by the Holger Danske sabotage group,[28] which we then joined. Best was given no chance to appease Hitler during his visit to Wolfschantz. Hitler refused to see him, and Ribbentrop was forced to act as go-between. This resulted in Best traveling back to Copenhagen on August 27 with an ultimatum, which was presented to the Danish government the next morning at nine o'clock. The government's negative reply was sent, after vigorous discussion, at 3:45 in the afternoon the same day, and this marked the end of the policy of collaboration.

The situation was a tense one, and we were confronted with a whole list of unanswered questions. On the last day of August, the newspapers began to appear again, this time under strict German censorship. On the front pages of the official press we could read that the Scavenius government had resigned and had left the running of the country to the civil service, who had been urged to remain in their posts. The population at large had been requested, as usual, to maintain law and order. There was no news about what had happened to the members of the government themselves.

The question that now lay on everyone's lips was whether we were now at war with Germany. Today we know that Werner Best had advised the German government to leave the question open, which would give him the opportunity to return to the ambiguous "policy of peace" that culminated in the elections of March 23, 1943. Von Hanneken's proclamation of the military state of emergency did not reveal much about the changed status of Denmark, or the Germans' future plans. According to the Danish translation, the proclamation was "in accordance with Articles 42–56 of the Hague Convention," which was the nearest we got to a formal declaration of war by Germany, and this was the result of a dubious translation to boot. It was quite an unclear announcement and was made no clearer by the final statement that "every citizen of Denmark who adheres to the above rules" will be guaranteed the inviolability of person and property in accordance with martial law as based on common law.

How could the citizens of Denmark observe martial law if Denmark was not at war, and what kind of law was it that guaranteed the protection of persons and property? Of the five items listed in the proclamation, three were the usual prohibitions of meeting, traffic after sundown and strikes. The prohibition of the use of post, telegraph and telephone no doubt surprised many people; but it was swiftly revoked. The death penalty for those who encouraged strike action was to be expected; but for some strange reason, not for acts of sabotage. The greatest surprise was, however, the order given to the civil service and local government to continue to fulfill their professional duties. This was interpreted as proving that the Germans had plans right across the board. The order to the civil service was supported by the old government which, after German pressure had been applied, sent the following farewell greeting:[29]

> We expect all members of the Civil Service, during the short time that the state of emergency will hopefully last, to stay at their posts and fulfilling their responsibilities continue to work for the good of our country and people, so that there does not arise friction between the organs of state and the German authorities, which, according to martial law and the state of emergency as proclaimed has the authority to act in this way.

This mention of "martial law" was the nearest Denmark got to an official declaration of war, before our leaders resigned and began to prepare their showdown with the people involved in the August Uprising. But war it was, and it was the army and the navy that felt this first when von Hanneken carried out "Operation Safari" on August 29 in order to disarm the Danish military forces.

Operation Safari

The chief archivist of the German forces, Goes, wrote a thorough report on the disarmament of the Danish army, and reached the following conclusion:[30]

> Forty-three Danish working areas, barracks and encampments have been disarmed in or near twenty garrisons.... In eighteen of these, the Danish army put up resistance; in four cases, stiff resistance was encountered. A total of 6,446 Danish soldiers were taken prisoner.... Five German soldiers were killed and fifty-nine wounded, and fourteen Danes were killed and fifty-seven wounded.

One more Danish soldier died of his wounds on October 15. The guards at the military arsenal were also killed. Goes ends with a depressing survey of all the weapons and other equipment that were stolen by, or handed over to, the Germans and ends with the following conclusion:

> Militarily speaking, the threat has now been removed that the Danish defense forces would go over to the enemy, should a landing by the Allies take place on the coast of Jutland. The Danish defense forces within the country have been knocked out. The Dannebrog now only flies over one detachment of Danes, and that is the Frikorps Danmark, which has been so insulted at home and is now fighting on the *Ostfront*.

It is obvious that at the time, we had no detailed knowledge of these matters. But we soon found out that the Danish army had, since April 9, again suffered humiliation. What angered us most were the rumors of a "voluntary" handing in of arms, weapons that the civil population in revolt would have had good use for. We were not the only ones who were criticizing the lack of will to resist. But our anger was mixed with a concern about the fate of the soldiers who had been interned. Would they be released and sent home, or would they be sent to the *Ostfront*?

One person we worried about in particular was my cousin Svend Kieler who was a naval cadet aboard the inspection ship the *Hvidbjørnen* (polar bear), which was used to train new cadets and which was, along with another training vessel, surprised by the Germans in the Great Belt when on its way to Sweden. A few weeks later, we were visited by Svend, and he told us how the Germans had come aboard and taken over command. The Danish minister of defense had issued the order that they were not to put up a fight. But a bomb had been prepared, so that they could sink the ship themselves. Svend told us:

> The captain came bareheaded and wearing a life jacket. He stood on a hatch and said something like this: "In five minutes, the *Hvidbjørnen* will be blown up. We can look our fellow Danes straight in the eye when we get home. We have done our duty." We all cheered the captain and the Germans began to release the safety catches on their weapons and point them at us. "So all that remains for us to do is jump overboard," said the captain, and that's what we did.

And a short while later, the *Hvidbjørnen* blew up. All the crew were rescued and taken prisoner by the Germans. Afterwards, Svend was interned along with the rest of the cadets in Copenhagen at navy headquarters, where most of the Danish naval vessels had been scuttled on the morning of August 29, on the orders of Vice-Admiral Vedel.

As the Germans took over Holmen, they fired on the Danish soldiers and killed two of them. Of Denmark's thirty-seven operational vessels, four managed to slip away to Sweden, while twenty-three were rendered unusable by being blown up, sunk, set on fire or run aground. The remaining ten were taken over by the Germans. They had hoped to later man these ships with Danish volunteers, but no one turned up. The Germans now lacked the ships and manpower to mount surveillance along the Øresund coast, something which would later on prove of great importance for saving Denmark's Jews.

We were kept well informed about these events by Svend. To our great surprise, he suddenly turned up one day in September at Raadhusstræde. At first, he did not say particularly much about his experiences on the Great Belt; but he did tell us that those interned on Holmen received permission to leave the internment camp once a week by showing a pass and swearing an oath that they would be back by a particular time. He told us that he was busy forging passes that were given to cadets who understood that they were only to be used to foster contacts with the Resistance in town.

He soon came to the point. What was important for him was to know whether we were willing to store a number of weapons that he and his friends were going to smuggle out from Holmen. We said yes on the proviso that we might ourselves be forced to use them for the resistance struggle. Svend completely agreed to this condition.

Svend was accompanied on one of his visits by a sea cadet called Erik Koch Michelsen, known as Mix. He had not been on the *Hvidbjørnen*, but had been in Copenhagen on August 29, and when he understood what had been happening on Holmen, he tried to sail over to Sweden in his canoe. He was caught in the fog and nearly drowned; but at the last moment he steered towards the Drogden lighthouse, where he was taken prisoner by the Germans. A few days later, he was transferred to Holmen, from where he began to smuggle light arms along with Svend. Mix later became one of my closest associates in the HD2 sabotage group. He reminded me of Peer Borup – the same big smile, the same lively eyes, the same keenness and impatience to get going. He was also quite confident in his behavior, and I was left in no doubt that he was the leader type. I had great confidence in him right from the start and knew that we would soon become good friends.

The Hostages

The attack on the Danish army and navy was the most conspicuous operation. But it soon became clear that the Germans had also taken a number of civilian hostages. While military operations were wholly the responsibility of von Hanneken, the hostage-taking that took place on the night between August 28 and 29 was organized by Best. Almost four hundred people were rounded up, including Conservative politicians, leading Jewish figures, professors, journalists, artists and intellectuals. Some of these were released immediately; but in Copenhagen itself, around 150 people were arrested, plus a further 135 in the provinces, of whom around a hundred ended up in the Horserød camp, where several huts were empty after ninety-five Communists had escaped.

The Swedish press described this operation in detail, so we were well up on what was happening. Strangely enough, the hostages did not include many people who had been suspected of taking part in Resistance activities, which were on the increase at the time. They had not been at home. Nor were there particularly many Jews, and although the leaders of the Mosaic

Congregation, C.B. Henriques and Axel Margolinsky, plus the chief rabbi, M. Friediger, were among the hostages, it is rather clear that this was not the start of the pogrom we were to experience a month or so later. Two of our professors from the faculty of medicine were also among the hostages. With few exceptions, the hostages were released during the month of September and the first days of October. Even Professor Warburg, who was completely Jewish, was set free, while the chief rabbi and his son shared the fate of those who, during October, were sent to Theresienstadt.

The Resignation of the Government

Then, and ever since, I have been convinced that the August Uprising forced the government to resign on August 29. But we also thought about all the other angles concerning this change of direction, which did not fit in with Scavenius's general policy aims. We have asked ourselves for a very long time how far the government was prepared to collaborate with the Germans. Where did the limit lie? Constitutional laws were being broken time and time again, and we knew that in reality the government had long since given up any pretense of independent policy decisions with regard to foreign affairs. Neutrality was an illusion.

Denmark had allowed itself to be forced to leave the League of Nations and enter into the Anti-Comintern Pact. She had broken off diplomatic relations with the Soviet Union and had accepted the setting up of the Frikorps Danmark. On countless occasions, Danish military equipment had been handed over to the Germans, and over and above all this, collaborators were now contributing to the German war effort by exporting agricultural produce and industrial goods to Germany. While the collaborators were satisfied with having received the government's blessing, the Communists now saw that for them no laws and justice existed. Against this background, there was a good deal of uncertainty as to how far the government was prepared to go. Would it accept the mobilization of Danish soldiers for operations on the *Ostfront* or the persecution of the Jews? The answer that immediately sprang to mind was that this would be unthinkable. But what about Frikorps Danmark and the Communists? This last question became an issue on August 28 and 29.

When the Free Denmark student group had been set up, we managed to cooperate with the Communists who, despite fundamental political differences of opinion with ourselves, proved to be loyal and idealistic colleagues who put all their energies into the common cause. We were therefore also very worried about the fate that awaited those Communists who were interned at the Horserød camp. While ninety-five had managed to escape, another 150 were now in German hands. One month later they were deported to the Stutthof concentration camp, which cost twenty-two of them their lives and the rest of them their health.

After the war, the former minister of justice, Thune Jacobsen, excused the deportation of the Communists by referring to von Hanneken's note to Scavenius in which he stated, referring to the state of emergency:[31]

> I expect that members of the government will desist from any action undertaken against the German Reich.

This is not only a cowardly excuse, but also wrong. Thune Jacobsen raised the issue during the closing session of government on August 28 where it was decided to dismiss the German ultimatum. There was no interest expressed there as to the fate of the Communists. The reference to von Hanneken's demand that members of the government were to desist from actions against the Reich cannot be accepted as an excuse, since the demand was first made in a letter that Scavenius received the next morning at four o'clock.

We obviously did not know about the government plans at the time. In moments of optimism, I nourished the hope that either the government had gone underground in order to join the Resistance, or that it had fled to Sweden, so that it could establish a government-in-exile at a later date in London. This would have been a significant step in enabling Denmark to be recognized as one of the Allies. But none of these hopes were met, and it would soon become evident that the government was merely hiding behind the scenes, where it continued to pull strings. It had handed in its resignation, which the king had immediately refused to sign. So the ministers could continue to draw their salaries while at the same time having gone on strike, leaving the administration of the country to the under-secretaries of the various government departments.

On August 29, we did however receive a provisional answer to our question as to where the government set the limits of its willingness to collaborate.

What the Danish government could not live with was that Danish police officers would hunt down militant members of the Resistance, and that these members would be condemned to death under Danish law and executed by their own compatriots. It was, after all, not only their political lives after the war was over that hung in the balance, but life as it was then, when the twenty-seven-year-old Poul Edvin Kjær Sørensen was condemned to death. Poul's fiancée, Else, fought desperately to get him pardoned. In vain. He was executed on August 28.

Rule by Under-Secretaries

Rule by under-secretaries was the loyal answer the civil service gave to the call by the government, itself on strike, to remain at their posts. Led by the under-secretary of the foreign ministry, Nils Svenningsen (a close associate of Scavenius), the under-secretaries (permanent heads of the various ministries) maintained contacts with the government and also with the former foreign minister, P. Munch. On the other hand, it took a good deal of time for them to establish contacts with the Resistance.

Postwar historians see the August Uprising in another light. Hans Kirchhoff,[32] for instance, describes the government's measures as

> a triumph for the tactics and pragmatism of the politicians. They managed to protect themselves from collaboration, and achieved a hibernation of the political system while preserving necessary influence via the under-secretaries.

This was the bitter conclusion we also arrived at up until 1945. But we never managed to shrug off the mistrust we had, and I found it difficult then as I do now to swallow any excuse for the measures taken by the politicians who were, in effect, collaborators. And yet we had no firm opinion concerning the heads of the civil service and their actions. We did not know these men and what they stood for. Some of them would later prove to have been good friends of the Resistance.

One of the first and most important tasks to be tackled by the under-secretaries was future cooperation between the Danish and German police forces, the latter now being installed in many places in Denmark. As loyal executives of the will of the government, the police had been at loggerheads with the Resistance and the SOE. Officially, jurisdiction was an internal affair of Denmark's and the Germans had promised not to interfere in this sphere of society. But immediately following the German occupation in April 1940, a contact organization had been created at the behest of Germany, called the "State Advocacy for Special Needs." This was to ensure cooperation between the Wehrmacht and the Danish police. We received no guarantees that the occupying power would actually respect Danish jurisdiction, and the cooperation became a burden for the Danish police. We were therefore very curious to see what the police's reaction would be to the state of emergency and the strike undertaken by the government.

The problems the police had were dealt with in negotiation with the German under-president of police, Kanstein, with regard to whom Nils Svenningsen and Under-Secretary Eivind Larsen had said that as Germany regarded Denmark as an enemy nation, the grounds for police cooperation in all matters of sabotage, espionage, strikes, demonstrations and so on were now null and void. This opinion was added to in a draft issued by the State Advocacy for Special Needs, which was presented to Kanstein on September 14. This resulted in a series of meetings between the Germans and the Danes, but no agreement.

The cooperation the Germans desired was unacceptable; but at the same time it was acknowledged that a total refusal could lead to a much harsher German policy regarding the population at large. The draft was sent around as a guideline on how the Danish police should conduct themselves in the immediate future. But what was more significant was the fact that individual police officers were no longer obliged to remain loyal to the government and could follow their consciences.

A Headache for Germany

The declaration of martial law meant that the highest German authority in Denmark no longer lay with Best, but with von Hanneken, whose primary objective was the disarmament of the Danish army and navy. This occurred in true Prussian fashion, but once Operation Safari was over, a whole series of political problems remained, which von Hanneken was not particularly well qualified to solve. He was doomed to cooperate with Best, not because he wanted to, but because he had to. Best had lost Hitler's trust, but not his belief in the politics of collaboration in which he and Scavenius were indulging. After his humiliating visit to the Führer's headquarters on August 24 and 25, he felt completely put on the back burner. Yet on August 29 he already found the opportunity for a comeback as it now became clear that

von Hanneken lacked an overview of all the political problems that had
arisen on account of the German ultimatum and the state of emergency.
Two days later, he received a telegram from von Ribbentrop, confirming
that on Hitler's orders it was now he, Best, who was politically responsible.
Best had therefore not been sacked, and he was swift to take the initiative.
The policy he wanted to carry out was expressed in a telegram to Berlin,
in which he said:[33]

> I now consider, however – especially with regard to the future politi-
> cal and administrative treatment of Denmark – that it will become
> necessary to decide whether the German Reich is at war with Den-
> mark, as this country is not a friend, but has a hostile attitude towards
> us…. To my mind, it is in the interests of Germany that the political
> and juridical relationship between the Reich and Denmark is kept in
> limbo, and that any closer moves in one direction or the other should
> be scrupulously avoided.

Best, with his forked tongue, remained true to form. His most pressing aim was to make sure that the civil service continued to cooperate and
also to look into the creation of a caretaker government with which he
could continue to collaborate. But first he would need to obtain the necessary political support. He had tested this out during, for instance, the
state of emergency in Aarhus when the Lower House elections took place
on March 23.[34] In answer to his petition to Ribbentrop, a battalion of uni-
formed German police were sent over from Poland (the ss-*Polizeibatail-
lon Chelm*) to Denmark. These proved not to be sufficient after August 29,
whereupon he sent a letter to Himmler as well as a telegram to Ribbentrop (Telegram Number 1001),[35] in which he explained that in order to
consolidate his position, he would need two battalions of gendarmes, plus
three hundred security police officers, since neither the Danish police nor
the Danish courts could be expected to mount an effective challenge to
the Resistance. He also proposed setting up twenty-five police stations in
various cities and towns throughout the country and creating a special ss
court, which would be under his command.

As he did not immediately receive what he wished, he again sent a petition to Berlin on September 8, this time setting out what he needed for
the impending persecution of the Jews. By the end of September, there

were between fifteen and eighteen hundred German police officers in Copenhagen. These were initially under the command of Paul Kanstein, who had been sent over to administer internal affairs following the events of August 29. On September 7, a new head of the Gestapo for Denmark was appointed. This was Rudolf Mildner, who was transferred on September 19 from Katowice, where he had been notorious for sending many Poles and Jews to Auschwitz. In January 1944, he was replaced by Otto Bovensiepen, whose acquaintance I was to make at a later date. The head of the new Gestapo section in Denmark was Karl Heinz Hoffmann, who arrived on September 14, and the head of the Sabotage Section (Section IV-2) was "criminal lawyer" Eric Bunke. I was also to make the involuntary acquaintance of these two gentlemen.

Best's dream to head the highest police authority in Denmark finally collapsed when Günther Pancke was appointed chief of police on October 6, 1943. Denmark was spared a Reichskommissar and was given instead a triumvirate consisting of a political administrator (Werner Best), a head of the armed forces (Hermann von Hanneken) and, from October 1943 also a chief of police (Günther Pancke), officials who did not always share the same aims.

The Danish Freedom Council

Both the Germans and the Danish government appeared to have the idea that in the summer of 1943 they were faced with an organized uprising with some kind of coordinated leadership being run from Britain. It was not clear to them that such Danish-British leadership did not exist at the time. What we were experiencing in August of that year was the birth of an organized resistance movement and the Germans were unwise enough to act as its midwife. After the results of the March election to the Lower House had been announced, Best and Scavenius had received the impression that the majority of the population supported the policy of collaboration. The August Uprising presented a different picture, which was confirmed by a statistical survey carried out by the Ring resistance grouping, which showed that the sabotage of the early summer had been accepted by a large majority of the population as a necessary weapon against collaboration and the occupying forces.

The August Uprising was therefore a sign that the growth of a popular movement was in full swing, but also demonstrated that there was no

overall leadership. This was especially true of sabotage. In the spring there
had only been tentative efforts to form a joint command and in the events
leading up to August 29, decisions tended to be made at a local level. It can
thus be said that the August Uprising was a grassroots movement against
policies that would make Denmark an ally of Germany when the war was
over. The uprising was too early to be of any assistance to an Allied invasion but from a Danish point of view, it came at the very last minute and
underlined the necessity of having a joint leadership. This lead to Frode
Jacobsen taking the initiative to found the Danish Freedom Council. This
body sent out its first proclamation on September 16; it contained, among
other things, the following information:[36]

> The Danish Freedom Council has been set up by representatives for
> the Danish movements which, in accordance with the wishes of the
> people, wish to actively fight the German occupying forces, until such
> time as Denmark is once again a free and independent country.
>
> The Council's members have taken a solemn oath to work for the
> freedom of Denmark and have set this aim above all partisan and pri-
> vate interests.
>
> The Council is working for democratic ideals and wishes to fight
> not only against the enemy without, but also against Danish Nazis,
> collaborators and those capitulating.
>
> The task of the Council is to organize resistance against the Ger-
> mans at all levels and with all means that the people can muster.
>
> September 1943   Danish Freedom Council

We in the Free Denmark group heard about the proclamation after a
short delay and as it completely agreed with the aims expressed by Free
Denmark we were satisfied. We were, however, disappointed that there was
no detail as to which specific resistance activities the council was going to
undertake. It seemed to be an organization to organize and coordinate the
initiatives of others, and the main focus of the council was directed at the
period after the war.

I read the fifth point of the proclamation with special interest. The fact
that the council would be struggling to uphold democratic ideals would give
rise to a discussion in our group as to what was meant here. On this score

the Communists and the rest of us could not find common ground, and the term "democracy" remained hanging in mid-air as an appeal against Nazism without any clear picture emerging as to how this popular leadership would be organized, once the Nazis had been defeated. The promise to struggle against not only Nazis and collaborators, but also people who capitulated was, on the other hand, received with joy. We interpreted this as suggesting that politicians who collaborated would also be made to answer for their actions. This would prove to be a naïve hope.

Because of the somewhat uncertain beginnings of the Freedom Council, I drew the conclusion that I could not afford to await its orders. The Resistance struggle constantly remained a question of private foreign policy and as I understood the situation, I could quite simply continue with my own efforts to organize a sabotage group that wanted to: 1) prevent a resumption of collaboration policies; 2) spare the Danish people attacks from the air; 3) contribute to the swift ending of the war and thus save people's lives; and 4) ensure international recognition of Denmark as an Allied nation.

On September 4, a German decree was published, which announced that all firearms, ammunition and explosives must be handed in to the police; the next day Best announced that the death penalty or a long term of imprisonment would apply in cases where people helped saboteurs and spies. This created a problem for me in particular, as Elsebet commented on as follows:

> Following the events of August 29, 1943, it was announced that also those who helped saboteurs would be given the death penalty. I remember an exchange of words with Jørgen, where I drew his attention to the fact that this would have consequences for Bente and myself. This was simply a fact and caused no problems at the time. It was merely a further step in the process of awareness of the necessity for violent action.

But it was not, in fact, that simple. It made no difference to my resolve, but I did become aware of the fact that this was not only a matter of weapons and explosives, but also of my sisters' safety. I had to find somewhere else to live. I therefore rented a small flat on Sølvgade Street, which was later swapped for an illegal flat in the harbor area at Nyhavn. September did not go by entirely without problems; but this could not diminish our joy at the resignation of the Danish government and the capitulation of Italy on September 3.

CHAPTER 5

The Persecution of the Jews

There were many of us in this country who thought that Denmark, during the first year of occupation, would be forced to adopt the Laws on Jews and that the Germans themselves wanted to begin persecuting them. The Jews, however, escaped with a fright, to the relief of many and the disappointment of few – but to everyone's surprise. Why?

There can be no doubt about the fact that German caution can first and foremost be attributed to tactical considerations. On April 15, von Renthe-Fink warned in a report against the paralysis of political and economic life that would arise in Denmark, should any but the most essential measures be taken against Jews, refugees and the extreme Left. And even in later reports to Berlin, he was as ambiguous as was Werner Best later on. His policy was simply to postpone the persecution of the Jews until after the war.

On April 9, 1940, there was a further reason for caution on the part of the Germans: Hitler had not yet given Himmler the order to carry out the *Endlösung* (the Final Solution). This did not happen until June 22, 1940. A month later, an instruction was issued by the German foreign ministry, which commissioned a report on the distribution of the Jewish population of the occupied countries, including Denmark. The instruction was issued by Franz Rademacher, who worked in a special department of the foreign ministry, named *Deutschland*, which coordinated all matters concerning the Jews. The instruction was sent to von Renthe-Fink in Copenhagen on July 22, 1940. Despite repeated requests, it remained unanswered until January 1942; but it shows that as early as July 1940, Danish Jews were already included in plans for the Holocaust. Sentence had been pronounced; but the time of its execution had not yet been fixed, and for the time being, Germany was satisfied with financing the vitriolically anti-Semitic campaign that was being waged by the Danish Nazis in their struggle to seize power.

The Beginning

After the Soviet Union was attacked on June 22, 1941, the mass murder in Eastern Europe began. On July 31, 1941, Göring issued an order that there should now be a *Gesamtlösung der Judenfrage* ("a total solution for the Jewish problem") for all the territories under German control, and Reinhard Heydrich was given the order to plan this "total solution." Denmark was also affected. During his visit to Berlin, when the Anti-Comintern Pact was signed, Scavenius had a conversation with Göring, where it transpired that Denmark would not be able to get around the question and he would be making concrete demands in this matter.

The suspicion that the Anti-Comintern Pact could be used against the Jews was confirmed by a press agency notice on November 28, 1941, according to which Wilhelmstrasse was of the opinion that "sooner or later all states that have joined the Anti-Comintern Pact will have to take a stance with regard to the Jewish problem in one form or another."

There was concern, both in the legal and the underground press, and the fear of pogroms spread. There were but few who thought that the Jews would not be affected; but the Jews themselves allowed their fears to be allayed, and Chief Rabbi M. Friediger concluded:[37]

> We felt safe, since we enjoyed royal protection. Nor would any Danish government, whatever its makeup, touch the status of Jews in Denmark.

The Danish Jews' feeling of security rested on slender grounds. On January 20, 1942, Reinhard Heydrich held a conference in Wannsee, during which plans for the *Gesamtlösung* – the total solution – for the Jewish question were to be drawn up, as Göring had ordered. At this conference, Heydrich first gave a speech announcing which countries were to be made *judenrein*, i.e., free of Jews. A total of eleven million Jews were affected, and the countries listed included Denmark.

As for the methods to be used, Heydrich declared that the Jews must first be transported to labor camps in Eastern Europe. Those fit for work would then be sent out in labor detachments to build roads in the areas in question. It was calculated that the majority of these laborers would succumb to the hardships. Those who survived would be regarded as individuals with great powers of resistance, and could possibly form the core of a new Jewish people. To prevent this from happening, these especially tough Jews would be sent for *Sonderbehandlung* ("special treatment"), which meant to the gas chambers, which constituted the *Endlösung*, the Final Solution, which was also the end envisaged for those unfit for work who had somehow escaped a natural death. This was, in principle, the same concept as *biologische Vernichtung* (biological extermination) which was to become the basic principle of all the concentration camps as well as labor camps that lacked gas chambers. The difference was that gassing was to be replaced with death by firing squad, hanging or drowning at the end of the war.

At the Wannsee Conference, Foreign Minister Ribbentrop's representative, the extremely anti-Semitic Under-Secretary of State Martin Luther, recommended the postponement of the operation in the Nordic countries, because of difficulties that had arisen. What had happened in Denmark was that von Renthe-Fink had sent a telegram on January 6, 1942, to Berlin on account of the rumors circulating that the king would wish to abdicate, should the Law on Jews be passed. In this connection, von Renthe-Fink had held a conversation with Scavenius, where he repeated what he had said earlier, namely that it would be wise for Denmark to prepare itself for the fact that at the end of the war at the latest there would be a solution for the Jewish problem throughout Europe. Scavenius made no bones about the fact that raising the matter of the Jewish question would encumber any continuation of his policy aspirations, which were oriented towards Germany.

Martin Luther and Franz Rademacher were, at the same time, pushing for setting into motion the persecution of the Jews in Denmark. But von

Renthe-Fink managed to have the matter taken off the agenda for the time being, and he did not send the long-awaited survey of Danish Jewry until the very day, or the following one, that the Wannsee Conference started.

In the latter half of August 1942, Ribbentrop's fears were justified. Himmler began to interfere, in that one of his colleagues, Secretary of State Wilhelm Stuckart, along with ss-Brigadeführer Otto Ohlendorf, paid a visit to Denmark. Ohlendorf was the head of the *Einsatzgruppen* unit, which terrorized the civilian population behind the lines on the *Ostfront*. His specialty was mass murder. He was very dissatisfied with the way the Jewish Question had been handled in Denmark and threatened that Himmler and his people would have to tackle the problem if the Danish government did not itself do so.

In a memorandum, von Renthe-Fink tried to deflect the threat. But Ribbentrop was already aware of what was happening and on September 24, 1942, he gave Martin Luther the orders over the telephone to organize the "most swift evacuation possible of the Jews from the various European countries, as there is information that the Jews are fomenting a revolt against us and may even be responsible for acts of sabotage." This instruction also stated that the foreign ministry of the Third Reich had decided that "we shall now turn to the governments of Bulgaria, Hungary and Denmark requesting them to evacuate the Jews from these countries."

This sounded the death knell for the Danish Jews. But at the last minute, they received unexpected help from one of their best friends, King Christian x, who, on his birthday two days later, set off the telegram crisis by sending his brief reply to Hitler's birthday greetings. The Danish Jews were yet again given an unsure respite, and von Renthe-Fink was relieved of a hot potato which he could, to his great relief, hand over to his successor; but Best had more pressing problems, first and foremost forming a new Danish government.

When Scavenius was appointed prime minister in a government that did not include the representatives of the DNSAP as Hitler had demanded, Fritz Clausen was dead in the water, despite enjoying Hitler's support. The Jewish Question was thus no longer linked to the desire of the DNSAP to seize power and would now have to be tackled on German initiative. But the Jews had not been forgotten in Berlin. On April 19, 1943, a personal telegram was sent to Best, asking him to submit a report summing up the situation of the Jews in Denmark and giving an idea of how, without caus-ing undue problems to Scavenius's position, to hand solution of the Jewish Question over to the Danish government.

Best replied on April 24 by submitting a long memorandum where he describes the political consequences of such an initiative, also stressing that in Denmark, the Jewish Question was of very limited scope. He sought to dispel any worries Ribbentrop might have had by pointing out that the thorough investigations he had done into the matter could be put to use when the time had come to tackle the Jewish Question.

This meant that the storm died down. One of the contributing factors was the fact that the two extreme individuals, Martin Luther and Franz Rademacher, were transferred elsewhere. Martin Luther was sent to a concentration camp on account of his attempt to conspire with Himmler against Ribbentrop. He was later released, but did not survive the war. Best too tried to foster closer ties with Himmler behind Ribbentrop's back. But Ribbentrop won a temporary victory, the result of which was that Him-mler desisted for the time being from further action against the Jews of Denmark.

This situation did not last. The Germans obtained further information on the Jews by way of two burglaries, the first on August 31 at the office of Chief Justice Arthur Henriques, where the records of the Mosaic Congre-gation were stolen; and on September 17, when the Mosaic Congregation's offices were ransacked. The fact that this material had not been hidden away long before these burglaries is a testament to the incredible naïveté of leading Jews, collaboration politicians and the under-secretary of the foreign ministry, Nils Svenningsen.

Von Hanneken's "victory" on August 29 weakened Best's position. He dreamed of returning to the status quo of before the August Uprising, but he was brought back to reality when, on September 6, Nils Svenningsen told him that the Danes would take no steps to form a new government. Best thus had to alter his plans, and two days later he sent the following telegram (Registered as no. 1032) to Ribbentrop:[38]

With reference to your telegram of 19.4.1943 and to my report of 24.4.1943 I feel free to inform you of the new situation with regard to the Jewish Question in Denmark. In my opinion, a consistent implementation of the new policy for Denmark must include taking into account the solution of the Jewish Question, and that of Freemasonry in Denmark. The necessary measures must be taken before the present state of emergency comes to an end, since later implementation would cause a reaction throughout the country which could lead to a renewed state of emergency, which is likely to be under less favorable circumstances than at present. In particular, a delay would result in the possibility of any government in office at the time to resign and the king and parliament would suspend further cooperation with regard to the governing of the country. Furthermore, the likelihood of a general strike must not be discounted…. If measures are taken during the present state of emergency, it would however be possible to appoint a select committee under my leadership, should it prove impossible to elect a functioning government as such, and legislative power would then be carried out by myself by way of decrees. To arrest some 6,000 Jews (including women and children) all at once and put them on transports would require the numbers of police officers as outlined in my telegram no. 1001…. I would be obliged to receive a decision as to what steps I should take in order to prepare for the solution to the Jewish Question and that of the Freemasons.

It would seem quite clear that he was here using the Jewish Question as a means by which to achieve an increase in police strength he had requested with other aims in mind, before the Jewish Question had become a current issue. It would be sensible to bear this in mind as we assess the use to which the numbers of police he actually received were put.

Warnings

This development obviously led to increased anxiety among Danish Jews, whose spokesmen stood by their opinion after the events of August 29 that mass flight would not be possible on several counts. The Danish population could not be reckoned on to cooperate, and the Swedish government would not necessarily be willing to take some six to seven thousand refugees from Denmark, besides which any such action could provoke a reaction against those who could not manage to escape. Furthermore, people shared the view of the politicians and civil servants, especially that of

Nils Svenningsen, that it was not in Germany's interest to start a pogrom against the Jews. They therefore chose to adopt ostrich tactics and stuck their heads in the sand, for which they were severely criticized. This same course of events also occurred in other countries. What happened next has been thoroughly researched by historians. Here is a summary of some of the more important events:

September 11, 1943. Best informs his shipping expert Ferdinand Duckwitz about his telegram of September 8. Duckwitz reacts sharply against this as, in opposition to Best, he thinks this could bring disaster.

September 13. Duckwitz flies over to Berlin to stop Best's telegram, but arrives too late. The telegram has already reached its recipient.

Mid-September. The Nobel Prizewinner Niels Bohr is warned via the Swedish Embassy that the arrest of refugees, including several of his colleagues, can soon be expected. Between August 29 and September 27, sixty-one Jews manage to flee to Sweden.

September 15. The police reinforcements requested by Best arrive in Copenhagen and march openly on the streets.

September 17. Best receives an instruction from the German foreign ministry to send a report of his plans for the deportation of the Jews, and of his needs regarding extra police and means of transport. Duckwitz begins to warn acquaintances about the impending pogrom.

September 18. In reply to the instruction, Best sends Telegram 1094, in which he lists the vessels and trains needed to deport the Jews to Germany. The telegram ends with a request that the police officers remain in Denmark under his command until after the deportation of the Jews has taken place, in order to keep under control any unrest in the form of riots and, for example, a general strike.

September 21. ss-Standartenführer Dr. Mildner – "The Executioner of Katowice" – who has arrived in Copenhagen to replace Kanstein as head of the security police, reports, with Best's permission, to Himmler warning that the impending deportation of the Jews is now common knowledge and could result in a fiasco.

September 22. Duckwitz travels to Stockholm, where he informs Swedish Prime Minister Per Albin Hansson about the impending pogrom. Rumors abound. One of the sources of these rumors is said to be the German Kommandant for the City of Copenhagen, Max Mauff.

September 23. In a *Notiz für den Führer,* Ribbentrop informs Hitler of Best's reply of September 18 regarding the practicalities of deportation, and uses the opportunity to remind him of the complications involved in such an action (riots, a general strike, the impossibility of forming a government, the likelihood of the king's abdication), which Best had mentioned in Telegrams 1032 and 1094. He asks, in this context, whether Hitler is still determined to continue and, if so, whether the operation is to be carried out during the state of emergency. He is, and it is.

September 25. Duckwitz returns to Copenhagen where Best informs him that the pogrom is to take place on the night of October 1–2. The operation is, in Best's opinion, now inevitable; Hitler has dismissed his doubts. Duckwitz informs Best that German forces are inadequate to ensure the surveillance of the whole of the Øresund strait. The head and deputy of the Mosaic Congregation – C.B. Henriques and Karl Lachmann – meet Svenningsen to discuss the situation. Svenningsen assures them that the under-secretaries of the various ministries will protest if the Jewish Question is raised, but cannot give assurances that they will resign in protest. Svenningsen still believes that Best's "peaceful" solution will be the result and warns against illegally trying to leave the country.

September 28. After pressure from Best and orders from General Jodl, von Hanneken extends the period of the state of emergency. Best informs Duckwitz that the operation has finally been planned for the night of October 1–2 and adds that he wishes he could build a bridge across Øresund, so that the Jews could escape to Sweden, at which Duckwitz assures him that such a bridge will be built. There are no records of where he got the idea from. Duckwitz then informs the Danish politicians Hedtoft-Hansen and

H.C. Hansen, plus the Swedish diplomat Ekblad and his friend, the German harbormaster Cammann, with whom he agrees that the German coastal surveillance vessels will not be made ready to sail. Hedtoft and H.C. Hansen then warn C.B. Henriques, who, after some hesitation, is convinced of the truth of the allegations, and raises the alarm. By this time, the news has already reached many people, and they have begun to leave their homes.

September 29. During an early-morning service in the synagogue, on the day of Rosh Hashana, the congregation is informed of the impending razzia and is told to tell all Jews to hide with friends and acquaintances. At a meeting of the under-secretaries, a protest note from the bishops and the University of Copenhagen is read out. Once again, the likelihood of illegal escape abroad is dismissed as unlikely and the threat of resignation should such things occur is regarded as futile. Instead, with Jewish approval and the encouragement of Nils Svenningsen, Under-Secretary Eivind Larsen puts forward a no doubt well-intended but desperate proposal that they should offer the Germans the Danish-led internment of the Jews. Svenningsen and Eivind Larsen meet Best, who continues to deny that he has heard anything about any impending pogrom, so that there could be no question of Denmark interning Jews. This was attempted on September 30 and October 1. But by then it was too late.

Niels Bohr

We had arrived at a watershed on Raadhusstræde. Everyone realized that the endless discussions between pacifists and activists about which methods we were prepared to employ now had to end. Not only did the debate between Elsebet and me about armed versus unarmed resistance stop, but so did the political ones between Communist and non-Communist members of our group. We were in agreement about having to fight Nazism, but had to admit that we meant very different things by the word "democracy," which could have led to dangerous divisions between us. But the split was avoided because the persecution of the Jews made us recognize one joint ideological attitude – our fervent embrace of human rights – and this pushed our political differences into the background.

Resistance had now taken on an ethical dimension, which overrode political matters. The Communists already knew how to suppress the truth that all was not well with the human rights situation in the Soviet Union.

This also held true for Tromle, who was the first one in our group to hear about the threat of the impending pogrom:[39]

> On September 26, the king's birthday and a Sunday, I went to a party, and right in the middle of the party I was told by telephone that there would be a pogrom that very day. I left the party and got in contact with my father and his brothers. None of them believed me, nor did any of them wish to take advantage of my information to escape to Sweden. They thought that I was making a sensation and that this was another of my exaggerations.

Tromle does not tell where the warning came from, nor what transport to Sweden he was in a position of offering. But we knew we had to warn as many people as possible as soon as we could. We did not know many Jews, but like Tromle and many others, we found out that our warnings were taken with a pinch of salt. The country had been occupied for three and a half years without anything happening. Why should anything happen now?

On September 30 I took part in a meeting in the auditorium of the Rockefeller Institute, where we discussed the situation. We agreed on both a student strike and protest letters. But the whole picture suddenly changed when a colleague in my group, Cato Bakman, came to the auditorium somewhat out of breath and said: "Greetings from Niels Bohr. He's managed to get to Sweden."

Niels Bohr, the head of the Institute for Theoretical Physics at Copenhagen University, had earlier refused an invitation to go to England, but now he had sailed illegally, along with his wife and other refugees, to Sweden, where he arrived on the morning of the thirtieth. He traveled on immediately to Stockholm where he had talks with the Swedish government and had an audience with the king and the crown prince. The next day, the Germans started their operations in Denmark.

Together with Ebbe Munck, Niels Bohr made concerted efforts to make public the Swedish offer to take Jews, as this was the key to all plans to flee Denmark. Swedish Radio announced, around the clock, that Danish Jews were welcome to come to Sweden. This led to an increased international awareness of the persecution and rescue of Danish Jews, which in turn led later to the special treatment they received in Theresienstadt. Niels Bohr also asked the Swedish authorities to avoid asking refugees by which route they fled and who had helped them. But he failed to convince the Swedes to threaten to halt supplies of iron ore to Germany, if the pogroms continued. They feared that this could lead to armed conflict. His last act to try to help Jews who had been arrested was to convince the Swedish authorities to request that the Germans send the German transport vessel the *Wartheland* to Sweden with the Jewish prisoners on board. The Swedish request remained unanswered.

Cato was the best informed member of our group. I do not know where he got the information about Niels Bohr's journey, or whether he was personally involved in the escape. But we gathered on the last day of September and Friday, October 1, at Raadhusstræde to discuss what we should do. We had no clear picture of the situation, did not actually know how many Jews needed help, and only found out about numbers after the war.

German Actions

On the night between Friday, October 1 and Saturday, October 2, the Gestapo and the ss sprang into action. Given the material available, and the fact that Hitler had given his approval, it cannot have been difficult for the German police to plan the razzia that took place that night, once the last police reinforcements had arrived in Copenhagen. These were under the command of Major Rolf Günther, one of Eichmann's associates. The following was written in the police minutes covering the course of the operation:[40]

FRIDAY, OCTOBER 1
20:00 hours. Police Inspector Rasmussen (Muster Unit) reports that 20 large German trucks have been driven in convoy from the Free Port.

21:25. Police Sergeant Toft (Station 2) reports that around 20 trucks manned by green-uniformed gendarmes are driving towards Strøget [the main thoroughfare in central Copenhagen]. It is thought that this concerns the Jews.

21:30. Police Sergeant Toft (Station 2) reports that there are now estimated to be 50 trucks. There are also trucks driving along Købmagergade [Street].

21:37. Police Inspector Rasmussen (Muster Unit) reports that all exit roads are now blocked by Germans, and all vehicles are being stopped and searched.

21:43. Police Sergeant Brønnum (Station 3) reports that at one of the posts on Sølvtorvet [Square], 32 trucks have been observed with canvas roofs filled with German soldiers at the Triangle [Square].

22:10. Station 2 reports that the operation has begun in Købmagergade. Chains have been spanned across the street and a number of small groups are going up into the buildings and fetching civilians. A German major in the 4th District has told a policeman that this is a matter for the Germans alone and that Danish police officers should not interfere. At that point the telephone connection was cut.

SATURDAY, OCTOBER 2
00:55. An on-duty police officer has heard loud engine noise along the quay at Langelinie. Police Constable Buschou (Station 3) reports that the whole quay is lit up and that there is much traffic in the direction of a steamship, the *Wartheland*.

08:05. Prisons Inspector Kaj Jensen reports that he has received a telephone call from the Horserød camp saying that the German authorities are busy transporting Danish Communists. The prison is most curious to find out where those concerned are being transported to.

10:00. Two steamships with people detained by the Germans have set sail by 10:00 from the quay at Langelinie. The latter sailed just before 10:00. Presumably in a southerly direction. The Communists from the Horserød camp were transported away between 08:00 and 10:00. Destination unknown.

10:24. Station 3 reports that the transport vessel, the *Wartheland*, is at present leaving the harbor.

That night, the Germans rounded up 202 Jews in Copenhagen and on Sjælland who were transported by sea, plus a further eighty-two Jews from

Fishing boat used for transportation of Jews to Sweden

provinces to the west of the Great Belt, who were sent by rail to Germany. Using information they had already received, German police officers were able to go from door to door, picking up the Jews. They had been given orders not to force their way into dwellings. In most cases, these orders were respected, although the leader of the razzia, Major Günther, had protested at this measure. The Gestapo managed to obtain 220 sets of keys from the concierges at the blocks of flats concerned, so that entry by force was rendered unnecessary. Luckily, most of the Jews had already been tipped off and were therefore not at home. One tragic exception concerned the residents of a Jewish old people's home who were arrested with a degree of violence. There is no explanation as to why this should have happened.

While being shipped in Copenhagen, the Jews were treated very brutally, and this situation continued when they were shipped on to Swinemünde (the present-day Polish town of Swinoujscie, then still part of Germany). Among the Communists deported was the later secretary of the Freedom Fund, Frode Toft, who told me how the Communists, on arrival in the German port, were told to leave the ship by the stern and line up on the quay. They then saw how the Jewish prisoners were driven with whips accompanied by shouts and screams, and were kicked and, in some cases, even thrown from the aft of the ship. These were mostly old people, many in shock, and they were then marched over to join the Communists. Out of anger and pride, Frode Toft then broke ranks and greeted the unfortunate Jewish prisoners, crying out: "Chin up, compatriots!" After this cry of solidarity, they were separated. The Jews were sent to Theresienstadt, the Communists to Stutthof. The latter camp proved to be the worse of the two.

"Little Dunkirk"

In October 1943, fifty-five illegal routes were established, transporting a total of 7,056 refugees to Sweden in one operation which, according to Leni Yahil, has often been described as "Little Dunkirk." This comparison refers to 1940, when the British fleet managed to transport some 340,000 British, French and Polish troops back from France, across the English Channel to safety. There is more than a fleeting similarity between the two operations. There is also the improvisation involved, the success achieved and the continued fight against Hitler. But it is obvious that the two operations cannot be compared in scope and scale.

While a number of the "nonviolent" members of our group joined other organizations, the Horsens group of students decided to establish a route of their own. We were joined, apart from Niels Hjorth, by Nan's friends Ebba and Ulla Lund and Klaus Rønholt. There were five things we had to obtain as soon as possible: 1) weapons, 2) money, 3) boats, 4) accommodation for the refugees, and 5) Jews. The last of these proved to be the greatest challenge.

A provisional division of labor was made. Niels and I would go to Varde to investigate whether we could get hold of some of the confiscated pistols that had been delivered to the police after the decree of September 4. Klaus and Elsebet would obtain money – a lot of money. Ulla and Ebba would find boats, and the rest of the group would find the addresses of Jews.

When the travel ban was lifted on September 12, Niels and I were able to take the train to Varde. We set off on Friday, October 1, and were very well received by Chief Constable Simony, who gave us seven pistols and ammunition, commenting: "At your disposal, gentlemen. No one is saying that they should only be used to protect transports of Jews. They can also be used for other things." This gave us an idea where we had the police in Varde. Niels then told me how he had kept cool on August 29 when he and his chief clerk Henning Schlanbusch had been arrested and detained on September 2, since they refused to sign a declaration of loyalty to the Germans. After a short visit to Schlanbusch, we traveled back to Copenhagen on Saturday, October 2. We were afraid we might be searched as we boarded the ferry to cross the Great Belt, but managed to get on board without incident.

The yield from our little trip was a good one. We hid our weapons under pieces of turf in our fuel store, knowing full well that our biggest problem was the fact that we had never handled firearms in our lives.

As for money, Klaus soon came up with a suggestion. His father was a tenant farmer at the Tybjergaard manor, and therefore Klaus knew most of the landowners on Sjælland personally. He wanted to go and sound them out along with Elsebet. In answer to the question of how they would travel from farm to farm, Klaus merely shrugged his shoulders and said, "We'll take a taxi." They set off on the Saturday morning. A quote from Elsebet's description of their efforts:[41]

> We took a taxi. I suggested this was rather an expensive business. "It's peanuts compared with what we're going to collect," replied Klaus, and it turned out that way, too. I remember what he said to Georg Garth-Grüner, the chief steward at the Lille Svenstrup manor: "You'll never get known for less than ten thousand kroner!" We reckoned on some thousand kroner for each "Jew ticket" to Sweden. Klaus pointed out what Count Joseph Holstein-Ledreborg at the Ledreborg manor had given – just as an appetizer…
>
> "You can easily understand that she's collecting money for the Jews," said Klaus's father, standing there in his riding boots with his fierce dogs when we arrived at Tybjergaard (where we also spent the night), "she's a Jewess herself, you can see that clear enough." Very flattering, but it happened not to be true. Our various hosts on our round thought we were doing the rounds on account of being engaged, until they were informed otherwise. "You could have put on a thinner pair of stockings," grumbled Klaus – I had dressed warmly for the long journey.
>
> The highlight of this little episode was our evening encounter with the Reedtz-Thotts at Gaunø. We got into the main building by way of the kitchen entrance, then went up into the house where we suddenly found ourselves in the midst of a dinner party. "You handle the

ladies," said Klaus, upon which he strode towards the lounge, where the gentlemen were gathered. So there I stood in my sensible clothing, surrounded by elegant ladies – and of course became, as did Klaus, the sensation of the evening.

It was somewhat naïve of us to ride round like we did, entrusting our little secret to all those we met; but on that occasion, our naïveté happened to prove our strength. It disarmed people's resistance; even the German police could not resist "die kleinen Idealisten." And, as I have said, Klaus knew all the families we visited – or they at least knew his family. Klaus must be given the credit for this trip; it was all his work.

When Elsebet and Klaus had arrived back from their trip, we all met up again at Raadhusstræde, where Ebba told us that she had managed to make contact with the son of a fisherman whom she knew from their holidays on the island of Christiansø. He also worked in the ships equipment business in Copenhagen and knew a reputed eccentric called "the American" who lived under an upturned boat out at the harbor at Skudehavnen, a part of the port of Copenhagen. It was here that the fishermen scoured and dried their fish and beyond was the quay with a row of fishing boats. On the southern side of the quay there was Syv-meter-bassinet – the Seven-Meter Dock – also known as Orientbassinet. This was used by German patrol boats. At the entrance to the harbor, the coastguard had a little hut. The nearest harbor on the Swedish side was Barsebäck, to which all our passengers were sent.

Using the American as middleman, we soon made contact with other fishermen. Ebba was good at convincing people and another thing that did not do any harm was that she could promise payments in cash – half before sailing, half after receiving a report that the Jews had arrived safely in Barsebäck. Over the period of a few days, we managed to assemble a flotilla of seven to ten fishing cutters that were ready to sail from Skudehavnen to Barsebäck with refugees.

We now had arms, boats and money. The problem with accommodation was solved as we went along. Relatives and good friends offered their flats. One of these, Hans Møller, was the director of the Copenhagen Municipal Baths, which became our most important assembly point. We had plenty of room on the boats, so the waiting times on our route were never too long.

We made our preparations during the space of a couple of days. Now the next phase was at hand. All we lacked were Jews. I contacted my parents and Peer Borup in Horsens, also Free Denmark in Aarhus. They all sent us refugees. Our parents sent us a Czech couple, and these became the first Jews we sent over the Sound. Ebba Lund describes this as follows:[42]

> As far as I remember, the first people I arranged transport for were two Czech Jews whom the Kielers had taken to Copenhagen. They were so Jewish that they looked like walking caricatures and had fled across a national border for the third time in succession. They were very sweet and expressed their thanks to God for having been able to experience this escape, where everyone helped them. They hit it off with the American.

The first transport must have taken place on either Monday, October 4, or the next day. The day after, the American managed to ship thirty refugees, who had waited to sail in Ebba's parents' house. After that transport, she took responsibility for embarkation and she gradually became known amongst the refugees as the Girl with the Red Cap, or simply Red Hat. It was she who made sure that people arrived at the Skudehavnen port.

Peer traveled on several occasions with the Jewish refugees from Horsens to Copenhagen. It was during one of these visits that he told me of a photographer who had provided the German Kommandant in Horsens with a list of all the Jews in Horsens. As far as I know, there were no arrests of Jews in Horsens; but the informer did not survive the war. From Aarhus, we took a Jewish tailor and his family who had been sent to us by the Free Denmark group. Between September and November, many members of this group were arrested, while others fled. One of the last ones we sent over was a former schoolmate of mine, Erik Reske-Nielsen, who was secretly married on October 22 and whose honeymoon consisted of a trip in one of our boats over to Barsebäck.

We then started a search action, scouring the city center for Jewish refugees from Poland and Czechoslovakia. This job was done mostly by Bente and Elsebet. They looked for Jews in backyards and under stairs and were grandly assisted by the art dealer Carlo Madsen, who knew Copenhagen incredibly well.

Once we had become established, our reputation followed our success, and a number of people actively sought us and "our" fishermen out while others were redirected to us by larger organizations that did not have enough boats. Private initiatives of this sort tended to first occur carefully via a go-between, then more openly. These initiatives could result in long negotiations. I remember visiting the actress Illona Wieselman, who enjoyed the help of a lawyer. He obviously wanted to know whether it was necessary to escape abroad and what security we could offer those fleeing. I could give no guarantees, but was able to point out that things had gone well so far. She found it difficult to make up her mind but finally agreed to let us help her. It was Elsebet who was to collect her the following day and take her to the boat. Later she would talk with enthusiasm about this delicate, rather special actress from the Royal Danish Theater. There she sat amidst her open suitcases (far more than we could take along), looking forlorn. "I don't even know whether I'm Jewish," she said. "I come from Vienna and know nothing about my ancestry; but everybody tells me I should go." We heard later from Stockholm that all had gone well, and that she was making a career for herself up there.

From various sources it has become clear that payments varied between five hundred and three thousand kroner, occasionally even more. This fits in with information I got from Ebba. At first people quite frequently had to pay two thousand kroner; but this swiftly dropped to around a thousand kroner and towards the end went down to five hundred. Those who could afford it paid for others and if they could not pay, we had our reserves. No one was refused for financial reasons. Sometimes we would also take Resistance people and deserters, even a Frenchman who had for some reason found his way onto our transport. Not every fisherman was willing to run the risk of taking gentiles, and others only did so for a higher price.

The costs involved not only the payments to the fishermen, who needed, among other things, a certain guarantee sum for their boats, which could get confiscated, but there were also bribes for the German guard posts and the Danish coastguard. The bribes were organized by the fishermen. There is no doubt that they made money on these transports, but neither the refugees nor we felt exploited.

I have no details of how many people we transported over to Barsebäck.

But with seven to ten boats each with a capacity for ten to fifteen passengers paying an average fare of five hundred to a thousand kroner (mostly paid by the money we had collected), our complete expenditure of 450,000 kroner indicates that during the first two weeks of October we transported between five hundred and a thousand refugees across the Sound. We did not lose a single life.

Transports were normally organized to occur in daylight, as there was a curfew at night. If there were no complications, the trip would take some two hours. If German patrol boats turned up, the vessels had to do some fishing to avoid arousing suspicion, and this could make the journey much longer. The passengers had to keep out of sight until the boat was in Swedish waters. In most cases, the cutters sailed right into port at Barsebäck. But sometimes they were met by Swedish naval vessels who would take the refugees on board.

Sending the Jewish and other refugees across to Sweden required a balance to be struck between security and efficiency. This was hard to achieve at first when swift action was regarded as crucial at the same time as having to reckon with a harsh reaction from the Germans. What Best and other Germans were thinking was something we knew little about. Security was not as tight as with other illegal activities. But there were still rules to be followed, and we tried to stick to them. For example, we tended never to allow refugees to visit Raadhusstræde, and did not tell them our real names. Anonymity was hard to maintain in a number of cases. This was true of Jews sent over to us from Jutland, and Jews who stayed at Ebba's and Ulla's parents' house near the port at Nordhavnen before being shipped over.

The Jews were often taken to the port by taxi, but these would never drive into the port area. The refugees had to move in small groups with a minimum of luggage. We accompanied them and tried to load as much of their luggage as we could onto our bicycles. Ebba made a kind of check before sailing, but could not always distinguish between Jews and other refugees. If she suspected that the motive anyone came up with for fleeing was sheer nonsense, they would be refused a place on board. But we could not do much about informers; although there is no evidence that we erred in that respect.

We did, however, have an encounter that forced me to come to terms with whether or not I was willing to liquidate a traitor. Ebba told me one day that fishermen returning to port at Skudehavnen the previous evening had found a barge without an engine, without sails, without oars, floating around in the middle of Øresund with a score of helpless refugees, including several children. Through one or another organization, they had made contact with a fisherman who had been willing to tow the barge to Sweden if he were to receive payment for doing so. He took his fee, took the barge with the Jews out into Øresund, cut the rope and left. The fishermen brought the unfortunate refugees into Skudehavnen where they spent the night in one of the fishing huts. There Ebba met the frightened people, who had no money. She immediately sent them over to Barsebäck, where they arrived safely. I do not think that anyone ever found out who the fisherman who betrayed his passengers had been. But I heard Ebba's story, and the question of the necessity for the liquidation of informers cropped up for the first time in my own life. The bastard could have betrayed other transports.

The presence of the Danish coastal police led to a particularly exciting episode. We knew nothing about the negotiations that were taking place between Under-Secretary Eivind Larsen and Kanstein in connection with the events of August 29, and did not therefore know where we had the Danish police. At any rate, we had to reckon with the fact that amongst the police there would be rotten apples. P. Hurwitz's tale lends credence to this. His transport was about to leave and they were waiting for a Nazi sergeant to leave his post and go for lunch. On the other hand, the presence of a German soldier presented no difficulties. He had been bribed. The fact that there were Germans who did not approve of the persecution of the Jews came to light when German marines warned them near the Seven-Meter Dock when a German patrol boat was about to set off.

Fear of German patrol boats diminished over time. But initially, we regarded them as the greatest threats to our activities. Along with Niels, Flemming or Klaus, I often stood guard in the port area near the embarkation point. We were armed with the pistols we had obtained in Varde. On at least two occasions, we saw how a passing German patrol spotted us and looked at us attentively. But on neither occasion did anything happen. Whether this was because we were armed, I have no way of knowing. But that was the conclusion we drew. Ebba had a similar encounter:[43]

> One day, I remember it was afternoon and shadows were growing longer, we had gotten some passengers into some of the boats, and they

were under deck, and the engine was running, when a German patrol – I remember the Wehrmacht uniforms – came along the path between the huts and the fish-drying area and walked along the quay. There were a number of fishermen on the quay and one or two coastguards and me. I moved close to a young burly fisherman and looked as romantic as I could – given the circumstances. The Germans – some five in all – did not say anything, but stopped and looked on. They looked at the policemen who were armed and looked determined, and looked at the fishermen. There were about a couple dozen of these, standing there solidly in their clogs. They also looked at me. Then they turned and went. I'm absolutely convinced that they knew what was going on, but understood that they would pay dearly, were they to start interfering. It was the eye contact that did it; I will never forget it. Anyway, the boats sailed off and everything went well.

The fact that our embarkation was under observation is also shown by the fact that on at least two occasions, ss patrols checked taxi cabs and other vehicles that passed through the entrance to the Free Port. We can be thankful that we did not lose any of our refugees. But not everyone was so lucky. On October 6, the German police arrested a Jewish woman and her two small children, as they climbed out of a taxi in Skudehavnen. And on the eleventh, a married couple were detained at the same spot. They were eventually set free, as only one of them was Jewish.

Among the refugees we sent across Øresund was one of our own people, Tromle, who was half-Jewish and therefore felt he had to escape. He has written the following:[44]

It was now clear – especially now that the pogroms had taken place – that I had to leave the country.... We ourselves had a route with which I myself did not have anything to do. It turned out to run from Skudehavnen to Barsebäck.... On the Tuesday morning (October 12, 1943), Jørgen Kieler fetched me and we drove out in a taxi to the neighborhood of Skudehavnen. There could, of course, be no question of luggage – it would have raised suspicions if "passengers" came walking along to Skudehavnen with suitcases. I spent an hour in a small hut where there were already a number of refugees. I clearly remember a little Jewish family, waiting to sail. They actually managed to sail with the boat after mine. They had a small child who cried loudly, despite the fact they had tried to sedate her with nerve tablets. I would have dearly liked to strangle her, but in the end she fell silent.

When I finally arrived on board the small fishing vessels, the hour in the hut felt as if it had been days. And so we waited on board. There would be checks and there were Germans on the quay, but I could hear and see nothing from below deck. What Jørgen Kieler…and Ebba Lund…were doing I simply didn't know. But we finally sailed. Not until many years later did I find out that the transport had been guarded by armed members of the Resistance.

Ebba ends her description with the following episode:

Among the people who turned up at the port, and whom I helped to travel on to Sweden, were a few members of the Danish minority in Schleswig, who had deserted from the German armed forces. They showed me photographs from Poland. They showed goods wagons filled with corpses and rows of people hanging from gallows. I hid the photographs for a while, but could not keep them. It was rather typical that, at the time, I did not really understand from what the people we were helping were fleeing. We simply didn't have the imagination to comprehend what was going on.

Our surfeit of places on board our boats meant that other organizations became involved and our cooperation with Cato, Holger, Trunte and Helge played a role in this. At first, these organizations would send us their refugees, but later on they arranged their own sailing from Nordhavnen, where there was a lot of bustling about, including a lot of taxi traffic in and out of the port area, and, in connection with all this, security was somewhat neglected. This was the reason that, once the "violent contingent" had turned to sabotage, Ebba moved our "firm" to the southern port – Sydhavnen. By that time, most of the Jews had already been shipped over to Sweden and it was the latter half of October. I was never involved in transports from Sydhavnen. They principally involved members of the Resistance and were therefore much more dangerous. But Ebba managed. She and Ulla remained in Denmark right until the end of the war, and so, in contrast to other members of our group, were there when Denmark was liberated.

Best Accused

When examining the persecution of the Jews in Denmark in detail, one has to distinguish between two phases: 1) the preparations plus the operation carried out on the night of October 1–2, and 2) the subsequent pogroms involving escaping Jews. It is principally in this first phase that Best came to play a significant role, when he sent Telegram 1032, and he became the chief accused after the war.

His defense pointed out that the day before the telegram in question was sent, he had received a secret phone call from Berlin, in which he was told that Hitler had already decided to carry out the Jewish pogroms in Denmark. So it was said not to be Best's telegram that sparked the persecution of the Jews.

This defense plea crumbled as the Copenhagen City Court could find no evidence that Hitler had issued orders to start the pogroms before Best sent his telegram, and on September 20, 1948, Best was sentenced to death. The following is taken from the court transcript:[45]

> According to information available, it can be assumed that the danger of an operation carried out against the Jews became particularly acute on September 1, 1943, but there is no reason to assume that the operation had already been decided when the Accused sent his telegram on September 8 in which he urged that action should be taken, and it may henceforth be assumed that his initiative is the reason for the subsequent deportation, for which he definitely used his position to prepare, cf. the telegram dated April 24, 1943.

But Werner Best escaped with his life, as the judgment with regard to the persecution of the Jews was overturned on July 18, 1949, by the Eastern District Court, where a witness for the defense was Franz von Sonnleithner, the former head of Ribbentrop's ministry, who told the court that a day or two before Telegram 1032 had been sent, he had received notification from the foreign ministry in Berlin that Hitler had, at the suggestion of Himmler, instituted the persecution of the Jews in Denmark on September 6 and that he passed on this information to Best during a cryptic phone call. As further proof, Sonnleithner told the court that in order to cover himself, he sent an official report to the foreign ministry in Berlin about Hitler's decision.

This note was not available during the session at the Eastern District Court, but Sonnleithner thought that it could perhaps be found in the archive for the Nuremberg Trials. Best was acquitted in the matter of setting in motion the persecution of the Jews and the Eastern District Court also absolved him of responsibility for preparations for this operation, including the razzias of August 31 and September 17, 1943, carried out against the offices of district court attorney Arthur Henriques and of the Mosaic Congregation.

The acquittal was ratified on these points on March 17, 1950, by the High Court, which nevertheless increased the penalty for the other crimes from five to twelve years imprisonment. Best was pardoned after a plea by Scavenius and Svenningsen on August 24, 1951 and deported from Denmark on August 29 by the authorities, who appeared to have forgotten the most important events that had taken place during the occupation.

Judgment has been passed, and Best is now dead and gone. Scavenius welcomed the fact that he was spared the death penalty; but the question remains as to how historians should judge the decision of the court. Here, special reference should be made to Leni Yahil, Hans Kirchhoff and Ulrich Herbert. No evidence has ever been found that Hitler had, on September 6, 7 or 8 ordered pogroms to begin in Denmark, nor of the telephone call that Sonnleithner mentioned. Quite the opposite. According to Ulrich Herbert, a check of the archive at the German foreign ministry showed that it would not have been possible that the German foreign ministry had known about Hitler's decision before September 17.

Sonnleithner's note, with which he wished to cover himself, was found as expected in the Nuremberg archive. But it did not confirm his phone call on September 7. The note was in fact dated September 18, i.e., the day after Best had received confirmation of Hitler's final order of September 16. Leni Yahil was therefore able to show that Sonnleithner had waited all of ten days to cover himself, and thus drew the following conclusion:[46]

It can therefore be assumed that the telephone conversation (between Sonnleithner and Best), if it in fact took place, occurred on September 16 or 17, following Hitler's decision, and not on September 7 or 8.

Yahil's interpretation of Best's responsibility has found wide acceptance.

The German historian Ulrich Herbert's conclusion is also worth looking at in this context:[47]

> Best's version of the lead-up to the events centering on Telegram 1032 is not alone dubious, but can be confuted on all points: it is one of the notorious results of a diversionary strategy – presumably agreed upon by those concerned at Nuremberg during April 1948. Best did not suggest the operation against the Jews in Denmark in order to prevent it, but to implement it.

Furthermore, as Ulrich Herbert points out, the warnings in Telegram 1032 were not against what would happen if the operation went through, but the difficulties that could arise if it were *not* carried out immediately, i.e., during the state of emergency that was in force at the time in Denmark.

When the Germans only managed to round up 202 Jews on Sjælland and in Copenhagen on the night of October 1, this was blamed not so much on a poor performance by the German police, as on the warnings that leaked out beforehand. It is reasonable to think that Duckwitz is to be credited for this result. But in his self-defense, Best tried to make it look as if it was he who gave the warning. He said this at the Nuremberg Trial in 1946:[48]

> The firmest proof that I sabotaged the operation rests in the fact that I informed several Danish politicians about what was going to happen and when it would happen, so that the Jews would have the chance to flee.

During this questioning session, he makes no attempt to convince his interrogators that he ordered Duckwitz to inform Hedtoft about what was going to happen; in fact he does not even mention Duckwitz, taking the credit himself for the warning. On this, as well as on many other occasions, he proved himself to be completely unreliable, and his theatrical desire to build a bridge across Øresund, over which the Jews could escape, raises the question as to whether he was as good a hypocrite as he was a liar. What contribution he actually made towards saving the Jews is hard to find. At the very most, his contributions were passive, rather than active.

"No revenge, only justice" was the motto by which Simon Wiesenthal pursued Adolf Eichmann and other war criminals after the war. Best saved his skin by a combination of speaking with a forked tongue, and relying on the Danish reluctance to bring the Germans to justice. But neither revenge was wreaked nor justice done in the case of the eighty Jews who paid with their lives during the pogroms in Denmark.

"Righteous among Nations"

There were people all over Europe who were ready to help the Jews in their hour of need. They were termed "the Righteous among Nations." The fact that 90 percent of Danish Jews avoided being arrested by the Germans and that almost 99 percent survived the Second World War is regarded as quite remarkable abroad.

Between April 9, 1940, and September 28, 1943, a total of 743 refugees fled from Denmark to Sweden; of these sixty-nine were Jewish. So there were around 7,600 still in Denmark running the risk of persecution. Of these, about 1,500 were immigrants without Danish citizenship. Of these, 202 became the victims of the first night of German pogroms, east of the Great Belt, which took place October 1–2, 1943. Three of these managed to escape, but the rest ended up in the Theresienstadt concentration camp, along with a further eighty-two Jews, who had been arrested west of the Great Belt and were deported by rail. During the second phase of the pogroms, the Germans rounded up a further 190 Jews and these were sent to Theresienstadt on October 13 and November 23.

Ten Danish Jews were transferred from the Sachsenhausen and Ravensbrück camps in 1944. So the total number of Jews imprisoned by the Germans came to 481 (about 6 percent of the Jewish population of Denmark), of whom 101 lacked Danish citizenship. Of these, a total of fifty-four prisoners, mainly elderly people, died during transport. Of those the Germans did not manage to arrest, twenty-six died, either drowning during their attempted escape or committing suicide out of desperation. This means that the sum total of Jewish deaths comes to eighty, which is but 1 percent of all the Jews living in Denmark at the time. Between fifty and a hundred Jews managed to survive without leaving Denmark, and 7,056 (around 91 percent) managed to get across to Sweden.

Anyone who has visited Yad Vashem in Jerusalem where the total Jewish losses have been added up per country of origin, will ask themselves the question: why did things turn out so differently in Denmark than in other countries? Bulgaria did protect many of its own Jews, but sacrificed many Jews from occupied Thrace. From Norway, 760 Jews were deported, of whom only twenty-six survived. Others escaped to Sweden but around 50 percent of Norwegian Jews died. In other countries, the percentages were much higher.

There are several reasons why Denmark was different. Some are obvious, others require a degree of commentary. Straightforward factors include those who betrayed their country, geographical considerations and Swedish policy. The more complex ones are German activities in occupied Denmark and the participation of the Resistance movement in rescuing Jews. These factors need to be looked at more closely.

While the ss was behind the pogroms during all phases of the persecution of the Jews, the immediate threats to Jews from Norway, Hungary and France were the traitors in pro-German groupings and, in France, the police force. In Denmark, the DNSAP was not in the center of the political picture. And Frikorps Danmark was "*anderswo engagiert* (otherwise engaged, i.e., on the *Ostfront*)." Hipo and the Sommer Corps had not yet been set up and the Schalburg Corps was under German command and not mobilized. The most important factor of all was, however, the Danish police force, not least those serving to guard the coast, who tended to refuse to cooperate and, in many instances, even actively helped refugees to flee. There were only a few sporadic instances of informers who did damage to the cause, but these did not constitute the same kind of threat to the Jews as in other countries.

The geographical advantages enjoyed by those helping the refugees speak for themselves. Only Norway lay nearer to neutral Sweden where refugees could seek sanctuary. From the Netherlands, Belgium and France, refugees would have to reach Spain and Portugal to then find a ship to take them to a safe port, and escape from Eastern Europe was even more difficult.

The fact that the number of Norwegian Jews who died was so much higher can not only be attributed to the activities of traitors, but also to the fact that the persecution of the Jews was started at a much earlier time, during which Sweden was still afraid of challenging Germany by accepting Jewish refugees. This was the time before Stalingrad. So the time factor was to Denmark's advantage.

There are differences of opinion on the above explanations as to how and why Denmark succeeded. But there is wholesale agreement on two factors: German attitudes and the help the Resistance offered refugees.

German Passivity

More recent historical research of the hunt for Jews during October 1943 has shown that apart from the head of the Gestapo, Juhl, in Helsingør, German efforts were scattered and, in many cases, halfhearted. This especially applied to the German navy. One problem for a historical evaluation of this passivity is that it has not been easy to trace the chain of command by which any orders to "turn a blind eye" were given.

The persecution of the Jews involved the Gestapo, ss troops and the Wehrmacht. I do not know of any instances where the Gestapo and the ss soldiers turned a blind eye with regard to attempts at escape, and Juhl's energetic efforts to catch as many Jews as possible in the northern part of Sjælland do not allow one to assume that he had been given orders from above to go easy on the Jews. But what is more remarkable is that the Germans did not use their full capacity, i.e., the approximately fifteen hundred ss soldiers in the Copenhagen area. There is no convincing explanation of this fact. Maybe they were being used for other tasks. Best had asked for these reinforcements before the operation against the Jews had been decided. However, it was not the Jews who were the threat, but the saboteurs.

We have the same problem evaluating the contribution made by the Wehrmacht. From our own experience, and that of others, we know that on a number of occasions Wehrmacht soldiers turned a blind eye when sailings took place, ones they could not have failed to notice. But we do not know whether they were acting under orders or doing this on their own initiative and if so for what motives. There can be no question of a direct order from von Hanneken to undermine the effectiveness of the pogroms; that would have cost him his life. The German patrols that did turn a blind eye must presumably have acted on their own initiative. Maybe the fact that those helping the Jews were armed played a role. But we ran a much greater risk of being killed than they did, as they were trained soldiers who could easily have mown us all down.

In other circumstances, bribery may have played a role, especially where the Germans turned up only in ones and twos. But the fact cannot be excluded from the equation that there was a certain generosity of spirit on the part of the Germans, although this would entail a certain risk of being court-martialed if they were part of a patrol, which could include a number of convinced Nazis who passed on information. Here we lack testimony from the German side.

Personal Risks

One contributing factor to the fact that the Jews were saved in October 1943 is said by some to be the small personal risk run by Danes helping to rescue them. This conclusion tends to be supported by the fact that those helping transport the Jews to Sweden, if caught, quite rarely suffered a harsh trial in the courts. Fear of German intervention ebbed away over time, something that was reflected in the fishermen's willingness to undertake sailings. The risks run by Danish helpers of the Jews were no doubt fewer than those run by, say, Polish or Dutch people in a similar situation. But the reluctance on the part of the Germans to interfere took quite some while to become evident. The evaluation of risks tends to be with the benefit of hindsight, and is in contrast to what those assisting the Jews actually felt at the time, fear being part and parcel of the operations themselves and also of the Gestapo investigations after the event.

The evaluation of the risks involved is based on rationalization after the event and is in clear contrast to what those assisting the Jews to escape felt at the time. Then, they clearly felt themselves to be in danger, both during the operation itself, and in searches conducted later by the Gestapo.

The assessment is, moreover, made from a point of departure that sees the persecution of the Jews in isolation, without taking into account the resistance to the German occupation in its entirety. Many of the people involved in helping refugees should have their personal risks assessed against a background of what they did in other fields in the Resistance. Deaths amongst Jews being rescued stood at twenty-six, as mentioned above. How many of those helping them died is much more difficult to calculate as many of them were involved in underground activities before, during and after the shipping of the Jews to Sweden. In our group, at any rate, eight lives were lost. Six of these had taken part in Little Dunkirk.

The August Uprising

One frequently overlooked reason for the weakness of German efforts to stop the refugees during Little Dunkirk can be found in the lack of surveillance of the coast and the Øresund strait. The fact that the Danish naval fleet and the coastal police did not help the Germans on August 29 also contributed to this. Given the long Danish coastline, the Germans were entirely dependent on cooperation with the Danish navy and coastal police, which had been set up at the behest of Germany and which grew to a force of some fifteen hundred men. On August 29, this cooperation collapsed.

Surveillance of the 215-mile-long (350 km) stretch of coastline between the Sjællands Odde peninsula in the northwest of the island of Sjælland and Gedser at the tip of the island of Falster in the southeast, in order to prevent the escape of seven thousand Jews, was for Admiral Wurmbach a pointless exercise and of no military significance. Minesweeping, escorts of merchant vessels and other naval tasks were more important. The Germans were naturally adamant to prevent Danish soldiers who had evaded arrest from fleeing to Sweden. And they would certainly have tightened up surveillance of Øresund had they known that the head of the SOE, Flemming Muus, and SOE agent Poul Hansen and several shot down Allied pilots and deserters from the German armed forces escaped to Sweden together with the Jews in October, while a number of Holger Danske saboteurs who had made the crossing to Sweden the previous month now returned to occupied Denmark to continue the fight.

The scuttling of the fleet which, according to Admiral Dönitz accounted for a German loss of twenty naval vessels and the manpower of fifteen hundred men, plus the lack of Danish surveillance of the coast, were added factors of great significance. These all contributed to the success of Little Dunkirk.

The sinking of the fleet and the strike by the coastal police were not the only contributions made by the August Uprising to the salvation of the Jews. Equally important was the clear change of attitude on the part of the Danish population as a whole to the Resistance from August 29, 1943, onwards. They had cast aside the shame felt from the initial occupation on April 9, 1940, and woken up after three years of humiliating collaboration with the enemy. This resulted in a wide-scale wish to help those persecuted by means of money, accommodation and transport.

When Duckwitz wrote that he wanted to build a bridge across Øresund to help save the Jews, this may be a question of hindsight. Apart from Duckwitz's Stockholm errand, no preparations were made on the part of the Germans which would help an escape, nor did the Danish politicians and under-secretaries do anything. And the Jews themselves were in denial right up until the last moment. Little Dunkirk was a spontaneous grass-roots reaction to the persecution and oppression and was inspired by the events of August 29.

Help for Theresienstadt

There has been no lack of Jewish recognition of the help given in October 1943 to Danish Jews and later to those who had been deported to Theresienstadt. I experienced this when I represented Denmark at the Second Holocaust Conference in Washington in 1986. But critical voices have also been raised.

The deportations unleashed massive protests from the under-secretaries, which meant that Red Cross packets with clothes and foodstuffs were sent to Theresienstadt from the spring of 1944 onwards. This made a big difference to the Jews' chances for survival. The death toll of Danish prisoners in Theresienstadt was 11 percent. By comparison, the death toll at the Stutthof camp was 12 percent and the average death toll for all Danes interned by the Germans was 10 percent. These figures do not, however, reflect the conditions under which people were deported to the various concentration camps.[49]

The time the deportation took and the ages of the victims also had a major influence on how many people died. When, one year later, Danish gendarmes and police officers were deported, they could be compared with regard to age with the Jews. Despite the length of the deportation, which was one third as long as that of the Jews, some 28 percent of the gendarmes died, which serves to illustrate that the conditions of the Danish Jews in Theresienstadt were somewhat better than in the rest of the concentration camps. By comparison, it should also be added that the death toll at Porta Westphalica, where I myself was deported, lay at 44 percent over a period of only six months.

The most important result of the Danish protests and not least of the international attention to the operation was that Danish Jews were not transported further east, that is to say to Auschwitz. And this proved to be their salvation. But others would have to pay for this. Many prisoners were sent to Auschwitz to make room for the Danish Jews in Theresienstadt.

This included all of those who had contributed towards making a

propaganda film in connection with the Danish inspection of Theresienstadt on June 23, 1944. The five Danish Jews who were repatriated as well
as the inspection team were obliged to keep to themselves the fact that
they had seen beyond the Potemkin façade they had been presented with
at Theresienstadt during their visit. After the war was over, this led to an
element of bitterness and criticism, which is quite understandable. But
what was the alternative? If the inspection team had publicized what they
knew, it would have undoubtedly cost the Theresienstadt prisoners their
lives. However, a secret message to Britain or the USA could perhaps have
had its effect.

The Germans had managed to keep the horrible truth of what was
occurring in the concentration camps a secret, and the brutal reality of
the camps came as a shock to the British and American invasion forces
as they liberated one concentration camp after another. I received a clear
impression of this when I again saw my old friend from Cambridge, Frank
Glassow. As a doctor and a British officer, his task had been to "liberate" the
Bergen-Belsen concentration camp. Here, most of the people to be liberated were already dead from starvation, sickness and abuse. If the Danish
witnesses had had links to the Resistance, they could have informed the
Allies, which, by way of threats of reprisals after the war was over, may have
slowed down the mass murder and given the Allies a better chance to prepare to face the reality of what they were about to see in the camps. I shall
describe my own experiences in this respect in a later chapter.

The Politicians Who Collaborated

Not everyone agrees that the August Uprising as described above contributed towards the saving of the Jews. The historian Professor Henning
Poulsen stresses the fact that the success of the transport of the Jews over
to Sweden is to a large extent due to the fact that German measures to
stop it were so unnecessarily halfhearted that the salvation of Danish Jews
can be attributed to a further example of the German policy of caution.
He also states that the small risks run by those who helped the refugees is
well documented, and prefers to locate the success in political rather than
Resistance factors.[50]

As an eyewitness who took part in Little Dunkirk, I disagree strongly
with such a conclusion, which is nowadays supported by people who favor
the rehabilitation of Scavenius and his policy of active adjustment to cir-

cumstances. Some of these would go so far as to make the Resistance actually responsible for the persecution of the Jews and give the politicians
who collaborated with Germany the credit for saving them.

With regard to the fact that August 29 marked the day that Danish
Jews lost the protection of the government, Chief Rabbi Friediger has this
to say:[51]

> We did not have a Norwegian situation here in Denmark, nor special
> laws for Jews. But on August 29, 1943, there was a sea change which
> was pregnant with consequences for Denmark, and from which Dan-
> ish Jews also had to suffer.

The chief rabbi did change his opinion later and everyone must say
that Best was right when he claimed that the pogroms were bound to come
sooner or later. The deportation of Hungarian Jews to Auschwitz during
the very last phase of the war is obvious proof of this. For a convinced
Nazi, the persecution of the Jews was an end in itself. This was also the
case with Hitler. Even when he realized that the war was lost, he continued
to carry out measures as part of his *Endlösung*. If anyone is in doubt as to
the fact that the extermination of the Jews was a high priority for him, all
they have to do is read his will (dictated to his secretary in his last hours
in his bunker):

> Above all, I would call upon the leaders of nations and all those that
> serve them to respect the race laws and to wage war on those that
> spread poison from nation to nation, i.e., the international Jewry.

Belittling the efforts of the contribution by the Resistance in saving the
Jews is, in my opinion, neither just nor fair. For me it is grotesque to give
the collaborationist politicians the credit for their salvation. In this context
it is relevant to remember the attitude of the Danish government to Jewish
refugees who sought shelter in Denmark before the war.

Denmark, like other countries, had a restrictive policy concerning im-
migration and refugees before World War Two. This was not an expression
of the anti-Semitism of the government, rather a fear of Germany and of
creating ghettoes, which would themselves lead to anti-Semitism. In those
days, as today, the aim was to integrate immigrants in Danish society. But

the major difference between then and now is that in those days this affected a few thousand Jews, while today hundreds of thousands of Muslims have to be integrated. There were limits to Danish hospitality even then. But the borders were not completely closed to refugees. This is shown by the fact that 20 percent of the Jews who made it to Sweden, as well as 20 percent of those who were in Theresienstadt, were without a Danish passport.

A much more significant criticism is that Jewish refugees who had escaped to Denmark before the war were handed over to the Germans on various occasions. The worst such action was when seventy German refugees were interned in the Horserød Camp north of Copenhagen in the first stage of the occupation. This involved a mixture of Jews, Socialists and others who opposed Nazism. Forty-eight of these became victims of the policy of active collaboration followed by Scavenius. These were handed over to the Germans and deported to Germany. Some were executed, others sent to concentration camps, others again to the *Ostfront*. How many Jews died in this manner is not clear. Civil servants working for the Ministry of Justice and the prison service in Denmark were responsible for this crime. But the overall responsibility clearly rests with the government itself. No one has been brought to justice and it is only now that the archives are available to everyone that we can see this. More surprises are, no doubt, in store for us.

Criticisms can be raised in the case of those responsible, not against Danish society as a whole. But all Danes should be ashamed of such politicians who denied protection to Jewish and other refugees before the war, and everyone must surely be shocked at the revelation that Jewish and other immigrants were actually handed over to the Germans during the occupation itself. We should be ashamed of this in the same way that we are ashamed of politicians and civil servants who abandoned the Communists in Horserød to their fate. This cannot be forgotten or forgiven.

Such feelings of shame should not, however, blind us to the historical facts, which show clearly that the coalition government was not anti-Jewish – quite the opposite. Anti-Semitism was, at the time, concentrated in the small, despised Nazi Party, which both the coalition government and the Resistance agreed had to be fought. However, it cannot be ruled out that Scavenius and others had the idea that by means of collaboration and handing over German refugees, the lives of Danish Jews could be saved. His rationale for accepting that the Danish Frikorps be sent to the *Ostfront* was that in so doing he hoped that he was sparing Danish conscripts from suffering a similar fate.

It is dangerous to be an opportunist, and nothing is more dangerous than playing with one's conscience. If you have to act opportunistically, then you have a certain duty to be cunning, and Scavenius failed in this. This cynical and experienced politician was not only blinded by his belief that Germany would win the war, but was also naïve in his dealings with Best. The decision as to when and where the persecution of the Jews in Denmark would begin was a German one, and if Jews wish to identify someone who helped save them from that quarter up to the telegram crisis in 1942, then this would be Cecil von Renthe-Fink.

But by December 1942, there was a serious risk that "friendly" cooperation between the Danish government and the Germans would break down. No one knows whether such a breakdown would have triggered pogroms. But it is possible that the German defeat at Stalingrad changed Sweden's policy on refugees, and this was contributed to by the fact that Scavenius was appointed to the post of prime minister, causing a delay in the implementation of the persecution of the Jews. This is the only point at which, in my opinion, the policy of active collaboration with the Germans had a direct influence on saving the Jews.

The collaborationist viewpoint reveals a naïve and unrealistic assessment of one situation after the other, culminating with the warning not to attempt to flee to Sweden, and the offer to intern all Danish Jews. The fact that the Mosaic Congregation in Copenhagen was no more sensible in this matter did not help the situation, either. Events in Budapest can be compared; in Hungary, too, the Jewish leaders were reluctant to listen to all warnings. I therefore think that it is not really right to claim, as the Jewish editor Herbert Pundik has done, that he was saved on account of the politicians who participated in active collaboration. We saw nothing of them in the North Harbor of Copenhagen, nor did we hear anything from them on Raadhusstræde.

The Significance of the Persecution of the Jews for the Resistance

Another aspect of the operations against the Jews was its significance for the further development of the Resistance. It is generally accepted that the rescue of the Jews led to the creation of many smuggling routes which, right up to the end of the war, were of importance for the Resistance. But the significance of the persecution of the Jews is more seldom commented on with regard to the Danish Freedom Council. The pogroms started some fourteen days after the Freedom Council had made its declaration on September 16 that it was going to lead the Resistance and had in mind not only to coordinate all the hitherto scattered initiatives, but also to plan for what Denmark was going to look like after the war was over.

When you consider how difficult it is to appoint oneself as leader for something while lacking the means to implement one's ideas, and without being able to demonstrate any form of authorization to carry these out, then a popular vote would have been necessary at the very least, if the enterprise were to succeed. Popular opinion arose during the August Uprising and this was a fine start for the Resistance with its unified aims and leadership. However, it was not to be taken for granted that the Freedom Council would enjoy the authority that it did in fact in the end achieve.

Crucial in such a situation is that swift and visible results occur. But while the state of emergency was still in place, the Freedom Council could do little except for making a few fine promises about what would happen when Denmark was free again. So it is indeed to the great credit of the members of the Freedom Council that their enterprise did in fact succeed. But it must be said that things might have turned out much worse, had not the Germans "helped" by making the unwise decision to start the pogroms. The Freedom Council rose on the crest of the wave of indignation these generated. Rabbi Friediger has given in his book on Theresienstadt a clear account of the inspiring solidarity involved:[52]

> That night, a Danish newspaper was smuggled in, and within a few nights it had arrived in the Danish colony. The newspaper went from hand to hand, until it was no longer legible and then ended up in the stove. But we had been given a breath of fresh air from home. We certainly did not understand everything written there. In nearly every column there was a notice that X had been shot or Y had died in the forest, that a factory had been burnt down, another bombed. We did not understand everything, but certainly got an inkling that Denmark was now resisting against the oppressor, and that the final battle had begun. How much we would have liked to have taken part in that struggle for freedom!

PART III: HOLGER DANSKE

Svend Otto Nielsen, alias John, disguised as police officer;
leader of HD2 actions until beginning of December 1943

CHAPTER 6

HD2

The resignation of the government on August 29 did not put an end to the sabotage. Before the end of that month five more acts of sabotage were carried out, and the total for September was eighty-five, which brought that month back to the high level achieved in July, when eighty-eight acts had been recorded. Although I did not know these figures at the time, the continuation of the acts of sabotage did raise the question as to their aim. We should also ask this question today.

Breaking off government cooperation with the Germans had been one of the chief goals of the August Uprising. This goal was now achieved and the Resistance had scored a win. Official cooperation between the government and the occupying forces was now at an end, but the politicians who were inclined to collaborate were still in the country and we did not know what they were planning to do. Nor did we know the attitudes of the undersecretaries, whose continued loyalty to their bosses who were now on strike is something we did not find out about until after the war.

So the struggle against collaboration was no longer a powerful motive for continuing the sabotage. A more important aim was to make sure that Denmark was regarded as an Allied nation and to shorten the war and therefore human suffering and fatalities. We were no longer in any doubt about the fact that Germany would ultimately lose the war, but I cannot deny that some months later I was seriously worried by the conviction the

Gestapo held that Germany was developing secret weapons that would guarantee a German victory. At the time, we knew nothing about German v2s or atom bombs.

The decision made by Peer and myself to set up a sabotage group still stood, and Flemming, Niels, Tellus and Klaus were ready to join. We received important support when, via Svend Kieler and Mix, we made contact with a group of interned naval cadets who were keen to join the Resistance. The events of August 29 had changed their circumstances entirely. There was no longer a government in place to which they should show their allegiance. Like the police, they therefore became more flexible in their attitudes. On the other hand, they were in effect prisoners of the Germans and would therefore run the risk of being deported to Germany. But this was a risk that many cadets were willing to take. They remained interned on the island of Holmen, but using Svend's fake passes they could begin to foster contacts with the Resistance.

Armed with the pistols that police inspector Simony had given us and two Suomi machine guns, which Svend had smuggled out to us in early October, our most pressing needs regarding weapons had been satisfied. But the cadets were keen to smuggle out more equipment if possible. So the next time Svend paid a visit there he smuggled two Madsen guns out in his kitbag. A helpful German, who was not aware of the contents, gave him a lift. The guns were hidden under the peat for our stove in our fuel store. They were not intended for sabotage operations but for larger-scale ones later.

On October 14, the naval cadets were released from Holmen and eleven of them immediately joined our sabotage group, which was now ready for action at last. Not all of them were in the group from beginning to end; but eight of them belonged to its core. Mix's girlfriend, Henny Sinding, who had been active with the transports of Jews to Sweden independent of ourselves, also joined. The naval cadets who went against the orders of their superiors to keep out of any action were:

Erik Koch Michelsen (Mix), born March 21, 1923
Svend Schack von Fyren Kieler, born November 13, 1922
Jørgen Michael Salling, born April 24, 1923
Stig Andersen, born February 17, 1923

Ib Gram Hansen, born December 22, 1917
Wilhelm Winther Christensen (Filler), born July 27, 1922
Paul Erik Reib, born October 6, 1923
Holger Mørch Sørensen, born February 20, 1923
Christian Friis-Hansen, born April 7, 1922
Tony Gath Kristoffersen, born May 2, 1923
Knud Kærgaard, born December 12, 1922

One significant factor that induced them to join the sabotage group, which had up to then consisted of students from Raadhusstræde, was that I managed to get in touch at the time with the Holger Danske sabotage group and the SOE.

The first Holger Danske group was created from among young men who had previously been volunteers and served in Finland and who had set up a sabotage group in 1943, with Tom Søndergaard as their leader.[53] This group took the name Holger Danske after a hero from a folktale who, according to legend, would come to Denmark in her hour of need. Their acts of sabotage culminated in the attack on the Forum exhibition hall which the Germans had requisitioned as barracks for their men, who had been brought to Denmark as a result of the August Uprising. Tom Søndergaard was seriously wounded in the operation and had to be evacuated to Sweden. During September, the rest of the most active members of the Holger Danske group followed suit.

A few people with looser links to the group stayed behind and one of them, Jens Lillelund, known as "Finn," decided to reconstitute the sabotage group. Through a mutual acquaintance he got in contact with me, and in mid-October he turned up at Raadhusstræde to ask if we wanted to form a new group called HD2 as part of a reorganized Holger Danske organization.[54] The timing could not have been better. The work with the transports of the Jews was slackening pace and I was busy organizing our group with the cadets. We now had weapons, but no instructions, sabotage material, targets for attacks or experience. Could Finn get the various things needed?

Finn arranged a meeting with a member of SOE. The man called himself Jens Peter, but otherwise told us nothing about himself. After the war was over, I found out that this was none other than the first officer Erik

Jens Peter Petersen who, after substantial training in England, had been dropped over Denmark the previous June to become a sabotage instructor, with Copenhagen as his base of operations. Along with Mix, I met Jens Peter twice in my illegal flat on Sølvgade. Jens Peter did not beat about the bush. Out of his bag he pulled detonators, fuses, ignition equipment, wads, plus various types of bombs and explosives. This was all spread out on the table and so the lesson began. I felt that it was something of a miracle that we did not all get blown up on the spot. But the lesson did convince us of how professional Jens Peter really was.

The Group Gels

A few days after the two instructional meetings, Finn turned up again at Raadhusstræde with a man not quite five foot six (170 cm), blond, thin and fit-looking, and about thirty-five years of age. His cheeks were a little sunken and the furrows in his face bore witness to worry or sorrow. But what drew most attention were his lively eyes whose ever-changing expression showed him to be very decisive, but not without a sense of humor and a capacity for friendliness. This was John. I only found out about his real name and his legal and underground background later on. His full name was Svend Otto Nielsen; he had been a teacher of mathematics and physics at a school in Charlottenlund, a suburb of Copenhagen.

John had already chalked up some experience with sabotage and we were all prepared to take him on as the leader of our group of six students and half a score of cadets. One of John's friends then turned up, a man of around twenty-two years of age with bright ginger hair, the result of a failed attempt at dyeing it. He was given the nickname "Flammen" (the flame). After the war, I found out that he was a trainee chef by the name of Bent Faurschou-Hviid.

Sabotage was considered a man's job. But the young women were also necessary, as they could play the role of courting couples in many situations, when a factory or person was under surveillance. But the young women had many other tasks to fulfill. Holger Danske 2 (HD2) included four women who were fully aware of the fact that the death penalty awaited anyone who accommodated or otherwise helped saboteurs. These four young women were my sisters Bente and Elsebet, my schoolmate Nan as well as Mix's girlfriend Henny. Elsebet has written the following about their work with HD2:[55]

As the persecution of the Jews was on the wane, Bente's and my task became to run a "speakeasy," so to speak, for the saboteurs. We experienced a friendship like those in the trenches, except in this case the front formed an invisible line through the middle of the population, when what seemed like a sleepy town under occupation would suddenly be shaken up by explosions at dusk and the wailing of fire engine sirens. And we women would be sitting at home counting the explosions. We knew how many there should be, if everything went according to plan, and listened for the fire engines – and for footsteps on the stairs. We would sit there in silence, evening after evening, counting the minutes until the boys came home and counting the boys when they came. We hardly did exemplary work to start with. We were the government, staff HQ and private soldiers all rolled into one. We lacked both experience and skills. Our friends marveled at the fact that we did not go underground; but we needed somewhere to meet, a home where we could live a normal mental life, because the work itself embraced values that could almost knock us off our feet, and which we all felt represented a concrete power within us.

And so we tried our best to live, if not normal lives, then at least a "civilian" life with normal functions. The cadets went to their classes, the students attended lectures at the university as often as they could. We considered this life "above ground" as good camouflage, something which would fool the enemy. It was nevertheless evident that this sham could only be maintained so long as none of us got arrested. Code names and forged documents obviously became part and parcel of our everyday lives. Although the students and cadets had known one another beforehand, a certain amount of anonymity could be maintained.

Although everything went wrong in the end, I could not blame then, nor do so now, our aboveground existence. We kept in touch with society and the people whose freedom we were fighting for. I certainly regarded not only informers, but also collaborators, as part of the enemy. But we had not declared war on Danish society, and I always reject Danish and German comparisons of the Resistance with a terrorist movement. We performed acts of sabotage because we wanted to ensure that Denmark would not end up on the side of Hitler, and also because it avoided air attacks of the population as a whole, reduced the Royal Air Force's losses over

Denmark and contributed – to a small extent – to a shortening of the war, which was costing some ten thousand victims per day in Germany alone. I thought of sabotage – and still do – as being the diametric opposite of terrorism, which is the murder of innocent people in order to achieve political or religious goals.

After Finn had introduced us to John, we rarely saw him. But we kept in touch with him and with the SOE via the Nordisk Boghandel bookshop in the center of the city. An instructional meeting was arranged towards the end of October and it was then that we took on the name HD2, as we said we wanted to take part in operations, while participation remained voluntary. We took no orders from anyone. But we did want to cooperate with a unified command, if such a thing existed.

The pistols were examined in more detail and the students were instructed in how to use them. This was a completely new experience and it was therefore not so surprising that a shot went off by accident. The bullet went right through my writing desk without damaging anything more than the surface which to this day bears the scar of a well filled-in "bullet wound." That was the only time we fired by mistake. But we did hold our breaths at the time because we were sure that the elderly couple living upstairs must have heard the shot, and there could hardly be any doubt about what was going on in our flat. But not a sound was heard, and when, in the end, everything went wrong for us, this was not as a result of our activities at Raadhusstræde.

Over the space of the following three months, HD2 carried out twenty-six acts of sabotage (see appendix, "Operations Carried out by HD2"). These included both small operations against the Nazis' offices and businesses, and more major ones against the war industry. The more experience we gained, the larger the targets became. Some of these deserve description in more detail.

Operational Practice

Operation IV – November 7, 1943. American Apparate Company, Søgaardsvej 52, Gentofte. After we had done three try-outs, we started on the real thing. We now wanted to demonstrate that we could carry out a sabotage operation "by the book." As far as I remember, it was the SOE that had chosen the target. This was a radio factory whose director was said to be a Nazi. We had also heard that the factory was producing jamming and other radio equipment for the Germans. The director denied to the police that he was collaborating with the Wehrmacht. He did concede that he was a supplier of parts to the Lorentz company in Berlin and to various Danish firms that were protected from sabotage by guards. There were four such anti-sabotage guards at his own factory, plus the gatekeeper.

On Saturday, November 6, in the afternoon, John and I went out to the factory to do reconnaissance. I was wearing the blue uniform of a Danish auxiliary policeman. We were spotted, without noticing it, by the anti-sabotage guards, who later explained to the police that we had observed the factory from various angles, after which we had disappeared. Early Sunday morning, John and I went out to the factory again, where we made notes. Once again, we were being observed unawares.

After we had made these preparations, we met at Raadhusstræde, and made our plan of action. I cannot remember how many were to take part, but the plan entailed that, wearing a policeman's uniform, I would ring at the gate and ask to inspect the blackout arrangements, about which complaints had been made over the past few days. John would follow me and keep the guards busy, while the rest of the group would place the bombs, which would be set to explode several minutes later. It was a Sunday, so we did not anticipate that there would be anyone else at the factory apart from the guards. It all seemed so incredibly straightforward. But it proved not to be.

We arrived at about 7:30 in the evening and, as planned, I went alone to the factory, which stood in a small yard whose gate was unlocked. It was only a few paces from the gate to the main door of the factory, and I rang the bell. But instead of opening up, the anti-sabotage guard opened a window one floor up. He shone a bright torch on me and asked me what I wanted. I explained that I had come to inspect the blackout. But he did not react to this. He wanted to know which police station I had been sent by and wanted my name and number. As he was clearly not going to be cooperative, I asked for the address of the director, so that I could contact him. He had no right to know my name, but I gave him my number at the police station.

At this point I began to walk back to the gate. The guard refused to give me the director's address, and ordered me to stay where I was, otherwise his colleague, who was pointing a pistol at me, would shoot. I replied that he would come to regret such an action and so reached the gate which I leaned against while the guard switched on the light in the office in order to look up the number of the police station in the telephone directory. At that moment I heard rapid footsteps behind me out on the street and a faint whistle. It was John who had come to get me out. As he passed me he whirled around, shone his torch at the guard and shot. The light in the office was immediately extinguished. The police report stated that John's shot had hit and damaged two electric cables, some six inches (15 cm) under the window sill. I ran out onto the street along with John. The guard explained to the police that he had shot several times in my direction. But I had been lucky; the pistol had merely clicked.

We all reached Raadhusstræde unscathed but apart from feeling annoyance at the failed mission, we also discovered that we had left behind our bombs in a rucksack behind a hedge near the factory. Something had to be done about this. It was far too dangerous to leave behind such traces, and besides we needed the bombs for future attempts. So the next day I went out to the factory with Nan – this time not wearing a police uniform. We found the rucksack and managed to get it back without any trouble. This caused some relief and we now began to think about what we should do and when to try there again.

A Change of Tactics

Operation VI – November 9, 1943. American Apparate Company, the second attempt. This time our plan was to abandon all attempts at entering the factory, but instead attack it from outside, by the long wall of the building. We split up into two units – a bomb unit which would, under cover by the armed unit, get near to the windows, after which we would hurl the detonation bombs in through the window after the guards and anyone else in the factory had been warned by, among other things, incendiary bombs. The thought behind this tactic was that it was better to render the factory unusable by blowing the whole building up, instead of wrecking the machines, which could always be used after the war. There was obviously a risk that the buildings would soon be rebuilt. But then they would "simply" have to be sabotaged once more.

The operation was carried out at around half-past seven in the evening. The armed unit consisted of four men who stood twenty yards from the factory, aiming at the windows with pistols, while the bomb unit sneaked right up to them. The procedure was one that would soon become familiar to us: when the signal was given, the bombers would smash the windows while the four men from the armed unit would give covering fire to prevent the guards from being able to shoot back. Once the windows were smashed, we would shout at those inside to go down immediately to the air raid shelter. We had chosen a length of fuse to give them three to four minutes to get there. A couple of small incendiary bombs were thrown in followed by a twenty-two-pound (10 kg) explosive charge. Then we took to our heels.

This was the first time we had used this new tactic, which became known as "direct assault" and was used by other groups. Splitting the group into a bomb unit and an armed unit and trying to destroy as much of the building as possible, as opposed to blowing up specific items of machinery or substations was a tactic that resembled a military operation. This tactic proved to be very effective on a number of occasions.

From the police report, we found out later what the operation felt like from inside the factory.[56] One of the two anti-sabotage guards said that at around 19:10 he had heard, via the listening apparatus set up in the factory, window panes being smashed and something thrown in. He went upstairs to warn the chief clerk of the factory and the two equipment inspectors who were present. They all went to the office and saw that there was a fire in the spools winding room. They got the bomb into a bucket and tried to put out the fire, which failed, as the fire extinguisher was out of order. The police and the fire brigade were summoned. At that point, a detonation bomb was thrown through the window. The explosion threw one of the guards and one of the inspectors to the ground without injuring them. The chief clerk then gave the order for them to all leave the building, which was in flames by the time the fire brigade arrived.

The next day, John introduced himself to the director of the factory as a reporter from the *Berlingske Tidende* daily newspaper. The director said that they had wanted to install searchlights after the first incident and that these would have been in operation the day after the second bombing took place. The two guards who had warded off our first attempt had resigned and had been replaced by new people who as yet had no experience of guarding buildings. The new guards were members of the Schalburg Corps, a volunteer force of Danes under German command. The new guards told John that if they got hold of the damned saboteurs they would shoot them on the spot.

A few days later, we received news that made us have to think hard. The same evening that our operation was carried out, another group had been going to do the same thing. As it happened, we got there first, which meant that the second group ran a serious risk of being caught when the police turned up. Nothing happened to them, but the whole incident made us realize that although we would continue to work independently, not taking orders from anyone, it was necessary for there to be a coordinated leadership in place, and we would have nothing against informing such leaders of our future plans, which John then took upon himself to do. The success of the operation against the American Apparate Company was of course a great encouragement, and we were keen to follow it up. But we were still being hampered by a shortage of explosives and were therefore consigned to the "minor operations division," with operations aimed at four small forms of collaborators, plus one major operation.

A Sabotage Failure

Operation xi – November 17–21, 1943. Reinhardt's truck repair shop, Lyngbyvej 36. Targets for sabotage included means of transport, and the SOE pointed these out as having major significance. Shipping and railways were of prime importance, but also works where road vehicles were produced for German use. The Germans needed many vehicles for their campaign on the *Ostfront*. One of these vehicle works became the target of one of our failed attempts at sabotage.

This was a large plant which repaired German trucks. We were unlucky right from the start. Just as we were penetrating the works, a large column of German vehicles arrived for repair. The German soldiers immediately opened fire on us and we had to retreat. We spread out and tried to escape by bicycle but we were apprehended by a Danish policeman and a situation arose, which showed us how equivocal the loyalties of the Danish police were after the events of August 29. The policeman came cycling along and soon realized that something was up. He followed me and I had several opportunities to gun him down, but this did not happen as we had all decided that we would not shoot at Danish police officers.

So it was the policeman who drew his gun first, and I had to throw mine down and raise my hands. We then walked for some time through a few side streets where there were luckily no German soldiers, with which the whole place was crawling. The policeman was nervous and started talking about what a cheek it was to commit acts of sabotage. He belonged to a religious movement that was against violence on principle. But he didn't really know what he should do with his prisoner. I informed him that he had the choice of letting me escape or taking me to the police station, which would mean I would be handed over to the Germans and executed. The policeman now had a crisis of conscience which resulted in him letting me go after finishing his homily. He kept my pistol. As usual, John then intervened. Even before the policeman had finished his lecture John had already got in touch with his contacts at police headquarters to tip them off about my predicament. But their help did not prove necessary.

Luck would have it that I again met the religious policeman some dozen years later. Late one afternoon, when I was sitting alone in my office at Fibiger Laboratories, a man suddenly entered the laboratory without ringing the doorbell. He was wearing a raincoat, so I could not see whether he was a policeman or not. He asked me whether I recognized him and when I said that I did not, he drew a pistol and asked, "Perhaps you recognize this?" It could have been a petty mugging; but I did not really have much to steal, so my first thought was that this was an act of revenge. Not everyone harbored particularly warm feelings towards former saboteurs. My guest then handed me the pistol, which I now recognized as the one he had taken from me in November 1943. I now realized that it was the religious policeman who had come to visit me. I asked him to take a seat and waited for his explanation with great anticipation. "I've been looking for you for a long time, so that I could give you back your pistol," he began.

> It's been lying in my desk drawer ever since we met for the first time, and has been bothering me. I knew neither your name nor your address. But a few days ago I saw your picture in the paper in connection with an interview about cancer research, and after that it wasn't difficult to trace you. So I've come to return your pistol.

After first having listened to how things turned out for his former prisoner, which he seemed to be satisfied about, he continued:

> What I said to you when I arrested you still holds true. But sometimes I have had my doubts. This happened when I later realized that several of my colleagues had gotten involved with the Resistance, and some

of them were caught. So I felt I had to lend a hand, and ended up as a member of a group that collected weapons dropped by the British. I became a member of the Resistance against my will, out of consideration for my colleagues. I still don't know even today whether I did the right thing.

Then he stretched out his hand, which was shaking slightly, and added, "But anyway, I'm glad you're alive and that I can return your pistol to you."

An Internal Struggle

A few days after the incident on Lyngbyvej, I met John in our secret flat in Sølvgade. It was here he told me that he had managed to foster contacts at police headquarters. Naturally, he gave no further details. But I was now doubly glad that I had not shot at the religious policeman.

We took the tram from Sølvgade over to Raadhusstræde in order to prepare for a new operation. A commotion occurred in the crowded tram, which a German soldier interpreted as a personal insult. He started threatening everyone with his pistol and the brave conductor found it hard to convince him that it was all a misunderstanding. As the soldier alighted from the tram, John winked at me. We followed. The chap had to be taught a lesson and we needed his pistol, now that I had lost my own. As we followed him a short way along the street it became clear that he was feeling embarrassed. He broke into a run, and as there were many people out on the street, we had to let him go. I was relieved, but could not get to sleep that night. I asked myself time and time again whether I was up to the job.

Was I afraid?

The answer is "yes." And in order to overcome my fear I began to ask myself what the root cause of my fears was. I lay awake for the rest of the night ruminating on this, but it was time well spent. We all felt afraid. But fear could have many causes. As the head of our group, I was of course quite convinced that our cause was a just one. The debate about this was over, and there was no point in going over all those things again, every time we got into hot water. But for the individual involved, operations often caused mental stress, everything from ignoring a "No Entry" sign to worrying about hurting innocent people. A great number of considerations and prohibitions, ones we normally accepted as part of our upbringing, had simply to be suppressed for the sake of the greater good, a mission whose justness we never doubted. Fear of guards – both human and canine – and of arrest and torture did not play an important role once we had started an operation. What was of greater importance was the fear of something unexpected happening, and then not being able to cope.

During the past three weeks, I had been held up on three occasions – first by the anti-sabotage guard at the American Apparate Company, then by a policeman in Hellerup, and then by the policeman on the Lyngbyvej. I was a little out of sorts, and now this German soldier was yet another problem I had to wrestle with mentally. The German had understandably felt threatened, when he thought people were posing a threat. And he could well have shot us out of a feeling of self-preservation.

I asked myself whether it was a fear of dying that had made me give up the chase, but thought that in all conscience I could answer that question with "no." I had gone into the struggle with my eyes open, knowing full well that it could cost me my life, and I was prepared, in principle, to pay the price. I only formed a more personal attitude towards the idea of dying later on, when as a German prisoner I was waiting for my execution, and by then I was not at all afraid. On this occasion there was no looming threat. It had been two against one, and John was a good shot.

Two against one! Yes, this formed part of my fear. The eternal Boy Scout in me was reacting. It was just not fair. But that was not the main thing. Quite a different problem was worrying me. It was the fear of losing all sense of proportion. Was that pistol worth my life, or that of the German soldier? The answer was again "no." But this was not an easy conclusion to arrive at.

It had to be understood that things in Denmark had changed radically over the space of only a few months. Before August 29, we had two enemies: the collaborationist politicians and the Germans. The underground press, the strikes and the increasing number of acts of sabotage, culminating in the blowing up of the Forum, had forced the Danish politicians to withdraw. The August Uprising was therefore a great victory in this respect. From that time onwards, mere provocations had become pointless, and now concrete action had to be taken against those who provided the German war machine with material and equipment. Even though we were still far from being professional, the time for training was over. It was now time that we regarded ourselves as up to the task and took on larger assignments.

Small suppliers who collaborated and the Danish girls who hung around with the Germans would have to be dealt with by others.

The New Tactics Prove Effective

Operation XIII – November 25, 1943. The Grauballe Uniform Factory, Allégade 8. For me personally, Grauballe was the turning point. After my nocturnal agonizing, I had now decided that the time was ripe for me to get a grip on myself. Otherwise I would never be able to do an effective job. No objections could be raised to the choice of Grauballe as the next target. This was a clothes factory with some hundred employees, and what they did was sew up German uniforms. As early as March 22, 1943, another sabotage group that cooperated closely with the SOE had attempted to burn this business down. But the fire was put out before any real damage had been done. On April 27 and again on October 15, new attempts had been made, but again in vain, so it was now high time that these collaborators paid for their actions. We were prepared to try and this time we had managed to obtain a small amount of plastic explosive.

The factory was housed on the second and third floors of a building where the ground floor at the back jutted out somewhat and was roofed in with a shed roof. We had studied the locality well and had assigned six or seven men for the job. So some of the cadets busied themselves with drawing a precise plan of the premises and the area around it. They used their English lesson period at naval cadet training for this exercise as their teacher, the translator Prom, noticed. He confiscated the sketch without actually looking at it in detail, but when the cadet who had drawn it asked for it back after the lesson, he took it out, looked at it briefly and gave it back without comment. This was, of course, a breach of the security of our group, but we counted on the fact that Prom would be on our side. And he was. The day after the operation he passed a secret note to the cadet with the words "My compliments."

This operation was executed according to our new technique. We put marksmen at appropriate points in the factory yard, while I, along with the other members of the unit, used a ladder we found in the yard to crawl up over the shed roof so we had access to the windows above the ground floor. As soon as the first window pane was smashed, the factory alarm went off and four searchlights were switched on. The armed unit began immediately to fire at these searchlights, while the bomb unit carried on.

First, we threw in an incendiary bomb. This was followed by a detonation bomb and a couple more firebombs. We got down rapidly from the shed roof and the detonation bomb exploded immediately afterwards. Within a few minutes, the whole business was in flames. The fire brigade turned up, but the premises were a write-off.

The police report states that at the time there were two anti-sabotage guards on the third floor.[57] They heard the window being smashed on the floor below them, heard the alarm and saw the searchlights. So they knew that this was an act of sabotage. One of the guards tried to put out the first incendiary bomb, while the other phoned the police and the fire brigade. But when the other firebombs were thrown in, they had to abandon their efforts and the fire soon spread to the rest of the building.

The police report said that the second and third floors were completely burned out and that the ground floor suffered water damage. This was a reasonable effort, and I felt I had gotten back in the saddle.

Experienced Saboteurs in Action

Operation xiv – November 28, 1943. The Hellerup Division of the Industrial Combine. Information about likely targets came from various sources. Sometimes it was workers in a particular factory, sometimes the police or the Freedom Council, all of which had their contacts, or from the SOE itself. There was an interest on the part of the British to sabotage factories, and these were our first priority. In this case, we targeted the Hellerup Division of the Industrial Combine where sound locators were being manufactured. They were used to pinpoint British aircraft, as they dropped supplies for the Danish Resistance, or planes crossing Danish airspace on their way to Berlin or Poland. More than thirteen hundred British airmen lost their lives over Denmark. When we were tipped off about Hellerup in the northern part of Copenhagen, there were already several sets of sound locators ready to be delivered to the Germans within a couple of days and we knew we now had to prove what we were worth.

The SOE wanted this factory to be sabotaged. But for the time being, Jens Peter, the SOE officer with whom we were in contact, could not obtain any explosives. Luckily, John could "organize" some TNT, taken from the Germans, if we could find the money to bribe a number of drivers. He was given a couple of thousand kroner and managed to get three tons of dynamite, of which two went to other groups, while one ton was deposited in a cellar which we had borrowed for the purpose. So that problem had now been solved and we could begin in earnest.

Along with John and Mix, I staked out the factory, while Finn tried to obtain more information from other sources. The factory had been installed in the western end of a large building, whose eastern part housed both the Danish and German harbor police. At the western end, there were three anti-sabotage guards armed with machine guns. We therefore had to count on stiff resistance from both the guards and the harbor police. The factory stood on a large, open plot of land, which was shut off from Havnevej Street with a high chain-link fence which, according to unconfirmed information, carried an electric charge. A plank fence ran along the western edge of the compound and separated it from a filling station which stood on Strandvejen. From dusk till dawn, the whole compound was lit up brightly with powerful searchlights.

It was easy to gain access by way of the plank fence behind the filling station. Then the bomb unit would have to cross a wide open space, what was termed the wash yard, without cover in order to reach the factory itself. Here we would be an easy target for the guards with their machine guns. But we thought it would be more dangerous to gain access via the chain-link fence, which was closer to the guards and possibly electrified. The aim was therefore to knock out the searchlights, then send in the bomb unit covered by two armed units who would fire over the fences and the wash yard.

Finn had been given some valuable information regarding the searchlights: they could be switched off from the Tuborg brewery, which was the northern neighbor of the Industrial Combine compound. He had managed to obtain keys for the machine hall where the switch was located. The whole operation was a dangerous one and Finn wanted to call the whole thing off. But we decided to give it a try. Preparations had been made, and as thoroughly as was humanly possible.

On the day of the operation, we met at Raadhusstræde for instructions and to allot tasks. According to the plan, our group, which had been reinforced by taking on a couple of strangers John had brought along, would meet up outside the Tuborg brewery at seven o'clock in the evening. One unit would then go into Tuborg and find any workers on duty there and hold them up. Then the switch to the searchlights had to be located. When this had been done, the saboteurs would pull out, leaving behind three of their number as guards; these would cut the power after ten minutes had passed. Then the operation itself could begin.

Two armed units would give cover to the bomb unit. Flammen and Niels would cover the bomb unit as they crossed the open space on the western side, while John and Flemming would keep the guards upstairs back from the windows on the long northern side, where the main attack would take place once the bomb unit had reached the building. The armed unit had pistols, but also the two Suomi submachine guns that the cadets had obtained for us.

The bomb unit was to consist of four sub-units of two men each and these were equipped with British firebombs and our homemade TNT ones, which each weighed over thirty pounds (15 kg). The bombs were equipped with detonators and had short fuses which were to be lit using fusees (combustible fuses). One of the sub-units would try to get the bomb in through a door on the western end of the building while the other three bomb sub-units would move to the northern long side and, when the signal was given, throw their bombs in through the ground-floor windows.

After all these instructions had been given, I asked who wanted to take part. No one was obliged to, but everyone said they would, and so the tasks were divided up. Three men were given guard duty at Tuborg and one to guard the street at the corner of Strandvejen and Havnevej. It was for such tasks that we had recruited a few extra men. Then it was my turn to pick men for the bomb unit. Apart from Mix, four cadets and two "civilians" undertook to carry out this assignment. I was a little hesitant about taking Klaus along as he was so tall that he would be an easy target for the anti-sabotage guards. But he insisted on coming along.

When the tasks had been allotted, Mix smiled his rather crooked smile and said, "You're the trigger-happy one." But we all knew that this was the only way to get things done, and everyone agreed with Mix when he added, smiling his candid smile, "I have to say that I'm shit-scared, but of course I'll do it."

A brave taxi driver, who had also helped us previously, transported the bombs out to Hellerup. The weather was ideal for the operation in that it was dark and visibility was poor. But it was raining, and the rain could present problems when we wanted to light the fuses.

At seven o'clock the group met up at the monument close to Tuborg as planned and the car with the bombs turned up a little while later. About a third of the group went into Tuborg. John knew the way and had the keys to various doors and gates. The police report says that there were two guards on duty at the gate.[58] We did not see them, and they did not see us. We did, after all, come unannounced, and with keys. Once we had entered the brewery, we first located the boiler attendant and the boiler room, then two machine minders in the machine room. These were a little surprised at the unexpected visit by a group of armed men, but were otherwise calm and not particularly impressed. They knew that this was obviously an attempt at sabotage.

When we told them that it was not the Tuborg brewery we were aiming for, but that we only wanted to locate the switches to the searchlights at the Industrial Combine, they became quite helpful. We asked them to stop the turbines, so that the lights would go out. But the machine minder protested at this, as it would overload the boilers. It would be better to use the switch on the distribution frame. But there was a problem: there were three switches, and he did not know which one switched off the searchlights. One of them offered to phone the duty engineer to ask him. The engineer was suspicious and asked if something was wrong. The machine minder denied this and suggested that the engineer call him back to verify, which is what he did. The machine minder then put his question, pretending that bets were being placed on the issue.

"Sorry, Larsen, but you've gone and lost your bet. It's the one on the right." So that problem was solved. The machine minder was then tied up, at his own request, while the boiler attendants were allowed to carry on with their work under the watchful eye of three of our men, while our operation took place. We then moved out leaving the three men to put out the lights in ten minutes' time.

We met our colleagues at the monument on the Tuborgvej. What had occurred in the Tuborg plant had taken time and we wanted to be home before the curfew began at eight. The waiting men were therefore a little nervous, and they were cold and wet too. But it was now or never. Our taxi driver drove a little way down Havnevej and we fetched the bombs. Then the armed sub-units moved to their positions and the bomb unit went up to the plank fence, which would be broken through. Then the lights went out. Our time of waiting was over and, as on so many occasions, our nervousness disappeared too.

We scrambled over the plank fence and began to move across the open space. The anti-sabotage guards were clearly somewhat disoriented at first. But when we had gotten roughly a third of the way across, their submachine guns began to "hic." All the men dived to the ground, and our armed units lit up the western façade of the building with a powerful torch, whereupon Flammen and John returned fire. Then everything fell silent and we continued to advance, arriving at where we had planned to in the lee of a wall. In order to signal the commencement of the bombing attack proper, one of the sub-units lit a firebomb which was thrown through the window into the machine hall of the factory on the ground floor. The fire soon spread and now the four bombing sub-units had to do what was most difficult. The fuses had to be lit, but both they and their matches were soaking wet from the rain, and this part of the operation took time. This was very frustrating but in the end they managed, and the detonation bombs were thrown in through the windows, and we began to make our way out of the factory yard.

Meanwhile, John had ripped four planks loose from the plank fence so that our escape would be made easier. He was crawling up the fence to cover our retreat. At that point he was a perfect target for the guards. But they had other things to think about. After all the men from the bomb unit had passed back out through the hole in the fence, they were counted. In the darkness, one had been overlooked and John therefore took a walk around to see whether all were now out. They were after all, and so we moved on to Strandvejen. And that is where we were when the bombs went off. The bombs had been fitted with a very short fuse, which barely gave us a few minutes to get away. We saw a huge flash, followed by three loud detonations. One of the bombs had clearly failed to go off. But three were more than enough to cause a significant amount of damage. Slivers of glass rained down, trams stopped and windows were shattered. Women screamed and wept, and here and there panic broke out. The guards at Tuborg were released, after which the saboteurs vanished on their bicycles or by taxi, the taxi waiting with its engine running on Havnevej.

According to the police, at the time of the explosions, there were only two anti-sabotage guards on duty and the third was a quarter of an hour late for work. He saw the explosions from Havnevej. The other two guards were on the ground floor, but when the lights went out they went up to the second, phoned the police and began shooting at our bomb unit with their submachine guns. The police arrived soon afterwards. When they heard the shooting, they realized that they had come too early. The sirens and the flashing light were switched off, after which they sneaked away. Not until the bombs had gone off did they come back rather slowly, this time with sirens wailing and their blue lights flashing.

The police report gives the idea that the workers at the Tuborg brewery were completely on our side. They gave no information of any importance. On the other hand, the anti-sabotage guards were much keener to provide descriptions of the saboteurs. But they had not seen much. The director of the Industrial Combine then told the police that his factory had been the target of acts of sabotage on four occasions. There were sixteen of the sound locators that they were making for a German company in the machine hall at the time and they were to be delivered the following day. They were all destroyed. The building, machines and equipment belonged to the Wehrmacht, all except the hand tools.

A few days later, John heard that the same evening as our operation was taking place, one of the leading engineers from the Industrial Combine, who lived near the factory, had a party. During the evening they began to discuss sabotage, and the chief engineer told his guests that it was impossible to sabotage his factory, which was extra well guarded. At that very moment there were a number of explosions and the windows of the room where they were meeting were blown in. "That came from your factory," said one of the guests. But the chief engineer insisted, and bet on it. So those attending were quite amused when a phone call proved that it was indeed his factory and that the saboteurs had been able to penetrate the plant under the "watchful" eye of the anti-sabotage guards. My description of the whole operation, written shortly after the war, ends with the following words:[59]

This operation was the icing on the cake of John's career as a saboteur. He took part in a couple more operations. But of all the operations he took part in, none had been as important. The attack on the Danish Industrial Combine's annex marked the start of a new course, a new spirit. First of all, submachine guns were now part and parcel of each operation, which meant tougher fighting, a greater risk for us, but also the opportunity to carry out larger-scale operations. This also meant that all the men in the units were utilized. Earlier actions had gone out from the following premise: the maximum result without a loss of life. This had now changed to: the maximum result, even if lives are lost. Earlier on, guile and surprise had been the tactics. Now it was more of an open fight, a military-style operation. This development was chiefly thanks to John, who occupies a special place in the history of Danish sabotage.

After the success at the Industrial Combine, we had a few days off. But suddenly, there were other things to think about.

Two of sixteen sound detectors that were destroyed by our sabotage
of the Industrial Combine in Hellerup, November 28, 1943

CHAPTER 7

The Show Must Go On

John's Arrest

On December 8, 1943, Finn had arranged to meet John. They were to meet on a street corner at 7:30 in the evening. On account of the curfew, which started half an hour later, they decided to stay the night in a flat whose occupants had fled to Sweden. They met as planned, but as John had the suspicion that the flat in question was under observation, they had to change their plans and find somewhere else nearby to stay for the night. They turned for help to a Norwegian seamstress by the name of Hedvig Delbo, who lived at Faxegade 3 in the Østerbro district. According to Finn, she was very keen to establish contact with the Resistance. She was supposed to have done a few jobs for the first Holger Danske organization and even taken part in a minor operation, evidently some vandalism to a business owned by collaborators. Whether Finn had any knowledge of this woman's past, I do not know, but she told the police herself that she had been arrested on four occasions by the Germans, including for a breach of public order.

On November 10, 1943, a pocket-sized English firebomb had been put under the doormat outside Mrs. Delbo's door on Faxegade timed to go off in thirty minutes' time. She had discovered it before it went off. The police were called and they succeeded in throwing the device into the gutter where it burnt up. Mrs. Delbo explained that one possible reason for this attack was that she had been married to a pro-German relative of a Danish politician with Nazi sympathies. She had now gotten divorced and changed her name to Delbo.

Mrs. Delbo was at home on December 8 and had served sandwiches and coffee to Finn and John, who after the evening meal put their bicycles in the entrance hall and listened to the radio broadcast from London. Then they went to bed in a little guestroom on the other side of the hallway. Mrs. Delbo was also going to go to bed. But before she did, she managed to find the time to call the Gestapo at the Dagmarhus Headquarters in the city and tell them what VIPs had taken up residence in her flat. The next morning at 8:30, Mrs. Delbo and her guests ate breakfast. Finn and John then took their bicycles and were about to cycle off. Mrs. Delbo followed them out onto the street, where they waved a friendly goodbye, before she went shopping across the street.

As Finn and John were cycling away, they noticed that they were being observed by two men and that there was a car with three or four occupants standing at each end of Faxegade. They suspected that these were Gestapo and that they were there to get them and this was soon confirmed when, as they cycled away they were followed along several streets, until the Gestapo began to shoot.

Finn tells that he saw John stand up on his pedals and fumble for his pistol with one hand. This was concealed in his trouser lining near his fly and "this was a familiar movement to us," as Mix said later.

Finn managed to get away after a dramatic chase and warn us via our information drop-off point at the tobacconists. But for John, things turned out quite differently. What happened to him that morning has been described by three eyewitnesses.

The German Gestapo agent Fritz Wagner survived the war and was interrogated in Neuengamme by the Danish police on May 27, 1946. He explained, and this concurred with Finn's description of events, that the two fleeing Resistance fighters had made their escape attempt along several side streets onto Østerbrogade, before they were caught up with by the Gestapo, who began to shoot. They hit John who fell to the ground in front of Østerbrogade 21.

John's arrest was seen by a Danish policeman by the name of Ravn, who told in the Danish police report that around 08:45 he heard a number of shots being fired and about a minute later a cyclist pedaled at full speed to the right of the corner, after which he fell over as if in pain. Soon afterwards, two cars drove up from a side street. They stopped on the corner and a passenger stepped out who told Ravn in German that they were German plainclothes security policemen. Two people jumped out of the nearest car. They walked up to John and arrested him.

Ravn and the Gestapo agent who had addressed him now arrived and Ravn asked John whether he had been hit. When John nodded and said a faint "yes," Ravn walked with the Gestapo agent over the road to a butcher's shop, where the butcher was standing outside. He asked the butcher to call an ambulance and then he and the Gestapo agent went back to where John had fallen. A crowd had now gathered around John, but from a distance Ravn saw that he had freed himself from the Germans and had drawn a pistol, loaded it and fired three or four shots in the air, then one at one of the German cars. Ravn could not see whether anyone was hit, but the Gestapo agent drew his pistol and fired at John, who dropped his gun. The Gestapo agent ran up to him and hit him three or four times on the temple with his pistol. John slumped in pain. Then he was bundled into the nearest Gestapo car.

Wagner's account of the incident is a little different. After being seriously wounded by the Gestapo agent's shot, John was bundled into a Gestapo car, after which John drew his pistol and shot at the Germans in the car. Gestapo agent Pelligrini was killed and another Gestapo agent was wounded in the forehead by a stray shot. Detective Inspector Voeght fired the last shot at John who was hit for the seventh time.

Cato – The First Casualty

The fates of people during the occupation were linked together in strange and unexpected ways. December 9 was a fateful day, and not only for the Gestapo agent Heinrich Pelligrini, Mrs. Delbo and John, but also for one of the "nonviolent" members of our group, Cato Bakman. Bakman had made a significant contribution to the underground press and helping the refugees. He was a co-founder of the Free Denmark News Service and during the pogroms against the Jews took up contact with the professor of surgery Professor Husfeldt at the university hospital and Dr Køster at the Bispebjerg Hospital, where he also worked with his wife Andrea, who was a nurse there.

During the incident in which John was shot, the Germans wounded an innocent cyclist who later told the Danish police that he was on his way to work on Østerbrogade when he suddenly felt a blow to his right leg. He got off his bicycle and then saw that he had been hit by a bullet. He was picked up by the Danish traitor Rudolf Petersen who took him to the entrance of Østerbrogade 21, where he held him. A pool of blood collected around him. He had been hit just under the knee on the outside of his leg and later in the hospital it was discovered that his fibula and a major nerve had been hit.

The cyclist was taken, along with the wounded Gestapo agent, in an ambulance. He was taken to Copenhagen University Hospital, while the German was taken on to the German hospital at Frederiksberg. As the Gestapo suspected that this cyclist was a colleague of John's, Rudolf Petersen came back to the hospital some while later in order to take the cyclist with him. The hospital refused to discharge him and they asked two medical students, Cato and Holger, to transfer him to the Bispebjerg Hospital. This all happened some eight hours after John's arrest. Cato went over to Køster's flat but he was not at home. Unfortunately, six Gestapo agents arrived shortly afterwards, who had been sent on an entirely different errand to the Bispebjerg Hospital, to arrest Dr. Køster. They did not find Køster but they did find Cato who was already wanted by them.

As Cato wanted to warn Holger who was waiting by the ambulance with the wounded man, he tried to escape. Putting trust in his strong physique, he jumped out of a third-floor window. The Germans shot at him and, now seriously wounded, he was brought into arrivals, where he was attended to by the duty nurse. This was Andrea, to whom he had been married for a couple of months. He had four injuries to his spine and three bullet wounds, plus a number of other injuries as a result of the fall. During the night he lost consciousness and died early the next morning. His parents came to his deathbed, where a German soldier was guarding him. When Cato died, the soldier asked his father if he knew the dead man. Cato's father said that this was his son, whereupon the German said he regretted the death and stretched out his hand to shake that of Cato's father. But he did not want to accept it.

Andrea buried her dead husband and continued to work for the Free Denmark News Service. Cato, who did not want to become a saboteur, was the first one of our group who paid with his life. Seven more deaths were to follow. Holger Larsen was imprisoned in the Vestre Fængsel (West Prison), and was released shortly afterwards. The innocent cyclist who had been wounded was discharged on January 18, 1944, without any lasting injuries. He told the Danish police that he had nothing to do with the Resistance.

The Fifth Commandment

John's fate after his arrest remained unclear for several months. We were shaken, but determined to expose and neutralize the informer. I knew nothing of Finn's dealings with Mrs. Delbo, and the explanation furnished by the Gestapo agent Wagner after the war was, of course, something we did not know at the time either. But even though Finn had indeed trusted Mrs. Delbo, this trust did have its limits and given the acute nature of the situation, he could not think that he had been betrayed by anyone other than Mrs. Delbo herself. We discussed the matter, and in the end we decided to put it to the test. HD2 was mobilized. First, a "courting couple" was sent to Faxegade to observe the house, after which Finn called Mrs. Delbo and told of the mishap that had befallen John. He said that he could not stay in Denmark now, but would have to flee to Sweden. He said he wanted to say farewell at three o'clock sharp that afternoon. She began to cry on the phone, and asked him to come up to her place before he left.

That was not the only telephone conversation that Mrs. Delbo had that afternoon. She immediately informed Detective Inspector Fritz Wagner, who told the police after his own internment at Neuengamme after the war that he, along with several other Gestapo agents, went to Faxegade, where they kept Mrs. Delbo's house under observation. According to Wagner, Mrs. Delbo received twenty thousand kroner to betray Finn and John.

Apart from seeing a number of Gestapo agents, our lookouts observed a Gestapo car at each end of Faxegade, and a handcart with Christmas trees outside Mrs. Delbo's, which later turned out to be concealing a machine-gun nest. This confirmed our suspicions. An hour later, Finn called and told Mrs. Delbo that he was sorry, but that he could not come. She tried to make a new appointment and pump him for information – when, where and how he wanted to get to Sweden. She was so unsubtle that it bordered on the ludicrous.

This was the first time that we had to start planning a liquidation. How much Mrs. Delbo knew about the rest of the group was something we just did not know. But given the fact that she knew Finn and John, there was a strong likelihood that the whole of the Holger Danske organization could be compromised. Finn insisted on carrying out the liquidation himself. But that did not release the rest of us from the moral responsibility for his act. We had discussed this problem again and again.

There was nothing more to be said. We now had a problem only we ourselves could solve. Do you want to help liquidate an informer, or do you want to stop doing Resistance work? We realized full well that this was not a question of revenge or punishment, but of self-preservation. We had no other way of rendering informers harmless. We could not imprison them, and forcing them to flee to Sweden would not guarantee that they would not continue informing. We already had discussed the principle of it all.

Our main problem was whether we indeed had enough evidence to be sure of the guilt of this informer. At that point in time, there was no higher authority that could furnish evidence, one way or the other. Now, for the first time, we ourselves would have to answer for what we were doing. We were in no doubt that Mrs. Delbo was guilty. Her liquidation was a necessity.

Operation XVII – December 10, 1943. Mrs. Delbo, Faxegade 3.[60] The planning and execution of the operation showed plainly that we were as amateurish in this field of operations as we had been earlier when we carried out our first acts of sabotage. For understandable reasons, Finn required as much backup as possible, and we called in extra men. Some fourteen or fifteen men were positioned throughout the area. One of the HD2 girls, whom Finn in his report called "the student girl," would go up to Mrs. Delbo to have a dress sewn. If she was at home, Finn would come forward and carry out the liquidation with a silenced pistol. This seemed so simple. But a couple of unexpected problems arose.

Mrs. Delbo was indeed at home, but she had another customer and this took time, which made Finn lose his nerve. In addition, the many lookouts were beginning to arouse the suspicions of the neighbors. The operation had to be called off. The "student girl" slipped away from Faxegade street unnoticed, while Finn forced his way into a flat where he held up an old couple and cut the telephone wires. They took it very well. He could see through their window over to Mrs. Delbo's; she was moving around her living room not suspecting a thing. The operation was already a fiasco, and things would soon get even worse.

A newsagent, who was afraid that all the young people hanging around on the street were planning to rob his till, called the police, and four of our lookouts, including Mix and one of the other cadets, were taken to the police station. As Mix was carrying a pistol, he could hardly play the innocent bystander, although the police did their best to help him cobble together a convincing story. A discreet hint from the navy suggested that it was imperative to release the four as quickly as possible.

They took note of this and the cadets were released at eleven at night. As they were unable to walk home on account of the curfew, they were given a lift by the police. However, before they were taken home, they managed to hear a policeman who came in and said: "Well, well, now they've gone and shot some woman on Faxegade. It's getting better and better."

It had been Finn and Flammen, who had realized that this presence of a large number of saboteurs was a big mistake. They had gone back to Faxegade and rung the bell at Mrs. Delbo's door. A Norwegian woman opened up, closely followed by Mrs. Delbo. When she saw Finn she let out a scream and fled into the flat. Finn shot her with his silenced pistol and when Mrs. Delbo fell over he thought she was dead, after which he and Flammen left.

The next day, they went to Detective Superintendent Andst at police headquarters to hear the news. They were greeted curtly with "Idiot!" He told them that Mrs. Delbo had only received a superficial flesh wound in her shoulder, and that she had recognized Finn. She happened to be sitting in the next office being interrogated by the Gestapo. "She'll be as right as rain in a week," said Andst, "and it's Sweden for you." The SOE agreed, and on December 22 Finn, along with his wife and two sons, was evacuated to Sweden.

According to Lillelund, Mrs. Delbo also had to leave the country. There is no certain information as to what she did then. She presumably went back to Norway. Lillelund told the Norwegian underground press, and she soon returned to Denmark, where she opened a tailor's atelier in the Vesterbro district of Copenhagen, under the name of Eva Dam. She seems to have renewed her contacts with the Gestapo. In a letter dated March 4, 1944, which she sent to a woman whose husband had been the victim of attempted murder as reprisal, she poured out all her hate over the saboteurs. She described the failed attempt on her life and after expressing her disapproval at how the police behaved in her flat, she added:[61]

When they tried to kill me on subsequent occasions, I have gone to the police, but have been so badly received there that I'm not going again. From now on, I will report the incidents elsewhere.

She also contacted a lawyer who was conducting a campaign on the radio against sabotage. But he was not interested in Hedvig Delbo's case. In a broadcast on May 16, 1944, he told of how she suddenly turned up at his office one day. He described her as a thirty-five-year-old beauty who was hysterical and nervous, and continued:[62]

She showed me a revolver which she had in her pocket and told me most glibly that she had been a saboteur and had been jilted by her lover. She now wanted to take revenge on him and his colleagues.

This raises the question as to whether Hedvig Delbo had other motivations than money when she started her career as an informer. The lawyer suggested she receive psychiatric treatment. But she did not need any as she was recognized by a bookseller, and via him Holger Danske found that she was living on Sankelmarksgade, where, on March 9, 1944, she was liquidated by another HD group. The police found thirty-five thousand kroner in cash in her flat.

Regrouping

John's arrest obviously made a deep impression on us. We thought that he was dead but had no accurate information about what had happened to him and tried therefore to focus our minds on the future activities of the group. It is with pleasure that I can now look back and say that not one of the members wanted to drop out. Quite the opposite: an act of sabotage against an even bigger target was necessary, and this had to be performed quickly. It was now a question of Denmark's status at the end of the war.

There were major obstacles to overcome. In a sense, we had to begin from scratch. We had lost one of our principal leaders. But this was not the only loss. After the failed attempt to liquidate Mrs. Delbo, Finn was now forced to flee to Sweden. He was the one who had had links with all the HD groups, with the sabotage group BOPA, the SOE and the Freedom Council, and was therefore an enormous security risk, were he to be arrested and tortured. Finn had to be evacuated, but this created an acute problem of leadership which merged with the fight against informers, of which Mrs. Delbo's betrayal had been the first major incident, and with the shortage of explosives which affected sabotage in the Copenhagen area, as the SOE depots slowly emptied, with no prospect of further supplies.

By way of our contact points, we got in touch with one Jørgen Staffeldt who was a member of the Military Committee of the Freedom Council, which was responsible for the formation of an underground army which would assist the Allies should it come to an invasion. This also meant that we now had links with the SOE, and as Jørgen Staffeldt became Finn's successor as early as December 1943 in leading the entire Holger Danske organization our cooperation with the other Holger Danske groups was also ensured. So the organization as such was still intact. But this did not solve the problem of obtaining explosives in the Copenhagen area. We had to accept the fact that if we wanted to carry out acts of sabotage, these would have to take place on the Jutland peninsula, and so our role as a sort of flying squad came about. And it did not take long before they needed us.

Varde Calling

Our contacts with the Varde Resistance had been established via Niels Hjorth, who had been working as an intern at the hospital in the small town of Varde, near Esbjerg in the west of Jutland. It was also through him that we had established contact with Chief Constable Simony who had given us the seven pistols, our first weapons. But it was Assistant Chief Constable Henning Schlanbusch who became the central figure in our cooperation with the Resistance in Varde. We happened to meet him when visiting Simony. Without going into details, Simony suggested that before traveling back home, we should pay a visit to Schlanbusch. We did so without knowing beforehand that Schlanbusch had another visitor there, Aage Møller Christensen, a parachuted SOE contact man whose code name was "Carlo Jensen," which could well have been the reason why Schlanbusch received us in his office. He obviously did not tell us about Møller Christensen, and after a short conversation had taken place between us, we went back to Copenhagen without knowing that we had missed the chance to establish a contact that we were very keen to have, direct contact with the SOE.

Our first meeting with Schlanbusch did not lead to any concrete plans. But it was nevertheless the first step of valuable cooperation between HD2 and the Resistance movement in Varde. Those active in the groups included

Communists as well as Resistance operatives of a more right-wing back-ground. They came, for the most part, from three circles of Varde residents: steelworkers, doctors and the police. Despite major political, social and cultural differences, cooperation was good.

Our visit to Varde on October 1 had resulted in the organization in Varde now having created a loose link with Raadhusstræde. And they would soon find use for this new contact. By way of Møller Christensen, they had found out that London wanted the Varde Steelworks to be sabotaged. A leading steelworker, Viggo Hansen, had done sabotage earlier, with a reasonable amount of success. But now the works was in operation again, hence the orders from London to blow up the whole works on November 20. Viggo Hansen had planned for this. But the operation was called off at the last minute, partly because of the threat of the death penalty which meant that not enough men could be recruited from nearby Esbjerg, and partly because two of his colleagues had been arrested that morning in Varde by the Gestapo, for illegally distributing newspapers.

This annoyed London, and Viggo then received the message that if the steelworks was not sabotaged within a short space of time, the RAF would bomb it from the air. The steelworks is situated right in the middle of town and an aerial bombardment would have cost the lives of hundreds of local residents. Viggo Hansen therefore asked Schlanbusch to send for us. Our offer of assistance was now taken up, and we said yes to the assignment.

If You Don't Do It Now, The RAF Will Be Along

Operation XVIII – December 12, 1943. Varde Steelworks. It was Niels who received the message. Students, cadets and Flammen then met up in our secret flat on Lille Strandstræde, where I had moved in after John's arrest. It was soon agreed that everyone should take the train to Varde. This all happened so rapidly that there was no time to register our luggage, which would in any case not have withstood any form of inspection. But the checks carried out at the ferry on the Great Belt were not efficient, so nothing happened. There was no railway link from Fredericia across central Jutland to Esbjerg, so we had to take a taxi. There was hardly room for us all, but we managed to squeeze in. A couple of German vehicles that overtook our cab caused some consternation, but nothing happened and that evening HD2 arrived without further incident at Chief Constable Simony's, where Viggo Hansen was already waiting. He told the following about this:[63]

We met them here and at about one o'clock we went over to my place, where my wife served us sandwiches and coffee, while we got our weapons ready for use and discussed the finer points of the operation.... My drawings were very detailed. But we did have a problem with the guards at the steelworks: there were four or five armed men who contacted the police station every half hour. Two HD people – Flammen and one of the cadets – wanted to occupy the telephone exchange, but they had to give up as the woman running the exchange refused to open up so late in the evening.

When we had agreed on everything, we went two by two over to the steelworks.... We entered the compound by cutting our way in through the chain-link fencing. The members of HD2 took the four guards completely by surprise in the guardroom when they kicked open the door. The guards did not have time to raise the alarm, the button for which was in the middle of the table they were sitting around. The guards voluntarily handed over the keys to the works, after which we locked them in the air raid shelter. There were two other guards patrolling the perimeter, but they had not heard anything suspicious. They too were overmanned and locked in with the others. We even found one of the anti-sabotage guards sleeping on one of the stoves we were about to sabotage.

It took an hour to rig up the bombs (eight in number, consisting of quantities of plastic explosive linked with Cordtex). So at half past, Flammen took one of the anti-sabotage guards and forced him to report to the police station that all was quiet. When everything was ready, we threatened the guards, telling them to stay in the air raid shelter till first light. If they came up earlier, they would be shot, is what we told them. The operation was a great success. We received praise from the British. Production at the steelworks was effectively stopped for some six months.

The operation was given international publicity. On the first page of the *New York Times* for December 13, 1943, blared the headline:

DANES BLOW UP PLANT MAKING GERMAN ARMS
Armed Patriots Overpower the Guards at Varde Steel Works

Both the newspaper and the anti-sabotage guards agreed that there must have been about forty or fifty saboteurs in action. But in reality there were ten.

With this act of sabotage we had become established as the leading sabotage flying squad. The success was followed up when several members of the group went to Horsens for Christmas, where Peer was waiting anxiously. There were several firms he wanted to visit with us. We obtained explosives and weapons from our friends in Varde and were then ready to carry out three operations in Horsens, all of which were a success. By this time, we had carried out a total of twenty-two operations between October 28, 1943, and January 2, 1944. We had been kept busy. But everything had gone well, except for the loss of John who by this time we thought to be dead. Perhaps we had become a little too foolhardy and self-assured. Perhaps we had not fully realized that detailed planning was the key to our success. But in every case, it was nevertheless a question of good or bad luck. We were to experience both.

Count Your Blessings

Following the successful operations in Varde and Horsens, we were keen to get started again in Copenhagen. It was the indefatigable Niels who managed to find our next target. He had made contact with a foreman at the large shipping wharf Burmeister & Wain (B&W), which repaired many ships for the German navy. This was the fifty-five-year-old Georg Jansen and the only condition he put on cooperation with us was that he could take part himself. The target was the engineering department of the wharf, which was located on Strandgade in the Christianshavn port area a little to the south of the Knippelsbro bridge. Georg Jansen told us that no work was carried out there on Saturday evening. The police report from the sabotage confirms that when the sabotage took place, on Saturday, January 15 between seven and eight in the evening, only two guard units had been present, including the air raid warden and the anti-sabotage guard, about ten men in all.[64] Two further guards, German field security officers, were added to this number.

The factory had already been sabotaged on December 21, 1943, by BOPA using a detonation bomb, and this had caused significant damage in the power plant. On January 8 a transformer and a number of drilling machines were blown up by BOPA in another B&W department. Unfortunately, B&W had started the production of diesel engines for the Germans once again.

We therefore started planning for a new operation against the wharf and presented the project to Jørgen Staffeldt for approval. This was a more ambitious and daring plan than any of our previous operations.

When Luck Was with Us

Operation XXIII *– January 15, 1944. The B&W Engineering Plant, Strandgade.* As I was detained by the German harbor police at the start of the operation, this act of sabotage was carried out under Mix's leadership.

This was a big job, but we were well armed and reckoned we could cope, once we had entered the compound. We had a diagram showing every man's tasks, minute by minute, and everyone knew what they had to do. This proved to be valuable. After expending a lot of effort, we finally got hold of a man from the Danish harbor police (Karl Krighaar) and persuaded him and his colleague to help us using their motorboat. The plan was as follows: one Saturday evening, four men would steal a large dinghy, which was moored in a canal near B&W. At seven o'clock they would have sailed this boat to a specific place in the harbor. The police boat that was patrolling the area would tow them into a private berth, which we had borrowed from friends. Here, the rest of the group's ten men would be waiting with all the equipment. We would then have the dinghy towed down past the Knippelsbro bridge to a canal from where we had access to the compound, which would then be taken over. When the bombs had been put in position, we would pull out via the canal to another bridgehead, which was covered by Flammen and three men from other Holger Danske groups. In his report Mix sums up as follows:[65]

> We were incredibly well armed. Everyone had a pistol and there were twelve submachine guns available as well, plus masses of hand grenades. We were determined to carry out the operation against all odds. We did not want to allow ourselves to be stopped by any accidental occurrence while we were on the job, but we were prepared to shoot it out with whoever stood in our way.
>
> We were very careful when we packaged the bombs. There were seven in all, containing a total of 412 pounds (187 kg) of TNT (what was left over from the explosives we had bought using what was left of the money intended to bribe people in our efforts to smuggle Jews to Sweden). They were all assembled in the flat on Raadhusstræde,

and all constructed so that they could be carried on our backs like rucksacks.

We had rented two wobbly tricycles to transport the bombs to our departure point in the Christianshavn district, to the east of the port. Two of the cadets cycled over the Knippelsbro bridge at the rush hour, which caused these two inexperienced "asphalt cowboys" some trouble, especially going up and downhill. One of the tricycles even keeled over. But they succeeded in the end. We were now ready for the next stage of the operation. We met in our illegal flat in the old harbor district of Nyhavn, which Niels and Jansen had now moved into.

Along with Klaus and two of the cadets (Tony and Holger), I would manage the dinghy in the canal out at Christianshavn. We inspected the area that afternoon and picked out a boat with sprit sails, which was moored and had the oars on board, locked up with a padlock and chain. We therefore also had to bring tools with us to free the oars. The dinghy was the largest present there in the canal. But we were nonetheless afraid that it would not be big enough for the whole of the group, plus all our equipment. So we decided that we would also take along a rowing boat, which was moored alongside.

We returned between five and six in the evening, and now encountered our first real problem. Right next to the dinghy we had chosen stood two men looking at a motorboat, which had sunk. They seemed to be in no hurry, but we were. We therefore jumped down into the boat and cut the oars loose with wire cutters. We had also brought along rope to tow the rowing boat. When Tony and Holger had cut loose the oars, they took the rowing boat and rowed out in a northeasterly direction, while Klaus and I prepared the dinghy for sailing. This took a while, as the men inspecting the motorboat seemed to have become aware of what we were up to, and one of them, presumably one of the owners, started to protest vehemently. But he was told that he would get his dinghy back. We reckoned with the fact that he could go and report us to the police, but as we had an agreement with the Danish harbor police, there was a limited amount of damage he could do. So we carried on, relatively untroubled by the slight setback.

We rowed along the Christianshavn Canal up to our agreed berth in the port and arrived at exactly seven o'clock. No Danish patrol boat came at the allotted hour, so the time passed. Then a motorboat turned up in the darkness – at last. We hailed it, but as it looked as if it was going to sail past at quite a speed, we signaled it with a torch. A searchlight was pointed at us, and a voice asked, "*Wer da?* (Who goes there?)" The crew of the motor-boat consisted of German marines, armed with submachine guns. It was the German harbor patrol, which had turned up unexpectedly.

After lightning consultations, we decided to bluff our way out of our predicament. We came up with some cock-and-bull story to give us time to drop our pistols overboard. We overlooked one pistol that lay on the bottom of one of the boats. The Germans had come alongside and they were just about to start searching. But all they managed to find was a briefcase containing a crowbar, a coil of rope and two torches.

The boats were then taken in tow by the motorboat. There was a risk that the boats would collide, and the Germans needed our help, which gave us the opportunity to slip the remaining pistol overboard. The Germans then set sail for the quay at Langelinie. But they still shone their searchlight one more time over the surrounding water. For a second, the light shone on the boom out at Holmen. Right in the middle of the beam of light was one of the hand grenades we had thrown overboard. There it was, lying in all its glory next to the boom. We held our breaths. But luckily the Germans saw nothing and we continued on our course, all the way to Langelinie, where we, under arrest as we were, were taken on board a ship. We were put together in a cabin to await the arrival of the Gestapo, who had been called in from German HQ at Dagmarhus. This gave us the time to come up with the explanation we would offer them during interrogation.

We did not know why the Danish police boat had not turned up as arranged. This could be the result of some mishap, which could ruin all our plans. The consolation for us was that we had had two strokes of luck after our arrest: the forgotten pistol and the hand grenade, neither of which had been discovered. The German patrol boat and its crew stayed on to guard us until the arrival of the Gestapo, and this meant that our operation against B&W had been saved. I only realized this later when, during the interrogation that followed at Dagmarhus later that night, I counted six explosions from down by the harbor.

The rest of the group had to work with us out of the picture. As already described, Flammen went to Langbrogade street with three saboteurs from another HD group to cover the retreat after the bombs had been put in place. Meanwhile the rest of HD2, nine or maybe ten men were waiting impatiently on the square at Asiatisk Plads for all of our equipment. The time went by but finally the police boat arrived, without us and our two boats. The harbor police officer Krighaar explained that he was unable to find us, but when I later met him in the Porta Westphalica concentration camp, he told me that his mate was getting cold feet. It took him a good deal of time to convince him, and that is why they arrived late.

We had not taken into account what should happen in cases like this and it had therefore not been agreed who would take command. But in situations like this, Mix showed his characteristic talent for leadership. He quickly explained to the two police officers that they had the choice of lending them their boat or following after them. They chose the latter course of action – Krighaar was happy to do so, and his police colleague tagged along out of necessity. But when they saw the large amount of bombing equipment and weapons, they went on land, whereupon one of the cadets took over the maritime tasks, while Mix began to quickly revise all our plans which had been so carefully laid. Navigation was no problem. Mix and his men managed to sail without hindrance to B&W, while the German harbor patrol was at Langelinie. He described the rest of the operation as follows:[66]

> While we were underway, we re-allotted the tasks and what was to our great advantage here was that each member of the group was well acquainted with each of the different tasks in hand. There was a lot to do and now nearly a third of our forces were not present. Well, everything turned out OK. We landed and the guards were held up as planned – some armed, some unarmed. I have to say that I have never met such all right chaps as the four B&W guards. They greeted us and caused no trouble. For example, two guards armed with pistols and two of our armed unit men with submachine guns and explosives met in the machine room. They pointed their weapons at one another, but when the guards saw that these were saboteurs, they immediately raised their hands above their heads. We were taking no chances and all the guards were kept under guard, but in a friendly manner.

One episode was rather amusing. Flemming, who was not one of our tallest men, was carrying one of the largest bombs on his back. It stuck out over the top of his head, and he had to bend forward to carry it along.

He was suddenly confronted by the sight of a very tall guard who pointed his pistol at him and asked him to put his hands up. Flemming, who had a philosophical frame of mind, first pointed at his bomb, then at his machine gun and said dryly: "You've made a mistake, my friend; I'm the one threatening you. If you shoot me, then this bomb will go off, and we'll both be killed. I could shoot you without anything happening to me." The guard understood the logic of this only too well, and put his hands in the air. When the guards had thus been brought under control, the bombs had to be placed in position. Mix relates:[67]

> We had two different whistle sounds as signals. The one meant "danger, hurry up!" the other "get to the boats – ignite the bomb where it is." This was also an indication for our people on the other side of the stretch of water, if anything unexpected should occur.
>
> It was hard for us to maintain proper communications with one another over such a large area. So I decided, being in the middle so that I could see the most on all sides, to give the first signal, so that everyone would be sure that it was now time to clear out. A couple of minutes later, I gave the second signal, after which I waited a couple of minutes and we counted our men in the boat.
>
> Everything was now ready, so we gave the guards orders to go to the air raid shelter and not come out again before they had heard ten explosions. We added three to their number as we wanted to force the fire brigade and police to come as late as possible. Then we sailed back to where we had previously moored the boat after having waited some quarter of an hour near the factory. We counted on the fact that those of us who were on the other side of the water would understand from our signals that the course of the retreat had been altered. We had to take the police boat back to safety again. When we got to the Knippelsbro bridge, we heard the first explosion and then a further five in quick succession. This meant that one bomb had failed to go off, because our fuses were made of poor material.
>
> We got back to our berth at the quayside where we returned the boat and thanked the owner for lending it to us. While we were packing up our gear, three men came up to us and asked what we were doing there. One of our men said we were "firemen." "OK," they said, "but we're the real ones," and with a wink they said that luckily for us they

were satisfied with the results. Then they continued on their round as if nothing had happened. Our people on Langebrogade street had been waiting at their posts without being able to understand where we had gone. Suddenly they crouched down at the huge explosion and a rain of glass splinters. Only then did they go home, and without incident.

Once we had returned the police boat to its mooring, we collected up our weapons and other equipment and put it all in four large suitcases. The idea was that these would be picked up by car. But on account of the delay, that part of the plan came unstuck and four of the cadets were obliged to lug the suitcases to Søkvæsthuset, the old Navy Hospital, where Mix and his girlfriend had found a flat where they could store the suitcases until further notice. The explosions had brought people out onto the streets, and the cadets had to pass by several naval officers. Luckily, they were not recognized by any of them. Mix stayed the night in the Søkvæst House, while the rest of the group hurried back over the Knippelsbro bridge. They just got there before the Germans shut it off. Mix finishes his story as follows:

> I spent a pretty sleepless night in Søkvæst House, as four of our number had disappeared. The next day, when we had surveyed the enormous damage, we started looking for them. But no luck. We also tidied up all our flats, just in case there were house to house searches.

The police and fire brigade had of course been summoned and a report was written of the damage caused. As with other TNT acts of sabotage, there was large-scale damage to the buildings. But a lot of damage had also been caused to the technical installations and the machines.

After the first attempt at sabotage by BOPA on December 21, four large diesel motors had been seriously damaged. Now the electrical relay in one large drilling machine had been wrecked, and the same was true of a dynamo and a large propeller, which had been sent for repair by the Hamburg-America Line. Generators standing on the quay had also been destroyed. In the testing hall there was one unexploded thirty-seven-pound (17 kg) bomb attached to one diesel motor. The fuse had failed. The bomb was collected by the German bomb disposal squad. It was to take between three and four months to get the wharf on its feet again.

How many months it actually took to repair and replace everything I never found out. Georg Jansen related that one of the engineers supervising the repair work had told workers to slow down. He commented that as a number of young people had risked their lives to help B&W to avoid having to collaborate with the Germans, there seemed to be no point in hindering this worthy aim by speeding up repair work. The workers agreed with the engineer, and the pace of work slackened.

There is no doubt in my mind that the Resistance movement had now, after the August Uprising and the pogroms against the Jews, gained a good deal of support from the population at large. Nor do I doubt that the underground press had had its effect, even the modest contribution made by the folk song movement, whose efforts to foster national unity deserve recognition. The fact that the factory guards were willing to cooperate with us and the delay in the repair work at B&W are also good examples of this.

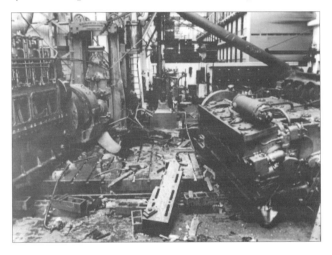

One of the sections of B&W destroyed by our sabotage, January 15, 1944

Gestapo Interrogation

When we had arrived at Langelinie, we were taken over to a German naval vessel where we were put in a small cabin guarded by two sentries. While we sat there waiting for the Gestapo, we managed to cobble together our story. We decided that if pressed we would admit to being students who, out of fear of a razzia at our university, had planned to escape to Sweden. We needed several boats for this operation. But first we would try the story that we had met the owner of "our" two boats as he was standing by the canal in the Christianshavn harbor looking at a sunken motorboat.

He was nervous about the possibility that something might happen to his dinghy and asked whether we would, for twenty kroner, get his dinghy to Nyhavn where he would meet us. We could use the rowing boat. We said yes and after having bought a pair of wire cutters at an ironmonger's, we got onto the dinghy and cut loose the oars. Then the towing began. And we had only just gotten out into the canal when we were picked up by the German patrol.

We had no experience of how careful you had to be with such agreements when under interrogation, but even if the Germans did not believe our cock-and-bull story, we hoped that we would get away with nothing more than the charge of theft and maybe also attempting to flee the country. We felt there was a good chance that we would not be suspected of having anything to do with the B&W sabotage as it had not yet taken place when we were arrested, and because the Germans had themselves been so kind as to furnish us with an alibi. I had a cyanide capsule, but it was not enough for the four of us and I also felt it was not yet the time to use it. Tony claims that we tipped the contents into the crew's salt cellar, but I cannot confirm that.

After a while, four plainclothes men came on board. These were the gentlemen from the Gestapo. One of them spoke Danish. We were ordered out onto the quay and into a couple of motor cars. We were driven to Dagmarhus under escort. There the chief himself, Kriminalrat Bunke, interrogated us. Tony went in first. Bunke started by offering him a cigarette and laid his pistol on the desk. He began very pleasantly by asking whether Tony would rather talk to him or to one of the Danes. Tony was in no doubt, so it became Bunke who continued in the pleasant tone of voice as he suggested to Tony that he tell all, so that he could get off home right away. Tony then told him in German the explanation we had agreed on as well as he was able. Bunke acted as if he believed what he said and left the office.

I cannot now remember who was next to be interrogated. But when it was my turn it was once again Bunke who was doing the interrogating. Tony's explanation was in line with what we had agreed. We knew full well that it was flimsy. The object of the exercise, however, was to spin the whole thing out so that our colleagues had time to complete the operation against B&W or at least get to safety. To my great satisfaction, I heard six explosions from the direction of the harbor, right in the middle of the interrogation. I took this as meaning that HD2, despite the bad start, had managed to carry through the operation and was now pulling out. This proved to be the case, and in order to win more time, I stuck to my improbable explanation, which Bunke listened to with great patience.

After half an hour had passed, he came back to Tony with three sheets of paper, on which the explanations given by the three others were written. There were, to say the least, large discrepancies between our versions. Bunke gave a smile and shook his head, whereupon two of the "Danish gentlemen" were called in. They took us to the ground floor of a small drill hall, where these traitors drew their pistols and got to work with the exercises.

"We'll start with twenty-five knee bends. Begin! Up onto your toes, down, one, two, three." He stood there counting while we crouched and stood up again twenty-five times. When I had finished, I could not stand straight, for which I was given a kick on the shins, and as punishment we had to do a further twenty-five knee bends. This carried on for an hour or two. I think we managed to do between three and four hundred knee bends. Suddenly the Danish traitor said "one, two" and no more but we automatically finished our knee bends; then he shouted: "Who the fuck said three?" As punishment, we got a further fifty knee bends. When we got to forty-five, Klaus staggered. He was given a punishment of a further twenty-five. During the exercise, the two traitors encouraged us with comments about how we would soon be home, as long as we told the truth. We did, of course, wonder what would happen if we were to refuse to obey their orders, but simply told them that we had told the truth, to which they, quite predictably, replied: "All right, so you don't want to go home."

In due course, the "Danish gentlemen" grew tired of the exercise, and we were taken back for interrogation, one by one. The highlight of the night was when a Gestapo agent entered the room where Bunke was interrogating me. In his hand was the unexploded detonation bomb, which had been brought from B&W by the German bomb disposal squad. The bomb had a fuse and detonator. It was clear that the Gestapo agent had no knowledge of bombs, because he stood there swinging it by the fuse and nearly banged it against the edge of the desk. Neither he nor I knew that the fuse was defective, so I had great trouble trying to look unconcerned. Although it was one of the smaller bombs, it was large enough to kill all three of us and wreck the building.

The bomb was put on the desk and there it was when Holger came in to be interrogated. A little TNT had leaked out. He recognized the bomb immediately; it was numbered with red paint. He had made it himself and still had red fingers as he had had no paintbrush to apply the paint and had used his fingers, which he now kept hidden under the desk. There was yellow TNT powder on his trousers that he had not brushed off. But Bunke was no great bomb expert either, so Holger escaped with a fright. We were interrogated for some good while separately, but in the end we were brought together, and although our explanations did not quite tally, they had been adjusted to the extent that the Germans felt convinced that here was merely a question of minor theft.

"*Das ist ja Diebstahl!* (This is certainly theft!)" yelled Bunke straight across the table, and threatened to hand us over to the Danish police. We had presence of mind enough to protest: "*Nein, nein, wir sind doch keine Diebe!* (No, no, we're no thieves!)"

And so, the happy ending to the interrogation. We were taken to the cellar, where we spent the rest of the night in separate cells. We did not get much sleep because we were all the time afraid that the Germans would find out what had really happened. But they did not, because we had the best alibi in the world. When B&W went up, we were sitting "comfortably" in Bunke's office at Dagmarhus. Mission accomplished by the rest of our group, unhindered by the German harbor patrol.

Count your blessings, as we say. But a week later or so, Bente told me how I had been even more blessed than I had imagined. While I was being interrogated at Dagmarhus, the Gestapo had paid her a visit at Raadhusstræde. This was the Gestapo section that dealt with the underground press and they had gotten an inkling that I might be involved with Free Denmark. It was me they wanted to talk to. But that they could not do, as I was under interrogation by the Gestapo sabotage section at Dagmarhus. But they were not to know that.

During Sunday, we were handed over to the Danish police, who played their part with mettle. We were received with great courtesy and were given a meal at Police Headquarters. Then came the report. First came the noting down of our cock-and-bull story. Police Superintendent Odmar was informed of what had happened, and we were put in the cells at the police station. The next day, the interrogation continued. We were again interrogated separately and were treated decently. But the police made no bones about the fact that they didn't believe a word of our tale, nor did they expect the courts to believe it either. With the help of the police, the "truth" finally came out. Klaus and Tony said that the aim of our operation was to get some students over to Sweden, while Holger and I stuck to our little fiction.

After that, we appeared before a judge who dealt with the matter behind closed doors, in order to promote the resolution of the case. The explanations were presented, but the judge insisted that they were justified in prosecuting us for theft and offenses against Law 123, section 3, dated March 30, 1942, and decided to keep us for further investigation for up to seven days of imprisonment.

After that, we were taken to one-person cells in the Danish section of the Vestre Fængsel. While we were being transported there, the warders asked if we were members of the Free Denmark movement. We denied this, but they did not believe us and were kind enough to us. It was not until many years after the war, when I was writing the history of the first Holger Danske organization, that I found out that the prison warders had very valuable contacts with Free Denmark and the saboteurs.

This was my first experience of prison, "Hotel Vestre" as it was called by the Germans. My "room" was the size of the average bathroom, with the same terrazzo floor and smooth off-white walls. At one end of the cell there was a barred window, high up in the wall, through which I could see the leaden sky. At the other end was a heavy door with a peephole, with a cover on the outside. The warder was supposed to look in at me; I was not supposed to see out.

Along one of the long walls, a desk had been fixed; along the other, an iron-framed bed that was folded up during the day so that you could neither lie nor even sit on it. This seemed quite unreasonable, as the only thing to sit on was a wooden stool without a back. So I often sat on the floor, leaning against the wall. When the warder saw this through his peephole, I was immediately told to get up. A rectangular chamber pot, placed in one corner by the ventilation duct, was the only other piece of furniture. I only later discovered how valuable this duct was for communication between cells.

We got up at six in the morning. After breakfast, we were allowed a little exercise in the prison yard, where we literally felt hemmed in. The rest of the day was spent thinking and pacing the cell, which was five paces by five, like the animals have at the zoo. I could well have paced a third of a mile (half a kilometer) a day, with breaks for breakfast and dinner in the evening. The food was miserable, but there was plenty of it.

Other amusements included making my bed and the daily visit to the toilet, during which I saw, at the end of the long corridor, a door which the guard told me led to the German section. I remember asking him whether the door was locked, and I noted the fact that the answer was that it was not. If I was ever so unlucky as to end up in the German section, one escape route would be through this door. But I also wondered how the Danish warders would react to such a situation. Their behavior varied from being polite, to actually being friendly. But this would hardly be enough, if there were any question of trying to escape. I also remember wondering whether John was behind that door. We had, by that time, received information that he had survived the shooting a month before. But I did not know whether he was in good shape, and spent a good deal of time thinking about whether he could be liberated via that door.

On one occasion, I was allowed to write to my parents. In the letter, I expressed what it felt like to be reduced to a number who only lived according to the rules of others. The letter was censored, and it was returned to me as "unacceptable." We were "interrogated" yet again at Police Headquarters, which resulted in an indictment, where we were charged with attempting to organize an escape to Sweden. On January 25, we came before the court. Klaus and Tony stuck to their story, Holger and I to ours. Neither the judge nor anyone else present believed what we were saying and we were sentenced to eighty days imprisonment of which eight were regarded as having already been served. Over and above this, we were to pay the sum of two hundred kroner to each of the two defense lawyers.

The boats were returned to their rightful owners as promised, but without our help. How the economic side of things was solved I cannot remember. But I think that Klaus's parents lent a helping hand. To my great surprise, we were released immediately and the sentences were to be served later, but I have never again heard anything from the Danish authorities. I have waited a long time and am now eighty-eight years old; but I still owe the Danish state seventy-two days imprisonment.

So that was the end of one of our most successful operations, a result that everyone except the Germans can be satisfied with. This good result is thanks not least to Mix, but also to the fact that where good luck and bad luck were weighed up, good luck tipped the balance to our advantage to an unusual extent. What had really happened was not discovered until some weeks later by the Gestapo, but by that time the participants in the operation were either already facing a death sentence or had fled to Sweden.

The Final Operation

The B&W operation had been a huge success, and we had been very lucky. On the other hand, we had now lost four pistols and had no more explosives left at all. We made an attempt to obtain pistols from the police in the village where Georg Jansen had been born, but without any luck. But a raid on the goods station on the Copenhagen railways meant that we now had a little TNT. It was clear, however, that what we needed was a short respite, a rest. Not least those who had spent their days in prison wanted a holiday. It was not as if our stay in prison had been unbearable. But our brush with the Gestapo did provide food for thought. And we were really annoyed that we had missed the action at B&W, and had simply been entertaining the Germans with our yarns at the time, confabulations they luckily did not see through. Our knees were also a little sore after all the knee bends a couple of our miserable compatriots and traitors had forced us into doing.

While Klaus went off home to Tybjerggaard, I went with two cadets to Horsens for a little vacation on January 29. We had only been in Horsens for a few days when a Gestapo razzia forced us to return to Copenhagen on February 2. We took Peer along, as he was the one most vulnerable in Horsens at the time. But in Copenhagen too there was opportunity for neither rest nor safety. The day after we arrived, Niels received a message from Assistant Chief Constable Schlanbusch in Varde, who wanted assistance with a couple of operations in Aabenraa in southern Denmark. These were to be the last ones that HD2 carried out.

It had been the local branch of the Resistance that had taken the initiative to carry out acts of sabotage in Aabenraa. They had been thinking for some good while to sabotage the Callesen and Hamag factories, which were run by collaborators and supplied the Germans with parts for U-boats and airplanes. Originally, there had been a plan to knock out the local power station, which supplied electricity to the whole of eastern Jutland. But this plan had been abandoned. It was later carried out by British initiative as part of a campaign designed to distract the enemy while the Normandy landings were taking place.

But Aabenraa had no connection to that. Via the Free Denmark groups in Esbjerg and Varde, we got in touch with the SOE agent Aage Møller Christensen. He was spending Christmas in Varde at Schlanbusch's place, and the latter then heard about the Aabenraa plans. As there were no experienced saboteurs in Aabenraa itself, it was decided that the acts of sabotage would be planned and carried out by the Varde group, led by Viggo Hansen. But this group was short of quite a few men, so Schlanbusch wrote to Niels Hjorth and requested our assistance.

Niels and I decided to go to Varde on February 4 in order to talk with Aage Møller Christensen and to get more detailed information about the plan. We did not meet the parachutist, but instead met Viggo Hansen, whom we knew to be an experienced saboteur from the operation against Varde Steelworks. Viggo confirmed that this had nothing to do with the power station but that it was the Callesen and Hamag factories that were going to be attacked. Niels and I were disappointed that this would not have anything to do with the planned invasion that everyone was by this time expecting to occur in the near future. But Callesen and Hamag were crucial targets, though they did not seem as important as those that had a direct connection with the invasion. So we raised a number of objections at our meeting with Schlanbusch, which he mentions in his statement:[68]

> February 5 happened to be both my wife's birthday and Simony's, so we went over to Simony's house and discussed Aabenraa as both Niels Hjorth and Jørgen Kieler had been reluctant to perform sabotage in Aabenraa as it was a small town where it can be difficult to move around unnoticed, and because, being near the German border, there were many ethnic Germans living there.

We did indeed have the doubts given above. But the operation had been approved by the SOE, so we regarded this as a sign that Britain wanted us to do it and we agreed to cooperate. There would have to be a place to spend the night in Aabenraa, as we reckoned that it would be impossible to flee the town immediately after the operation; both the roads and the railway would be under surveillance immediately after the bombs went off. We also expected that our transport to and from Aabenraa would be organized by local activists. We were, after all, not on home ground as we had been in both Varde and Horsens. We had neither thought up the operation nor planned it in detail, but were simply helping, without actually knowing very much about the topography of the town in question. But we did have quite a lot of experience from the two other towns and could trust our colleagues from Varde. So we called our HD2 colleagues and arranged to meet them on the railway station at Fredericia the following day.

Niels and I stopped over at Schlanbusch's place. We had arranged with Viggo that we would meet him the next day at the house of a car mechanic, Koch, in Styrtom, south of Aabenraa, and here would also be operational headquarters.

On the Saturday morning, February 5, 1944, Viggo and Jens arrived in Aabenraa by train. They were spotted by a pro-German teacher who reported them at ten o'clock to the German security police, the *Sicherheitsdienst*, or SD: two suspicious men with heavy suitcases had been standing for half an hour outside Restaurant Domach before hailing a taxi. The SD soon found out that the two men were now sitting in the Sølyst Kro pub in Styrtom, not far from Koch's house. But the taxi driver could not give any further details. Viggo and Jens soon found out that the pub was swarming with Germans, so they left.

Meanwhile, twelve or thirteen of our group took the Jutland Express at seven in the morning to Fredericia. The weapons and ammunition were registered as luggage and were collected without incident in Nyborg. Niels and I met with them at the station in Fredericia, where we decided to split up into two groups to avoid arousing unnecessary suspicions. So some of the group took a taxi to Aabenraa, while the others took the train, which arrived in Aabenraa in the afternoon. We agreed to meet at Koch's place in Styrtom, which was to be the headquarters for the operation. Niels and I took the taxi as we wanted to take a look at the Aabenraa Tuberculosis Clinic before we arrived at Koch's house and inform Kai Hammer, the chief physician there, that we were in Aabenraa in order to look for a job at the hospital. We arrived at Koch's house without incident.

Those who took the train encountered greater difficulties. We had been told that the local group would meet those members of our group with cars at the station and transport them to Koch's house. But that part of the plan went wrong. Once the HD2 had arrived in Aabenraa station, they split into smaller groups, which went in different directions and had some difficulties finding their way about. Their arrival was soon noticed. But two hours later, they had all arrived at Koch's house.

Viggo then set out the plans for the two operations and produced the explosives we had brought. There were more than twenty bombs and the Cordtex fuses were now to be attached. Viggo had brought plans of the two factories and a sketch of where the Callesen guards would be found. The information had been provided by the police. He had then planned an operation, which closely resembled the operation in Varde that had met with such success. The guards would be overpowered, then bombs would be attached to particular machines and all be joined up with Cordtex fuses. This work had taken over an hour in Varde. But this time there were more saboteurs, so we calculated it would take us half as long to do (in the end it took only fifteen minutes to rig up the whole string of bombs). This was important as here there was a risk that the Germans would get involved. As in Varde surprising the guards was of key importance as they could well be pro-German, which was of cardinal importance.

Koch's house in Styrtom would have been handy as a base from which to attack the power station, but it was a good mile and a half (between two and three kilometers) to Callesen and Hamag. Although the start of this operation had already been flawed, we still reckoned we stood a good chance of carrying it off with the success we had enjoyed with the Varde Steelworks. We decided to meet at Aabenraa Castle, which was near the two factories concerned, and once the tasks had been allotted, people were sent out at midnight, two by two, with long pauses in between, just as we had done in Varde. We met the local saboteurs at the castle. This was the first time they would take part in such a large operation where we ran the risk of exchanging fire with the anti-sabotage guards and German soldiers. One of the group says:[69]

> I believe that I can say that we were in a rather sticky situation. While it was still some way off, it was easy to be tough, but as the time drew near, one hour after midnight when we were to turn up, we were no longer so enthusiastic. But no one dropped out, and all seventeen men met at one o'clock outside the gate of the prefect's living quarters at Brandlund Castle.

We and the local people all walked together from the castle to where the operation was to take place. The two factories lay next to one another not far from the castle. We only met one policeman on the way. He looked surprised at the large number of men. But as he said nothing, and we had been given to understand that the police were to be trusted, we did not react. Our operation could now begin.

Operation XXV – February 6, 1944. Hamag, Lavgade 30, Aabenraa. The attack on Hamag was straightforward as there were no anti-sabotage guards at all at the factory. So only three cadets, and Jens Jørgensen from Varde were assigned to that operation, plus two locals. They were armed with pistols and one submachine gun. When they arrived at the factory, one local stood on guard outside while the rest forced the door with a crowbar and entered. Five four-and-a-half-pound (2 kg) bombs containing P808 were placed on various lathes. They had timers set for half an hour. The police report states that the whole building and five of the eight lathes were wrecked. This stopped production. There was damage to windows in the surrounding building, but there were no casualties.

As the saboteurs were pulling out and had not gotten very far from the factory, they heard a lot of shooting and rushed to the Callesen factory to assist their colleagues. They met them on the road some way off, and they shouted, "Here come the Germans!" We later found out that the shooting was the work of seven policemen who had agreed to fire their pistols in the air.

Our "Waterloo"

Operation XXVI – February 6, 1944. Callesen's, the Aabenraa Motor Works, Kolstrup 1, Aabenraa. Sabotaging Callesen's was a much more difficult assignment. We divided up into our usual armed unit and bomb unit. The entrance to the factory was via a very heavy barricaded gate with two sentries on guard. There was no way that we could enter there without being spotted, so our plan was for the armed unit to get into the compound from a neighboring property and surprise the guards from behind, then open the gate for the bomb unit.

The armed unit soon encountered unexpected problems. We were first going to get over a wall with barbed wire on top. There turned out to be a large heap of scrap metal at that point, so we could not maintain complete silence. And this could have alerted the guards. What was worse was that I had lost contact with our local guide, who had gotten cold feet and left.

We in our group were very familiar with the problem of fear, and no one would hold it against anyone who dropped out during the planning stage. But once you had committed yourself, then your colleagues' lives were in your hands. And this man let us down. This cost the lives of three of our HD2 group.

Once the guide was gone, we found it difficult to know exactly where we were. Looking at the sketches we had brought along did not help. However, we did manage to locate the Callesen factory by following rails for trolleys and found the building where we thought the guards would be. All the doors were locked, but we could see a chink of light and I suddenly heard a voice saying, "Yes, I'm speaking from Callesen's. Persons unknown have entered the compound." So now we knew where the guards were, but also that the police had been notified.

So the element of surprise, which had been so crucial at Varde Steelworks, was now lacking. We still had a few minutes in hand, and decided to give it a try. The alternative was to pull out, mission unaccomplished. But the police had been informed, in any case. The decision was made within a few seconds. We took our chances. I shot off the lock with my submachine gun and kicked open the door. Two deathly pale guards were lying on the floor. Nothing had happened to them, but they were scared to death. The phone standing on the table was off the hook. They must have heard my submachine gun being fired, at the police station. We got the gate open and let in the bomb unit while the armed unit guarded the guards.

There were a total of twenty-two bombs and these were fixed to lathes around the turner's shop so that linking them up with Cordtex fuses could begin.

Just after the bomb unit had started work, the watch at the gate told us that the police had arrived. Two men held up the policeman, who did not resist. We had learned that there was no German garrison in town, but the police told us that there were fifty German marines, and that they had presumably been warned about the attack. This is no doubt what our watchman meant when he had said that the Germans were coming. The order was therefore given to light the fuses and pull out as quickly as possible. The police fired several shots in the air. No one was hit. The police could then begin to evacuate the surrounding buildings and cordon off the street.

Meanwhile, another police squad had arrived and at 2:25 in the morning the police entered the factory. The bombs were still attached to the lathes, but had not gone off. Ten minutes later, the Germans arrived and took over.

CHAPTER 8

On the Run

The Retreat

It would undoubtedly have been best if we had been able to leave Aabenraa immediately. But a swift evacuation would require four cars and we had no access to such. We had the choice of wandering around on the roads leading from the village, in order to get to a railway station that was not being guarded by Germans, or hiding somewhere in Aabenraa itself, until the acute danger had passed. We chose the latter option and therefore beat our retreat and went to our various lodgings.

Viggo Hansen and Jens Jørgensen, plus Peer, Klaus, Niels and myself were staying with Koch, and the rest were supposed to have gone with the man who deserted us out of fear. But as has been said, we had already lost contact with him right at the start. One of the other locals, Svend Hoffmann, swiftly reorganized where everyone would be staying.

According to our plan, the various groups of saboteurs not living in Aabenraa would spread out in the course of the day and follow their various routes to different railway stations. Then they would travel to Varde, Copenhagen or their hometown. We all managed to get to where we were staying without encountering Germans. We heard the Hamag explosions, but not a sound came from Callesen's and we realized that the sabotage there had failed.

After discussing the events of the night, we who were staying with Koch decided to let the other saboteurs go home according to plan, while we would make a new attempt, this time by frontal attack. In order to achieve this, Jens Jørgensen was to take the morning train to Fredericia, in order to obtain more explosives. If he succeeded in getting some, he would send Koch a telegram with the text "Happy Birthday!" and then return to Aabenraa. If he failed, he would send a telegram saying "Have a nice anniversary!" and would go to Varde. We then went to bed.

On the Sunday morning, the HD2 saboteurs who had not been staying with Koch managed, by various routes, to leave Aabenraa. Only Flemming and Jansen decided to bide their time. They first wanted to contact us at Koch's place for fresh instructions once they realized that one of the two acts of sabotage had failed.

Jens Jørgensen went off with an empty suitcase to get more explosives. We waited in vain for his telegram. What had happened, none of us had the slightest inkling of. But later on we found out that he had been arrested by the Gestapo at the railway station. On their way to German Headquarters, Jens had managed to get free. He was shot in the chest, but managed to flee to a forest to the west of Aabenraa. He was lucky enough to be found there by three of our cadets who had hidden in the forest, as they had missed the train.

They managed to get hold of a taxi to drive to Tjæreborg, near Esbjerg, where they had friends at whose house they could hide. The taxi driver had difficulty finding his way. When he stopped at a farm to ask for help, a German car with two officers suddenly appeared. Two of our cadets escaped, but in the back of the taxi was the seriously wounded Jens Jørgensen and the naval cadet Jørgen Salling. Fortunately enough the Germans were not interested. They too had lost their way and were looking for help. Jørgen Salling managed to persuade the driver to drive on to Tjæreborg, where Jens was brought to safety by the local Resistance. Later, he stayed with a doctor who looked after him. Salling traveled back to Copenhagen where he went into hiding, staying with Carlo Madsen, a good friend of our group, in the Lavendelstræde.

The explosion at Hamag was heard by the Wehrmacht garrison at the Ortskommandantur and they phoned Georg Könert at the local branch of the Gestapo. The Wehrmacht arrived at Callesen's at 2:25, three quarters of an hour after the explosion. Könert arrived shortly afterwards, accompanied by a Danish traitor. He soon saw that the fuses were intact and Oberfeldwebel Schönfeldt cut them through, which is why the bombs there did not detonate. Könert collected all the unexploded bombs and drove back with his men to the Ortskommandantur.

Meanwhile, the Gestapo chief for southern Jutland, August Naujock, had been informed. Along with his assistants and a driver, they had come from Gestapo Headquarters in Koldinghus Castle to Aabenraa, where they first inspected Callesen's and Hamag and then met Könert, who described the night's events. They decided to drive out to Koch's house in two cars.

At this point in time, most of the saboteurs were safe, at least for the time being, but things turned out very differently for Flemming and Jansen, Koch and his landlady, and the five guests from Varde, Horsens and Copenhagen.

Encounter in Styrtom

Shortly after Jens Jørgensen had left, Peer, Niels, Viggo and I went to a small toolshed that stood behind the Koch house. Klaus was in Koch's workshop arranging our equipment. He suddenly came running into the shed and said, "Two German cars are coming up to the house." We knew it must be us they were looking for and loaded our pistols immediately while thinking about what we should do next.

There were two escape routes. One option was to flee over the roof of one of the outbuildings. But the roof was made of corrugated iron and the noise would draw the Germans' attention. And on the roof we would be an easy target for their pistols.

The other way was to climb out through the window into Koch's garden and then cross fields to the south and disappear in the adjoining woods. But such a route would also mean that we could be seen from the German cars, so this would only be used as a last resort, if we were spotted and a gun battle ensued. So I suggested we all stayed calm and encouraged the rest to prepare their weapons.

It was only now that I felt I had overall responsibility. The operation had been planned by others, and a collective decision had been made to sabotage the Callesen factory; we were only part of this. From that point onwards, we were jointly responsible, without ourselves having any say in what was to be done. From the police report and other archival material, we can see that I gave the order to climb out through the window. I felt that a leader was needed and if my decision was interpreted as an order, this was due to the fact that in the tense situation three of my colleagues thought in that way. I am not sure that was what Peer felt. He kept on insisting that we stay in the toolshed. "No, no, let's stay here," was the last thing I heard him say.

Glancing out of the window, we could now see that the cars had indeed come to a standstill outside Koch's house and shortly afterwards we heard German being spoken in the house, then a crash, and Miss Lund, Koch's landlady, screaming. Klaus burst out with, "They've shot her!" I sneaked out into the yard to have a look. All was still. There was nothing to be seen in the house, so we hoped that they would now leave and leave everyone in peace. After the war, Könert told the Danish police that initially, they found nothing of interest in Koch's house. It was only when he found a fur cap, which he thought he had seen before, that he began to inspect the house more closely.

We could hear how they were first looking in the toilet, then they moved towards the toolshed where we were holed up. Miss Lund had been standing in front of the locked door to distract their attention. This we could not see because the door opened outwards. What we did see shortly afterwards was that the door was opened and an arm with a pistol stuck in through the gap. It was Könert. He saw us immediately and shot Klaus in the leg. Naujock and his assistants then quickly came over and a total of sixty-two shots were exchanged through the closed door. The door with the bullet holes has been preserved. It shows that two-thirds of the shots fired came from outside. During the exchange of fire, Miss Lund was seriously wounded in the chest.

A pause ensued. We had no idea how many Germans we were fighting against. But we did realize that they would be calling reinforcements from the military police who were at the Sølyst Kro pub, near to Koch's house. We had to get away. Klaus kicked out the window and was badly cut. We clambered out into the garden and ran into the fields around the back of the house. Here I could see Niels and Viggo in front of me and Klaus was a little way behind. I saw a figure disappearing behind a knoll and thought, "Peer has also managed to escape." But it was not him.

During the pause in the shooting, Könert noticed that everything had gone quiet in the toolshed, and when he heard the tinkle of glass, he assumed that something was going on at the other side of the house. And indeed when he ran around he saw someone disappearing fast. Könert shot after him but missed. The German military police, who were billeted at the Sølyst Kro pub, heard the shooting and sent several men to assist. They received orders to pursue us.

In the toolshed the Gestapo agents found Peer Borup, fatally wounded. He had been hit in the back of the head. His eyes were crossed and a rattle was emerging from his throat. It was obvious that he was dying. By that time, the Danish police had also arrived, but were told to keep away in no uncertain terms. They were nonetheless ordered to fetch an ambulance, which took Miss Lund and Peer to Aabenraa Hospital, from where they were later transferred by the Gestapo to the German hospital at Vojens. By that time Peer was dead.

Unaware of Peer's fate, we were running across the snow-covered ground, when Klaus suddenly shouted to me, "Jørgen, look at my legs!" I had already seen them. He was swimming in his own blood. It sounded as if he had stuck his feet in some mash. "Keep going a bit longer, Klaus," is what I shouted back. And we carried on. But the blood in the snow gave us away. We aimed for the nearest farm, which stood in a range of hills about a third of a mile (half a kilometer) to the south-southwest of Koch's house. When we were about 220 yards (200 m) from the farmyard, Klaus shouted, "My legs are like lead; I can't go on." I ran up to him and propped him up, and tried to encourage him to hold out till we got to the farm.

After we had staggered a few steps further, Klaus said: "No, Jørgen, I can't manage, everything's going black in front of my eyes. It'd be better if you shot me in the head and got away yourself." So I gave him a piggyback. He was not very heavy, but very tall. Soon, we had managed to cover the remaining 160 yards to the farm. There we met a very nervous man, then an old lady who had just gotten back from church. Although her silence did not tell us whether they were Danes or ethnic Germans, she pointed over to an outhouse where four cycles were standing, and we were free to take them. While I was walking with Klaus on my shoulders, still bleeding, another woman arrived. They both screamed with fear. We had no time to calm them. Niels and Viggo grabbed the bicycles, which were luckily not locked, while I tried to apply a temporary bandage to Klaus using my handkerchief. He was recovering slightly by then.

And so the escape continued. We took it in turns to carry Klaus and managed to get through a copse and over a couple of hills. This sapped Klaus's strength and when we heard a car approaching, we had to step up the pace. So Klaus and I hid in a ditch while the two others, at a signal from me, sped on to the woods nearby, where they would be able to hide. The German military police were after us; but they did not see us.

I now had the time to do something for Klaus, who had lost a lot of blood. I still remember it as being a fine winter's day with a severe frost, but no wind. The snow-covered landscape was as beautiful as eastern Jutland can ever be. It was worth fighting for. But I had more important things to think about. I set about dressing Klaus's wounds, and ripped my shirt into strips. He had been wounded in both legs. The wounds extended about halfway around each ankle. On the one side, the wound had been caused by broken glass. This he had suffered as he kicked out the window. The other leg had been shot through by a bullet. Strangely enough, there were no signs of a fracture. But, as I have said, he had lost a lot of blood.

We lay in the ditch for about three quarters of an hour, while Klaus recovered. But we had to move on. It would have been far too easy for them to find us, if we had stayed where we were. As I bandaged Klaus, I discovered that a stray shot had hit me in the fingers. That too was bleeding and all in all, our trail of blood was leading the Germans right to us. I crept out of hiding and did a little reconnaissance. There was not a soul around. I helped Klaus onto a bicycle and gave him a push to start him off, then jumped on one myself. We managed to cycle a while, then came to the top of a hill where we could see, in the distance, the railway line and a road which turned off to the right, some hundred yards further on, into the woods. But we also saw a German vehicle traveling along the road to the railway line. We went back to the ditch to hide, but it was too late.

We heard a car stop, and from the shouting that ensued, we understood that they were mounting an attack. I had an English hand grenade in my pocket. But before I threw it, I would have to know where the enemy was. So I stuck my head out over the edge of the ditch and immediately a volley of shots was fired. Klaus now saw that we were also being attacked from the right, where we were unprotected. So we were now surrounded by six Germans. There was no chance of killing them all with the hand grenade and I had not taken the pistol from Koch's house, as the magazine had been emptied. I rummaged through my pockets and found my identity card and a train ticket; I did the same with Klaus's pockets. All these things were hidden under dry leaves. Then we gave ourselves up.

We were quickly surrounded. Klaus was lying on the ground; I stood behind him. We were searched, but they found nothing. Then one of them asked in excellent Danish, "Where are the other two?" At the same time, he pointed his rifle at us. Klaus simply shook his head. The angry German repeated his question, and it looked as if he was going to shoot. Klaus later told me that he heard another soldier whisper to the enraged one, "*Tue das nicht!* (Don't do it!)," to which the other soldier replied, "*Ich tue es auch nicht* (I wasn't going to)." This all seemed incredibly violent to me, so I interrupted, saying: "*Er versteht nicht Deutsch; Sie müssen mit mir sprechen.* (He doesn't know German; you'll have to deal with me)."

Considering the fact that one of the Germans had spoken Danish, albeit with a German accent, my comment was not so clever. But they were too worked up to notice. They now started on me. "*Wo sind die zwei anderen?* (Where are the other two?)" I answered that we had been attacked by four men who wanted our ID cards and coats. When we resisted, they had shot Klaus in the legs. Where the four had gone I did not know. They had disappeared in a southerly direction. The Germans told me to cut the crap and repeated their question: "*Wo sind die zwei anderen?* (Where are the other two?)" "*Die vier anderen, meinen Sie. Ich weiss es nicht* (The four others, you mean. I do not know)."

This repeated itself a couple of times. Then I was hit on the head with a rifle butt. When I had finished studying astronomy, I perceived that I was lying on the ground. One shoulder and the top of my back were very painful and I therefore believed that they must have kicked me as well as hit me over the head. But they gave up trying to find out where the others were. Klaus was put on a bicycle, which the two Germans pushed, while I walked in front of the soldier who had hit me on the head. The car drove slowly behind us. My back was growing stiffer and stiffer and my head was getting worse and worse. I asked the German: "*Sagen Sie mir, bitte, warum haben Sie mir eigentlich geschlagen?* (Tell me, why did you actually hit me?)" He was not, however, in the mood for discussing psychology with me, and as he clearly was not used to talking in a polite way with people, he merely replied, "*Du sollst die Schnauze halten!* (You should shut your trap!)"

We passed the farm where we had taken the bicycles and these were delivered back to their owners. A little further on, a truck with soldiers stopped. The Aabenraa garrison had indeed been summoned and deployed. We were now hoisted up onto the back. Klaus lay there shivering. He was in quite a bad way. I took my jacket off to lay over him and then discovered it was full of blood and that there was a hole near the collar. I had been hit by a bullet when I had peeped over the edge of the ditch. Now I understood the pains in my back and shoulder, plus the stiffness in my neck.

A later medical examination in the German first aid post in Frederiksberg showed that apart from a minor crack in my skull after the blow with the rifle butt, I had also been hit in the left-hand side of my neck. The bullet had damaged the process on the lowest vertebra of my neck or the top one of my chest and emerged through my right shoulder blade. It was something of a miracle that my arms and legs had not been paralyzed. But I obviously belong to the type that survives everything. I have had many lives.

We were then taken under guard to Aabenraa. A lot of people noticed and yelled after us. We were taken to the local Ortskommandantur where we were received by a hysterical officer who shouted, *"Ihr sollt aufgehängt werden! (You should be strung up!)"*

I consoled him with the fact that we no doubt would be. But this did not seem to calm him down. We were taken upstairs and put on two berths. An officer started to interrogate us while a man from the German minority in southern Jutland stood by and kept on lecturing us, "Best tell the truth."

I told him the same story I had told the soldiers out on the country road. Strangely enough he seemed inclined to believe me. I said I lived in Copenhagen and he then began to ask me what I was doing in Aabenraa. Here, my conversation with Doctor Kai Hammer at the hospital came in handy, and I told him that I was looking for a job at the tuberculosis hospital, and I had taken my friend Klaus along for company.

The first session was over, and they appeared to be satisfied. A doctor from the German minority came to treat our wounds. He gave us a little temporary treatment and reminded me that I should rather be home taking care of my studies, rather than undertaking such a trip. I, of course, played the blue-eyed innocent. We were then given some warm soup, which we had to drink out of the bowl. I spilled half of it and it ran down my stomach. It was disgustingly fatty, and burned my lips. Soon afterwards, the officer who had interrogated us came back and announced solemnly that by way of his powers of logic he had reached the conclusion that I was lying. I suggested that his powers of logic were somewhat confused, and continued to play the innocent.

Klaus was now taken by ambulance to the German-run hospital at

Vojens and I was now alone playing the Sphinx, while German soldiers came and went to view the phenomenon. A large group of people had gathered outside, among whom there was one who was very inquisitive. He was arrested on suspicion of knowing the saboteurs, but soon released. My interrogator came back in. He informed me, during the interrogation, that one man had been shot dead at Koch's house. I realized that it could not have been Peer I had seen disappearing behind the knoll. The information made a deep impression on me. But I pretended not to know what he was talking about.

I spent a couple of hours at the Ortskommandantur. I had, as it turned out, fallen into the hands of the Wehrmacht and the military police, not the Gestapo. They had other things to do. While the soldiers had been chasing us, they had taken the trouble to search Koch's house and interrogate Jansen and Flemming who had turned up to find out what had happened at Callesen's and why the bombs had not gone off.

They had spent the night with friends in the Resistance. On the Sunday morning, they had decided to look us up at Koch's house. A guide followed them out and then returned to Aabenraa, while Flemming and Jansen continued on to Styrtom.

They saw the Gestapo car outside Koch's house and their suspicions were aroused. They therefore went down a side road, but were spotted by the landlady of the Sølyst Kro pub and her daughter, who informed the Gestapo. This cost the pub owner a ten-year prison sentence after the war. Flemming and Jansen were then arrested by the Gestapo and taken to Koch's house where, along with Koch, they were ordered to take off all their clothes. They were interrogated in German and as they did not seem to understand they were kicked and punched and ordered to walk round the room by the Gestapo agent. Every time they passed him they received a blow. Then they were made to do knee bends and push-ups while the Gestapo agents and German soldiers searched the house.

Now and again, they were asked new questions in German, and they continued to pretend not to understand. Then they were ordered to crouch, stark naked as they were. The windows and doors were opened and they had to crouch there for between half an hour and an hour. If they moved or were about to keel over out of exhaustion they were hit with fists and rifle butts. One time, when Jansen lost his balance, one of the Gestapo agents broke his jaw with a blow from his pistol. The Gestapo agents ate some apples they found in the house, and threw the rest of them at the prisoners' heads.

The Gestapo finally found proof of Flemming's links to the Resistance movement when they found a bag with an ID card and Flemming's photograph. Whether the card was real or a forgery is not mentioned in the police report. But they recognized Flemming, who was then subjected to more beatings. Finally, the three were ordered to put on the minimum of clothing. As this was not being done quickly enough, they were given another thrashing until a truck turned up and they were taken to the Ortskommandantur, where I had been already for about an hour knowing nothing about their capture and beatings.

I was, of course, unhappy to see them when I was ordered up onto the back of the open truck. We were given orders not to talk with one another, but Flemming managed to whisper, "Has Niels been shot?" "No," I replied, "but Peer has."

He nodded, as a sign that he knew. So the transport began to Kolding. The guards made sure we did not talk to one another. I tried with my finger to write on Flemming's leg the explanation I had given at our arrest, and to encourage him to keep silent as long as possible, but he did not understand my message.

The saboteurs were all prepared for arrest and torture. Everybody feared the collapse, and everybody knew that there is a limit to courage. Therefore, the general instruction was to keep silent for the first twenty-four hours. That would give those who had not yet been arrested a reasonable chance to escape and to continue the fight. The Gestapo knew of this instruction, and cited it as an excuse for the torture in the trials after the war.

When we arrived in Kolding, some twenty-five miles (40 km) away, we were taken to the stables at the ruin of Koldinghus Castle. Jansen helped me down from the truck and as what was now important was to give our colleagues who had not been caught the chance to get to safety, I whispered to both Jansen and Flemming: "Play for time, deny everything as long as possible."

Niels and Viggo Escape
After Niels and Viggo had said goodbye to Klaus and me, they continued their escape. They had to hide several times to avoid being detected. But they managed to get to Kliplev to the south. Niels tells the story:[70]

When we arrived in Kliplev, we looked up the vicar of the parish. He behaved in a brave way and did the best he could to help us. It took some explanation to convince him that it was not a question of a provocation. Anyway, the vicar called a doctor who would take us somewhere else. The doctor seemed afraid and indecisive. To ourselves and the vicar he made the excuse that there was a danger of informers. After the conversation with the doctor, I wrote a farewell letter to my parents as I realized that the chances we would get away were minimal. I left the letter with the vicar, who then phoned the local taxicab owner who was known as being "a good Dane." I can't remember whether he was informed as to the exact details of what had happened. But I do not think so. He took us in his little vehicle some short distance. When we reached the main road, he stopped abruptly about twenty yards to the north of a German barracks. He asked us to get out, as he said we were suspicious, and many people had been shot by saboteurs. He had heard this only recently from another driver. The fact that we were not caught by the Germans here was thanks to the fact that they had not been notified. The taxicab owner's unusual brand of good Danish character is something I have never forgotten.

The two saboteurs had to continue on foot. This meant a long tramp over fields and along minor roads. Finally they did end up in Tinglev where they got on a northbound train. They had wrapped up their submachine guns in some paper at the priest's house in Kliplev. They were put in the luggage net in one compartment, while they took a seat in another, which happened to be full of German officers. As camouflage, Niels had put on his finest clothes as he used to do whenever he carried out a sabotage operation. And because he had gold-rimmed spectacles and spoke fluent German, no one was the slightest bit suspicious. Both Niels and Viggo had to change trains, Viggo at a small station called Lunderskov and Niels at Fredericia. But they both missed the train. So Viggo stayed the rest of the night at the station, and Niels took a taxi to Odense, where he spent the night with a friend of his. They arrived unhurt to Copenhagen and Varde respectively the next day, and were thus in relative safety.

At Gestapo Headquarters in Kolding

As we left Aabenraa, we said farewell to the bright eastern Jutland landscape that winter's day, also to our much cherished freedom and, in our thoughts, to our family and friends. We imagined that this would now be the beginning of a grim end to our lives. Given the fact that they had been looking for me for some while, and that I had already been arrested once before, I thought that my comedy of innocence could not be kept up for much longer. Klaus was not with us on the transport from Aabenraa, but we saw him in Kolding. We were driven straight to Gestapo headquarters at Koldinghus Castle, where Gestapo agent Naujock commenced our interrogation by boxing Flemming's ears when he turned around from facing the wall to see what had happened to me. I could see how he had to prevent himself from hitting him again. We both knew that the time for humiliation had come. Otherwise, the first interrogation for Klaus and myself was of short duration.

While Flemming and Jansen stayed at Gestapo Headquarters, Klaus and I were transferred to a hostel that the Germans had requisitioned (the Højskolehjemmet), where we were given one of the guest rooms. The room had two beds, one along the long wall, the other at the end. Against the other long wall stood a table and under the window a chair. I do not remember what the paintings on the wall were. But they were no doubt dreadful. We were given permission to visit the lavatory under escort, and I took a few sheets of toilet paper from there. Then we undressed and went to bed. A German soldier sat at the table to guard us. We were not allowed to talk to one another. Now and then the soldier was visited by the maid, a *tyskertøs* (a Danish girl who collaborated with the Germans), who sat on another chair and kept the Wehrmacht soldier amused as best she could.

We were given a thermometer each. I realized that our greatest handicap was that we did not know what had happened to our colleagues. We had to play for time. They had spared Klaus and me during our first interrogation that first evening at Koldinghus, presumably because we had been wounded. There was no point in getting tough right from the start. I hid under the covers and started rubbing the thermometer.

"*Was macht er?* (What's he doing?)" the Wehrmacht soldier asked his girl. "*Ich weiss nicht* (I don't know)," she replied with a giggle. Then he asked me the same question. I cannot remember what I answered back. But he did not do anything.

Soon afterwards, a German medical orderly – a so-called *Sanitäter* –

turned up to fetch the thermometers. I found out what Klaus's temperature was. But when the orderly took mine, he found it to be 101.5 (38.6° c). He uttered a few words of comfort to me. I don't remember exactly what he said, but the gist was that I was running a fever on account of my wound, which was quite common. He seemed to be experienced in these matters.

I tried to involve Klaus in my attempts to play for time. The *tyskertøs* had left when the medical orderly arrived. He exchanged a few words with the soldier. "*Hübsches Mädchen* (a pretty girl)." The soldier agreed, and followed the orderly to the door. I took the opportunity to get hold of a pin that was stuck in my clothing, which was lying next to the bed. I wanted to write a note to Klaus on the toilet paper I had managed to save from the lavatory. I disappeared under the covers again and tried to puncture a vein. But the soldier's suspicions had been aroused. "*Was machst du?* (What are you doing?)" he asked suspiciously. "*Ich friere* (I'm freezing)," was the reply.

The *tyskertøs* came in again, and a short while later I continued with what I was doing. I managed to get a few drops of blood, so I could begin to write my note. I was helped indirectly by the *tyskertøs* who was now sitting in the Wehrmacht soldier's lap. The love affair and the writing of the note progressed in parallel. Her blouse was unbuttoned, and I began to write my "vital" note to Klaus. The blood coagulated and the *tyskertøs* made coy whimpering noises. I tried to puncture another vein under my blanket, so that I could write to Klaus that he should pretend to be ill, in order to play for time. "*Er guckt* (He's looking)," said the girl and stared hatefully at me. "*Du pass mal auf! Was machst du?* (You watch it! What are you doing?)" shouted the soldier angrily at me.

I pretended to be asleep and remembered how my puritanical sister had reluctantly accepted that the girl collaborators should have their hair cut short and be chased out of town. She was no doubt right. But I cannot honestly say that I agreed with her that evening in Kolding. I'm afraid that I wrecked the cozy atmosphere. The *tyskertøs* had gotten cold feet. The soldier's attempts to change her mind did not work, and he followed her out.

I used the opportunity to pass my note to Klaus, who accepted it with a mere nod, as the soldier had already returned. I was very well aware how little importance could be attached to this note. But it had some psychological effect if you did anything at all. Writing in my own blood and the short affirmative nod from Klaus meant that the isolation was not complete. We were both very tired. We had both lost a lot of blood and soon fell asleep. It had been a long Sunday – all twenty-four tense hours of it.

Monday, February 7, 1944. We were not taken for interrogation the next day either. I wondered why, and began to worry. Naujock obviously had a lot on his hands. I was worried about Flemming and Jansen. But I principally thought about Peer. It was hard to imagine that he was dead. I could still hear his eager voice, telling us to stay in Koch's toolshed and attack the Germans from there. I had thought he had escaped with the rest of us, but I now realized that he had decided to fight it out to the end.

Flemming and Jansen were put in cells at Gestapo Headquarters at Koldinghus Castle, where they met four other detainees. Two of them introduced themselves as Jan Møller and Henry; they had been arrested after a sabotage attempt in Kolding, Fredericia and Aarhus. The fact that they, under the threat of a death sentence, were well on their way to becoming informers, was something that only they themselves and the Gestapo knew.

The Germans in Kolding were not at first aware of what a catch they had obtained and they had not begun to look into our past as saboteurs. For our part, the most urgent thing was to get a message out of the prison to tell our colleagues where we were. Flemming therefore accepted an offer from Jan Møller, who was, so he said, waiting for a visit from his sister, to smuggle a letter out. So he wrote a brief note about our imprisonment at Koldinghus to Carlo Madsen, who had not been involved in the sabotage, but who had contact with Elsebet. The message was passed on to the Gestapo. But otherwise, the informer did not manage to finagle any information from Flemming. Jan Møller told Gestapo agent Urbansky that it would be hard to get anything out of Flemming, to which Urbansky replied, "Don't worry, when we put the thumbscrews on him, he'll talk, all right."

Wanted: Horsens and Varde in the Gestapo Spotlight

News of the incident in Aabenraa soon spread throughout Denmark. The HD2 saboteurs who had managed to evade capture gradually made their way to Copenhagen on the Monday. Viggo Hansen arrived by train to Varde, where he was reunited with his family. For safety's sake, he and his family were taken to Esbjerg and stayed at his uncle's. Viggo did not want to flee to Sweden. The badly wounded Jens Jørgensen, who was first kept hidden somewhere near Tjæreborg, was soon transferred to the village of Ølgod near Varde, and looked after by a Dr. Øllgaard.

There was clearly a lot of uncertainty as to the future of HD2. But the first major worry was the fact that several of our colleagues were in captivity. Niels was staying with a good friend of ours, the journalist Anders Georg, who immediately traveled to Aabenraa, where he went to the chief constable and others, to interview them, in his capacity of an "innocent journalist."

The list of casualties for HD2 now included Peer, who had been killed, plus Klaus and myself, who had been wounded and taken into custody, plus Flemming and Georg Jansen, who had been taken by the Gestapo and now experienced German interrogation methods for the first time.[71]

Tuesday, February 8, 1944. On February 7, Naujock had tried to obtain further information about Peer from the Danish police. On February 8 it was discovered by the Germans that Peer was dead, and his brother Poul then came to Vojens to identify him. The next day, Poul Borup went back to Horsens by car, taking with him his dead younger brother's body. According to the police report, they were met at the edge of town by a group of people who went with them to the chapel. There was no unrest in connection with this.

In Varde too, everything remained quiet and Viggo Hansen returned with his family from Esbjerg to Varde. In Copenhagen, they heard that all was peace and quiet in Varde, so Niels and Nan traveled there to find out what had actually happened in Aabenraa. This is what Nan wrote in her diary:

Tuesday, February 8. A frightful day. Traveled all day with Niels (first class). Arrived in Varde in the evening. Heard who was dead and who wounded. This gave some relief. The Simonys are great people. Spent the night there.

Both Niels and Nan were, quite understandably, very worried about the saboteurs who had been taken prisoner. Niels told her how I had stayed in the ditch with Klaus, who had been wounded. But Nan knew nothing about what had happened to us after that. The relief she felt was because she heard that the dead man was Peer and not her beloved Klaus. But she would soon find out that there were many other worries in store for her.

If Tuesday, February 8, was a terrible day, the ninth proved even worse. Without knowing it, Niels and Nan had walked into a trap, an action which the Gestapo had set up a good while before to destroy the Resistance movement in Varde. This had seemingly nothing to do with the operation in Aabenraa, but exposed the link between Varde and HD2.

Wednesday, February 9, 1944. Quite independent of the events in Aabenraa and Kolding, the head of the Gestapo had decided to conduct a razzia in Varde.[72] When Schlanbusch looked out his window on the morning of February 9, he saw that the Gestapo were there to arrest Dr. Nordentoft who lived opposite. Schlanbusch warned Simony to give Niels and Nan a chance to escape. This happened at the very last minute. From upstairs, Niels could see that Simony was detained and taken away by the Gestapo. Luckily, they did not search the house and Niels got away without them discovering him. The details of the rest of his flight are vague, but it is known that after traveling through quite a lot of western and central Jutland by railway, he turned up that evening at Nan's parents in Horsens, where he spent the night.

There is nothing in the archives about Nan's flight. Presumably she simply went to Varde station after the Gestapo had left Simony's house and took the ten o'clock train to Horsens, arriving at four in the afternoon. She met not only Niels, but also her brother Tellus and one of the cadets who, after the operation in Aabenraa, had stayed in hiding in Esbjerg. "Father was very nervous," wrote Nan in her diary, and he had every reason to be.

Unfortunately, the Germans were not only looking for Simony and Nordentoft. It did not take long for them to trace Viggo and his wife Ebba. Viggo describes the arrest:[73]

> When the Gestapo arrived they did not seem to care that we had three children – the youngest only six months old – who would be left behind alone. We were not even allowed to tell the neighbor to ask them to look after them. They had to fend for themselves. They ended up at my brother-in-law's place in Esbjerg and only saw their mother again a year later, me after fifteen months had passed.

Schlanbusch was also arrested. This happened as he returned home for lunch. By this time, four other members of the Varde group had been seized, plus Jens Jørgensen and Dr. Øllgaard. They were taken to Esbjerg where the Gestapo had set up a temporary place of custody in connection with their headquarters at Hotel Hafnia there. Viggo was beaten up by Danish helpers, while Schlanbusch (and presumably also Simony and Nordentoft) were treated decently.

Thursday, February 10, 1944. The arrests mentioned above meant that the majority of the Varde group were now in custody. But a couple of names were still on the Gestapo list of wanted men: Chief Constable Poul Gerner-Mikkelsen and a worker named Peter Petersen, both of whom were arrested on February 10.

From a German point of view, the razzia in Varde and environs would seem to have been a success, which has led to many speculations. How could it have gone wrong for so many? The whole way the razzia was carried out suggests an action that had been planned for quite a while and was quite separate from the events in Aabenraa. So the obvious question is: who was the informer? From Viggo Hansen's story, it would seem that a *tyskertøs* called "Nina," now dead, who had known their family for a long time, was revealed to be one of the Gestapo's main sources of information. As the family felt unsure about Nina, she was packed off to Sweden before the war was over.

Not until after Nina's death in 1990 did it emerge that her liaison with the Wehrmacht not only involved sexual passion, but also betrayal. This cost Simony and Nordentoft their lives. They both died in the concentration camp at Husum. Poul-Gerner Mikkelsen and Peter Petersen were both sent to the Porta Westphalica concentration camp in Germany. Neither survived. Schlanbusch and another three members of the Varde group, plus Viggo Hansen and Jens Jørgensen, who later ended up in the main camp at Neuengamme, managed to survive the war, but not unscathed. That *tyskertøs* Nina must have had a lot on her conscience. If we had known at the time, we would have liquidated her.

Clearing up in Horsens
Nan wrote the following in her diary about what happened in Horsens on February 10:

Holger and Niels went into town with me at 10:30 in the morning. That was the day that Peer Borup was being buried. The whole of the town had put the flags out, but the Germans went into the shops and ordered people to take them down again. Everyone wanted to follow him to his grave, but that was prohibited. There was a great commotion in the town. Niels left with the midday train. Went up to talk to Mrs. Kieler.

Peer Borup – killed February 6, 1944 in Aabenraa

Peer's funeral had been arranged for twelve o'clock on the Saturday morning. But the Germans wanted to have it earlier on the Thursday before. At eight o'clock in the morning, the head of the Gestapo from Aarhus arrived, Kriminalrat Schwitzgebel. He ordered everyone to take down the flags, and during the service in Klosterkirken church, he ordered the clergyman Aage Dahl to announce from the pulpit that those who wanted to pay Peer their last respects were prohibited from following the coffin out to the Eastern Cemetery, where Peer would be buried.

With the words "even in death they persecute our compatriots," Pastor Dahl turned to the church, which was filled to the brim, and informed the congregation of Schwitzgebel's orders. Many nevertheless accompanied the coffin as it was carried out of the church. But in Havnegade street, Schwitzgebel was standing with his men, ready to drive the mourners apart. Schwitzgebel had drawn his pistol and was waving many away. But via various shortcuts, a large number of mourners managed to arrive at the cemetery where Pastor Dahl gave a sermon, his voice trembling with rage, which led to his being arrested and sent, on March 27, to a German concentration camp.

Peer Borup was only twenty-one years old when he had joined the Resistance in Horsens. He was a few classes lower than me at school, and I did not then really know him very well. But during our underground activity, a close friendship developed. I have rarely met a member of the Resistance who was so eager. He was a jolly lad, as thin as a lath, and could also be very serious. He thought a lot about life and was quite interested in philosophy. When he met others, his joy of life was in evidence and he spread good humor around him. But his struggle against the oppressor was something he took part in with much gravity of purpose and he was willing to give up a lot. His premature death unleashed great sadness amongst his friends in his hometown. When grammar school boys in Horsens joined the Resistance, this was to a large extent inspired by Peer, and a reaction to his heroic death. Despite his youth, he had become one of the key figures in Horsens during the German occupation. His family never got over the loss of this friendly, keen and inspired son and brother.

Friday, February 11, 1944. The day after Peer's funeral, Nan went back to Copenhagen. She describes the day briefly:

> Took the midday express to Copenhagen. Mother and father came with me. The Gestapo fetched Dr. Kieler – and I was supposed to have been there that morning.

My youngest sister Lida remembers my father's arrest. At 6:30 in the morning, three men from the Gestapo arrived. Lida had gotten up early to study some French vocabulary, and my mother was also up and about downstairs, while my father was still in the bedroom on the floor above. The Germans rang the doorbell and my mother spoke so loudly that my father realized what was going on downstairs. While the Gestapo were being shown into the living room, he descended the back stairs unnoticed and went into the coal cellar in the yard, where he hid while the Germans were questioning mother and Lida. One of them spoke Danish, but wanted to talk German to Lida, who pretended not to understand and suggested they speak English. This the Germans did not want to do.

A long questioning session ensued, and the subject of the members of the family who were not present at the time inevitably came up. But the main subject of the conversation was the underground press and especially Elias Bredsdorff. Meanwhile father sat twiddling his thumbs in the coal cellar. They searched the house quite thoroughly but did not find anything. They were very interested in obtaining photographs of Elsebet and Bente who had not been arrested at the time. But they found no other photos nor underground newspapers in the house. The visit from the Gestapo had not come unexpected.

In the end, my father began to grow anxious about his wife and youngest daughter and emerged from his hiding place, whereupon he was arrested. The Gestapo then took him to Aarhus, where he underwent a long interrogation, without, however, suffering any physical abuse. He remained in custody in that city until on March 8 he was transferred to the Horserød concentration camp in the northern part of Sjælland. This was neither the first nor the last arrest undertaken by the Gestapo in Horsens. But none of this had anything to do with the events in Aabenraa.

After four days' work chasing the HD2 saboteurs, Naujock finally found out that the Gestapo in Dagmarhus in Copenhagen were looking for us. So on February 10, the four of us (Flemming, Jansen, Klaus and myself) were transferred from Kolding to Copenhagen and locked up in the Vestre Fængsel prison (aka "Hotel Vestre"), with which I had already made my acquaintance in connection with our operation against B&W. I do not remember the actual journey to Copenhagen. After our arrest and transfer to Kolding, I had been totally unaware of what had happened in Aabenraa, Varde, Horsens and Copenhagen. And I was wondering why the interrogation of Klaus and myself was being delayed.

The reason was presumably that the Gestapo had started their pursuit of the various members of HD2 who were still free. Flemming's short note led to a razzia at Carlo Madsen's house in Copenhagen, where the Gestapo picked up two of our cadets, Tony and Jørgen Salling, who had been with us in Aabenraa. Tony managed to escape, despite a serious wound to his leg, while Jørgen Salling and Carlo Madsen were arrested and taken to the Vestre Fængsel prison.

Jan Møller, Alias Snogen, in Action

Saturday, February 12, 1944. Nan's diary adds nothing of significance to the information about what happened on February 12. But judging by the trial of the informer in the cell, Jan Møller – also known as Snogen (the snake) – it would seem that he and the other informer, Henry, had been brought to the Vestre Fængsel in Copenhagen along with us. Jan was put in the same cell as Flemming, while Henry, from what I later found out, had been installed in John's cell. The chase of the members of HD2 was now entering its final phase.

Flemming was soon taken for interrogation, and there can be no doubt that the Gestapo thought at the time that they had caught a big fish, as the head of the Anti-Sabotage Department, Kriminalrat Bunke, interrogated him himself. During the interrogation, he hinted at the fact that Jan would be set free on February 12. Flemming did not see what was coming to him, and when Jan offered to take a message out of the prison for him, he wrote a short note to Elsebet and Bente, telling them to go to Sweden right away. The note was addressed to Mrs. Else Møller, who was married to our close associate Hans Møller during the transport of Jews, at Nørrevold. Jan was paid 175 kroner by the Gestapo, left the Vestre Fængsel and went to stay at a cheap hotel, where he started operations, which were to lead to seven arrests and one attempted murder, for which he paid with his life after the war.

During the court case in 1947, it emerged that Jan Møller had been a woodwork teacher, but had otherwise worked as an odd-job man doing various temporary jobs, e.g., as a draughtsman and doing menial work. He was twenty-six years old, married with two children. He took part in various sabotage operations in Fredericia and Kolding, including against the very hostel where Klaus and I had been taken right after our arrest. This building was occupied by German switchboard operators and shop girls.

He had been arrested by the Gestapo that previous December, and they had found a suitcase with explosives in his possession. He soon broke down under interrogation and started working for the Gestapo – perhaps on account of the threat of a death sentence. He himself claimed that the cooperation was on account of the fact that he was angry at having been branded as an informer in the underground press.

He had previously managed to infiltrate the Resistance in Kolding, which he had had contacts with earlier on, and this had led to the arrest of several members. After we had been arrested, Flemming was his special assignment and by way of the address of Hans Møller in Nørrevold, he began his informer's career against HD2.

Sunday, February 13, 1944. The day after he had been released, Jan went to Hans Møller's house and delivered Flemming's note addressed to Elsebet and Bente. Mrs. Møller was in bed, ill with concussion following an accident. Jan said he had been in the same cell as Flemming, but had now been released. Apart from conveying Flemming's greetings, he said he knew something that he wanted to tell the Resistance. Hans Møller called Elsebet and Bente, who then received Flemming's warning that they should flee to Sweden. After the arrests in Aabenraa, Bente had moved to her grandmother's in Valby, while Elsebet, with Carlo Madsen's help, went into hiding in a convent on Jagtvejen street in Copenhagen. This would prove an important move for her.

During Jan's visit, one of the cadets turned up. He had come back from Horsens and wanted to know what was going on in the capital. They all trusted Jan, who mentioned that he wanted to try to draw up a plan to help Flemming escape. The cadet should try to get in touch with the people who were interested in his stock of arms. What Jan did not know was that the cadet in question was a member of HD2 and had been in action in Aabenraa.

That same afternoon or evening, Jan went over to Malmøgade street where Hans Møller's sister, Margrethe, lived with their old mother. He met Hans Møller again there along with Bente and Elsebet. During his visit, the writer Kelvin Lindemann dropped by. He was the one who had originally put us in touch with Finn and therefore with the Holger Danske group. Kelvin promised Jan that he would obtain a forged ID card (an *Ausweis*) for use with the Germans, which was necessary to be out of doors during the curfew. Jan was to pick them up the next day from another address. He then left the house along with Elsebet, while Bente stayed on at Malmøgade. No one had had any suspicions about Jan.

Monday, February 14, 1944. The next morning, Jan was paid a visit by a Gestapo agent who had brought him a pistol, as it was dangerous to move about unarmed in Copenhagen. He was also told that he was not working quickly enough. But it cannot be said that he was lazy. He continued to make efforts to contact the people with the stock of arms, and via the cadet from Horsens, his request was conveyed to Jørgen Staffeldt. Staffeldt was, however, cautious, and Jan had to make do with the message that the matter was of no interest. This he reported to Gestapo agent Neuhaus, who gave him the order to maintain the contact with the cadet and to try to get more information about Flammen.

Tuesday, February 15. The day after she had met Jan at Margrethe Møller's house, Elsebet moved in there. Preparations for an escape to Sweden were in full swing. Nan too had been told to leave. Tellus had come from Horsens and had now gone into hiding with friends who had both the right connections and knew a transport route to Sweden.

The Gestapo Pounce in Copenhagen

Wednesday, February 16, 1944. After his failed attempt to get in touch with Staffeldt, Jan wanted to try the Kelvin Lindemann tack. So he went off to the address where he had been told he could collect the false IDs. Jan was received in a little office by a friend of Kelvin's who became suspicious about him. Jan was therefore sent away empty-handed, as he had said he wanted to talk to Kelvin alone. As he was leaving the office, he happened to meet Kelvin on the stairs. They recognized one another. Jan became confused and as he did not know what to say, he simply told him to put his hands up. A tussle ensued during which Kelvin fell down the stairs, while Jan started shooting at him. Kelvin ran out onto the street and a taxi happened to be passing, so he was able to get away. He phoned Margrethe Møller from a telephone booth to warn her – but he was unfortunately too late.

Jan did not manage to do any more damage in Copenhagen. The next day he went back to Kolding where he reported for duty at Gestapo headquarters there. He was given a fee of three hundred kroner for his ten days' work in the capital. What happened at Malmøgade 10 is described by Elsebet:[74]

By that time, Bente and I had decided to escape to Sweden. I had changed my hairstyle and Margrethe had helped me to slap on a lot of makeup. In this guise, I had my photo taken at the Central Station for a false passport. Once back in Malmøgade I was seen there, including by Jan, who then left, while we stayed on to eat evening dinner with Margrethe and her mother. We had just sat down to eat when there was a ring at the door and in stepped a couple of Gestapo agents with revolvers at the ready. I think it was Falkenberg and Neuhaus. We were given permission to finish our dinner, and the two agents were sitting there playing with their revolvers when the phone rang. I was ordered to lift the receiver and to tell whoever it was on the other end to come over immediately.

I heard Kelvin Lindemann's voice: "Jan's an informer," is what he said. "He has just shot at me on Kongens Nytorv square!" "You've got the wrong number," is what I replied and replaced the receiver. The Gestapo agents were furious. So when, unfortunately, Kelvin called again, it was old Mrs. Møller who had to answer the call and give the notorious reply. But by that time, Kelvin may have suspected something, because he left for Sweden and never turned up.

After dinner was over, I asked if I could go to the toilet. I wanted to take off my red nail varnish as I could imagine sitting there in Vestre Fængsel with it wearing off, day by day. I had to be alone, both physically and mentally. [*Elsebet did not expect Falkenberg to follow her all the way to the toilet but he did.*] So both Falkenberg and I wandered into the Møllers' bathroom. He stood pointing at me with his revolver while I wiped off my nail varnish. The situation was not without its funny side. We were then ordered down the stairs, into a car and were taken off to Dagmarhus.

Bente suffered the same fate and along with Margrethe and her eighty-year-old mother, they were taken for a provisional interrogation at the Vestre Fængsel.

The ladies at Malmøgade were not the only prey caught by the Gestapo that day. Although Jan had not succeeded in getting in touch with Jørgen Staffeldt, the Nordisk Boghandel bookshop suddenly aroused their intense interest. From Mogens Staffeldt's testimony to the city court, we can read that a man came in at 5:40 in the early evening and asked for a

Peter Jørgensen, this being Jørgen Staffeldt's undercover code name. Jørgen was, unfortunately, also present. He was asked to step outside. Here stood Neuhaus and the informer Arno Hammeken waiting for him. The pistol in Neuhaus's hand convinced him he was under arrest. When the man returned to the shop and called whether anyone could take a message from Peter Jørgensen, Mogens Staffeldt also had to go out onto the street where he too was arrested. What the Gestapo did not know was that at that same moment, Mix was in the Nordisk Boghandel, along with Henny, to discuss the impending evacuation in more detail.

During interrogation at Dagmarhus, it transpired that Mogens had been arrested by accident. The Germans had not known his name, position or his connection with the Nordisk Boghandel. But the Germans were convinced of the fact that the bookshop was a contact point for underground groups and the parachutists from Britain, and under interrogation, Mogens was shown photos of Lillelund, John and Flammen on their way to or from the Nordisk Boghandel.

The operation carried out against the Nordisk Boghandel was a major victory for the Gestapo. Archive material suggests that the bookshop had been under surveillance for quite some while, and the arrest of the Staffeldt brothers, as well as the arrests in Varde, cannot be traced back to the failure of the operation in Aabenraa. After the war, we naturally suspected Jan as having been the one who informed on the bookshop. He denied it and the court dismissed that charge. However, the court did not believe that he was merely firing warning shots into the ceiling during the Kelvin Lindemann incident and this was one of the important factors leading to his being sentenced to death.

He had other unfortunate incidents on his conscience and bitterly regretted what he had done. So he did not ask for clemency and was executed on May 13, 1948. Elsebet met one of his children, many years later. She thought that her father had been executed by the Germans, and Elsebet let her continue to harbor that illusion. That was the right thing to have done. After the war there were many voices raised for a general pardon to be given to traitors. The only thing that people unfortunately forget in such circumstances is that the only people who could possibly forgive are the victims themselves of the work of traitors. Elsebet was such a victim with the right to forgive, and it is for that reason that Snogen, alias Jan Møller, has not been identified by his real name here.

The Order to Evacuate

Thursday, February 17, 1944. Elsebet and Bente, plus Nan and Tellus, had decided to escape to Sweden, and the cadets also had to follow an order from navy command to cross Øresund. Everyone who had not been arrested had gone into hiding, while they looked into various ways of getting over to Sweden. Over the following week, most of them found some way of getting there.

Most of the evacuees from our group met later on in a camp at the Möckelsnäs manor house near Diö in the Swedish province of Småland. Only Tony took his time to turn up. He had been brought down by a bullet wound in the leg. He finally arrived with a dredger (a ship with equipment to remove sand from the bottom of the sea). That is the end of the story of HD2. Here is a survey of the fates of the group:

Killed: Cato Bakman and Peer Borup.

In German captivity: John, the four Kieler brothers and sisters (Elsebet, Bente, Flemming, and myself, Jørgen) and our father Ernst Kieler, plus Klaus Rønholt, Georg Jansen, Jørgen Salling, Jørgen and Mogens Staffeldt. Also our friends: Carlo Madsen, Margrethe Møller and her mother, and her brother Hans.

Escaped to Sweden: The naval cadets Mix, Stig, Filler, Holger, Christian, Reib and Ib Gram Hansen, plus Henny. The students Nan, Tellus, Niels, Tromle plus Trunte, who soon returned to continue her Resistance work and courier work for the SOE. She narrowly missed being arrested. Mix too returned, but could not avoid capture. He was executed by the Germans on February 2, 1945.

Stayed behind: Knud Kærgaard and Svend Kieler stayed in Denmark where they continued in one or another branch of the Resistance. Ulla and Ebba Lund carried on helping refugees to escape, while Helge and Holger Larsen, who had previously been detained for a short while, carried on working for the underground press under more discreet circumstances. Flammen too continued to work in Denmark, but the Gestapo were hot on his trail. He did not survive the war. He was surprised by the Gestapo and took a cyanide pill on October 18, 1944. But he managed to knock out twenty-two informers.

The arrests of Jørgen and Mogens Staffeldt were quite independent of the events in Aabenraa, but their case was soon linked to HD2 activities. The addition of the fourteen prisoners from Varde about which I have already written brought the number of those arrested to thirty. Schlanbusch told in his memoirs that in the office where the interrogation with Neuhaus was taking place, there was a poster with the text "Sache von Fyren Kieler." According to Schlanbusch, this meant that "the Germans regarded Jørgen Kieler, and quite rightly so, as the leader of the Holger Danske 2 group and all their operations and activities, i.e., both the work of the group at Varde and at Aabenraa." This may have emerged from the previous pages, but should be taken with a pinch of salt. I will, however, not deny that I often took the initiative and felt an overall responsibility, which also continued during a further sixteen months spent as a prisoner of the Gestapo, which shall be covered in detail in the next section of this book.

PART IV: PRISONERS

Elsebet, Bente, Jørgen and Flemming Kieler arrested by Gestapo

CHAPTER 9

Prisoner of the Germans in Denmark

The increasing need that the German occupier had for prisons to house captured Danish freedom fighters meant that German sections were opened at various prisons, in addition to the takeover of the Horserød concentration camp, which was later replaced by the Frøslev camp. None of these prisons and concentration camps can be compared with those in Germany itself. The prisoners did not have to suffer cold and starvation, or the slave labor I later experienced in Germany. On the other hand, prisoners were subjected to harsh interrogation with the eternal threat of torture, and a risk of being executed. Resistance against the occupier was not yet over, even though I had been locked up by the Germans in Denmark. My family and I became very familiar with the Vestre Fængsel prison in Copenhagen. It housed the largest German section in the whole country and was termed *Hotel Vestre Gefängnis* by the Germans themselves. I was transferred there along with Klaus on February 10.

Back to Vestre Fængsel

On arrival at Vestre Fængsel, Klaus and I were put in the same cell and could now talk freely to one another, which rather surprised me. We talked over what had happened and prepared ourselves for the forthcoming interrogation, which to our astonishment was delayed still further. Seeing Vestre Fængsel again was a strange experience. The cell that Klaus and I occupied was the same size as my old one in the Danish section the previous month. But there was less room as there were now two bunks, one along the long wall, one along the end wall. The bunks were not folded up against the wall during the day as they had been in the Danish section, so there was even less room to move: four paces one way, four back. But at least you could sit down and make yourself comfortable during the daytime. I saw the door at the end of the corridor that led to the Danish section. I had seen it from the other side, and thought this time too about chances for escaping.

A *Sanitäter* (a medical orderly) – a cycle repair man in civil life – changed our bandages. But otherwise we did not receive any medical treatment the first week. We still had our blood-soaked clothes from the time of our arrest, no soap or the opportunity to shave, cut our nails, brush our teeth or perform any basic grooming. Our stubble grew longer and finally turned into a beard, which cured me for life of ever wanting to grow one again. We felt dirty and humiliated.

The pain from the bullet wound had not been so bad at first. Now it grew worse. It became more and more difficult for me to sit up and I became worried that I might have suffered damage to my spine. I also had a headache and as the wound incurred when I was hit on the head with the rifle butt healed, I felt unevenness there, which made me suspect that my skull had been fractured. Both suspicions were subsequently confirmed when I was X-rayed at the German first aid station.

Klaus complained about the heaviness of his legs and he found it hard to stand or walk. We began to talk more openly with each other, tell about our home life, our youth and our dreams for the future. It was not while still at home that Klaus had been inspired to join the Resistance, but he was wholeheartedly committed. However, I did not know whether he would have gone so far as to join a sabotage group if he had not met Nan. I felt great sympathy and felt it was quite unreasonable that he should die so young on account of falling in love in his youth. I had not thought like that as we lay in the ditch in Styrtom but now, four days later, I felt responsible for the fates of all the members of my group and I was glad to have stayed with him then, although this would later prove to have been futile.

On February 14 I was given permission to send a letter to my parents. My mother hid the letter afterwards. I had to reckon with the fact that the letter would be censored, so I wrote with that in mind. I related that Flemming and I had been detained by the Germans in southern Jutland, suspected of sabotage. In an attempt to cheer them up, I wrote that Flemming was unscathed and that I was not suffering too much from the bullet wound I had suffered while being arrested. I went on:

> I am now being held in the German section of Vestre Fængsel and am receiving fair treatment. What the future will bring, I cannot tell. I have no worries in that direction. When you are at peace with yourself, the outside world cannot upset you. There are, however, one or two small problems with everyday life that could be alleviated from outside the prison. We can receive parcels once a week. They can be delivered between 14:00 and 16:00. I am very short of underwear and toilet articles. It is also possible to send a few provisions.
>
> Give my greetings to the girls and whoever else can share your worry. Don't be too worried on my account.

The letter ends with a birthday greeting to my father who was celebrating his fifty-sixth birthday on February 17. I did not know at that point that he had been arrested on the eleventh of that month and taken to the German prison in Aarhus.

I had no idea what was going on outside the walls of the prison and only later did I find out that February 22 had been a critical date. On that day, the Gestapo carried out another razzia in Horsens. A total of twenty people were picked up, including the lawyer Kaj Dahl. My mother nearly ran into the razzia at Dahl's office, where his assistant was busy burning compromising documents. He had just finished doing this, when there was a knock at the door. It was my mother who wanted to talk with Dahl himself. It was about nine in the morning. Valdemar Sørensen managed to say, "He's been taken by the Gestapo," then pulled himself together and added, "Sorry, I wasn't supposed to mention it." My mother managed to disappear before the Gestapo turned up.

She hurried out onto Søndergade street, where she met our neighbor opposite, who had seen the Gestapo stop in front of our block of flats. The Gestapo sat on the stairs waiting for my mother who had pinned a note to the door saying "Back soon." Meanwhile, she went to the neighbor's and called the school to warn Lida. Lida's English teacher took her home to his house and my mother, cared for by good friends, escaped arrest.

But it was not so much her own safety that was on my mother's mind. The following days she made attempts to get parcels to the imprisoned members of her family. At the end of February I received a reply to my letter from the fourteenth in the form of two parcels, which had been sent on February 23 and 24, respectively. I have never in my life felt greater need for a change of underwear or a shave. My much-hated, suffocating and ugly beard disappeared down into the sewers.

On February 27 my mother traveled with Lida to Copenhagen where our good friend Dr. Johannes Clemmesen generously put his flat at their disposal. This was where they lived for the following fortnight. My mother and Lida were safe in Copenhagen. The trail had gone cold for the Gestapo, but a passive life in hiding did not suit the temperament of Margrethe Kieler. Instead of keeping out of sight, she decided to demonstrate her "contempt for the enemy," so along with Lida she went to Dagmarhus and spoke to Police Inspector Wolf there in order to arrange an opportunity to visit and send parcels to the imprisoned members of her family. They were not arrested and were even treated with great courtesy and my mother was consistently addressed as Frau von Führen Kieler – no doubt the only time she ever allowed herself to be called that. In that situation, the name was rather handy. Lida too was treated properly. The Gestapo agents could see that she was very sweet, which she actually was. For my mother, this was all a little too much of a good thing and she only took Lida along on one more occasion.

According to Elsebet, my mother used the opportunity to ask the Gestapo what they were thinking that she and Lida were going to live on. Her empty purse was proof that they were in acute need, so they paid out the last portion of our "Jew money," which they had presumably confiscated when they performed the razzia at Raadhusstræde on February 9.

A further contribution to solving her financial problems was the decision made by my father's colleagues shortly after his arrest. With all votes for the decision except one, they decided to care for my father's patients on his behalf as long as he remained in prison. His doctor's practice was therefore saved and no replacement was appointed. There were bad apples in Horsens as in every other town, but my father mostly experienced a degree of solidarity to which certain risks were attached. We had always liked the town. Now we were really glad we lived there.

My Prison Diary

On my arrival in the cell I had found a pocket diary in which I briefly noted down what happened to me in jail. On the basis of these notes, I wrote out a full diary in 1945 and this has formed the basis of my description of what happened to me in Vestre Fængsel.

Tuesday, February 15. In my pocket diary I noted down: "Interrogations starting. Move without Klaus to Cell 56 with Henry C." Henry was about twenty years old. He told me he had been a saboteur in Aarhus and had been arrested there along with the rest of his group. According to what he said, his colleagues had been executed one after the other and he too had been tied to a pole, after which the order to fire was given. But this had been a mock execution. He lost consciousness and woke up in a coffin.

While he was telling it, his story sounded plausible enough, but I was not entirely convinced. I was still too shocked to care very much about his narrow escape. On the other hand, what did shake me up was the fact that he had shared a cell with John, who lay wounded and beaten up, in a cell near to ours. Henry then told me that he knew that John had worked together with me. Otherwise he did not ask me much about John, and I did not dare to ask him much either, for fear of revealing something I did not want to.

Two Gestapo agents had been assigned to our case. One was called Falkenberg. He was between thirty-five and forty years old with fair hair, stocky, with a severe face and cold grey eyes. He spoke fluent Danish with a southern Jutland accent. After the war, I found out that he was the son of parents belonging to the German minority, in the south of the Jutland peninsula, near the German border. He was a professional policeman who had received his training in Germany. The other Gestapo agent was called Neuhaus. He was a little younger, of above average height with dark hair and smiling eyes. By all appearances a friendly man from Hamburg who only spoke German. I later got the suspicion that he understood Danish, but would never admit to doing so.

They used the classic Gestapo tactics, where one interrogator was harsh, the other more understanding. First the "tough guy" would soften up the prisoner, then the "soft guy" would extract information from him now that he had been intimidated. Falkenberg started off. The first interrogation took place in Vestre Fængsel. When I was taken down to the interrogation cell, I passed one of the Gestapo men in the hall who had interrogated me in Dagmarhus after the sabotage at Burmeister & Wain. He came towards me smiling and complimented me on the success of our operation, then asked me whether it was part of the plan to get ourselves arrested by the German harbor police. I was, of course, not particularly interested in revealing unnecessary details and simply replied that it was not, whereupon he replied dryly: "*Ja, wenn das der Fall ist dann war es vielleicht nicht so elegant, wie ich glaubte. Aber jetzt haben wir Sie jedenfalls festgenommen* (Yes, if that is the case, it perhaps wasn't as elegant as I had thought. But anyway, we've now got you in custody)."

After that little exchange, which confirmed the fact that I had been recognized as the student who had been detained before, I was taken in to Falkenberg who started by advising me to tell the truth, otherwise my life would become particularly unpleasant. I was in no doubt that he was right, and I only wondered why he was taking such a roundabout route. Why did he not start torturing me right from the start, as I imagined that this would follow anyway. The first interrogation dealt, understandably enough, with Aabenraa and Burmeister & Wain. There was no getting away from these operations, and Falkenberg did not seem either to feel that there was much to discuss. To my surprise he did not ask me anything about John.

The day after my first interrogation, the people I have already mentioned were arrested: Elsebet, Bente, Margrethe Møller and her mother and brother, plus the Staffeldt brothers. Elsebet wrote the following about her first interrogation:[75]

> It was late when Bente and I were summoned for interrogation. Neuhaus was sitting at his typewriter and we were sitting next to one another, opposite him. I had my handbag on my lap and had my fingers inside, trying to tear into small pieces a letter to the writer Lindemann in which I outlined our reasons for joining the Resistance. When Neuhaus had been given the information he wanted (our personal

details on that occasion) he walked up to me and turned my handbag upside down. Small pieces of paper rained onto the floor... "Ach du lieber Gott," he said, "we'll now have to go to all the trouble of sticking it back together again." Just try, is what I was thinking. But they did manage to do so.

Ten days later, when I was back at Dagmarhus for interrogation, he presented me with my letter, perfectly pieced together, and asked me why I had torn it up. I replied truthfully that I was afraid that the people named there would get into trouble. They are dead, or have fled to Sweden, was Neuhaus's reply – and a weight fell from my chest. The letter had an unexpectedly positive effect, in that I had emphasized there that our resistance was not motivated by a hate of Germans but was a struggle for human rights. "Kleine Idealisten," mumbled Neuhaus, and shook his head.

Thursday, February 17. I was visited by a German doctor. After examining me, he said that I had presumably suffered a fracture of the spinal column, which had to be X-rayed. He told me I should stay lying down on my mattress. I could not help smiling and told him that he should convey that information to Dagmarhus and the medical orderly there.

Apart from that first interrogation, I was interrogated at Dagmarhus alternately by Falkenberg and Neuhaus. I had a feeling that initially there had been some uncertainty as to who was taking the overall responsibility for our case. But after a few days had passed, it became clear that it was Neuhaus. One reason for this was that at the time, both my sisters, my brother and I all spoke fluent German. There were therefore no language grounds for letting Falkenberg take over.

I had no overall picture as to who had been arrested and my most urgent problem the next few days was to find out how much the Gestapo knew about my connections with John. Henry's mention of the fact he was sure that John and I had worked together did not necessarily mean that the Gestapo knew as well. Although I was somewhat suspicious of my cellmate, I was not yet convinced that he was an informer. But after a few days, when his rather taciturn behavior gave way to a curiosity with regard to my links with John, my suspicions began to grow apace, and I became even more distrustful when I noticed that he was often summoned to leave the cell just before I myself was to undergo interrogation. I also thought it interesting that on each occasion, he would return with some cigarettes.

Later on, he became more open about the torture that John had been subjected to. I regarded this as a threat, and asked to drop the whole subject of John. We did not bring up the subject again, but I was not unduly surprised when at length I was confronted with my friend and group member. In my diary, I wrote the following:

Friday, February 18. Today I was confronted with John. He lay alone in Cell 65 in one of the usual bunks, which had been put in the middle of the cell. Around the bunk were masses of tufts of hair lying on the floor. For today's visit, he had been shaved and had his hair cut for the first time since December 10, 1943. I was happy to see him, yet depressed. He looked pale and tormented. There was something in his gaze and his facial expression that reminded me of a cornered animal – a marked contrast to the self-assuredness that had made him the ideal leader of operations. I did not dare to say anything for fear of disclosing things the Gestapo was not already bound to know. John, however, gave me a clue as to how to play it when he said, after a slight hesitation: "Yes, we know each other from the Cannibals' Kitchen (the student refectory)." I was then led out.

To my surprise, this confrontation was not followed up by an interrogation session and I did not see John again for another month. In between, I received a message via one of the orderlies who distributed the meals that he had been harshly treated. The next day I wondered a lot whether he was going to undergo many painful interrogation sessions in connection with our arrest, but to my great surprise, I was not subjected to more interrogation about it, and Henry seemed to have lost interest in John.

Instead, he now began to ask me about my family. It seemed to be Elsebet he was most interested in, which led me to suspect that other members of my family had indeed been arrested. In his eagerness to obtain information, he was careless enough to say, the next day, "The one I'm most interested in hearing about is your cousin Svend." Where he had gotten Svend's name from I did not know, but there was now no doubt about the fact that Henry was an informer. His pushiness began to become a torment for me. It was clear to me that he had received instructions to extract as much information as possible out of me about HD2.

Monday, February 21. To my great relief, I was moved to Cell 69. "Really nice, as the sun shines in here and I'm no longer as cold," is what I wrote in my pocket diary. I was glad to be rid of Henry, but was still rather listless on account of the loss of blood, and I suffered to an increasing extent from the lack of personal hygiene. At first, I had Cell 69 to myself. It was a relief to be on my own. During the whole time I was imprisoned, I suffered more from the presence of other people than I did from being alone. I do not understand more recent ideas of the isolation cell as a form of torture. The worst thing was that I still knew nothing about which of the members of my family had been arrested.

Some three to four days later, I nonetheless found out that Elsebet and Bente were in Gestapo custody. Elsebet, who wrote a prison diary like I did, gives a description of our first meeting in Vestre Fængsel:[76]

> The interrogation sessions followed in quick succession, mostly in Vestre Fængsel. There was one longer session at Dagmarhus the following Friday, February 25. It was on this occasion that I was presented with my glued-together letter. It was also that day that I again saw Jørgen. We were made to stand with our faces to the wall, when he and some others were taken past. We caught each other's eye, and he thought, "Damn it" – that was obvious. He now knew that the girls had been arrested too. My interrogation was over in all important aspects in February. Five sessions in all.

Tuesday, February 29. I obtained permission to send a censored letter, twenty lines long, to my mother, in which I wrote:

> Dear Mother,
>
> Hopefully, you will get this letter today. I have understood that you only have Lida with you, and am thinking a lot about you for that reason. Bente and Elsebet are also here. Their stay can hardly last long. They will no doubt be charged with helping with illegal transports and the German authorities are, as far as I can see, very understanding about the humane motives which give rise to such activities. You will no doubt be seeing Father soon. He hasn't done anything. For Flemming and me things are rather more serious. But I am hopeful for the future and ask you to be, too.

Thanks very much for the parcel. It was a pleasant surprise in what is a somewhat monotonous existence… I mostly lie on my bed, as the bullet damaged one of my vertebrae at chest level. No paralysis, just some pains in my back. They have promised to X-ray me…

Love,

Jørgen

Monday, March 6. In my diary, I noted "Mother and Lida visited." Their talk with Inspector Wolf had therefore not been in vain. The visit was of great significance. It was a moving experience. Although there was a guard present and we could therefore not speak freely, there was nothing to stop us expressing the warm feelings we were filled with. We had a lot of trouble keeping ourselves under control. Mother deliberately talked about the attention paid to our arrest throughout the country and about the many bunches of flowers she had received. She also had news about my father, who was in custody in Aarhus. The visit was a short one, but when we parted, she embraced me and whispered into my ear: "Jørgen Salling's been arrested, the rest are in Sweden." She hugged me again and then repeated, "are in Sweden." I realized that now I had someone working on my behalf beyond the bars of the prison.

On March 8 my father was transferred to the Horserød concentration camp in the north of Sjælland, where he met many friends and acquaintances from Horsens. He was no longer of interest to the Gestapo. When my mother found out about the move I do not know. She and Lida stayed in Copenhagen until March 17 in the hope that she would receive permission to visit us again. She did not succeed in this, although she made a third visit to Dagmarhus – this time without Lida. After she had sent two more parcels to her children in Vestre Fængsel, which contained, among other things, books, which were very welcome, she and Lida traveled to Aalsgaarde, where they stayed with my uncle in order to be near my father. They visited him at Horserød, which was not far away, on March 22.

On the twenty-fourth she again received permission to visit us at Vestre Fængsel. The visit took place in Elsebet's cell, where Bente also was. Neuhaus was, of course, there too, so we could not talk freely. But I was happy to see them again. Two days later, my mother and Lida traveled to

Horsens to a life no less tough than ours. On April 2, she wrote me a letter, from which I will quote:

> …I am happy I could see you again so soon and in good spirits. I had been very unhappy about your illness and that of Flemming. If only you could get permission to see the birch tree sprouting. You can't imagine how wonderful it was for Lida and me to arrive in Aalsgaarde so that we could visit Father. We both enjoyed getting away from the city.… Thank goodness Father has got something to do, and that he can read – and he has plenty of time to philosophize.…We had greetings from lots of old friends… I can't remember all the names, but you can't imagine how many people are thinking about you and send their greetings.

Not until many years later did I discover that the whole situation affected my youngest sister Lida the most. Margrethe Kieler was well respected and a loyal wife as well as a mother who gave up a lot for others. She had been hit by misfortune and this moved others. Her bravery aroused a good deal of admiration, but not many people saw how enormous was the support she received from Lida, and it took a long time before I understood what a price the young girl, not even an adult, had to pay. She is not one to complain, and because of the general worry about what was going to happen to those members of our family who were in prison, plus respect for my mother, Lida was often forgotten.

In the past, she had done well at school, but during her time at secondary school, she had to accept that what she had missed on account of fleeing from the Gestapo and the trips to Copenhagen and northern Sjælland had taken their toll, so she was obliged to have extra tuition over and above normal school attendance. Most of the teachers were understanding in this respect, but not all. Her history teacher said quite plainly, and with irritation in his voice, that he was fed up with the Kieler family. There was no longer any reason to treat her in a special way. His irritation also had its political background. One of his sons, a volunteer on the *Ostfront*, had perished; another was put on trial for betraying his country after the war.

Nor did the families of all her classmates have sympathy for her. One lawyer, who was the father of one of Lida's friends, pointed out with glee that if you mess around with Communists and other scum, you will get what is coming to you. Fate caught up with him later.

Lida also suffered at school from the spartan clothes she was forced to make do with. She grew up in the shadow of the misfortune that had befallen her family, and her youth lay in tatters. And yet she was expected to show a degree of strength and provide the support that my mother could not do without. She has kept that strength all her life. But a little less pressure and a little more happiness in those days would have done no harm.

Interrogation – The Strategy and the Tactics

Since Aabenraa, I had felt myself to be the leader of the group and had a responsibility for damage control. Given the background of the invasion and liberation we were all hoping for – too soon, as it turned out – I decided to adopt the following strategy and tactics: play for time, admit to things they have evidence for, but not until it was really necessary, do not confess to the guilt of others, unless the person concerned was known to be safely in Sweden.

I realized that the more the whole matter could be kept within bounds, the smaller the risk would be that more members of our group would be arrested. It was therefore imperative to try to make sure that the interrogation of my colleagues came to an end and that Neuhaus would concentrate on me, which was achieved when I admitted to being the leader of the group. There was no great sacrifice involved in taking on the role of scapegoat. I knew that the Gestapo recognized me from my sabotage at B&W, which would inevitably be punished by the death sentence. Whether I was condemned to death for one or more acts of sabotage made very little difference. But I hoped that the Germans would be satisfied with one death sentence, or just a few, and allow those who had merely been "beguiled" to get away with life imprisonment.

My mother's information about who had been arrested and who was in Sweden was invaluable. Furthermore, it would soon become evident that the fact I spoke German was a great advantage. Where I was most at a disadvantage was the fact that I did not know whether Klaus, Flemming and Salling had admitted to taking part in the operations at B&W and Aabenraa. Georg Jansen's "confessions" included these two operations, so there was no problem there. Interrogation took place, often twice daily, for twenty-five days in a row. This was quite drawn out, but my tactic worked. I can claim, with a certain amount of satisfaction, that not one more arrest was made on the basis of these interrogation sessions.

March 7. I was taken to the German hospital where I was X-rayed. The examination confirmed my suspicions that I had suffered a minor fracture of the skull and a fracture of the lower part of one of my neck vertebrae. The wounded warrior could therefore be subjected to the rest of the Gestapo treatment without further medical restrictions.

March 8. I was driven by car to Aabenraa to visit the spot where I had been arrested. The Gestapo agents spent a long time searching the ditch where Klaus and I had hidden, and to my great annoyance, they found a hand grenade. I spent the night in Aabenraa in a very small cell, which reminded me of a medieval dungeon.

March 10. I noted down in my pocket diary that I met Flemming, Salling and Jansen. Neuhaus was, of course, present and the aim of this meeting was to finalize the preliminary investigation. I noticed that Flemming was suffering from jaundice, which worried me a lot.

The same day, Elsebet got a new cellmate. This was the wife of Police Commissioner Grunnet, who had been seized by the Gestapo along with her husband, just as they were returning home from a funeral. In the evening Mrs. Grunnet started to complain of severe pain in the stomach. Elsebet spent the whole night trying to get the medical orderly to come from the Danish section of the Vestre Fængsel, as she thought that Mrs. Grunnet was suffering from appendicitis. The Germans thought she was pretending and did not call an ambulance until the morning. By that time, Mrs. Grunnet was at death's door.

March 13. I admitted to taking part in eight acts of sabotage. I do not remember all of them, but I could not avoid confessing to Aabenraa and B&W, while Varde Steelworks was not even mentioned. Flemming, Salling and Jansen admitted to taking part in the B&W operation.

March 16. To my great annoyance, I got a new cellmate, code-named

Johansen. I was automatically suspicious, and soon found out that he had made a deal with the Gestapo. They were now seeking information about Flammen.

John

As part of the continuing interrogation, I was confronted with John. My diary entry for *Wednesday, March 22* states, "Visit to Svend."

It was Neuhaus who fetched me. He presumably hoped to obtain new information about my cooperation with John. When he locked me in John's cell, he said: "He will perhaps say some unpleasant things about me, but you have to remember that he shot my best friend."

John after torture in Vestre Fængsel

John was still bedridden. When he knew we were alone, he shook my hand, gave a slight smile and then whispered, "Speak softly, I'm sure they're listening." I then whispered back, telling him how things stood. He asked me who had been arrested and what I knew about Finn and the rest of the group. Then he took my hand again and said, "You can't imagine how unhappy I was to see you in here." After a short pause, he began to tell me what had happened to him. His story about what had happened at Triangeln on December 9, 1943, agreed with the statement I managed to get hold of after the war. But this was the first time I had heard it. What happened after he had been arrested, only the Gestapo and he knew. But this is what he said:

He had been taken to Dagmarhus where he was put on a cold floor with seven bullet wounds. One bullet had broken his right thigh bone. A

German doctor declared that he had only a couple of hours to live and he was handed over to Falkenberg and Neuhaus. Neuhaus opened the conversation by saying that he most certainly was going to die for a capital offense, so it would be better to unburden himself now. As this appeared not to make any impression on John, the torture began.

> First they kicked my broken leg as hard as they could. I never knew that the pain could be so great. Then they twisted my lower leg outwards, so it almost stood at right angles to its normal position. You cannot imagine how I yelled. Then they stopped for a moment and began to ask me questions again. As I kept on denying everything, they started to torture me all over again. I ended up losing consciousness, but they poured a bucket of cold water over me, I regained consciousness and then they began all over again. I only hoped I would die there and then. I lost consciousness again and at that point the interrogation ended.

John was then taken to the German hospital where his bullet wounds were dressed. They did nothing with his leg, and he went on to Vestre Fængsel. When he had come to this point in his story he was lying motionless in bed and looked up at the ceiling helplessly. He then turned his face towards me. With a little, proud smile he said, "They didn't get anything out of me."

Then he drew back the covers and showed me his injured leg. It was somewhat shorter than the other. The lower bone was pulled up about four inches (10 cm) alongside the broken thighbone and poked out of the skin. The break was still very painful, so even slight movements caused great distress. If his leg had been put right and bandaged, the pain would have been considerably less. But they had told him that it was not worth it "as you'll be shot anyway." You could feel a bullet under the skin of one hip; it rolled under your fingertips. The other bullet wounds seemed to have healed and were not causing him much pain. He pulled the covers back over him and continued his story:

> They took me to Vestre Fængsel and I was put in a one-man cell. I could not move. No one was given permission to take me to the toilet. So I tried to wash, using the soup they had given me for dinner. In order to reduce my bowel movements, I stopped eating. I had, in any case,

no appetite. But at length the mattress and blanket became so soiled that there was a terrible stench in the cell. The German doctor refused to come into the cell and nobody was allowed to open the window. I lay there like that for a month before the prisoners in the kitchen unit were allowed to help me.

Silence fell again in the cell. For the first month after John's detention, I had not known what had happened to him. Now I did. Only three months previously, he and I had taken part in the same sabotage operation. This seemed like an eternity ago to me, and I could not imagine what it felt like to him. I was, of course, deeply shocked by the story of suffering I had just heard and it therefore was a little while before I asked him what things had been like after that first harsh month. He had shared a cell for a short while with Henry. We both agreed that he was not to be trusted and although being alone had become a torment for John, he was nevertheless glad to avoid having Henry present. John was now washed, and was carried to the toilet once a day.

I asked him whether there had been more interrogation. He smiled proudly and broadly and said, "No, they've given up trying to get anything out of me." Then his face fell and he added, "I don't think I could stand any more interrogation."

Now it was John's turn to ask me, and I told him that it was Falkenberg and Neuhaus who were interrogating us and he said, with worry on his face, "Yes, they were also the ones who interrogated me." Silence again fell. He then seized my hand and said pleadingly, "I'd so like to go outside and get a breath of fresh air," and he added, "Please come again if you can."

My diary entry says: "After we had talked for half an hour, Neuhaus opened the door of the cell and entered with his eternal jovial grin. I had to stop myself from attacking him."

On March 29 and 30, Neuhaus needed my services as interpreter during the final interrogation of Jansen and Klaus, respectively. Klaus and I were interrogated together at Dagmarhus. When things slowed down a bit as Klaus's contribution to the final report was dictated, Neuhaus interrupted and said to me: "*Machst du es; du weisst ja alles davon* (You do it yourself; you know the whole story, after all)." I did not need to be told twice and so it was only me who was left as "case still open."

I requested Neuhaus to let me be transferred to John's cell, but received no answer. On Saturday, April 1, my fortunes changed as I was put in the kitchen squad, as what the Germans termed the *Kalfaktor*. This was undoubtedly done on orders from Neuhaus. At first, I felt this to be a great privilege, but later I was to realize that it was all part of the search for Flammen. The kitchen squad busied itself with washing the stairs and corridors and taking the meals to the various cells. The head of the kitchen was one Captain Olstrup, and he gave me the job of regularly taking John to the toilet once a day. This gave me the opportunity to talk to him and smuggle books, tobacco and a little extra food to him. My existence had taken on new meaning and it became easier for me to stand up to the daily interrogation sessions, to which no end seemed in sight.

My diary says that on Monday, April 10, I spoke with the medical orderly about whether it would be possible to take John out into the exercise yard for a while. The orderly, who was quite a decent fellow, answered that he could not give permission for me to do so, but had nothing against it. I therefore went to the head of the watch and told him that the "doctor" had said that John should be allowed out for exercise, along with the kitchen squad. The head of the watch then gave me permission without asking Meister, the prison governor. To my great surprise, this was allowed for fifteen days running, until April 26, when John was sentenced to death.

So, on Tuesday, April 11, we carried him out into the exercise yard where I spent three quarters of an hour with him in the blazing sunshine. I have never seen anyone enjoy the sunshine and the fresh air so intensely. John had been an open-air person and during his youth in the forest at Rold Skov, he had enjoyed good health and had plenty of contact with nature. For him, invalidity and detention were twice as hard to bear as for many other people. Forty-five minutes sitting on a stool in the prison yard was hardly any substitute for the life he had led, but no one could have been more grateful.

During the next few days, I received permission to carry him out into the yard several times. His whole mood seemed to improve and he began to talk about both the past and the future. I now learned that his real name was Svend Otto Nielsen and that he had been born on August 29, 1908. His father had been steward at Rold Skov, and it was there he had grown up, along with his brother Knud. Like their father, both lads were keen hunters. When he was going to hunt with his father he would have to get up very early. When it took too long for the boys to get up, it was not uncommon for their father to fire a shot in through the open window to their bedroom upstairs.

In the police report it states that John had said he had wanted to become an officer in the commercial navy, but he had to give up that idea on account of illness and had instead taken a degree as a teacher at the Ranum Seminarium. He had done his military service in the navy. From 1934 onwards, he had had a full-time job as a teacher of mathematics in the middle school and secondary school in Skovshoved, which I visited on several occasions after the war, to tell the pupils about John. There is an attractive memorial plaque to John at the school, and he is remembered not only as the lonely freedom fighter but also as a very popular teacher, who warned his pupils against dictatorships at every available opportunity. When he was sitting there in the prison yard at Vestre Fængsel, he talked a lot about his pupils. He liked children and had a three-year-old daughter, Kirsten, whom he missed a lot.

While he would tell me a lot about his happy childhood, he was more reticent about his marriage to Grethe. After John had been arrested, Grethe took Kirsten to Sweden and was for that reason in no position to be of any support to him during his detention. One – maybe more – of his friends had brought him clean clothes and extra food as soon as they had the opportunity to do so. This meant a great deal to him. During the first spell at Vestre Fængsel, he not only suffered from the physical pain of his wounds and mistreatment, but also from the loneliness and the feeling that everybody had abandoned him. He was glad when he realized that he was not forgotten.

During our talks, his zest for life began to gradually return. His right leg still hurt a little, but in general his physical condition had improved. He had not admitted to being a saboteur, and the German doctor had told him that he would not be condemned to death for the murder of the Gestapo agent, as he had acted in self-defense. He clung to this hope, though he did not entirely believe what had been said. He wondered why the Germans had not executed him long ago, but had the right answer to his own question: "They are waiting for the day they can avenge the sabotage operations; then they'll shoot us." John really wanted to live. But he did not want the acts of sabotage to stop.

The many, often false, rumors that circulated in the prison gave us slight hope and we were keen to convince ourselves that liberation was about to take place. During such conversations, we would speculate about what would happen when Germany was defeated. John's biggest worry was about his health in years to come. I tried to convince him that he would walk again. He was glad at that, and we began to plan our holidays in a cabin in the Norwegian fells. But despite all the beautiful dreams for the future, we both still retained a good dose of Jutland skepticism: "No, Jørgen, let's look the truth in the face. They're going to shoot us. If you play for time, maybe you stand a chance – I don't." And the sad look returned to his face, which only moments before was so radiant in its hope for a vacation in Norway after the war.

The light of hope and the darkness of his inklings struggled in his mind. This struggle seemed clear enough to me, and also that his sense of realism had gained the upper hand. Gradually, his optimism receded, and he would begin to talk more often about his execution as inevitable. He was very sober about this and would ask me, "How can they tie me to a pole – I can't even stand up." He listened to the rumors of an Allied invasion with justified skepticism, although he was convinced that Germany would ultimately be defeated. When we now talked about the time after the war, he often gave the impression that he was pessimistic about the chances of the Resistance getting the better of politicians who had collaborated with the enemy. He was not unhappy about the fact that he personally would be spared such a defeat. On the other hand, he never regretted for one moment his participation in Resistance activities – for him it had been a necessity were he to keep his ideals.

We did not spend very many hours together out there in the prison yard, but it felt like a lifetime. Despite the grim future that was awaiting us, we made many jocular remarks and quite often he would even laugh a little, when he remembered a funny episode from his childhood.

Hitler's birthday, April 20, 1944, was celebrated by the liquidation of two people who had collaborated with the Gestapo. On the twenty-second, we heard of an attack that had taken place on German soldiers. Three days later, there was unrest in Copenhagen, and eleven Danish freedom fighters were brought back to Denmark from their prison in Schwerin, Germany. I knew that there were going to be reprisals in the form of executions and that John's turn had come.

April 23. Neuhaus took some time off. But there was no reason to relax.

The next day, Johansen, with whom I had shared a cell, was freed by the Gestapo for helping in their hunt for Flammen, while I was moved to Cell 186 where I had a cellmate I can remember nothing about; I was too taken up at the time with John's impending fate and the treachery committed by Johansen. The same day, a total ban on reading and smoking was instituted in the prison. It was obvious that something was afoot, and there were rumors that one of us was going to be executed. This is confirmed by the notes I made in my diary:

> There are said to have been street protests in Copenhagen. John has been forcibly shaved and he is said to be being moved to another part of the prison. We talked about this in the toilets. The other members of the kitchen squad tried to console him with the fact that all of this meant nothing. Now that we were alone, the mask fell. John had grown calm. The nervousness was gone, as he knew what was in store for him. "If only we could be shot together," he said and pressed my hand. Then we took him back to his cell.

During our time in the prison yard on April 26, John was reasonably calm. We no longer talked about what would happen after the war, as we had done earlier. Nor did we talk about the hunting we would be doing with his brother Knud up in Rold Skov. Nor about trips to the fells in Norway or Sweden. We talked about the execution: *"How will they be able to shoot me if I can't even stand? Do you hear the bang and feel the bullet go in?"*

When we brought him back to his cell, Falkenberg was standing along with another Gestapo agent in the guardroom. For one moment, John became nervous. "Hurry up and get me into bed, I want to be in bed when they come for me," he said. It was as if he wanted to make his life last a minute or two longer; but there they were. John nodded towards Falkenberg and whispered, "It was him, Falkenberg, who tortured me." I managed to shake his hand; then I was thrown out of his cell. Before my own cell door was shut, I saw Falkenberg and his colleague carrying John out of the prison. At 11:30 I heard him return. From his letters, we know that he was condemned to death by the ss court.

It became an endless night for both myself and him. *"How can they tie me to a pole if I can't even stand up? Will I be able to hear the bang and feel the bullet go in?"* I had not been able to answer his questions. The only experience I had had with bullets was from Aabenraa. I did not hear the bang, and did not feel the bullet go in. But there were also so many other things I had had on my mind, as I lay in the ditch with Klaus in Styrtom.

John's suffering went through my mind and burned itself into my consciousness. I remember it as if it were yesterday. At 5:30 the next morning, April 27, I heard the barred door at the main entrance to the prison open and studded boots walking across the terrazzo floor. It sounded like a whole regiment, and I heard the rattle of chains. I wondered whether they needed so many men to shoot one saboteur. Then I heard the voice of the prison commandant and the rattle of keys. Shortly afterwards, I heard them carrying him past my cell door. Then the barred door at the entrance was opened and slammed shut again. The pounding of boots ceased. A car engine was switched on, then all was silence. *"How can they tie me to a pole if I can't even stand up?"* I didn't know for certain, but that was probably what the chains were going to be used for. At any rate I now realized that I would never see John ever again.

Later that morning, I received the opportunity to peep into John's cell in my capacity as food orderly and saw, on the table there, a plate of sandwiches. Next to it lay a cigar. Both were untouched. John had had more important things to think about, as can be seen from his farewell letter to his mother, his brother and sister-in-law, and to his wife Grethe and daughter Kirsten. I first saw this letter after the war. It provided me with new information, but changed nothing of what I had myself experienced at the time. During the period from March 22 to April 27, my life was completely taken up with my friendship with John – my admiration for him, my sympathy and hope that I would be able to live up to his example, should it ever be necessary to do so. For the rest of my life, I have lived with the memories of those thirty-six days and when, after the war, I had a need for serious reflection, solace, moral support or inspiration to take my life risks, I have time and time again returned alone to his grave in the Mindelunden cemetery in Ryvangen.

Just like me, John had entered the spirit of Free Denmark's cross-party political stance, without harboring any illusions that this would have much influence on the politics of Denmark after the Second World War. He did not imagine there would be a Communist revolution once Germany was defeated, but had his reservations about whether Denmark would be free of the Russians. So one had to be prepared for a régime shift. But he thought it would be most likely that the old political parties, and many of the old politicians, would return to power.

But neither he nor I could imagine that Buhl, who had encouraged Danes to become informers on behalf of the Germans, would become prime minister in a post-liberation government. But we were satisfied at having made our modest contribution to the defeat of Hitler which we, at the time, thought was imminent. We were sad about the fact that we would not live to experience it, but we were agreed that the victory of a humanist way of thinking over inhumane tyranny was worth the price. And we also agreed that we would do it all over again, should the need ever arise.

On April 28, when Elsebet was on her way to the exercise yard, I kicked her shin gently in passing and whispered: "Many greetings from John. He was shot yesterday." And so, April 1944 came to an end.

Kalfaktor and *Kachiber*

What I remember from April 1944 is of course dominated by what happened to John, but there were other things that had made an impression on me. One of the happier moments was a visit by Elsebet on April 3 and 4. It was very encouraging to see how determined and brave she was. I cannot say it surprised me, but I was happy, as I shared some of the responsibility for what had happened to her.

My other important task was being a *Kalfaktor*. The dictionary tells us that this is the German word for any prisoner who does work around the prison, even informers. I was already experienced enough with prison life by now to anticipate that the kitchen squad would be crawling with informers, something which Olstrup confirmed to me. He later became a fellow prisoner in Neuengamme and Porta Westphalica. He did not survive the war.

In the case of prisoners involved in the same case, it was of vital importance that they could exchange information about who had been arrested and what they had admitted to. Such communication in prison consisted of chance and fleeting exchanges during visits to the toilet, short notes written on the walls of the exercise yard, where we were allowed to walk around twice a day for half an hour at a time, plus by way of Morse code by tapping on the water pipes.

None of these methods were, however, of as great importance as working in the kitchen. Olstrup introduced me to the illegal internal postal service. We soon came to trust one another and agreed that if I could set up communication between the cells and the kitchen, he would set up a link with the outside world. I could not see how he was going to do this, but an agreement with a German soldier seemed the best chance we had.

I possessed three important qualifications for being such a postman. I could speak German and could therefore start chatting to the warders at the cell door in order to allow time for messages to be passed while they were distracted. I also had a large hole in the lining of my jacket, and I finally convinced the German *Sanitäter* (medical orderly) and the guard that white bread, which was regarded as special diet food, could only be handed out by people with medical competence such as a student of medicine like myself. Many messages can be hidden in a loaf of bread and as nothing went to waste, the return message was also guaranteed thus. The very next day after my conversation with Olstrup, I started my new job as postman and in so doing became friendly with Olstrup. So many prisoners in Vestre Fængsel have this friendship to thank. One of the first people I got in contact with by way of my job as postman was my own sister Elsebet, who has the following to say:[77]

Like everyone else, I was very afraid of revealing anything about other people that could do them harm. The constant threat I was under from the Gestapo was that if I did not tell them things, perhaps mother and Lida would also be arrested. One thing I note from my journal is that during that time I now began to believe in the existence of a guardian angel – for the first time in my life. I felt protected during interrogation and it helped with the moral issues I was having to face: thou shalt not lie... But there was also the matter of solidarity with my colleagues; their lives and deaths would depend on it. So again a great conflict arose in me.

One thing that helped me colossally was when Jørgen came to visit me unexpectedly. I had caught a glimpse of Flemming on an upper floor when we were both going back after exercise. He looked pale and had grown a beard. But Jørgen suddenly turned up at my cell door along with a German soldier and delivered diet bread to me from the Red Cross. It was Palm Sunday, April 2. He must have thought up the ruse himself, as I had not asked for any diet bread. As I sank my teeth into it gratefully, I found that it was hollow. Inside lay a farewell letter from Jørgen. He was counting on a death sentence. The next day he was there again and asked me professionally for the end crust of the loaf so he could give me a new one. I now understood that he had set up a postbox for me too.

Meanwhile, I suddenly received a proper visit from him in my cell. On April 4 he was locked in with me for the evening. And we were left alone. We sat on the iron bed, side by side, and could speak freely. I need not mention that I was happy to see him! This visit also meant a lot for setting right information about things I had been trying to piece together at the time, so I came to know what the boys had been up to, who was dead, who had fled, who was in prison. This was of invaluable help, although I did understand that things had reached a point I could never have dreamed of. For those in prison, there was not much that could be saved.

Why Don't You People Cry?

After eight members of the Hvidsted group had been fetched for execution, the German warder asked Elsebet: "Why don't you people cry? That's what they do in every other country, when people are taken for execution."

Elsebet hardly had an answer on the tip of her tongue. But she was in no doubt that those who were about to die felt it was better to die for a just cause than to live for injustice, violence and oppression. One of those who did not cry was Georg Quistgaard, who had meant something special to me. The day before Georg's execution, Olstrup had told me that Georg had written a prison diary, which he would like to get smuggled out of the prison. I was asked if I could arrange this, and I said I was willing to try. As we approached his cell as breakfast was being served, I told the warder that I had been given half a loaf for the condemned man. Then I stood back a little, so that the food trolley reached the next cell before the door to Georg's cell was closed. This offered me the opportunity to whisper to my unknown friend, "There's a message in the loaf."

We hardly caught a glimpse of one another. I moved on, so that the warder would not suspect anything, and the door to Georg's cell was slammed shut. The message was a brief instruction to hide his diary in the loaf and give it back to me next time the food came around. That evening, when it was mealtime again, I told the warder that white bread had been allowed for the cell next to Georg's, and so I managed to join in distributing the food in the part of the prison where Georg was waiting for his execution. When the door to his cell was opened, I pointed out to the warder that the prisoner had not eaten his bread, which, given the circumstances, was quite understandable. He also agreed with me that I should take the loaf back, as in wartime you never wasted anything, and so, as planned, I took the half loaf.

Not many moments of my life have made such an impression on me as those few seconds during which the loaf changed hands. The tall young man who towered over me seemed even taller. He seemed to fill the whole cell. He looked at me with a friendly, serious and very clear gaze. It was the noble calm before the fate awaiting him that struck me so forcibly. He radiated authority and there I stood, with his most precious thoughts hidden in a half loaf of white bread. I thought to myself: If you can behave in this way when your time comes, you will have nothing to be ashamed of.

We looked one another right in the eye and I had to hurry on so that no one would notice. This demanded a great amount of self-composure. I did not sleep that night. I knew they were going to come for him at around five in the morning, but where were they going to shoot our people? Would we have to dig our own graves? Is the coffin standing ready, or will they just shoot us down on the bare earth? Will we receive a blindfold?

I wondered what was written in his diary and whether it had been smuggled out safely. My job was over, once I had delivered the loaf to Olstrup. Georg's diary was published after the war. Many years after the war was over, his mother and sister found out that I had helped smuggle the diary out and they wrote a wonderful letter to me back in 1963. At the same time, they sent me an extra copy of the diary that Mrs. Quistgaard, eighty years old by then, had kept.

I accepted it with gratitude, wrote back to thank her, but then laid the little book aside without reading it. Both the interest and the desire to read it were present, but I lacked the courage. The memory of Georg Quistgaard was fixed in my mind and I was afraid that this image would be disturbed. Sooner or later I would have to read it and in 1980, when I was collecting together source material to produce our joint story, entitled "Story of a Resistance Group," I finally plucked up the courage to read it. When I had read it, I was happy to find that the diary in no way altered the picture I had formed in my memory, but to the contrary, it affirmed and strengthened it. This was not only a memoir filled with courage, dignity and authority, but also showed the literary talent of the author, whose loss Denmark mourned. Today, I feel it a privilege to have contributed to saving these valuable thoughts for posterity.

On May 29, my period of kitchen service came to an abrupt end. An informer had told the chief warder, who proceeded to search my person. He found the hole in my lining, but no letters. My cell was also searched, but in vain. Nevertheless, a report was drawn up and sent to Dagmarhus, stating that I was to be regarded thenceforth as a suspicious person – termed a *Kachiber* in German. I do not know how many letters I had managed to smuggle, but I received many whispered words of thanks. I do not think the message about my dubious loyalty reached Neuhaus, so the storm that I felt was brewing did not break. But that was the end of my time in the kitchen and the penultimate act of the drama of my stay at Vestre Fængsel was about to begin.

Everyday Life in Hotel Vestre Gefängnis

My mother's (and Hitler's) birthday fell on April 20 and was "celebrated" with an interrogation session at Dagmarhus concerning Free Denmark. I cannot remember precisely what the questions centered around. But I do remember one little episode. When the interrogation was over, Neuhaus took me into an adjacent office where he asked me to wait a short while. I was now alone and could not help noticing an ID card that was lying on the desk in front of me. The name on it meant nothing to me, but the photo was of Trunte – one of my colleagues in Free Denmark. Obviously, my first instinct was to snatch up the ID card and swallow it. But luckily, I realized that this might be a trap, so I pretended I had not noticed anything. Neuhaus stayed away for a good ten minutes, but gave up in the end. After that, I was no longer interrogated on the subject of Free Denmark.

That day was a good one for Bente and Elsebet, as Bente was transferred to Elsebet's cell, where she stayed until she was released on May 23. She had by then shared a cell with several people whom Elsebet described later as being somewhat on the insane side. The mistrust of her cellmates and the fear of revealing anything that could harm others had put a great strain on her. A painful inflammation of the bladder did not make her life any easier either. She had been sent to Neuhaus for interrogation on April 1 and 6, and seemed now to no longer be of interest to the Gestapo.

The weather during May 1944 was wonderful. This I experienced through the bars of my cell and in the exercise yard. I also noticed this during my daily trip to Dagmarhus for interrogation, which also gave me the opportunity of seeing some of Copenhagen. The city seemed so near, yet so incredibly far away. I would sit on the back seat of an ordinary car along with one or two Gestapo agents. Sometimes there were traffic problems and then the Germans would swing out to the left or right of the road. On a couple of occasions I pointed out that they were violating traffic regulations, upon which they swore they would get the rules in this ridiculous little country changed, because now they were in charge here. On one occasion, I asked them why they had not stayed home, if conditions here were so terrible. It looked as if I was going to get my ears boxed, so I remained silent after that. Clearly, the Master Race were in control. God, how I hated them. But I was able to control myself, as I knew that their days were numbered.

But ours were too. Despite this fact we tried to look on the bright side, which was expressed, for instance, in a letter I managed to have smuggled to my father out at Horserød. In it I wrote the following:

Dear Father,

At last I have the opportunity to send you greetings. I think a lot about you and am glad that you are as well as can be expected under the circumstances. We are also OK, though it is not very pleasant that there are so many executions. One of those who was executed was a friend of mine (John). The future is uncertain, but we are optimistic. Elsebet and Bente will not be brought before a court, and they are maybe already on their way to Horserød with this letter. Flemming and I are expecting to be sentenced in the near future. We will both probably be condemned to death, but I have received news from Dagmarhus that such a sentence will not be carried out...

This was wish fulfillment on my part and meant as words of comfort. I could also tell him the glad news that Flemming no longer had an inflammation of the liver, nor Bente her bladder inflammation. I had no major trouble with my bullet wounds, but did have some sciatica, as I have ever since.

At the same time as Johansen was installed in my cell on March 16, the hunt for Flammen began. Neuhaus asked me on one occasion if I had recognized Flammen during my time working in the kitchen. He was clearly counting on the fact that Flammen was already under arrest, but not yet identified. But there he was wrong. Johansen did not try to pump me for information as Henry had done. Instead, he tried to convince me, and perhaps especially even himself, that it would be right to condemn Flammen as a mass murderer, to whom one need not be loyal. I could, obviously, give him no support in this area. But I did not want to reveal anything about Flammen, either. It was clear to me that Johansen was a nervous wreck, in fear for his life. I never did ask him about what he had done in the Resistance, nor was he very forthcoming. He was not tortured but was afraid he might be executed. He was undergoing the growing pains of a Resistance man who had become an informer.

On April 24, he told me he had been granted leave of absence, after having sworn an oath that he would return. This explanation seemed quite incredible. But I was pretty sure I knew what lay behind it. The hunt for Flammen had run into difficulties and the Gestapo needed a man out there in the field. What made me wonder was the fact that to all appearances he himself believed this story about his word of honor. The explanation can be sought in his military background. I began to think desperately about how I could get a message out to warn Flammen. But knowing the Vestre Fængsel prison as I now did, and that it was crawling with informers, I saw no other way than simply to spread the rumor that they were hunting for Flammen in the hope that the warning would be passed on by one or another of the prisoners who were set free. I knew neither Flammen's real name nor where he was, and I could not make use of our contact address on a street named Farimagsgade.

On May 3, Johansen returned from his wonderful leave of absence. We were again put together in Cell 69, which I shared with him right up to August 24. He told me nothing about what he had been doing during those nine days of freedom. But the Gestapo had not yet caught Flammen.

When Neuhaus returned from his own leave on May 4, a long series of interrogation sessions began. These centered around details of our sabotage operations, about our activities in the underground press, but most specifically about Flammen. The hunt so far had been in vain, and in desperation the Gestapo had begun to arrest any red-haired young men they happened to see on the street. These would be put in a lineup and I would be asked whether I recognized any of them. I did not and so ultimately I was no longer interrogated about Flammen.

The Bill Is Presented

Saturday, May 13. I wrote in my diary: "Was taken to visit Standartenführer Bovensiepen. Saw Ebba and boyfriend on Raadhuspladsen. Execution in the offing."

Seeing Ebba and her fiancé Søren, as I was being taken to Dagmarhus, made a deep impression on me. They did not see me, and I had, of course, to keep as quiet as a mouse. At Dagmarhus, I had to wait a while for Bovensiepen who, like Neuhaus, had just returned from Germany where they had been to arrange a new visit by the ss tribunal to Copenhagen, in order to sentence us. Bovensiepen was as cold as ice and simply stated briefly that we had been condemned to death and that our execution would depend on whether or not the acts of sabotage ceased.

Neuhaus tried to comfort me saying that it could be quite some while before the ss tribunal arrived in Copenhagen and first a counsel for the defense would be appointed, who would have time to study our case. He had definitely begun to sympathize with us, and this was also the impression that Schlanbusch had received. Schlanbusch also said that I had a long talk with Pancke, which ended with Pancke saying: "Yes, Mr. Kieler, I have begun to sympathize with you a good deal, so I am sorry that I will have to have you executed." I do not myself remember that conversation. But it could well have been Flemming instead who was talking to Pancke.

Neuhaus's secretary was also put out by the fact that we would be executed. "*Du muss schön reden, Jørgen* (You must make a good case for yourself)," is what she said, and Neuhaus put in his oar when he asked me what I would answer if the tribunal asked me what I would do if I were set free. He shook his head when I replied that I would try to get in touch with the Resistance again in order to continue the struggle, little knowing that a few minutes later I would be taken at my word.

The interrogation had finished and Neuhaus took me down to the car that was waiting outside Dagmarhus. There was no chauffeur, nor was there a sentry at the door. Neuhaus told me to go and sit in the car and wait a little while he fetched the chauffeur. So there I was, sitting in the car unguarded. My first instinct was, of course, that this would be a marvelous opportunity

to run away and rejoin the Resistance. My next thought was that this was
a trap, which would help to lead them to Flammen. My final, and decisive,
thought was that if I now escaped, my friends at Vestre Fængsel would
most certainly be executed. So I remained seated and waited for Neuhaus
to return some twenty minutes later. I had pleasant thoughts about Ebba
as we drove back to Vestre Fængsel.

It gave me great strength to be able, on May 20, to meet my two sisters and Flemming. I urged the authorities to set Bente free, as did Elsebet. Three days later, I noted happily in my pocket diary: "Bente out after
a word with Neuhaus." And with her I could smuggle my last letter to my
father at Horserød:

Dear Father,

A thousand thanks for all your greetings. This is the latest news
from the front. *Bente has been released*, which brings us all great joy. She
has done her duty and was only kept back because she refused to say
anything about us. Our case is nearly at an end. We have been waiting
for a fortnight now to go to court. But partly because of the complications of our case, and partly for reasons I don't understand, they've spun
the whole matter out, which is obviously something I'm glad about. You
are to go to court with us and I have looked for you every time there has
been a transport from Horserød. Even though I would very much like
to see you again, I breathe a sigh of relief that you are still at Horserød.
Our case will be a long one. I reckon there will be ten death sentences.
Whether or not we are executed will depend on the situation in the city
and the whole country. I am an optimist in these matters, and I ask you
to be, too. Should things go wrong, we will have to take it like men, in
the knowledge that we are dying for a just cause.

Otherwise everything is OK. Elsebet and Flemming are keeping
a stiff upper lip. But the many executions do put a certain strain on
the atmosphere in here… We live in a little world, surrounded by bars
and grilles. But life is large here too. You just have to live your life as a
human being, shut everything else out. You see your friends as a shining example, a light that will suddenly be extinguished by ten bullets.
But then a miracle happens. The light fades, but a glow remains in our
eyes. On the other side, a total collapse can also be seen. You get to
know people in here. If I escape with my life, this will be an experi-

ence I would not have wished to have been without for anything… I promise you that whatever the future may hold, I will accept it with my head held high. Our cause can never die.

A thousand greetings…

It is clear that the letter was written under the powerful impression I received by meeting both Georg Quistgaard and Johansen. It is also a final act in my work for the Resistance. Apart from the blows I had received during my arrest in Aabenraa, I had not suffered physical abuse during my imprisonment in Denmark. And yet the endless interrogation sessions at Dagmarhus and my work as a courier of messages in Vestre Fængsel felt like a continuation of the struggle, which now had as its chief aim to prevent the Gestapo from inflicting further losses on the Resistance movement. But now I had become a mere hostage.

What happened to Bente immediately after she was released I know fairly little about. But after the war she did tell me that she was released by Neuhaus from Vestre Fængsel and that the few confiscated possessions she had had with her on arrest were returned. So there she stood out on the street with just enough money to buy a bus ticket to Valby where she asked to stay the night with our old grandmother, who immediately phoned Horsens with the glad news. My mother and Lida then traveled to Copenhagen to be reunited with Bente, and they traveled on together to Aalsgaarde, where they lived for about four weeks near to Horserød, where my father was kept all that summer.

After my conversation with Bovensiepen at Dagmarhus, I returned to Vestre Fængsel to prepare for death. The end would not be a surprise. The "preparations" had been made long before, but there was an amount of tension present nonetheless as my function as a member of the Resistance had come to an end, and my life as a hostage had begun; now my fate rested in the hands of others. It would have been a great defeat for me if the acts of sabotage were to cease on account of hostages. I was prepared to pay the ultimate price, as Peer and John had done, but I did not feel myself to be a martyr. I had done the best I could to deserve this fate and I would have despised myself if it had been any different. So it was not so dramatic for me to now be playing the role of hostage as I was luckily not an *innocent* victim of German terror, but of course my situation did give me food for thought.

I was young, not even twenty-five years of age, and no doubt felt I was too young to die. I really wanted to live long enough to see Hitler defeated and would have liked to have started a family of my own. But first and foremost I felt that I had not managed to thank my parents sufficiently for their love and protection that they had given my brother, sisters and me during our childhood. On the other hand, I drew consolation from the fact that if my experiences rather than the number of years were taken into account, I had perhaps lived long enough. I had met so many people I had liked and had no need to meet more whom I did not. During the preceding months, as a kind of culmination to all this, I had had the great privilege of joining a group that confirmed my ethical principles which, without the support of religious belief, had become an important part of my worldview. I did not need to believe in an eternal life. But it was nevertheless with satisfaction that I thought about the fact that the ideals I had fought for would not end with the bullets of the firing squad.

Although I was clear about the hopeless situation in which I now found myself, I did not entirely abandon a rather unusual brand of optimism. If the long-awaited invasion should come in time for me to be saved, this would be quite a sensible thing, as I would have prepared myself pretty thoroughly for my final examinations in medicine. So, during my "spare time" at Vestre Fængsel, I studied for my exams. There was a thorough description of the functioning of the heart in my pharmacology textbook. I was well prepared for execution.

The concern within the walls of the prison was reflected on the outside. I was deeply moved after the war when I found out that our fellow medical students had pleaded with the German authorities to pardon us. Bishop Fuglsang Damgaard had also written a request to Best to let forgiveness take precedence over justice, and a letter was sent by my mother to the same addressee asking for clemency.

My immediate reaction after the war was that I wished these pleas had never been sent. But on further thought, I had to recognize that our lives are not only our own, but belong to all of those whom we love, and so these others may share ownership. And today I am deeply moved by these pleas to save my life. Nonetheless, I could not have written them myself.

The Tactic Wins
"If you play for time, maybe you stand a chance – I don't" were some of John's last words to me. The chance was there, since rumors of an invasion of

northern France by the Allies were circulating in our prison. On June 6 I wrote, "The British have taken Calais, Cherbourg and Le Havre." There was an excited atmosphere in Vestre Fængsel, almost one of revolt. The Germans went around swearing and slamming doors hoping to quell the "mutiny" but in vain. But we had been too optimistic and had to admit, within the space of a few days, that our own hopes had been premature.

Our optimism had its basis in the nervousness that the Germans were exhibiting. During the continuing interrogation concerning Flammen, I had the opportunity of discussing the military status quo with Neuhaus. He had expected an invasion, but assured me that quite the opposite would happen and that Germany would invade Britain from Jutland and Norway. In this context he talked about secret weapons that the Führer had promised the German people. I think this was mere wish fulfillment and that he himself doubted the veracity of the news, but I shall not deny that he had succeeded in worrying me. I myself was even more worried when we found out that our hopes of a swift collapse of the German war machine were not to be realized. Instead, there would be long, drawn-out and tough resistance from Germany. An invasion could not save us from being executed, but would in fact bring it closer. What happened the following days and weeks confirmed this pessimism and this can be seen from what I wrote in my pocket diary, which told of fresh executions:

Thursday, June 22. Flemming and I were given permission to celebrate his birthday by visiting Elsebet's cell, and with a visit by my mother and Lida to the new Gestapo headquarters at the Shell House. They had been brought to Copenhagen to visit us one more time – their last, by all accounts. But no tears were shed. They stayed in an abandoned flat on Kristianiagade in the Østerbro district of the city.

During their visit to Shell House, I spoke with our prosecutor, who regretted the fact that he had to ask for the death penalty. I too regretted this. But there seemed to be no way around it. That same day, according to my diary jottings, the Industry Combine building was blown up, and in revenge eight members of the Resistance from Aars were executed the following day.

Saturday, June 24. We received news that courts-martial had been introduced for the island of Sjælland – which included Copenhagen – and

Neuhaus told us that we were to be sentenced on the twenty-eighth. So that was that. I talked to Kriminalrat Bunke, who mentioned the chances of a pardon. Then I went up to Bovensiepen. He thought we were idiots and that we would inevitably be shot. My diary states: "On Wednesday, the final act begins. Strange that it doesn't make a deeper impression on me." Behind this note lies the fact that I wanted to get it over with. The endless demands made during interrogation, the endless swings between hope and despair and the weight of responsibility for the lives of others were taking their toll. I hoped it would all end soon. But it did not.

The execution of the group from Aars was clearly not adequate revenge from a German point of view. On June 24 the Tivoli, the Royal Porcelain Factory, the Students' Union and the Citizens' House were all blown up by the Nazi-inclined Schalburg Corps and on the following day, a Sunday, the official German announcement was made that a curfew would be imposed from eight o'clock in the evening until five in the morning. This was the last straw. The workers at B&W organized a "Go Home Early" strike, ostensibly to cultivate their kitchen gardens to reduce food shortages. The demonstrations and street protests spread over the three days that followed to embrace the whole city, which was by that time on the brink of a popular uprising. The curfew was ignored, trolley cars were pushed on their side, streets were barricaded and the German army ridiculed.

Wednesday, June 28. My diary notes that more executions had taken place, plus the following comment:

> Should have been sentenced. Postponed on account of the disturbances. Spoke to four of the others (Flemming, Klaus, Salling and Jansen) in Flemming's cell in the presence of Neuhaus, who mentioned that the matter had been postponed until July 5, as some of the papers were not yet in order.

Since I had stopped working in the kitchen, I was badly informed about what was going on and did not therefore know who were the latest ones to be sentenced to death. But I soon found out that these were the publican Marius Fiil, his son and son-in-law, plus five other members of the Hvidsten Group. These were sentenced on June 27 and executed two days later. Marius Fiil's daughter Tulle had also been condemned to death, but the sentence was commuted to life imprisonment. Five others, including Tulle's seventeen-year-old sister Gerda, were sentenced to long prison terms. All the accused conducted themselves with great courage and dignity during the trial. "Only the interpreter wept" was one pithy comment on the trial, found in a medical report after the war.

The unrest in the city grew apace. Best tried to pour oil on troubled waters by making the evening curfew begin at eleven o'clock instead of eight o'clock, but at the same time, he, Pancke and von Hanneken started an operation termed "Monsoon." German troops from all over Denmark were sent to Copenhagen and the public utilities were occupied. As was written in my diary and elsewhere, the citizens of Copenhagen did not allow themselves to be intimidated.

The General Strike in Copenhagen

Friday, June 30. "All permission to smoke, read and write has been withdrawn. There is going to be a streetcar, telephone and railway strike."

That same evening the electricity, gas and water were shut off and on Saturday, July 1, a state of siege was proclaimed. The whole city was cut off from the outside world and German cannon and machine-gun posts were positioned on streets and squares, while at the same time German tanks and patrols started to carry out acts of terror, during the course of which 102 people were killed.

Saturday, July 1. "There is no gas, light or water in the prison. The kitchen squad have dug latrines out in the yard. There is very little food. So the rumors of a strike must be true. If only they can hold out. The warders are growing nervous."

Rumors spread quickly through the entire prison and were received with enthusiasm. We blew the water out of the syphon traps and brought the news via the water pipes to the cells on the floor above. Morse code was used between the cells and the desperate guards were no longer able to prevent us talking when we went out into the exercise yard or visited the toilet.

Mother, Bente and Lida spent the time of the strike in the flat on Kristianiagade. Like many others, they fetched water from the Sortedam Lake and there was a shortage of food. Mother was worried about our old grandmother who lived out in Valby, alone. There were neither trolleys nor local trains, so she and Lida went all the way to Valby on foot to see the elderly woman. This was not without its dangers. On account of shooting taking place, they had to seek cover in stairwells and doorways time and time again. But they arrived in Valby unscathed. They saw that, given the circumstances, grandmother was doing fine and walked all the way back to the Østerbro district of the city, where they arrived home rather exhausted, but without mishap.

The next few days in Vestre Fængsel were marked by uncertainty. My diary says:

Sunday, July 2. "Today seven people have been deported to Germany. Why didn't they shoot them?"

Monday, July 3. "Gas, water and light returns. People are still bringing street-cars to a standstill by pushing them on their sides."

On that same day, Elsebet noted the following:

> The strike was over by July 4. The water returned – and the exercise hour. On the way up from the exercise yard a woman in front of me suddenly turned her head and whispered, 'They've shot my husband, my father and my brother." I was horrified. Once up on the women's corridor, I took the opportunity to seize her arm as I passed her cell door to express my sympathy. She whispered back: "They can't do any-thing. We'll hold out!" That was Tulle Fiil.

Elsebet received the information about the executions of the Hvidsten Group from the German warders:

> One German soldier, who had been guarding the publican Marius Fiil during his last night, said that when they came for him early in the morning, Marius Fill embraced him in parting, a last merciful farewell to the enemy, whom he forgave for his part. "If I ever die such a death," the German soldier had said, "I will be satisfied."

Tulle Fiil asked Meister for permission to have Elsebet moved to the cell that she and her sister occupied. They were one cellmate short and Meister, who was a little uneasy about her state of mind, gave his permission. So

Elsebet was moved to Cell 265, the Fiils' cell, which she shared with Tulle and Gerda until they were deported to Germany on July 15.

For the days immediately following the general strike, I made two short entries:

Wednesday, July 5. "They have not come to fetch us. Why not?"

Friday, July 7. "Neuhaus was here and said that we will not be sentenced. The strike has saved us."

The executions ceased and on July 22, Elsebet was transferred to Horserød. I interpreted this as a sign that the Germans were unable to continue their terror for fear of an open revolt. We had been saved for the present, but how long would this be allowed to last? The Allies had landed in Normandy one month before, but no German capitulation had ensued. We could not follow events on the military front from our prison cells, but the rumor that an attempt had been made on Hitler's life did filter through on July 20, giving us renewed hope that the Germans were in despair about their impending fate. The rumors were confirmed during my talk with Neuhaus, but I still did not feel we were out of the woods yet.

Nor did my mother. She went to pay a visit to Neuhaus in order to get the latest information, and was told that we would be sent to a labor camp in Germany. She had no clear concept of what a concentration camp entailed, but was deeply skeptical. "So they're just going to beat them to death," was her commentary. Neuhaus said she should be satisfied that we had managed to avoid being executed. But she was not, and had good grounds not to be.

After the war, I have of course speculated a good deal why things went as they did. There were, no doubt, a number of factors that played their role here. And in order to reach a conclusion, we have to go back a little in history.

Our own efforts to save ourselves were limited to trying to play for time in the hope that there would soon be an Allied invasion. As we managed to succeed in spinning out our story during interrogation, the whole case was fused with the case against the Varde Group and therefore became of significant proportions. Our admissions also meant that long interrogation sessions were being held with eight saboteurs which, in the case of my sisters, my brother and myself, could be conducted in German, affording us the opportunity to start endless discussions with Neuhaus about the war and the moral and political questions involved. I am happy to say that the interrogation in Copenhagen did not lead to one person being arrested, and this fact is primarily thanks to my mother.

We had set our hopes on an invasion, but had no immediate influence on our own chances of survival. Neuhaus did happen to tell us that the postponement of our case from June 28 to July 5 was on account of the fact that not all the documents pertaining to the case were in order. This can be an explanation as to why the Hvidsten Group was executed before our turn came, but I am not sure of this. I suspect that Jansen's signature was lacking on the document to proceed, which is presumably on account of the fact that he did not understand German. This explanation is rather a poor one and it is more likely that Elsebet was right when she suggested that Neuhaus was trying on his part to play for time in order to save us. Another explanation could be that when our case was merged with that against the Varde Group, Chief Constable Simony and his deputies Schlanbusch and Gerner Mikkelsen risked the death penalty, which would dash any further hopes the Germans had for cooperation between the German and Danish police forces.

While it is clear that several factors contributed to our case being delayed, there cannot be any doubt that it was the general strike in Copenhagen, rather than the invasion, that saved our lives. Duckwitz tried to convince Best to be accommodating. But it was not until many years had passed after the war that I found out that the decision to postpone our execution came not from Best, but from Hitler who, on December 30, 1943, had instructed Best to combat sabotage with terror, not with trials and executions. It was not the deaths of the 102 citizens of Copenhagen that angered Hitler. It was the execution of the Hvidsten Group and twenty-one other executions which, in Hitler's eyes, were the cause of the general strike in Copenhagen. That could not go unpunished. On July 2, Best sent his report of the general strike to Berlin. This was put before Hitler, about whose reaction the German foreign minister gave Best a full report in a telegram shortly afterwards:[78]

On the basis of your report about the situation in Denmark, the Führer is most critical of your policy hitherto vis-à-vis the Danes. I request an immediate and detailed report, especially with regard to the reasons why you ignored Hitler's instruction to combat sabotage by terror alone and not by trials in the courts.

Best had to obey orders. The ss tribunal was sent back to Berlin and all sentences passed on Danish citizens were postponed. This did not, however, prevent the Gestapo from murdering Danish prisoners without charge. We remained hostages.

My twenty-fifth birthday fell on August 23, 1944. For many months preceding that day, I had not been very hopeful that I would ever reach that age, which was all the more reason to celebrate. This occurred in the shape of a visit from my mother, the last one she made to Vestre Fængsel. She spoiled me to the extent she could. The connections that the Kieler family had with the *Hotel Vestre Gefängnis* came to an end at this point. The following evening, we were transferred to the Frøslev camp, to which my father and Elsebet had been brought, along with other prisoners at Horserød, twelve days before.

The "Holiday Camps"

Compared to the German concentration camps, the two prison camps in Denmark, Horserød and Frøslev, can almost be regarded as holiday camps. There was no requirement to do very much work, and the food was arranged by the Danish prison authorities. There was no starvation. The guards were German. The worst thing was the uncertainty as to what would happen next. At any time at all, we could be sent back to Vestre Fængsel, be interrogated again and even sentenced to death, or could be sent southwards to an uncertain future in a German prison or concentration camp.

The Horserød Camp was put under German command on August 29, 1943. It had previously been used as an internment camp for anti-Nazi refugees who were, by one of the most shameful decisions made by Denmark, handed over to the Germans, when the camp was needed for the imprisonment of the illegally interned Communists. As these had now either fled or been deported to Stutthof, Horserød became a German prison camp for captured Resistance fighters. My father was taken there from the prison in Aarhus on March 8, 1944, and Elsebet joined him there on July 22. She has written the following about her stay at Horserød:[79]

Horserød – first of all, being reunited with father. At Vestre Fængsel there had been a girl in my cell for a couple of days who had come straight from Horserød. "Oh, so you're Uncle Kieler's daughter!" He was their camp doctor. "Wonderful" and more of the same sort of thing. I managed only with difficulty to talk to him in private when I finally saw him. During his daily visit to the women's huts he was surrounded by women and praised to the heavens. My father! He had emerged from his philosophical existence in Horsens and become a man of the people. How strange.

Meanwhile, the Germans had decided to move everyone over to Frøslev – no doubt because this camp was near the German border, which facilitated deportation. This move occurred under dramatic circumstances – seven hundred prisoners were put in buses and sent to Helsingør (with German soldiers with machine guns in the ditches along the road), then by ship down to Flensborg. This sailing trip gave us excellent opportunities to foster contacts on board.

The Frøslev Camp had been built in order to satisfy German demands for a prison camp of their own in Denmark. The Danish authorities accepted this camp near the Danish-German border in the hope that it would be used as a reception center for repatriated Danish prisoners. But it could equally well be used as the last station before deportation. It was in fact used in both ways.

The sea voyage from Helsingør to Flensborg took place during the night between August 11 and 12, and at the end of that month more prisoners arrived from Aarhus and Copenhagen. Flemming told the following to the members of the family who were still free, in a censored letter dated August 26:[80]

We have arrived at the camp with the other colleagues. We left on Thursday night and traveled the whole night and the following morning in a truck. Everyone who was involved in our case is now down here. We had quite a decent trip. It was wonderful to see the open countryside, and to be able to talk with the rest after such a long time in isolation. We arrived at about midday on the Friday and were quickly given our places. We greeted Father, and now sleep in the same hut and help him with medical matters. You can imagine what it must feel like to be able to mix with everyone and talk to them; this is a big change. The food is also better here. From a small rise in the camp, you can see a hilly area covered with heather, ringed by a forest of firs. It's nicer here than I thought it would be.

A thousand greetings,

Flemming

I can add my own report from Frøslev. Although we were meant to do menial work as a team to expand the camp, we had ample opportunity to shirk and visit our father as he saw patients. Being reunited with Father was, understandably, emotional enough, but it was more than that.

I had known my father as a friendly, smiling and charming man who, at the same time, was terribly shy. Now I met him in captivity I found that he had a whole crowd of friends who, more than most of the other prisoners, had their finger on the pulse of the camp. As he was the camp doctor, he had a good chance to make the acquaintance of most people and develop a trusting doctor-patient relationship and this all helped to get rid of his shyness. Many had had the same worries about their wives and children, and many shared his joy when they saw him reunited with his sons. We were received very heartily, and you can understand that I went to his office as often as I could.

One time, however, things nearly went wrong. The camp commandant was about to make an inspection of what was going on there. He knew that I was a student of medicine, and I therefore told him I was helping my father. I was treated to a lecture to the effect that I was not doing that. As I had neither then nor since learned to reply "*jawohl* (yes, sir)," I made do with a modest "*doch* (yes, but)," which caused a fuss. I better understood this when I heard later that the representative of the Master Race was in fact an ironmonger in civil life. Everything seemed to be collapsing around us and we thought that our hour had come – then he left.

Not until a few days later did I realize why he had actually come, and also realized that it was not only by helping people in his capacity as a doctor that my father had become so popular. My father was the camp news service. Under the floor of the office he had a radio that supplied the camp with news about how the invasion was proceeding. This was what the camp commandant was searching for, and it was via that radio set that we received news of the military situation, which was professionally commented on by Captain Dichmann and other interned officers.

We experienced the war itself from somewhat closer quarters when a British plane was shot down near the camp. I saw a wing fall, then the fuselage. But there remained a man in the sky, descending on a parachute. The alarm was sounded in the camp and a couple of hours later our radio news service told us to our great sorrow that the Germans had caught the only survivor.

On September 8 the camp commandant finally found the radio set. The whole Frøslev camp was very worried about what would happen to Dr. Kieler when they heard he had been taken to Flensborg for further interrogation. I felt all the same sort of fear he had when he had been in Horserød and received my farewell letter. So the relief was that much greater when he turned up again at the camp two or three days later – unharmed.

Another sad episode occurred on September 11, when the Germans introduced areas that were out of bounds. Before they had marked where the line ran, one unwitting prisoner who crossed the as yet unmarked line was shot and fatally wounded. There was great anger in the camp, even among the German guards, and things got very tense.

It was at about the time that my father came back from Flensborg that we learned that Frøslev was intended as a transit camp for deportation to Germany. Many rumors circulated about what this actually meant, but even the worst could hardly prepare us for the reality we saw when we were deported.

On September 15 there was reveille at three o'clock in the morning and we were lined up on parade. The Germans were quite agitated. They took a number of prisoners who had particularly serious charges against them, including five of us from HD2 (Jørgen Salling, Georg Jansen, Klaus Rønholt, Flemming and me). We did not know whether we were going to be executed or deported. When the roll call was complete, we were ordered to pack up our things, while the rest were sent back to bed. We were then ordered to march over to the guardroom, where our luggage was inspected.

Then some two hundred prisoners assembled, including three women. I saw to my great relief that neither Elsebet nor my father were among the two hundred, but it was sad to recognize that Margrethe Møller was – someone whom Neuhaus had on several occasions called an evil and spiteful woman. I now realized that although she was less guilty than my sisters, she was going to share our fate on account of her proud behavior in the hands of the Gestapo.

I could also see Koch and his landlady from Aabenraa, our friends from Varde and Jørgen Staffeldt, whom I had met for the first time in Frøslev. At seven o'clock we marched out of the camp to a number of trucks that took us over the border to a small country railway station, Harrislee, where we were ordered to get into cattle wagons, forty per wagon. At eleven o'clock in the morning, the doors of the wagons were locked and the train set in motion. The time had come for us to pay the price for remaining alive thus far.

Jørgen Kieler before deportation from Froslev to Germany

CHAPTER 10

KZ – The Concentration Camps

The system of concentration camps (KZ is the German abbreviation, from *Konzentrationslager*) was set up by decree on February 22, 1933, and this provided for Hitler's political opponents to be taken into *Schutzhaft* (protective custody) and to remain there, according to SS-Reichsführer Heinrich Himmler, until they had learned to become decent people in the eyes of the Nazis. The first camps, including Dachau near Munich, were started by Göring; the internees of this camp were mostly German Socialists, whom they wanted to render harmless. The Gestapo, the SA and the SS had free reign over these camps.

In 1934, reorganization was already taking place, which entailed that they were put under the command of Himmler and the SS. The first camps, with the exception of Dachau, were closed down and now a number of larger camps were built, including Sachsenhausen and Oranienburg, a little over twenty miles (35 km) to the north of Berlin. The aim of the camps changed, too. In one of his speeches in 1934, Himmler said that it was now no longer sufficient that prisoners should be turned into decent people, but that their will should be broken.

From 1934 onwards, religious opponents, mostly Jehovah's Witnesses, began to be interned and in 1937 came the turn of gypsies, asocial elements and criminals. After the attack on a German diplomat in Paris on November 9, 1938, *Kristallnacht* was unleashed, and a growing number of Jews were sent to concentration camps. During the pogroms on November 10 of that year, thirty-six Jews were killed, thirty-six badly injured and twenty thousand arrested. This was the beginning of Hitler's use of the concentration camps in connection with his policies on race.

By the start of the war, there were a total of six concentration camps with some twenty-one thousand prisoners, the great majority of whom were German citizens. There were three categories:

Stufe (grade) 1: Labor camps
Stufe 2: Labor camps with hard labor and poor living conditions
Stufe 3: Extermination camps (*Vernichtungslager* or *Knochenmühlen* – "bone mills")

Over the course of the war, the German munitions industry needed more labor. In 1942, a special organization, which was to exploit the growing numbers of KZ prisoners, was set up – the SS-*Wirtschaftsverwaltungshauptamt* (WVHA). On April 30, 1942, an order was sent out to the camp commandants, according to which the security aims of the KZ camps must now give way to the mobilization of a labor force of prisoners to help intensify munitions production and help rebuilding activities after the war was over. Total effectiveness was required, with a minimum loss of working time, e.g., for meals. "*Dieser Einsatz muss im wahren Sinne des Wortes erschöpfend sein, um ein Höchstmass an Leistung zu errichten* (This effort must, in the literal meaning of the term, be exhaustive, so that the highest effectiveness can be attained)."

The need for slaves in Germany grew apace, not least once the war had begun to turn against Germany in North Africa and at Stalingrad. As the labor force grew, many *Aussenkommandos* ("outsourcing" camps) were started – i.e., smaller camps under the aegis of the *Stammlager* (main camps) – wherever there was need for extra labor. These outsourcing camps, sometimes simply called labor camps, were spread over the whole of Germany. A map from 1945 of prisons and camps in Germany and adjacent territories shows more than four hundred concentration camps and outsourcing camps plus more than 150 Gestapo prisons. Neuengamme was one such main camp and served the whole of northwestern Germany. It had eighty-seven outsourcing camps, from Ladelund in the north, close to the Danish border, to Wittenberg in the east, Goslar in the south and Meppen near the Dutch border in the west.

As resistance grew in the occupied countries, the need for terror grew proportionally. Deportations were an important means of terrorizing the local population in, for instance, occupied Denmark. A paradoxical situation arose in that the Germans wanted, on the one hand, to have maximum production and labor efficiency, while on the other they wanted to starve their prisoners, mistreat them and even murder them, so that the chances of survival for the gross of prisoners would be reduced to a minimum. "*Arbeit macht frei* (Labor liberates)" was the promise emblazoned over the portals to the concentration camps, but it was "*Vernichtung durch Arbeit* (Annihilation by labor)" that many prisoners had to face once they had entered the camp.

When you think of the fact that there was an almost endless slave labor force to be drawn by Germany from the occupied territories, chiefly from the ranks of members of the Resistance and ethnically unwanted people, but even random people caught up in razzias, you can imagine that there was a certain grim logic in the way the Germans thought. Before we accept this logic, it is worth remembering that the wvha, by the end of 1944, had some six hundred thousand slaves in concentration camps, which is less than one tenth of the number of prisoners who were murdered. Terror was, and remained, the chief aim of the kz camps.

The question as to how much the rest of the world knew about the existence of these concentration camps has been raised on numerous occasions since the Second World War. The fact that they existed was already known before the war, both in Germany and abroad. When I was living in Munich in 1937, I read about their existence myself in the German press. Both German and foreign journalists had visited some of the early camps, which were presented to them as re-education centers, from which the prisoners were released as soon as they had foresworn their resistance and declared themselves to work loyally for the Fatherland.

The fact that the prisoners had been interned without trial could not be disguised, and a true picture of how prisoners were treated could be heard from the stories of prisoners who had been released and had fled abroad. But they were far from always being believed. In order not to jeopardize family and friends still in Germany, they were often rather tight-lipped. Not least the Jews had become embittered by the skepticism with which the rumors of extermination camps were met in the free world. But there can be no doubt that the developments that had been taking place in the concentration camps once the war had broken out, and especially after the attack on the Soviet Union, were unknown to the vast majority, as they were also to the 199 Danish prisoners who were deported to Neuengamme on September 15, 1944. We simply did not know what we were getting into.

The Deportation

The 196 men and three women who were deported from Frøslev on September 15, 1944, included the five members of HD2 and the Varde Group and Margrethe Møller, as listed above. There was also Karl Krighaar – the policeman who had helped us with the operation against the B&W plant. Others included Captain Olstrup, who had been the chief chef at the Vestre Fængsel prison, the mechanic Koch and his brave landlady, Hilda Lund, who had been wounded when we were surrounded by the Gestapo in Aabenraa.

On one occasion the train stopped and we were all ordered out to relieve ourselves, guarded by Wehrmacht soldiers with rifles. This is where I met Margrethe Møller. We managed to exchange a few words, but I shall never forget the look of pride and defiance on her face. I suddenly realized why the Gestapo had termed her "*eine böse Frau* (an evil woman)." She had, no doubt, let the Germans know exactly where she had them during interrogation. While the Master Race were pointing their rifles at us, we did our business. We looked at one another again, filled with anger and humiliation, but also with warm feelings of friendship and mutual concern. I never saw that stouthearted woman again, but she survived the extreme conditions of life in Germany and after returning back to Denmark took up, once again, her occupation as private tutor of literature. When she died, she was praised by colleagues in that academic field for her in-depth knowledge of the subject. I personally remember her as someone who stood up bravely to the Gestapo.

After our little "toilet" intermezzo, we continued on to Hamburg where the train was shunted onto a siding. This is where we spent the night. No food was handed out and the little that some of the deportees had brought with them from Frøslev did not stretch very far. That night there was a bombing raid. The ack-ack shot over us and shrapnel rained down; when things were at their worst the wagons jumped on the rails. It was an extremely risky situation, but no one came to any harm.

The next morning we traveled on to Neuengamme, a small town about fifteen to twenty miles (25–30 km) to the east of Hamburg on the main road to Berlin. The journey went at a snail's pace and our only relief was to fetch a little water at one of the stations at which we stopped. We arrived at the camp at about five o'clock in the afternoon.

Neuengamme

Neuengamme was set up in December 1938 as an *Aussenkommando*, an outsourcing camp under the auspices of the Sachsenhausen concentration camp, on the decision of the Reichsführer of the ss, Heinrich Himmler, and Gauleiter Karl Kaufmann from Hamburg. War was in the offing, and a steady stream of prisoners was expected. The Gestapo in Hamburg wanted to be well prepared. At the start there were only a hundred prisoners, who were housed at a brickworks; but in March 1939, a further four hundred prisoners were brought from Sachsenhausen and construction of the main camp began. On June 4, 1940, Neuengamme was given the status of an independent concentration camp of the second grade.

From October 1942, ss-Obersturmbannführer Max Pauly was the camp commandant. He had arrived from the Stutthof concentration camp. His closest associate was ss-Obersturmbannführer Anton Thumann who had come from the Majdanek concentration camp near Lublin, Poland. They both had a long list of crimes to their names, and were both executed in 1946.

About 106,000 men, women and children were registered as prisoners at Neuengamme between the years 1938 and 1945. The first prisoners were Germans, 9,200 in all. Later other prisoners from more than fifteen countries arrived. Most were from the Soviet Union, a total of 34,350; but prisoners also came from Poland and France, which countries delivered large numbers, with 16,900 and 11,500, respectively. About 13,000 Jews passed through Neuengamme. Some 4,800 prisoners from Denmark and 2,200 from Norway were registered there. A total of more than 55,000 prisoners died at Neuengamme.

We were obliged to hand over all our personal possessions, including wedding rings. The tobacco was stolen on the spot by the ss. We later learned that this activity was termed "organization," not "theft." Our heads

were then shorn, which revealed unexpected shapes of the head, and that
hair had not been washed for a long time. Our heads were filthy. It was a
comical sight, but humiliating at the same time. The comical aspect disappeared and the humiliation grew when we then had to strip naked and
lie down on a bench like sacrificial lambs to have our armpits shaven and
around our genitals. For a moment, I thought we were going to be castrated,
and there were others who thought the same; but in this instance, the treatment was merely a contribution to keeping down the number of lice. The
process left behind scratches and sores, which smarted when our portion
of anti-lice cream was subsequently rubbed in. This was, however, nothing
compared with the mental smarting we felt in our souls on account of the
indignities we were being exposed to.

The hot shower that followed gave us back a little of our self-esteem.
We were given a small piece of toilet soap, which was to last us a couple
of months; but as we had nowhere to keep it, it soon vanished. After the
shower, we were given a new set of clothes. This consisted of a shirt and a
pair of underpants made out of thin washed-out material, a pair of foot-rags
instead of socks, plus a pair of trousers and a jacket that must have come
from the rag-and-bone man. A large yellow cross was painted on the back,
which denoted nothing more than that we were convicts. The size of gar-
ments was regarded as something of quite minor importance, and braces
and belts were not part of the prisoner's normal outfit.

Finally, we were given a pair of slippers and headgear. One prisoner
received a cap, another a ladies' hat, a third one a hat that a Catholic priest
might wear. I cannot remember what I received to cover my head with;
but I soon learned that the most important role that the hat played was
to enable us to greet our guards with respect. In the space of quite a short
period of time, we had been transformed into a flock of ragged clowns in
fancy dress, in comparison with which Storm Petersen's cartoon tramps
would look positively well dressed.

One worried fellow prisoner made an impression on me when he said
that he had diabetes and had been deprived of his insulin supply. I tried to
calm him down by saying that he would no doubt soon be receiving some
as long as he consulted the camp doctor. None of us realized the kind of
world we had now entered. But six months later I remembered that episode when I heard that he had died of diabetes, since there was nothing
resembling insulin in the whole camp.

Our first time at Neuengamme lasted two days. We met, among all the prisoners, Social Democrats from Schleswig-Holstein who had some experience of the camps. They believed the war would soon end and were expecting a prisoners' revolt during the last phase. They were keen to be good friends with us and reassured us time and time again that they had no responsibility whatsoever for developments in Germany: "*Wir waren ja nur Zuschauer* (We were only observers)," is what they said. "*Ja, eben* (Yes, sure)," was my reply – irresponsible observers who now themselves were in the clink. No friendship came out of this encounter.

We learned that there were various categories of prisoner: political prisoners had a red triangle on their chests, criminals a green one, asocial elements a black one, religious prisoners a purple one, Jews a yellow one and homosexuals a pink one. The difference between us and the Master Race was instilled in us right from the start. In the presence of an ss man we were obliged to remove our headgear and stand to attention. If this did not happen swiftly enough, a whip was put to use. Having a piece of string to keep up our trousers was, in such situations, of vital importance and we soon learned to "organize" things.

We also learned that there was one unified system of camp guards who went under the name of *Kapo*, i.e., *Kammeradschaftspolizei*. At the top of the hierarchy was the *Lagerältester*. And at Neuengamme there were people assigned to keep order in each hut called *Blockältester*. These had several assistants who were called the *Stubendienst*. When we were transferred to the outsourcing camp of Porta Westphalica, we also learned that each Lagerältester was assisted by a number of Kapos who ran the various work teams. They too had their subordinates who were termed *Vorarbeiter* and *Schieber*. Most of the Kapos were Germans, often with a criminal background, but there were others. They had been promoted above the mass of prisoners after themselves being subject to mistreatment and ran the constant threat of being demoted if they did not treat their fellow prisoners as the ss expected them to. In Porta we soon learned to fear the Kapos as much as the ss.

In Neuengamme, we first learned the meaning of the term *Appell*. In the morning and the evening, the prisoners all had to march to the square for roll call. As we later realized, this could take hours. The roll call was an important part of the general terror that held sway in the camps. To our amazement, we saw that the camp even had an orchestra consisting of prisoners, which played at roll call. We also noticed that the square had two sets of gallows with room for four at a time and we heard that shortly before our arrival, six Russian lads had been hanged: nooses had been put around their necks and they had then been tied so that they would draw up their legs and hang themselves. Some of us had noticed the hanged men as we entered the camp.

We soon also got a taste of the culinary delicacies that awaited us and of the stench and filth in which we would be living. We made our acquaintance with the traditional turnip and cabbage soup and every Sunday we were treated to a portion of goulash. I think I found three shreds of meat in the portion I was given. The filthy bowls and the foul-tasting food took my appetite away. This only returned when the hunger became serious. For the time being all there was for it was to stop being choosy and fastidious.

We also received an insight into problems of hygiene. Vermin was a problem that could not be hidden, and toilet paper was a luxury that we had not earned. The first impressions were worrying enough and when we were taken later that day to Porta Westphalica, Flemming and I were glad to be among those chosen to go there. It could not get any worse than Neuengamme – at least that is what we thought – and the fact that the *Blockältester* had told us that the accommodation at Porta was to be "Hotel Kaiserhof" sounded very encouraging.

We did not, of course, know what the principles were on which people were picked out for this transport. But from the questions that the ss asked us, we realized that the education of the prisoners in question was of importance. There was a shortage of those skilled in operating machines, which the Germans were in need of in great numbers. Office workers, tradesmen, academics, officers, police officers and such could only be employed doing menial tasks such as the dangerous work involved in tidying up bombed districts of towns. If we had known that we had been chosen to do hard labor down the mine, our enthusiasm would not have been as great.

During the organization of the transport, the air raid sirens went off, which gave rise to a barrage of curses and blows to drive the several hundred prisoners through cellar windows into the air raid shelter. Both the Kapos and ss seemed to be in fear for their lives, but they were equally afraid of prisoners escaping.

After this introduction to the brutality we would witness for the next six months, we were sent to have a shower and after a superficial medical examination, we were given our new uniforms. We then had to take another shower within a couple of hours and the rags we had been given were replaced with a striped prison uniform consisting of a pair of trousers, a jacket, a coat, and a cap made of thin synthetic wool – one of the many substitutes made during the war. We had a patch with our number and a red *D* sewn onto our jackets, the *D* standing for *Dänisch*. The red color of the letter showed that we were political prisoners.

We also received a pullover, which seemed to originate with the same branch of the rag trade as the clothes we had initially been given on arrival. As usual, they were lax about the sizes, and the pullover was sometimes nothing more than a quite unnecessary brassiere. On the Sunday afternoon, we were given boots as replacements for our slippers. The boots consisted of wooden soles and leather straps, sewn together with coarse stitching. Laces were a luxury that few of us had. So more string had to be "organized." If you complained about the size of the boots or seams that pressed into your feet, you were given a wallop. I later experienced how you were in danger of your life wearing this pathetic footwear.

The prisoners who had been chosen for the transport – some two hundred of us in all, of which ninety-eight were Danes – were transferred to a crowded hut (Block 11). On Monday, September 18, shortly after lunch, we went off to Arbeitslager Porta Westphalica, little knowing that this would cost just under half of us our lives.

Porta Westphalica

In February 1944, the Royal Air Force and the US Air Force changed their tactics. Instead of systematically carpet-bombing the German industrial districts of cities they began to employ precision bombing of the German aircraft industry. This was made possible by advances in radar techniques, and had catastrophic consequences for the Luftwaffe. The German Ministry of Supply therefore found an answer to this threat. They planned the construction of twenty underground industrial plants, each between 54,000 and 540,000 square feet (5,000–50,000 m²) in area. The head of the concentration camp program was now Himmler, and he became the biggest supplier of cheap labor, which he termed "*die neuen Höhlenmenschen* (the new cave-dwellers)."

One of the first of these plants to be established was at Barkhausen, near Minden, where the River Weser breaks through what are termed the

Westphalian Alps on its way to the North Sea, dividing these hills into an eastern ridge called the Wesergebirge and a western one, the Wiehengebirge. This is where Porta Westphalica (the Westphalian Gateway) is situated. Before the Second World War, it was known for its natural beauty and its spas. The labor camp Porta Westphalica was established here, an outsourcing camp of the main camp Neuengamme.

At first, an old sandstone quarry was exploited – Jakobsberg – in the Wesergebirge on the eastern bank of the River Weser. Then the underground parts of this mine were expanded to also include the Wiehengebirge. Galleries – what the Germans termed *Stollen* – were bored out of the rock at a total length of twelve miles (20 km). These galleries connected factory workshops and machine halls of varying sizes with ceiling height of up to 130 feet (40 m) to enable large cranes to work there. This was where the fuselages and technical equipment of new fighter planes were assembled. But first of all, an underground city had to be prepared.

For this purpose, professional mineworkers from the Saar were called in. Himmler gave these professionals an auxiliary workforce consisting of some fifteen hundred concentration camp prisoners. The first 250 or so of these came from the Soviet Union and Poland. They had been sent to the concentration camp Buchenwald as early as March 1944 and their first task was to prepare the banqueting hall to receive prisoners. This was part of Hotel Kaiserhof, a rather elegant timber-framed building whose rooms the ss had occupied. The restaurant continued to serve the local population who were therefore well acquainted with the prison camp in the banqueting hall behind, where large banquets had taken place before the war for up to twenty-five hundred guests. This was the place where the "cave-dwellers" were going to live.

Over the spring and summer, the number of prisoners had increased to around a thousand. These were from various East European countries, and in September, five hundred extra prisoners arrived mostly from Denmark, France and the Netherlands. The Danish prisoners, ninety-eight in number, were members of the Resistance and were regarded as political prisoners. We represented various political affiliations within the Resistance, but there were, in fact, few Communists. Most of these had ended up in Sachsenhausen or Stutthof.

Our transport to Porta was by cattle wagon with fifty men in each, twenty-five at each end of the wagon, leaving room in the middle for the

two ss guards. We were ordered to sit on the floor with our legs wide apart
so that the first row would sit between the legs of the next, as on a toboggan.
We were ordered to neither talk nor move. An old jam bucket served as
our toilet and that, plus a petroleum lamp, were the creature comforts we
were afforded for the journey. The ss had been equipped with submachine
guns for their convenience and they also had whips, and were allowed to
use both. They were indeed used on us.

The trip to Porta took forty-two hours. This was the worst trip I have
ever taken in my whole life. During the day, the doors were open, so we
could catch glimpses of the surrounding landscape. The train crawled
along and when darkness fell, we had come no further than Hamburg.
The position in which we had been forced to sit became unbearable. But
at the slightest attempt to move we were threatened with submachine guns
or given a crack of the whip. When one of our colleagues tried to take off
his boot because it hurt, he was hit over the head and ordered to put it on
again.

When we arrived in Hamburg, we were ordered to go to sleep without changing position. If anyone dared to stretch their legs into the space
reserved for the ss in the middle, they were immediately hit and kicked.
Then the doors were locked and we had to wait until daylight. No one got
much sleep that night. The only relief we got was by thinking about how
the German railway network was on the point of collapse on account of
the bombing raids by the Allies.

The next morning, the journey continued at a snail's pace. We were
given a portion of food consisting of a quarter loaf of rye bread and a slice
of black pudding. We used our fingers as utensils. The guards were changed
every other hour. When one of the less spiteful guards understood that
a revolt by the prisoners was in the offing, we were allowed to appoint a
spokesman. This was Captain Ploug, who managed to get us the privilege
of being able to stand up, one at a time, for a short while in order to stretch
our legs. Our muscles and joints ached terribly, we got bloody rims on our
backsides and thighs, and our feet went to sleep. The tightly packed wagon
was claustrophobic. We were in desperate need of *Lebensraum* – we each
had one square meter and the air contained in it.

In the afternoon, we thought that we had reached Hanover and by ten
o'clock at night reached Porta, as far as we knew. We were glad to have arrived at our hotel. Everyone was exhausted and tormented by the journey.

So we were hugely disappointed when the guards jumped out and locked the doors and told us to adopt our sleeping positions from the night before. As this did not occur without protest, they shouted that they would shoot through the walls of the wagon if we did not shut up. There was immediate silence, but we had to endure yet another night of torment before we were finally allowed to enter Hotel Kaiserhof.

Hotel Kaiserhof – Porta

The Camp

When the doors were finally opened, a tormented group of prisoners crawled out of those cattle wagons on September 20, with stiff and painful limbs. After a journey of just under two whole days, we finally got the opportunity to stretch our legs. We were in a depressing railway siding somewhere in Germany. I looked around frantically, hoping to identify the spot. But I did not succeed. I saw a river, which broke through a low line of hills, but I continued to be disoriented. But by the following day, I knew that this was the River Weser.

My geographical musings were cut short by a storm of swearing and cracks of the whip which, for some incomprehensible reason, meant that suddenly two hundred men were standing in rows and ranks, five men in each, with the Danes lined up by height. We marched in a column, like a company of soldiers, up to an old suspension bridge, which swayed under our footsteps, causing the ss to get into a rage about these "*verfluchte*

Dänische Sabotöre (these damned Danish saboteurs)," who were continuing their operations within the borders of the Third Reich. As we were
marching over the bridge, we saw ahead of us a two-story timber-framed
building with bay and dormer windows and small turrets. This was Hotel
Kaiserhof. On our way to the hotel we passed one of the local end stations
of the local railway. Only some time later did we realize that the railway
led to a larger town, Minden, a little to the north.

The sight of the hotel had been encouraging. So the rumors at Neuengamme were true. We would be staying in a hotel. But there was no red
carpet, and it soon became clear to us that the front door with the pomp-
ous stairway was meant for the masters of the manor and that we were
consigned to the back entrance. Behind the hotel was a large building by
whose entrance there were still a number of posters that told us that this
was a theater. Between the long wall of this building and the ridge was a
path leading to a yard surrounded by barbed wire enclosed on two sides by
the backs of the hotel and the theater. It was along this path that we were to
make our entrance into KZ-Lager Porta Westphalica. Our initially positive
impression of the sight of Hotel Kaiserhof gave way to fears when I read,
in the yard, an inscription written in charcoal on the white wall. In large
letters the Latin inscription could be seen: HIC MORTUI VIVUNT.

I am not at all sure that very many of my companions saw or understood this inscription. Flemming did. But we kept our fears to ourselves.
We understood the words – HERE THE DEAD LIVE – but the true meaning
in all its horror was only revealed over the following six months.

We were received by the man at the top of the hierarchy of prisoners, Lagerältester Kapo Schorsch. He was a short, freckled redhead with
an underbite and rather few teeth. We soon nicknamed him Lurifax after
a well-known cartoon character. The red triangle on his striped jacket
showed that he was a political prisoner. Under the command of Kapo
Schorsch were a number of other trusties, mostly the Kapos who were in
command of various types of work groups. These were mostly Germans
with a criminal background. Then there were their helpers, as mentioned,
the *Vorarbeiter, Schieber* and *Stubendienst*. The top command was naturally
in the hands of the ss.

The camp commandant was Obersturmbannführer Hermann Wick-
lein, whom we only saw when something was the matter. The head of the
commando was ss-Rottenführer Hermann Nau, a brutal and stupid man;

it was he who took the daily roll calls. He was as feared as Schorsch himself. Other ss soldiers of a lower rank had other duties.

The theater was a large hall, about eight-five by thirty yards (80 × 30 m). The windows were blacked out and covered with barbed wire. There was no heating. One side of the hall had blocks of bunks, stacked up vertically in fours and in rows of two. The bunks normally had a straw mattress and two thin blankets. The prisoners were not given a fixed sleeping place and as there were not enough bunks for everyone, there was a daily scramble for a place to sleep and for blankets as two or three men ended up sleeping in the same bunk with or without blankets.

The middle of the hall was reserved for roll calls, meals and the distribution of clothes and tobacco. Under the ceiling there was a block with a rope so that prisoners who tried to escape or were guilty of other misdemeanors could be hanged. At one end of the sets of bunks there were tables with stools where a couple of hundred men could be seated. At the other side of the area for the roll calls there was a former counter where the barbers were installed, whose main task it was to use mechanical clippers to give prisoners a haircut that alternated between a cockscomb in the middle of a scalp that had otherwise been shaved clean and an "autostrada" where the clean part had grown back. Behind this counter were also stores of potatoes and vegetables. These were later moved outside into the yard.

At one end of the theater hall there was a stage next to the main entrance. Here the Kapos had organized their private quarters behind a wall of boards. In the two corners on each side of the stage two small rooms were used as a primitive camp hospital, called the *revier* (abbreviated from *Krankenrevier*, sick bay). One of the rooms held thirty bunk beds for in-patients, while the other room was used as a consulting and emergency room for out-patients. At the other end of the hall there was an exit to the yard. On one side of the exit door there were three toilets and on the other side a small kitchen. At this end of the hall there were also various storerooms and small workshops for tailors and shoemakers. All these facilities were soon found to be absolutely insufficient and two months after our arrival they were moved out into the yard in two new barracks, one for the *revier,* and one for the other activities. New latrines, a shed for potato peeling and a shower were badly needed extra facilities, which were eventually added.

Outside the hall was an ungroomed yard, which was about as big as the theater itself. This was later doubled in size. A number of large leafy trees indicated that the yard was originally for the delight of theatergoers who had come out during the intermission. Now it had become an assembly point for the columns of prisoners going to and from their work. On rainy days it would be reduced to a muddy pool. But whatever the weather, the prisoners had to line up here for their food rations. They would walk past the kitchen where the chef stood and deal out the food. Any attempt to keep the theater clean was, under such circumstances, doomed to failure right from the start.

The yard also had a place where the prisoners could wash under a water pipe with a dozen or so holes, out of which a thin stream of cold mountain water would run. Later this primitive washing area was expanded and showers were installed. At the opposite end of the yard were the latrines with room for twenty-six. These were in constant use. The yard was surrounded by barbed wire. Outside of the wire, guards patrolled with dogs and had orders to shoot if any attempts at escape were made.

There were only three to four hundred prisoners in the camp on our arrival. This was the night shift trying to get some sleep. At lunch time we were given a little turnip soup, which was both unaesthetic and tasted terrible, and I had the greatest difficulty in getting it down. In the afternoon we did odd jobs until the various columns of workers came home. Suddenly, the limited area of the camp was filled to bursting.

The return of the work columns meant that fights were unleashed to get hold of a bowl, to get into the food line and then to get a sleeping place. The evening meal consisted of a chunk of rye bread and something to put on it, so long as stocks lasted, and this varied between black pudding, brawn, beetroot, pickles, salted fish innards, cottage cheese or forcemeat made from bombed cattle. Now and then we got a piece of margarine or artificial honey instead of the meat. Towards the very end of our stay at Porta we were given three-quarters of a liter of turnip soup instead of bread.

Everything had to be drunk or eaten using our fingers, as there were neither knives nor forks. The food bowls were made of metal. There were not enough for us all and it was a question of first come first served with the prisoner hardly having time to finish his meal before the bowl was handed on to the next man. Nor were there enough tables and benches so we had to eat on our bunks, sitting on the floor or standing. Under such circumstances, civilized table manners soon vanished and the descent into misery caused by the humiliating shave, the embarrassing haircut and the ridiculous clothes soon followed in rapid tempo. The climax was reached on our first day in Porta when we had to pay a visit to the stinking filthy latrine. "Here you have to learn to shit your ass dry" was Schlanbusch's ironic commentary at the total lack of toilet paper.

After the meal, the night shift was sent to work. This occurred after an endless roll call plus shouts and blows. At eight o'clock in the evening the rest of the prisoners were called for roll call. An old sex criminal from the Stubendienst made a hell of a noise by banging a length of rail that was hanging on a rope, while the head of the camp, accompanied by a number of Kapos and other trusties, went around lashing out left and right and shouting: "*Appell, Appell. Schnell, schell. Los, los. Beeilt Euch!* (Roll call, roll call. Quick, quick. Come on, come on. Hurry up!)"

We were made to stand in rows and line up to be counted forever and ever. When Schorsch had finally done his sums, he told this to the ss soldier who was on duty and the recount would start. This lasted between half an hour and an hour, but later on, roll calls of two to four hours were quite common.

After the roll call we crept into bed. Flemming and I shared a bunk on the third level. It had a straw mattress and two soiled blankets. We were completely exhausted and soon fell asleep not really knowing where we were and in despair as to what had befallen us.

Theater hall at Hotel Kaiserhof, Porta

The Work

At 4:30 the next morning we were woken up by someone from the Stube-dienst who, seemingly with great pleasure, belabored the hanging rail with a hammer. At the same time, others from the Stubedienst began to run around like apes between the rows of bunks shouting "*aufstehen, aufstehen* (get up, get up)" while they lashed out at the bunks with sticks and then at the prisoners themselves if they were not quick enough. We soon realized we had entered a noisy hell. Within the space of a quarter of an hour, around a thousand men had been driven out into the yard and were standing in rows. This occurred with a maximum of violence on the part of the Kapo.

At five o'clock breakfast was distributed. We passed the kitchen in single file and were given a chunk of rye bread, a piece of margarine and a drop of "coffee" or tea, if we had been so lucky as to get a bowl or dish. There was nothing resembling cups or mugs. The margarine was spread on the bread with your thumb and the coffee substitute was drunk as quickly as possible, before someone else snatched the bowl from your grasp.

The shouts of the Stubendienst and the Kapos increased to a crescendo: "*Beeilt Euch – schnell, schnell – Drecksack* (Hurry up – quick, quick – shitbags)."

Eating in peace was something quite unknown. The whole meal for some thousand men was to last no more than half an hour. Then Kapo Schorsch took over the leadership of the whole hysterical performance. This gorilla obviously had difficulty passing by prisoners without hitting, threatening or swearing at them. Roll calls were the highlights of his existence and with the morning roll call, scenes of violence would ensue. The sex criminal hammered the rail so that our eardrums were about to burst and his colleagues ran around swearing and lashing out in order to get their fellow prisoners to roll call by six o'clock.

So there we stood, lined up while Kapo Schorsch tried to count us. This took him a good while, but in the end he handed the counting over to Kommandoführer Nau or some other ss man and we were then divided up into labor columns, which were once again counted. Flemming and I ended up in the same group and this was called Weser Stolle, so our geographical position became confirmed. It was not only from the point of view of an escape attempt that we wanted to know where we were, but whether we could look forward to liberation by either the Western Allies or the Russians.

Weser Stolle lay some three miles (5 km) from Hotel Kaiserhof. We marched out in a column of about seventy men, most of whom were

Russians. The column was under the command of a Kapo and there were also soldiers with rifles present. After marching for about an hour along the river, we were told to halt. On the bank we saw a small area that reminded us of a gravel pit. Here we were counted for a third time before being sent into a mine gallery, which was between ten and twenty feet (3–6 m) in width and had a rail for dump wagons.

The first day we were quite perky. We sang during the march out to Weser Stolle but were stopped when we started singing a song from our native country ("*Dengang jeg drog af sted*"). There were men from Schleswig-Holstein among the guards, and they understood Danish. Then the Russians started to sing. They were much better at it. Soon our poor quality footwear began to plague us, so we were no longer so eager. The foot-rags we had been given instead of socks soon disappeared and the lack of shoelaces meant that our primitive boots chafed and rubbed. This soon became a torment on the long march and it was therefore a relief when we were transported the last part of our journey in an open truck with trailers.

Our job consisted of hacking out the mine gallery and shoveling the rubble into a dump wagon. We were all unaccustomed to this sort of work, but to the bemusement of our Russian colleagues, we started working with gusto, in order to show the Germans that we had not been cowed. Besides, we wanted to get some exercise. Most of us had been "unemployed" for several months. I had been locked up in a cell for a good seven months and I had paced it like a lion in a cage with no chance to exercise apart from my service in the kitchen, plus half an hour daily in the exercise yard.

"*Langsam arbeiten, Kammerad, sonst gehst du kaput* (Work slowly, otherwise you'll wear yourself out)" was the good advice given us by the Russians, and when a number of Danes seemed not to be convinced, they added, "*Willst du für die Deutschen arbeiten?* (Do you want to work for the Germans?)"

This had its effect, and we soon came to our senses. But it took us some time longer to learn to use our eyes. The whip in the hand of the ss soldier made it clear to us that he should not be disregarded, but it took us some while longer to take into account the *Schieber, Vorarbeiter* and Kapos. Their endless shouts of "*Los, los, Mensch – Beeilt Euch* (Come on, come on, men – hurry up)" accompanied by a hail of curses soon made it obvious that there was also a hierarchy among the prisoners themselves. So we learned the hard way how to use our eyes. When no one was looking we would take a break and when the ss soldiers or the Kapo approached we would work at a pace that satisfied our tormentors. When we were filling the wagons, we were nearly always being observed and so this part of the work was done at a swift rate, which soon gave us a realistic idea of our physical strength.

Weser Stolle presented other problems too. There was nothing which could be called rainwear, but even when the weather was dry, Weser Stolle was a damp place to work on account of the river overflowing, so water would drip from the ceiling. And now that summer was over we realized how cold and draughty it could be. So we were happy when we could take a short break to eat, which initially was done in the open air outside the entrance to the mine. The sun and the terrible turnip soup warmed up our bodies. This was the only time of day that we had the chance of seeing the sun. Otherwise we would be down the dark mine or in camp, both of which had poor lighting. When, later in the year, it had started to become foggy and rainy, the meal break was held in a warmed-up wooden shed into which seventy men were crammed. Mealtimes ended with the usual wearying roll call and the prisoners were counted all over again.

After twelve hours had passed, work broke off at six o'clock in the evening and the prisoners assembled at the entrance for yet another roll call. We soon learned that it was sensible to be on time when the counting began. This went reasonably smoothly as long as the number of prisoners tallied; those who came late were beaten. Then came the hour-long march back to camp where the fight to get bowls awaited us. We passed by the kitchen and the food was distributed and we could then enjoy our hunk of rye bread with something on it fit for Lucullus, so to speak, eating standing or sitting on our bunks, or on the floor, or on one of the few stools available. At around eight o'clock in the evening there was yet again another roll call and this could take up to two hours. Then, the exhausted prisoners could look forward to six hours sleep at best, though not infrequently our sleep was cut short with renewed roll calls held when the Kapo noticed that some misdemeanor had been committed.

Prisoners' Society

All ninety-eight Danish prisoners who arrived at Porta on September 20 had a Resistance background. For security reasons we did not talk much about this. Our cases had been closed for now, but there was always a chance that the interrogation could start again if new arrests had made this necessary.

Gestapo agent Heinrich Oeltze, who was living at Hotel Kaiserhof, had been given the task of making investigations into all the prisoners. He could also take up dormant cases again. Of all the ninety-eight Danes, I knew some half a dozen already. But soon a friendship was struck up between all the Danish prisoners and this continued after the war was over.

There were the inevitable differences of political outlook. But among the Danes there were very few Communists. We had frank discussions, but this did not hamper feelings of solidarity. Cross-party cooperation stood the test of our sojourn in Porta.

Before being deported to Germany, we had heard over my father's secret radio set at Frøslev that Paris had fallen to the Allies, so we were reckoning on Germany capitulating soon afterwards. On arrival at Porta, most of us still believed that the war would soon be over and that we would be liberated and repatriated. But time dragged on, and despair became evident. I could divide my fellow prisoners into three sorts: optimists, realists and pessimists. Although I realized that our chances of survival were small, I told myself I was an incredible optimist: "You'll see, you'll make it."

I believe this to have been the necessary encouragement for most of us, but I did not shut my ears to what the realists and the pessimists had to say. The realists thought the war could last another six months, by which time we could be dead. The pessimists thought the same except they thought that our chances for survival were nil as they would shoot the survivors as the war came to an end.

In retrospect, I have to admit that the realists' and pessimists' views were nearest the truth. But the naïve hopes of the optimists nevertheless came true thanks to an unexpected rescue at the very last minute. But during the last months of 1944, all we could do was keep up our spirits in a hopeless situation. I therefore asked my realist and pessimist friends to keep their views to themselves, while I maintained my little campaign of hope.

The fact that the Danish prisoners stuck together was of great importance for our chances of survival. Especially important was to team up with someone who was trustworthy. This was of crucial importance when we were at work and needed to keep an eye on the guards and the Kapos, or when we needed a helping hand to carry heavy objects. It was of even greater importance at the camp itself when food was being distributed, so that you could get a bowl, keep your place in the queue, when you wanted to get a bunk and a blanket for the night, as protection against theft and attack, and when using opportunities for bartering, plus in many other situations. It was equally important to have a good friend to share your bunk with, so that you could exchange worries in the evening about those back home and about our own prospects for the future. I had the great advantage that I had my own brother Flemming as companion for most of the time. We owe one another our lives.

However, the prisoners came from seventeen different nations. Including those who came towards the end of October, there were now some fifteen hundred prisoners. Most of these were from the Soviet Union, including the Asian parts. There were also many Poles, around two hundred Frenchmen and some Germans. Otherwise, there were men from the Netherlands, Belgium, Spain and Italy, Czechoslovakia, Yugoslavia, Bulgaria, Greece and the Baltic countries. We were a motley crew. Some had been partisans, others from the Resistance, like we were. Some were prisoners of war or subject to forced labor, or had tried to escape or broken the rules at their place of work. Others were free laborers who had broken their contracts. In addition there were a number of criminals. Most of the German prisoners wore the green triangle of the criminal (*Berufsverbrecher*), or the black one for asocial elements. The chef wore a purple one; he was a Jehovah's Witness. There were no Jews or gypsies in the camp. As for language, this was the Tower of Babel, although the common language was naturally German.

We Danes were a homogeneous group and were regarded as a unity, and also with a degree of respect as we had been in the Resistance. Only the Soviet and French prisoners had such a clearly defined national identity as we had.

The Soviet prisoners were, for the most part, prisoners of war and partisans, who had already been in prison for a long time. Most of them described internment in camps in Russia where there was barbed wire and watchtowers. Without huts and tents there was nowhere to escape the harsh Russian winter. Obviously many had died under such conditions, and those who survived were especially tough. Most of them exhibited discipline and were very patriotic and anti-German. The concentration camp was their first experience of Western culture, which they judged by the lack of hygiene. They were not impressed and by no means suffered an inferiority complex, nor did they need to. Several of them had learned German during their captivity and so it was possible to make contacts with them, so that even personal friendships developed.

The two hundred Frenchmen included about a hundred who had come when we did. These were mostly members of the Resistance, and their group was no less unified than ours. We got on well together and I was impressed by their attempts to keep up a civilized standard of living. They spoke politely to one another, which was not only a question of the traditional respect for their language, but also a question of mutual respect. In the evening, before they went to bed, you could see them in larger or smaller groups discussing everything under the sun. The discussions centered mostly around our chances of survival and the way the war would go. There were also discussions about delicious food. But they were also inclined to discuss politics, philosophy, religion and the like. I got the impression that the French had a large amount of cultural resistance in them and I eagerly sought their company. And in this way I learned some French. Other Danish prisoners did the same, and many Franco-Danish friendships ensued.

We were therefore well received by our foreign companions in captivity. But things soon changed. Three weeks after our arrival, another group of 127 Danes arrived, all wearing a black triangle. These were prisoners who had been arrested shortly after September 19, 1944, when a razzia was conducted against the Danish police. They were arrested on the street or in dwellings where black marketeers tended to congregate, or on the strength of Danish police card files of former criminal elements who had been in prison. The idea was to provide Germany with an extra labor force and at the same time reduce the amount of criminality in Denmark. At any rate they were not members of the Danish Resistance and solidarity among them was lacking.

The two groups of Danish prisoners at Porta have often been described as 50s and 54s, referring to the batch of prisoners arriving by the thousand. There was some friendly contact between the two groups, but relations were normally determined by which side of the law we had been on in peacetime. The effect for us was that the Danes were soon all tarred with the same brush, and regarded as asocial elements. The Frenchmen were clear about the distinction, but in general the reputation of the Danes at Porta took a knock. There were several reasons for this.

One of Himmler's basic principles when he set up the concentration camps was to break the prisoners' spirits. One important pillar of this was preferential treatment of some. The Kapo system was part of this and the

most effective means that the ss had found. It affected us only slightly. On
our arrival, some of the tallest and strongest Danes had been selected to
serve in the camp as Kapos. I clearly remember how the other prisoners
were suspicious of them. Luckily, it turned out that my taller and stronger
fellow prisoners proved unwilling to live up to Kapo Schorsch's expectations
and were sent back down the mines with the rest of us. A number of other
Danish prisoners gained positions as *Schieber* and *Vorarbeiter*. These privileges were used to the advantage of the other Danish prisoners and they
were not subject to criticism, either then or after the war. I myself ended
up working for two months as a medical orderly in the camp, although I
did not receive the status of Kapo for my work.

But as Danes, my compatriots could attain special attention. Whether
we liked it or not, we were Aryans and therefore of the northern race that
the Germans regarded as needing different treatment than the rest of humanity. This meant that we had the special privilege of receiving and writing short letters, which had to be written in German. When Flemming
and I, some one and a half months after we had been deported, received
letters from our parents, they still did not know where we actually were.
They were, of course, not allowed to write about the course of the war or
the situation in Denmark, but were chiefly interested in simply keeping in
touch. My father's letters are therefore especially important as they note
when parcels had been sent to us and that they had heard nothing from us.
The most important piece of news, however, was that Father and Elsebet
had been freed from Frøslev on October 1.

We never did receive the parcels our parents had sent. But other Danish prisoners were luckier. The welcome supplements to the terrible food
and warm clothes were received with gratitude. Later that year, the Danish Red Cross began sending parcels to all Danish prisoners. This had
its significance in that it reduced the number of fatalities in, for instance,
Sachsenhausen, but for us in Porta the parcels rarely arrived and always
with a long delay and after having been plundered. The few things that did
arrive were accepted gratefully. But they also created problems. Prisoners
had nowhere to store foodstuffs. While I was working as medical orderly, I
was asked on several occasions to store parcels for my lucky comrades. In
the notes I wrote in 1945 after I had returned home to Denmark, I wrote
the following:

I was so kind as to take on the supervision of parcels and this aroused anger in the petty thieves in the camp. I imagine that I had, time and time again, to repeat the Ten Commandments to myself. Does it not say somewhere: "Thou shalt not covet thy neighbor's eggs"? Well, I coveted and was happy once my fellow prisoner and his buddy had consumed the coveted object and thus removed the temptation that my role as guardian of foodstuffs brought with it.

What was worse was that the contents of parcels could unleash short but serious bouts of diarrhea. Our starving bodies were not always capable of standing up to the consumption of rich food. The biggest problem was, however, that the parcels caused a good deal of envy. We had suddenly become a privileged class of prisoner, beyond the class of normal prisoners. So Danish prisoners, both those who were political prisoners and those with their black triangles, were often the victims of theft. Not only food was stolen, but also clothes. It soon became clear that the motto for the level of justice at Porta was: *Rechtlos, Ehrlos und Wehrlos* (No Rights, No Honor, No Defense).

There was no guarantee of justice with regard to the theft committed by prisoners against their fellows and there were no punishments for misdemeanors. But punishments were meted out should a prisoner steal anything from a Kapo or a depot or place of work. "*Fünfundzwanzig im Asch* (twenty-five in the rear)" was the standard punishment. A roll call was made, and the unlucky miscreant was made to lean over a trestle and received twenty-five blows of a rubber truncheon or cane on his backside.

This was on the initiative of the Kapos. The most sadistic of these was Kapo Schorsch. I once saw him beat a German prisoner to death. This was a starving prisoner who also suffered from the failure of such victims of starvation to hold their urine and feces. Using a lath from a bed, Schorsch belabored the unfortunate individual. First his clothes tore, then his skin, then his muscles were beaten into a pulp so that in the end you could see the bones sticking out. He was then sent off to the infirmary where he died soon afterwards. Schorsch was often drunk. He had access to spirits. But on this occasion what struck me most was the fact that he was a mentally ill sadist. Even the other Kapos thought this was too much.

There were other forms of mistreatment. Locking a prisoner in the mortuary without clothes during winter was a punishment that could result in death. Also being attached to a ring, which was at one end of the theater. This was originally meant for pressured gas canisters, but was now used as a neck ring for prisoners who had been caught thieving from the depots or other places. The unfortunate victim was made to crouch with his hands tied behind his back and stay in that position all night, running the risk that he would hang himself.

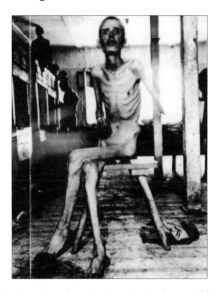

Mussulman: the kz designation for the terminal phase of famine disease. "The prisoners assumed a peculiar dragging gait. In order to remedy the failing heat regulation they often wrapped themselves up in a ragged blanket, draped over the head and held together in front. This 'attire' coupled with the emaciation and the 'humbly' bent posture made the patients reminiscent of ascetic old Mussulmans on pilgrimage. Mussulman, probably owes its origin to this." [81]

Escape attempts resulted in being shot on the spot, or hanged later. Twenty-five to thirty prisoners had tried to escape before we arrived at the camp. Ten were lucky but at least seven were executed as a punishment. Hangings took place in the theater, at roll call. Nau would hold a speech in which he made it clear to the rest of the prisoners that escape was impossible. After the speech was finished, it would be translated into various languages and Kapo Schorsch would hoist the prisoner up by his neck where he would die slowly of strangulation. The corpse was left hanging there for a while as a warning. I never experienced one of these executions myself, but one morning I saw, out in the yard, the bodies of prisoners who had been shot while trying to escape. The guards certainly kept an eye on us.

"The gallows" was also used in another way. One morning as I returned from the night shift down the mine I saw that Schorsch had put a number of chairs up on tables. On top stood a prisoner with his hands tied behind his back and to the noose that was used for hangings. When he was ready Schorsch got back down and kicked the tables and chair away so that the arms of the prisoner were soon dislocated. He was still there when I marched off to work again, but was gone the following morning.

The Pathology of the Concentration Camps

As a student of medicine, I naturally gave a lot of thought to the symptoms that gradually arose at Porta and was often asked by my fellow prisoners about certain symptoms that resulted from hunger. After the war, I and six colleagues undertook a large-scale investigation of surviving Danish former concentration camp inmates,[81] and on the strength of that investigation we were able to describe the conditions under which prisoners were deported and the ailments and diseases that were the cause of death at the various concentration camps where there were Danish prisoners. The average death rate was around 10 percent. At Porta this was 44 percent. Porta was therefore the grimmest camp to which Danes were sent.

Hunger and infections dominated the picture. The first sign of real starvation was our ability to overcome the nausea we felt at the ill-tasting food we had to make do with. At first, we received fifteen hundred calories per day, which was a third of that necessary for working in freezing conditions down the mine for twelve hours at a stretch, plus the hours of wearying roll calls. Then the number of calories dropped to about six hundred, which was not sufficient to maintain a normal body temperature, and thus life. We talked and dreamt about normal food and for many of us a large layer cake with masses of whipped cream was the most wonderful thing that anyone could receive.

I do not know whether these dreams reflected anything specific that was missing in our diet, but my research after the war showed that apart from calories, what we lacked most was protein. While a lack of vitamins set its stamp upon the health of prisoners in Japanese concentration camps, it was a lack of protein that was characteristic for German concentration camps, and this was to be attributed to differences in the food provided.

We soon began to lose weight and the weight loss was the most dramatic during the first two months at Porta. Subcutaneous fat soon disappeared, our skin grew loose and personal traits began to vanish, so that we all began to resemble one another. Then the skeleton would begin to poke out more and more and in the final phase, all that was left was skin and bone – camouflaged to some extent by edema in the calves and one or two other places in the body.

Once the body's supplies of carbohydrates and fat were used up, the protein of our cells and tissues began to be eaten away – a kind of internal cannibalism. As our muscles shrank, an enormous weariness would overtake us (adynamia), which meant that movements became sluggish, and we walked with a stoop and dragged our feet. The extremely starved and permanently freezing prisoners looked like living human skeletons. With our blankets draped over our heads to keep off the cold we looked like ascetic old "Mussulmans" on pilgrimage. The concentration camp designation for the terminal phase of famine disease owes its origin to this. In many capitals all over the world you will find monuments erected to commemorate "the Unknown Soldier." In the center of Copenhagen there is a monument commemorating "the Unknown Mussulman."

The hunger syndrome as it developed in the German concentration camps was characterized not only by a loss of weight and the weakening of the muscles, but by a complex dysfunction of the fluid balance of the organism and of certain vital tissue. Even in the early stages of starvation, we began to complain of abnormal urination. This not only meant urinating large amounts, more than four quarts (4–5 liters) a day, but also frequent, insistent and not infrequently painful urination, which was impossible to control. We did not know – and still do not – the reason for this phenomenon, but one factor is the large amount of liquid input. We were always thirsty and drank large amounts of water. This stilled our hunger to some extent. Furthermore, most of the food we received was semi-liquid.

But in addition to this disturbance of the fluid intake and output, there was chronic diarrhea. This meant that even more fluid was lost and led to dehydration, which in turn led to even more thirst and, paradoxically, also to fluid retention in the form of edema, especially in the legs. So the starving "Mussulman" was typically a prisoner with a seriously emaciated and dried out torso and arms who stumbled around on legs swollen with edema.

This imperious need to have a pee would force us to go and urinate up

to between ten and twenty times a day. This was worst at night, especially
for those up on the fourth level of the bunks. Many things had to click,
in such a situation. Firstly, you had to have a good bunkmate who would
guard against your sleeping place being taken over while you were out in
the yard. Then there was the question of physical strength. First, you had
to overcome a universal bodily exhaustion, where a few hours' sleep were
vital for survival, but you also would have to crawl down from the fourth
level as the need for a pee knew no assuaging.

If you did not manage to get down, first your mattress and then the
man directly underneath would receive a night greeting and if he protested
you ran the risk of a night roll call and "*Fünfundzwanzig im Asch*." This was
not, however, the greatest danger. What was worse was if you were tempted
to use one of the food bowls as a pisspot. If someone was caught doing this,
there would be a roll call and he would be made to drink his own urine in
front of all his comrades, then receive twenty-five blows to his behind. As
described above, this was something that not everyone survived.

The most prevalent illness in the concentration camp was undoubtedly diarrhea caused by hunger. This was termed *Scheisserei* among the
prisoners. Neither we nor the doctors who finally came to rescue us in
white buses understood what caused this. *Scheisserei* affected so many of
the prisoners that you could imagine that an epidemic was taking place.
Typhus and dysentery were what was diagnosed and both the patients
and the doctors thought this to be the most likely reason, but the diagnosis was wrong in most cases. Not until animal experiments were carried
out after the war did my colleagues Jørn and Eigil Hess Thaysen find out
that diarrhea caused by hunger arises on account of the deterioration of
the mucous membrane of the intestines, now incapable of absorbing food.
The illness was not contagious, but had hit the whole of prison society on
account of hunger.

There was not only talk of hunger patients "eating themselves from
within," but there was also a reduction in the production of fresh cells to
compensate for those that had become worn out.[82] Later I wrote a doctoral
thesis on this subject.[83] We soon became aware of the fact that both finger-
nails and hair grew much more slowly than normally and that sores and
wounds healed much more slowly too. On the other hand, what we could
not see was the damage done to internal organs, whose function normally
needs a swift turnover of cells. One of these organs is the intestine, whose

mucous membrane is usually changed within a matter of days. This could not occur on the Porta diet, which was poor in both calories and protein. The intestine became nothing more than a slippery drainpipe which the food ran through, with chronic diarrhea as a result.

Other organs that were particularly susceptible were the lymphatic glands and the spleen, which led to the reduced production of antibodies, and thus a reduced resistance to infection. On the other hand the brain, which has no exchange of cells in an adult, was the last organ to be attacked in the last phases of the shortage of protein and starvation in general.

Scheisserei also meant many visits to the latrine, day and night. If things went wrong, you ran the risk of a roll call, with the prisoner having to lick his pollution up from the floor. When Kapo Schorsch was in a particularly bad mood, the miscreant ran the risk of having water thrown over him and having to spend several days and nights in the mortuary, naked, beaten and freezing. Naturally survival was far from certain.

Starvation was the direct cause of the symptoms described above. They were so characteristic that a hunger syndrome could be defined. However, other life-threatening diseases were rife. Infections were especially important given the poor hygiene and the reduced capacity for the formation of protective antibodies.

The skin was especially vulnerable, and edema particularly common. A hunger patient would have many subcutaneous lumps and swellings as a result of the wounds in the mines and many bites from fleas and lice. In the areas with edema, infections would spread like wildfire resulting in what is termed a "phlegmon." When the edema was lanced, a whole liter of pus could run out. Death often visited such patients.

Infections tended to first affect the respiratory tract. Prisoners in Porta often complained about long-term and very irritating coughs, which kept them awake at night. This was due to the dust-laden air in the mines, but could lead to bronchitis and pneumonia. But the infection that was most feared among prisoners was tuberculosis of the lungs. In such an over-crowded hall as the theater, the risk of infection was maximum. There was no chance of receiving a precise diagnosis, and there were no ways of treating the disease. But if a patient was suspected of having tuberculosis, this would lead to him being isolated until a transport to Neuengamme could be arranged. What happened to the patient after that was something we knew nothing about. How many men died of tuberculosis at Porta has never been established with any exactitude, but in the cases of twenty-five deaths that were examined, tuberculosis played a role in the case of nine of them. Both Flemming and I were infected, but weren't diagnosed until after we had returned home to Denmark.

Tuberculosis was the most frequent and most serious aftereffect of the deportation. Some 25 percent of all former Porta prisoners were diagnosed with the disease on repatriation. Five such patients died after arriving home. For Flemming, this meant two years in the hospital. But he survived.

While the diagnosis of tuberculosis was inadequate, there was no doubt about the throat infection that had a particular effect on the Danish prisoners when it struck our excellent spokesman, Captain Ploug, during the trip to Porta. He had a bad sore throat and we sought help with the Czech "doctor" at the camp, but were sent away. In the end a large swelling of the throat ensued and we managed to get the Kapo to understand the gravity of the situation, and with his help we managed to get Ploug transferred to the infirmary. The Czech "doctor" proved to be a mere dental technician and did not know what to do with the patient, and within a few hours Captain Ploug died in my arms on November 14, while a rat sat on a cornice looking on. I had no knife and was helpless.

I was unhappy by now and had ever greater difficulty in continuing to be optimistic. Poor morale began to eat away at us and things got no better when another Dane died five days later. A further eight Danish political prisoners were sent on transport to Neuengamme that November. Only four survived and we soon saw how things were bad among the 54s. Against this grim background, I was asked at the end of the month to assist in the primitive infirmary we had.

The Infirmary

When I started working in the infirmary, it was still in the theater hall. As this was inadequate, sick men were also to be found in among the others. The lighting was so bad that you could hardly read the thermometer. There were not enough blankets and there was also a shortage of medicine, bandages, instruments, food and people to help. It was a hopeless enterprise.

The infirmary was at first run by the incompetent Czech dental technician mentioned above, but he was soon sent back down the mines and replaced by a Polish doctor, whom many of the Danes remember with gratitude. He was assisted by a Russian pharmacist who was only interested in feathering his own nest. The medical staff also included a Russian medical orderly (*Kalfaktor*) who was basically a decent chap, if somewhat light-fingered. The staff was increased to include a French doctor, Robert Naudin, and myself.

Robert Naudin was a provincial doctor from St. Loup de la Salle near Beaune in Burgundy. He was a fine doctor and a good man, but had no power over what went on in the infirmary, even though he was the only person who had medical competence. But he looked after his patients. He was always smiling and would work up to eighteen hours a day without so much as a murmur. Working in the infirmary meant that Flemming and I had to change bunkmates. While the infirmary was still in the large theater hall, we could still share a bunk, but at the beginning of December it was moved out into a hut in the yard, and so our spell as bunkmates came to an end. I moved into the infirmary where I was lucky enough to share a bunk with Robert Naudin. And Flemming had good luck too. His new bunkmate was Nikolaj Nikolajsen, more about whom will be told in the next section.

I worked just under two months at the infirmary. The food was slightly better and I wasn't always cold. But it did mean an eighteen-hour stint every day. The worst thing, however, was the knowledge that we could do very little for our fellow prisoners. Hunger, given the nature of our circumstances, was something we could do nothing about and as for treating infections, we only had very small supplies of German sulfonamide preparations.

The dressing of wounds was hampered by a lack of disinfectants and bandages. We used paper. Arms and legs were not infrequently broken as a result of accidents in the mine. In one or two cases we received permission to send our patients for X-rays to the town of Minden. But otherwise we simply had to make do as best we could. We could not perform larger-scale operations, there were no anesthetics, and medical expertise was also in short supply. Appendicitis would usually result in peritonitis and death.

The most we could do for our patients was, in many cases, give them a rest from work by staying at the infirmary, or put them on *Schonung* ("light duty"). This meant that the patient was transferred to potato peeling. It was a cold and wet job, but had certain advantages. Work was not so hard, and the chances of getting extra rations or the thicker part of the turnip soup were greater. There were even chances of taking a shower and obtaining a little more underwear. For Danish prisoners, this offered the opportunity of storing their Red Cross parcels. For prisoners who were about to succumb to the hard work in the mine, this was a last chance to save their lives. One of my Danish friends managed to get himself *Schonung* by putting an axe through his own foot down in the mine. It was an act of desperation, but he survived.

Flemming also got himself *Schonung*. But he regretted it when he saw the strength of a fellow prisoner fading away in the potato store. I believe it was at that time that he contracted tuberculosis. To my great worry, he volunteered for one of the toughest teams in the mine.

As winter approached, the cold and damp did too. There was an icy fog over the Weser valley, and food rations were getting smaller and smaller. If we could get hold of a dog or a rat, the poor animal was soon killed and eaten. I did not experience any cannibalism. The fact that the list of deaths increased during this time is to be understood. In early December, two Danish Resistance fighters died, and five more, including my HD2 partner Jørgen Salling, were sent on a transport for the sick to Neuengamme. Only he survived. He returned to Denmark, but the memories of Porta haunted him and in 1959 he committed suicide. Losses among the 54s were even greater.

The enormous exhaustion that I felt grew worse and worse, and I tried to put a description of this down on paper once I was back in Denmark:[84]

I have always regarded the skeleton as an ugly object, and even worse when covered by only a thin layer of flesh, a little skin and a bit of hair. You should let the dead look after themselves. But now when you could see a skeleton wearing a piece of shirt that hardly covered the upper part of his chest, leaning over the edge of the bunk so that his ribs bent under the pressure, and moving his arms slowly and fumbling like the limbs of a daddy longlegs; when you could see two large eyes filled with boundless despair, tearful eyes, and you could hear some vague moaning sounds emerging from the compressed ribcage, uttering, in a whisper, "I can't go on any longer!" then you realize that this skeleton with a little flesh on the bones, a little skin and a little hair, is still a human being, still alive, who needs you to help him up into his bunk. In such a situation, have you the right to feel disgust?

It is true that as he stands there his feces are running out of his bowels and down his legs at the same time as the pus from a large boil on his left ankle has caused a puddle on the floor which he is standing in. It is also true that you can see from a long way off, on account of scratches, that he has fleas and lice. Nor is there any doubt about the fact that the crusts in his ears are a month old and that he has straw stuck to his bedsores, there where the bones of his pelvis are penetrating his skin. But is this any excuse for feeling disgust?

You can grow so worn out from physical labor, cold and starvation that every step is a victory in itself, every word uttered an effort. When you work for eighteen hours per day and have to live on twelve ounces (350 g) of cellulose bread and a little turnip water you can, within the space of a month, become as weary as a whole old people's home. It takes five steps to reach the skeleton and it is to be lifted five feet into his bunk. Five steps and the lift, and I am so tired.

But the eyes remain filled with tears and the arms and legs continue to fumble and stumble. The dead man again whispers, "I can't go on anymore." He is like an insect that creeps up the window pane, only to fall down and start crawling again, endlessly.

I try to ignore him. I have so many other things to do. The Russian prisoner with the phlegmon needs a change of bandage and there are seven blood tests to be done. By the time that is over, I hope that he has in some way or another managed to get into his bunk. If only he would stop fumbling. He is distracting me and I'll never manage to locate the vein at this rate. At last the blood comes, only six more blood tests to go.

Only five steps and he is so thin. He must weigh next to nothing.

Now he's falling!

He is almost six feet three inches (190 cm) tall and strongly built. He weighs no more than a child. Now he is lying there relaxing a little, and so he whispers, very quietly, "Thanks," and his hand tries to clasp mine. The tormented look on his face gives way to a slight smile, only a second long. But there it was. He had felt my sympathy and paid me back with all the emotion he could muster. He only had one wish, to get up onto his bunk and die in the puddle that was to become his deathbed. Now he was lying there, recompensing the man who had just helped him with all the love he had.

How filthy he is. The lice are crawling all over him and he stinks of excrement. Why don't I take my hands off him. My arms are smeared with his feces right up to my elbows. Where has my disgust gone?

So many thoughts, yet the whole of this only lasted two minutes. I have not had so many thoughts for a whole week. We look at one another a little, then I squeeze his hand and now it is me who whispers, "Thanks." He looks at me with some incomprehension. But then his face clears and he asks, "Were you outside?"

"Yes, right up to the edge of where you stop being human but still live on." He says nothing more. He has tears in his eyes and squeezes my hand. We love one another. Then we part and go our separate ways – he to the grave and me to my next patient.

Liberty, Equality, Fraternity

"In here we're really cut down to size" was the conclusion that Schlanbusch drew a few days after our arrival at Porta. He was right. Prisoners were not only stripped naked but they were stripped mentally too. In some of them, self-preservation became the dominant character trait, of which we saw a most frightening example in Kapo Schorsch. But it affected many other prisoners to a greater or lesser extent. But for others, maintaining human dignity was the first priority. There are, luckily, many instances of this. But there was one man who made a deep impression not only on myself, but on many prisoners of various nationalities. This was Nikolaj Nikolajsen.

It may have been out in the Weser Stolle that I first set eyes on this forty-year-old man. He was large and strong. But it was the gentleness in his friendly eyes that first drew my attention to him, to a greater extent than his sheer physical strength. There was no doubt about the fact that he was used to working with his hands and it came as no surprise that he had been a farmer. But his eyes told that he had used his time for many other things than merely cultivating the soil.

Nikolaj had a small farm in Sjølund, to the south of Kolding, at the foot of the *Skamlingsbanken*, the hill on which Danes assembled during the nineteenth-century dispute with the Germans over the province of Schleswig. He lived there with his wife and five children. He could not afford to keep horses, but dreamed of mechanizing his little farm. But what was stored at his farm was not agricultural machinery but second-hand weapons and explosives. He had been the chairman of the local Young Conservatives' Club and was active in local politics and Schlanbusch was no doubt right when he wrote that Nikolaj would have had a career in Conservative politics ahead of him, had he survived the war. Nikolaj had said very little to anyone about his Resistance activities during the occupation. But by way of an informer, the Gestapo found his cache of weapons, and that was why he had ended up in Porta.

He spoke genuine Jutland dialect and no other language with it. But it did not take many days for him to establish contacts with both the Frenchmen and the Russians. The other prisoners soon found out that Nikolaj was always on hand when they needed help with, for instance, heavy rocks, or when the Kapos were urging them on to work harder, when the dump wagons were being filled. One day, near the beginning of his time in Porta, he was working at the "Large Stolle" and when the shift was ready to go back to the camp in the evening one of the Russians was so ill that he could hardly drag himself back to camp, so Nikolaj carried him the whole way. Nikolaj was ready to help anyone. He was not the kind of man to ask, "Who is my neighbor?" Anyone needing his help got it and there was plenty of need for it down the mine.

At one point, the whole Danish group was in need of his help. I do not remember exactly when it took place, but at any rate it was shortly before Christmas. The first Red Cross parcels had been distributed to the Danes at the end of November, beginning of December. This had caused dissatisfaction among other prisoners and given rise to thefts and attacks; but since the parcels had already been plundered in Neuengamme the dissatisfaction was more of a general antipathy towards the Danes than any specific expression of envy. But when the parcels began coming with more in them, less having been stolen out of them, the situation changed.

In mid-December we received reefer jackets, warm underwear, a scarf, a pair of gloves, a cap and, most important of all, a pair of clogs that the Danish Red Cross had sent to all Danish prisoners. Even though a lot of these things ended up among the prison population in general on account of thieving, it did mean that circumstances for the Danes were better than for the average prisoner. The equality had been broken and the different ranks now not only included the Master Race and the rest. Suddenly a group of privileged men had arisen out of the ranks of ordinary prisoners, and this brought with it risks. Now Danes were without rights, without honor and without protection in the real meaning of the term. Hatred grew and reached its climax one dark, rainy evening.

Kapo Schorsch had ordered the Danish prisoners for roll call out in the yard. A new Red Cross consignment had arrived with food, and the parcels were distributed by the Kapo who, once they had secured their share, withdrew to a corner of the yard to see what would happen next. Kommandoführer Nau and several of his colleagues assembled in another corner to watch the performance. It took no more than a few minutes for the small group of Russian prisoners at the other end of the yard to grow. The group became bigger and bigger and came closer and closer to the Danes, so that these were now faced with a group five times the size of their own, a group of starving comrades from some seventeen nationalities.

The time for the great massacre was at hand. The final showdown. We all realized what this would mean. Then we suddenly heard a voice, full of fear, shouting, "Nikolaj, Nikolaj, come and help us!"

Out of the crowd of frightened Danes stepped a tall, strongly built man with bushy eyebrows and heavy limbs. He went alone with his arms stretched out up to the mass of men who were approaching the much-hated Danish upper class in a threatening manner. But when they saw Nikolaj they hesitated and when he told them to come to a halt, they obeyed. There they stood, weighing one another up – Nikolaj Nikolajsen, alone on one side, and several hundred starving Russians, Frenchmen, Dutchmen and many others on the other. A deathly silence had fallen over the yard. At the entrance stood a group of Kapos, eagerly awaiting the advent of the bloodbath. But in vain. A couple of minutes passed – it felt like an eternity – before we all realized that Nikolaj had proved to be the stronger. He now clearly felt that he had the situation under control, slowly let his arms fall to his sides, turned to his frightened compatriots and said, "And now we are going to share everything!"

So there was Christmas fare for everyone. But the people celebrating Christmas were a sad bunch. Against all expectations, we were given one and a half free days. This gave rise to gladness, but also worry. Even though the prisoners were divided up into a day shift and a night shift, there were not enough bunks for all. If all the prisoners were in the camp at the same time, we could anticipate an enormous fight for a place to stay without ending up outside in the freezing cold.

In the theater, the camp authorities had put up a Christmas tree with electric lights. But it was impossible for this to create a Christmas atmosphere. We had also received a little tree out in the infirmary, plus a few fir twigs. We even managed to requisition a little wax and shoe polish and from this we managed to make a few smoky candles that lit up the twenty-four square yards (20 m²) of the room, in which there were twelve bunks with patients who had contracted tuberculosis and other contagious diseases. It was here that I lived along with Robert Naudin and it was here that I was working as doctor, nurse, drudge, mortuary assistant and professional mourner, and it was here that some fifteen to twenty people would be celebrating Christmas – Danes, Frenchmen, Poles, Russians and a few Germans.

The highlight of Christmas Eve was the dinner, which was derived from the contents of the Red Cross parcels. The menu was oats cooked into a porridge with skimmed milk, diluted and with a little malt extract (Ovaltine) added. It was a thin soup, but we were glad to have it. Some of the Danes had been given the remains of the parcels they had been sent from home. They shared them with us. Nikolaj's plea had not fallen on deaf ears. This boosted our morale a little.

When the meal was over and our bowls licked clean, we tried to sing some Danish, French and Polish Christmas carols. The Russians were a little disoriented. They were not used to celebrating Christmas, though they knew what it was, and they also felt the poignant difference between the concept of Peace on Earth at Yuletide and the reality we found ourselves part of. The memories of the fact that we had once been human beings, loved by others, brought tears to the eyes of many of us and made us feel deeply moved.

The candles soon burned down, the smell of singed fir twigs filling the room. The sick dozed off and dreamt dreams they had not thought of for a long time, dreams that reduced the hard glint in their eyes and made their starved faces look less tormented and more human. I went out into the yard with Flemming. It was a sharp frost and not a cloud in the sky. This was a rarity in this otherwise foggy valley. We walked around, enjoying the fresh air, trying to locate constellations. The Great Wain was very clear and by that we could also find the Pole Star. Our thoughts went to our family and friends in Denmark and Sweden. But the cold soon brought us back to Porta and we shrugged off our feelings of weakness and emotion, and asked ourselves the eternal question: when will this all end?

The end came within a few hours for Jørgen Staffeldt, who died on the morning of Christmas Day. He had taken over command of Holger Danske after Lillelund and had been arrested by the Gestapo as HD2 was wound up. We had become good friends in Frøslev and in Porta he had become a shining example of a man with an invincible regard for his fellow human beings who had never let himself be infected by the evil that surrounded him. But he had no way of warding off tuberculosis. He was one of the patients I looked after on Christmas night. And the next morning I was filled with sorrow when I told Flemming that Jørgen Staffeldt was dead. He was the thirteenth Danish freedom fighter to die at Porta. Another twenty-three were to follow.

After the war, the corpses of the concentration camp victims who had been identified were brought home to Denmark on July 16, 1947, and reburied at the "Mindelunden," the Memorial Cemetery in Ryvangen in Copenhagen. Jørgen Staffeldt was one of these. It fell to me to bid welcome to our dead comrades and to give a last salute to the dead. In my attempts to contribute a small grain of solace in my great sorrow, I thought of a star – however small and far away it was, it was still a dot of light in our dark memories, which could not be extinguished. Then I thought of Jørgen Staffeldt, who inspired me to this description of the death of a prisoner:[85]

> He lay still and calm in his bunk. To all appearances, he did not differ from those who still had more strength and yet there was something about him that was not present in the orderlies who brought him his last bowl of soup, or the friend who brought him his last hunk of bread. In the midst of this small but utterly evil world where human beings were slowly being reduced to hunted animals, he emanated a strange restfulness, which was marked by both humility and pride. His eyes reflected deep concern for those who were to suffer what he had suffered. His thoughts strayed to those back home; his worries were about their future. His fumbling hands sought those of the friend who was straightening his blanket, so he could show gratitude and sympathy to a man who would live on. At the same time, a slight but victorious smile crossed his lips. They had tried to remove his right to be a human being, to love humanity, and they had lost.

Jørgen Staffeldt was the answer to Kapo Schorsch, and for that reason, his loss was felt all the more deeply, affecting others too. "In here we're really cut down to size" had been Schlanbusch's comment. He was an experienced police officer. The news of Jørgen's death made it obvious that each and every one of us had to ask the question whether we would be cut down to our *natural* size. Was our natural human dimension that of Kapo Schorsch or of Jørgen Staffeldt? By far the greatest majority of human beings live their lives without ever having to answer such questions. They never get to know themselves. But we got the chance.

We began to become more aware of the fact that war was being waged, as Allied airplanes began to fly more and more regularly over our camp, and even attacked on occasions. A couple of days after such an attack, we could enjoy a little more meat in our turnip soup, on account of the horses that had been killed in the air raid. Down the mine we were safe from aerial bombardment, but not during the marches to and from the camp. One French prisoner was killed in that way.

The many flights over our heads were a sign that the Germans would suffer ultimate defeat, something which pleased no one more than it did us. But rumors of the Ardennes offensive being conducted by the Germans robbed us of the hope that the war would be over soon. The Allies had air superiority; that was in no doubt. The question was how and when the end would come. Would liberation come before we all died of starvation; would the surviving few be freed or murdered to eradicate traces of the actions of the criminals involved? We simply did not know. But as 1944 drew to a close, our thoughts on this matter proved to be very realistic ones.

After the "gluttony of Christmas dinner," hunger began to make itself felt for real. The infirmary was soon filled up with emaciated prisoners. Food portions grew smaller and smaller. The ss tried to solve the problem of too many people receiving treatment by conducting a number of inspections whereby anyone whose temperature was below 102 (39° c) was declared fit for work and sent back down the mine. No one would dream of pretending. This would at best result in a transport away from Porta, and rumors of conditions at Bergen-Belsen were beginning to circulate.

Soon, all the "Mussulmans" had to fend for themselves as best they could. I ended up with a "doctor's practice" with patients consisting of exhausted prisoners who still had to drag themselves to work. The rational cure for this condition was food; but there was hardly any food. All I could do was try *Schonung*, encouragement and consolation. One case sticks in my memory, a colleague from Horsens, who was now at the terminal stage of starvation. I managed to get him *Schonung* but this only helped a little. I tried to encourage him to keep himself clean, wash, eat our disgusting food, bullied him into action, but this had equally little effect. He was a lost man. One day, when I had tried in vain to get him to take some soup, I took him back to his bunk in the theater. I helped him up to the second level and there he lay, totally exhausted from the effort to get there. His legs had been badly affected by edema. He lay still, half unconscious. Then the dripping began. He had gotten a hole in one of his legs and the water from his dropsy was seeping out. The mattress was drenched with the fluid and with the sufferings of this self-sacrificing man. He was dead within twenty minutes.

The situation we found ourselves in gave us a lot of food for thought. You could have imagined that there would have been a lot of suicides on account of the hopeless circumstances. I only saw one example of this. One of the older Russians hanged himself from the bedpost. You could also have expected people to resort to religion. Those condemned to death at Vestre Fængsel found strength in religion. But it was different in Porta; it was difficult to find Our Lord there. Religious inspiration undoubtedly gave comfort and support to my brother Flemming, but it was only expressed after liberation. As for me, my stay at Porta only confirmed the same point of view I already had when awaiting execution back at Vestre Fængsel. I believed in the historical figure of Jesus, in my own responsibility, but not in Christ Our Lord and eternal life; I can still live with those convictions.

In discussions with Communists, both Danish and Russian, before all rational conversation had petered out, we often talked about the ideals of the French Revolution: Liberty, Equality and Fraternity. For me the resolution of the discussion came around the end of 1944, start of 1945. For me, it had been Jørgen Staffeldt who had represented Freedom, something he regarded as worth giving up his life for. The "Mussulmans" were the ultimate and undeniable representatives of Equality. We were not truly equal until we lay in the grave; but we were getting perilously close to the "ideal" once we had reached the "Mussulmans" stage. With Nikolaj Nikolajsen as the representative of Fraternity, the apostles of Equality could not entirely convince me of their case.

One generation after the war it became Equality that seized people's imaginations, rather than either Liberty or Fraternity. This is something I do not understand. Is it that the strongest drive in human beings is the herd instinct – which Hitler played on – or envy? I do not know, but a few weeks later I felt the blessings of Equality with my own body.

On the Road to Eternity

At the end of January 1945, the ss declared a total war effort had begun. The death throes of Germany had begun, and for us this meant in practice that all patients who were able to stand up, plus half the staff of the infirmary, were sent to work down the mine. This triggered a wave of intrigues in which the Russian pharmacist was one of the most active participants. He saved his own skin, but for me my work in the infirmary had come to an end and my acquaintance with the "Grosse Stolle" could begin.

The Grosse Stolle was an enormous network of mine galleries where people were blasting their way into the rock in the Weser ridge just across the river from Hotel Kaiserhof. The march to reach this part was shorter, but that was the only advantage with this new place of work, which consisted of endless larger and smaller tunnels that bored their way into the hillside at seven different levels. The tunnels joined up the factory areas, which were as large as churches. Grosse Stolle was the biggest of these. There was plenty of room for two railway lines next to one another. Ceiling height varied between 33 and 130 feet (10–40 m).

The first job I did when I was thrown out of the infirmary was working on a small tunnel a couple of floors above Grosse Stolle. This was a dead end and was to be opened up to reach another part of the network. I worked in a small team consisting of three to four prisoners and two to three civilian miners under the leadership of a ganger. The professionals had been called in from Saar to help their Westphalian colleagues. They only worked for eight hours at a stretch, and even now, towards the end of the war, they were not undernourished.

Their attitudes vis-à-vis the prisoners varied. The ganger exhibited the holy fire of the Teuton. Germany was to be saved at any price. He was presumably a Nazi, but this was hardly something we could ask him about. He was cold and inimical towards us prisoners, but he did not hit us. But he did constantly try to push up the tempo of work. His civil colleagues were less aggressive. In an unguarded moment, one of them confided in me that he feared that all Germans would be held accountable for the atrocities we had had to suffer and expected that all adult males would be castrated. But on one occasion, he did share his food packet with me.

The work consisted of drilling six to ten feet (2–3 m) into the rock with a pneumatic drill, a cavity into which an explosive charge and a fuse were placed. This was most familiar to an old saboteur like myself. After the explosion had taken place the loosened rocks and stones were shoveled and lifted out onto a dump wagon, which the prisoners would then push out of the mine.

My own job meant holding the drill with my bare hands during the pre-blasting phase, until it took in the rock face. Cold water ran down my sleeves and I soon became soaked through and freezing. The vibrations of the drill took the skin off my palms, which in no time at all were full of sores. Then the shoveling and lifting would begin, which hurt both my hands and my back. The ganger was urging us on and once he even lit the fuse without checking that we were all out of the way. This cost the lives of several prisoners.

I worked on the day shift and the night shift, by turns. The night shift had the advantage that it was better in camp during the day. We could more easily obtain a bunk to sleep in and a blanket to cover us, and the food line was not as long. On the other hand we risked having to do extra work in the camp itself. So we got very little sleep when on the night shift and it was therefore hard to keep awake in the mine.

When we had finished opening up our little tunnel, I was set to work on a ledge in the Grosse Stolle. There was no rail and you ran the risk of falling down and killing yourself. I learned the art of chewing tobacco to keep me awake. This worked, but I would hiccup and felt that my diaphragm was about to burst.

Then I was set to work unpacking machine parts in one of the large halls. By doing this I discovered that machines and equipment from the Philips radio works in the Netherlands were to be installed underground. The work offered opportunities for sabotage, and they were taken, which the German engineers only discovered when it was too late. If sabotage had been discovered there and then, it would have led to a cruel death.

The parts I had to unpack were lying in chests filled with glass wool. I had never seen so much "angel hair" and given the cold and my tiredness, I gave in to the temptation to "tuck up" in one of the chests. But I soon came out again as my whole body began to itch. I should have known this beforehand, but I was so tired. The itching definitely saved my life. Had I fallen asleep, I would have been discovered, sooner or later, by the ss guard. This would have meant *"Fünfundzwanzig im Asch"* and hanging, as the most likely consequence, ending my life on Earth. And I dare not think what would have happened if they had also discovered that a condenser was missing from one piece of equipment.

I was finally moved to a mining gallery. Here there was room for larger dump wagons, so that shoveling occurred in two different tempos. First the stones and pieces of rock were shoveled by three civilian miners onto planks that were lying on two trestles next to the wagon and from there we would shovel it all into the wagon. My workmate here was a baker in civilian life and now a prisoner, on his way towards the "Mussulman" stage. The ganger was my tormentor in this gallery. Everything had to happen quickly and the civilian miners appeared to think that they could shovel their way to a German victory. The baker and I did not stand a chance. We were in the minority, we were starving, we had to work for twelve hours at a stretch and our only hope was that Germany would soon lose the war.

The stones and rocks piled up around us and the ganger kept on cursing. In the end he took a shovel and started working himself and soon I realized that it was less a question of filling the dump wagon than of sacrificing the two Danish prisoners. In his desperate struggle against defeat, he was now punishing the enemy, i.e., us. We tried to protect ourselves with our shovels and our hands, but we were hit by flying stones; first our shins, then our bodies, then our faces were hit. The blood ran and in the end the baker collapsed while I was shoveling like a madman.

Then came the signal for work to end and for a roll call. The stoning stopped and the civil miners packed up their equipment while I began to dig myself and the baker out of the heap of stones. I succeeded and half carrying, half dragging my mate we reached the place where the roll call would take place, outside the Grosse Stolle, in time. My unfortunate workmate was unconscious by now. He was moaning and along with another prisoner, I had to carry him back to camp.

We took him to the infirmary where he received some form of bandage. The baker was then put in a bunk in the infirmary where he died within a few hours. I went out into the yard in order to recover. I had a pain in my back, mostly in the place where I had been shot. I was afraid that the old fracture would give again.

Rumors of being stoned spread, and the ss doctor who happened to be there to inspect the camp asked me how I had received my injuries. I was surprised at this, but told him about the stones and my old gunshot wound. The ss doctor knew that I had worked previously in the infirmary and when he heard I was a medical student, he asked me about where my father had worked. While he was talking to me, the Russian pharmacist was dancing around us nervously. He was clearly worried that I would once again be employed at the infirmary – and that he would therefore be sent down the mine.

Even the ss doctor was moved by my plight. I was the son of a fellow doctor, i.e., a colleague of his, and he had my fate in his hands. He shifted his weight from foot to foot and said apologetically, spreading his arms: "*Das einzige was ich für Sie tun kann, ist Ihnen acht Tage Schonung zu geben* (The only thing I can do for you is give you eight days *Schonung*)." The pharmacist looked relieved and went back to the infirmary while I stood there asking myself: "Can this be true? Am I asleep or awake?"

It was not the eight days of *Schonung* or the nervousness of the pharmacist that had made an impression on me, and only to a lesser extent the fact that the ss doctor had shown concern. No, it was something quite different. He had said "*Sie*" to me, and had not called me a *Drecksack* or a *Schweinhund*. The polite form of the pronoun is used when polite people address one another. It was as if he had taken a flute from his pocket and played a little Rococo music, and then recited a poem by Schiller. It was grotesque, unreal, a memory from a world long gone, but a great encouragement nonetheless, something the enthusiasts for equality after the war would have difficulty in grasping.

When I started my eight-day "holiday," I did not realize, however, that a much greater problem lurked on the horizon.

It was hard for me to judge what chances I myself and my fellow prisoners had of surviving this ordeal. But at that point in time, I became clear about the two key factors involved: starvation and tuberculosis. I was growing increasingly worried about my brother, whose coughing was getting worse and worse. But it was the fate of another patient that occupied most of my thoughts and feelings during my little period of respite. I realized by now that it was not always the strongest and largest men who stood the best chances of survival. Tuberculosis made no distinctions, but hunger hit large men harder than it did small ones, as they needed a larger intake of calories. And it also hit the strongest of us all: Nikolaj Nikolajsen.

Nikolaj was taken to the infirmary at the end of February and I used my days off to visit him. He knew the end was nigh, and took it all with great presence of mind. I was sitting with him when he died on March 3.

The Russian pharmacist came past and saw that I was sitting weeping. "*Ist es dein Vater? (Is he your father?)*" he asked. I looked up at him and said, "Yes." Because although I had my own father, whom I loved and greatly respected, I did in truth feel that Nikolaj had been one for us all.

Nikolaj Nikolajsen, to whom many prisoners in Porta owe their lives;
Nikolaj Nikolajsen died in Porta from starvation March 3, 1945

The Russian shook his head slightly and left the infirmary, also in tears. A little later, I saw how they had thrown Nikolaj's naked corpse out into the yard. There he lay in the mud without a stitch. I went up to him in sorrow, but then realized that I was not alone. One after the other, they came from all corners of the camp, men from Siberia, Hungary, France, the Netherlands, from all over Europe, and said farewell to their father. Many of them knew, as I did, that this could be the turning point, where our survival was no longer a matter of months, but of days.

Flemming and I now shared a bunk again. We were lucky that we also ended up working in the same place once my *Schonung* was past. This was called Häverstädt and was a long way away from the camp. We first had to take the trolley for a short distance, which gave ordinary civilians plenty of opportunity of seeing in what state we were. After the war, the idea of collective guilt was rejected by many Germans, saying they did not know what had been happening in the camps. It is true that all contacts with prisoners

White buses from Danish Red Cross on their way to
Neuengamme to rescue Scandinavian prisoners

were strictly forbidden, but people had had plenty of chance to see us as
we went to work and many of them could not avoid having contacts with
us at work and had plenty of time to watch us as we marched home every
evening with our dead and dying workmates. People often spat at us.

The last couple of miles (3 km) to Häverstädt had to be covered on foot.
We would take side roads along the north side of the Wiehen ridge and
finally ended up on the edge of a village at the foot of a hill. This is where
we stopped, at a piece of ground where there was a depot where rails were

Count Folke Bernadotte – head of Swedish Red Cross – in
conversation with members of the Danish Women's Voluntary
Services at the Danish-German frontier in Padborg, April 1945

stored. Just under the brow of the hill was a large entrance to a mine. This was the other end of the network that we had made our acquaintance with a good five months previously when we had begun our career as miners in Weser Stolle.

This time, our task was simple but deadly. We were supposed to drag the rails up the steep hillside to the mine at the top. There was no road, but at length we wore a path into the hillside. In order not to slip back down the hill we would take hold of plants and outcrops of rock while holding the rail with the other hand. I cannot honestly remember how many men it took to take each rail up the hill, but it must have been six or eight. But what I do remember clearly is the searing pain in my shoulder when one man stumbled or slipped. It was unbelievably hard work, and there were also the whips of the ss to contend with.

I soon realized that Kommando Häverstädt was not destined to survive for very long. The flights overhead had, to our great chagrin, diminished somewhat and we only saw a few bombing raids in the vicinity of our workplace. But we did hear cannon fire in the distance, and this gave us the hope that liberation would soon come. We knew nothing about the military state of affairs and could not possibly know that a major breakthrough would occur three weeks later. What we did know was that a locality was being built in the camp yard, which was said to be an ablutions block. But we were convinced that this was going to be a gas chamber in which we would be murdered at the very last minute.

I looked at my brother who was coughing continuously and in whose eyes starvation was writ large. I looked at myself and saw that I had serious edema as a result of hunger. I had suffered from constant urination problems and reckoned that my weight had dropped by about 30 percent. All I needed now for me to become a fully qualified hunger patient was for the *Scheisserei* to start. This last and cardinal symptom of starvation took a few days to make its presence felt.

We still tried to have conversations – about the past and the future. We talked a lot about home, and we read the letters we had received again and again. The censor had a very narrow definition of what was allowed to be told in them. But they were nevertheless a sign of life. But hopes of ever seeing our families again began to fade. The exhaustion increased and our conversations would peter out. We now began to daydream more, but hunger caught up with us all too soon. I ran out of things to think about

The Cap Arcona after the bombing which caused the death of several thousand Neuengamme prisoners who were to be drowned by the ss in the Bay of Lübeck

in my past and things were no better with regard to my future. Every day at Porta was the same, the same old routine every single day.

Dreams of liberation and of the eating orgies that awaited us ceased. The passing of time became an ever vaguer concept and in the end vanished entirely. We were living in an eternity with no beginning or end. Starva-

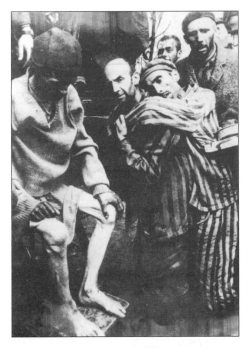

Starving concentration camp prisoners liberated from the Wöbbelin camp

tion had now gotten to our brains. Little knowing that rescue was on the way, I had begun to lose hope. I do not think that at any point during my captivity in Denmark or Germany had I been so low, had such feelings of hopelessness and despair as the day I discovered that I could no longer see my parents, sisters and friends in my mind's eye. I was in the "Ring of Hades."

Hic mortui vivunt.

PART V: THE ROAD TO LIBERATION

CHAPTER 11

Miracle and Catastrophe

On March 18, 1945, the Danish prisoners received orders to take a bath and get ready for departure to Neuengamme the following day. We had heard rumors that the Scandinavian prisoners would assemble at Neuengamme and so sensed a chance that we might be rescued. But at this time we knew nothing about the negotiations between the head of the Swedish Red Cross, Count Folke Bernadotte, and Reichsführer Himmler, who had agreed that all Scandinavian prisoners should be concentrated in Neuengamme and later transported to Sweden. Neither did we know that a large Danish rescue organization in collaboration with the Swedish Red Cross was preparing the transport of hundreds of prisoners first to Neuengamme and then to two camps in Denmark, from where they would finally be sent to safety in Sweden.

Of the total of 225 Danes who had been deported to Porta Westphalica, 144 of them had given up the struggle. They were either dead or had been sent to an unknown fate at Neuengamme or Bergen-Belsen as incapable of work, which meant that by March 18 there were only eighty-one Danish prisoners left. We noticed a change in the attitude of the ss and the Kapos – they had stopped hitting us.

On Monday, March 19, the day began as usual with a lot of noise and a roll call. We only realized something special was afoot when the Danes were given the order to group together separately from the rest. When the work columns had marched off, we were given the remainder of the Red Cross parcels. I remember a Frenchman who came over to me with outstretched arms. "Doctor, I don't want your parcels, I just want to shake your hand as a farewell gesture." I realized that now our fate would either be a miracle or a catastrophe. I never saw him again. This, however, was not the case with those who tormented us most, Kapo Schorsch and Kommandoführer Nau. They were standing at the entrance to the theater and were "saying goodbye" to us. None of us knew then that we would meet again three years after the war. Had they known, I would not have managed to get home alive. They both ended with the guillotine.

At 10:30 we marched over to the railway where we were put in two cattle wagons. We had hardly gotten inside when there was an air raid. The wagons jumped about on the rails during the heavy fire. When the all-clear had sounded, the train started moving. On account of air raids, we had to halt several times and bombs fell all around. But we were not hit. During the journey, we enjoyed our Red Cross parcels. We had not eaten so much in a long time, and I warned my companions not to be too greedy. Compared with our journey from Neuengamme to Porta six months earlier, this was sheer luxury. We had straw to lie on and could stretch out as much as we wanted to. No mistreatment, no curses and blows. Defeat was near.

Neuengamme Revisited

We arrived at Neuengamme late in the afternoon on March 21 and were initially housed in three old wooden huts. We met a number of our former acquaintances who had been at Neuengamme the whole time. They were shocked when they saw us. They had seen many Danish and Norwegian prisoners who had been returning from the various outsourcing workplaces or been brought from other main camps, but none of them had been in such bad shape as those from Porta.

I was glad to see several of my fellow Resistance fighters from Varde, but was sad to hear that Klaus Rønholt, Simony, Nordentoft and Koch had died at Husum. Another thing that made an impression on me was to see many people from Horsens again. The Gestapo had clearly been keeping a close watch on that town where, for instance, Peer Borup's death had given rise to tough resistance to the German occupation.

After being moved around to various wooden huts, the Danish and Norwegian prisoners were put together in one large stone building, which first had to be emptied of dead and dying prisoners of other nationalities. We heard that we were going to be sent to Sweden and began to imagine that we had a chance of survival, even though we feared the whole time that the Germans would change their minds. And what about the rest?

We were now no longer prisoners, but internees and therefore had a number of privileges. Red Cross parcels were soon distributed and the eating orgies we had but dreamt about at Porta could now begin. As expected, not everyone could cope with the food; but the hard slog, curses, noise and beatings had now come to an end.

But there was soon a need for my own specialty. There were many sick men among the Scandinavians and an infirmary was set up in the stone building. Once again I became a camp doctor with a long working day – but no longer eighteen hours at a stretch. Gradually between six and eight Scandinavian doctors worked at the infirmary and my job was more to be a kind of junior partner, rather than doing any actual healing. But they needed me badly too, as many of my patients had tuberculosis. At Porta, I had had a lot of contact, day and night, with TB patients without getting infected. But now things went wrong. I noticed increased coughing, accompanied by a high temperature, and strong pains on the right side of my chest told me that I had contracted pleurisy. It hurt when I breathed. But I continued with my work, though I was too tired to join in the doctor's meetings and discussions about the various diagnoses.

The biggest event at the infirmary happened a few days after we had been moved into the stone building. We were paid a visit by Count Folke Bernadotte. He came to inspect the camp and to arrange the transport home of all the sick men. He smiled, had authority, and was able to command respect from the ss. He was eager to tell us about his negotiations with Reichsführer Himmler. This was the first time we heard about the exceptional action undertaken by the Swedish Red Cross under Bernadotte's command. But in the end it was not the Swedes, but *Det Danske Hjælpekorps* (the Danish Assistance Corps) that got us out of our hell.

But we are extremely grateful to Bernadotte. I am for that reason reluctant to relate a small episode that jarred. The fact I am consigning it to paper at all is because I believe it to have historical significance. And it must cast some light on the situation that the Jews were in at the Theresienstadt camp towards the end of the war, and on Bernadotte's tragic death a few years later in Israel.

When the transport home for the sick had been arranged with Bernadotte, there was time for informal conversation. Our belief in a quick rescue had improved our mood, which was in glaring contrast with the reality around us that the prisoners outside the stone building were facing. No great or witty thoughts were expressed in our circumstances and it was understandable that our "guest" hid the feelings that the sight of all the living human skeletons must have aroused in him. There was a need for action, not tears.

Nonetheless, it came as a shock to me that the count began to contribute to the mood of the day by telling crude Jew jokes. I remember three of them, but feel no desire to repeat them here. It was a thoughtless and tactless act, but worse still was the lack of respect and sympathy for the persecuted Jewish people, which was here expressed as liberation approached. The sheer horror of the fate of the Jews was not yet clear to everyone, not even for all of his audience who were eager to have something to laugh at. For this reason, it is fitting to remember the situation that the Jews found themselves in at the concentration camp at Theresienstadt.

Theresienstadt

During the afternoon after Bernadotte's visit to Neuengamme, there was a staff meeting at Friedrichsruhe, near to Lübeck, where Bernadotte had established his headquarters in Bismarck's old manor house. Colonel Björck explained that he, along with half the Swedish staff and a third of their equipment, would return to Sweden within the next few days and hand the rest of the Swedish detachment over to Major Sven Frykman. At this meeting, the Danish doctor Johannes Holm offered Danish assistance in the form of a large number of buses, ambulances and trucks with Danish drivers, plus all the equipment necessary to replace that of the withdrawing Swedes. Bernadotte was not sure that the Danish "stove vehicles" could be used for transports, but after further consultations the Danish offer was accepted with gratitude and on March 31 Johannes Holm was authorized to form what was termed *Det Danske Hjælpkorps* (the Danish Assistance Corps).

Bernadotte did make the condition that all transports would be conducted under Swedish control and that all negotiations with the Germans would be done by Swedes. Whether this was a question, for Bernadotte, of Swedish prestige or whether it would be awkward for the Germans to negotiate with what were, after all, their enemies was never fully explained. But Dr Rennau, the German Gestapo leader who was in command of the forty Gestapo agents who supervised the operation, was clearly satisfied with the Danish initiative. Under difficult negotiations with other Gestapo bosses and the heads of camps he had managed to maintain good cooperation with Holm, and the new Swedish head of the detachment, Major Frykman, was equally eager for the Danish Assistance Corps to lend a hand, once the last phase of the large-scale rescue action was set in motion.

The arrival of Scandinavian prisoners to Neuengamme aggravated the commandant there, Obersturmbannführer Pauli. First of all the camp was overcrowded. Therefore Pauli insisted that the Swedes should transport some of the non-Scandinavian prisoners to other camps. He refused to accept any more Scandinavian prisoners from the Swedish Red Cross and refused access to the Swedish doctor Professor Rundberg and his nurses to Neuengamme. Personally he wanted all eyewitnesses killed. Himmler himself was furious when the Allies published pictures from Bergen-Belsen, and threatened to stop the rescue of the Scandinavian prisoners, which no doubt did nothing to improve Pauli's disposition towards us. Nor did he want to let Rennau into the camp, which meant that he asked Holm to drive to Berlin to arrange for all orders to be confirmed by Pauli's superior, Gruppenführer Müller, at the *Reichssicherheitshauptamt* (national security headquarters). This was a problem, because it was difficult to obtain contact with Berlin due to the advancing Allied and Russian armies.

On March 29 Rennau and Holm therefore made a flying visit to Berlin without taking into account air raid sirens and *Tiefflieger* (low-flying aircraft). At Rennau's suggestion, they had taken along a lot of Red Cross parcels as bribes. They succeeded in obtaining the relevant orders for the commandant of the Neuengamme camp. Rennau also managed to get permission for Professor Rundberg to repatriate sick prisoners he himself would select. In order to make room for the Scandinavian prisoners, the Germans wanted the Swedish Red Cross to move some two thousand prisoners of other nationalities to a camp at Walderstädte in Hanover. We heard no more about their fate.

The most urgent task was to rescue the Danish Jews from Theresien-stadt. The commitment that Bernadotte had received from Himmler re-garding the grouping together of all Scandinavian prisoners at Neuen-gamme also included the Danish Jews from Theresienstadt. But Rennau let Holm understand that although Himmler had given his permission, resis-tance from the lower ranks was so great that he was doubtful whether the Jews could be transferred to Neuengamme. The only chance for them was to have them taken directly to Sweden, which was ready to receive them. As the front was approaching by the day, both from the east and from the west, action had to be taken quickly.

On April 8, a meeting was held at Friedrichsruhe where Bernadotte was present. When Holm raised the matter of the Jews at Theresienstadt, Bernadotte said that he had promised Brigadeführer Walter Schellenberg from the *Reichssicherheitshauptamt* to give up the idea of transporting the Danish Jews as, according to Schellenberg, this could affect the transport of the rest of the Scandinavian prisoners.

As the Danes could not manage to change Bernadotte's mind, Ren-nau was persuaded to get permission from the *Reichssicherheitshauptamt* to transfer the Jews to Sweden. On April 10 Holm drove to Berlin with Rennau. Unfortunately, they were unable to get hold of the Gestapo chief, Gruppenführer Müller, but Holm did manage to create an element of co-operation by offloading schnapps and Red Cross parcels, with the prospect of more. The next day the phone call from Berlin was awaited in vain. As this phone call did not come, the situation became even more precarious. Holm negotiated with the Swede, Captain Harald Folke, who warned Holm not to try to force their way to Theresienstadt using Danish buses fueled by wood gas. But he also thought he could get permission from Major Fryk-man to have Swedish buses at their disposal.

On April 12, the Swedish-Danish help convoy set off, consisting of a mixed Danish and Swedish crew, plus gasoline-fueled Danish ambulances, taking a team of Danish doctors and nurses. Captain Folke was himself the leader of the convoy. Meanwhile, Johannes Holm and Rennau drove to Berlin in a final attempt to get Gruppenführer Müller's permission to fetch the Jews. This succeeded, partly due to the large amount of schnapps and Red Cross supplies. The necessary papers were signed, but the governor of Bohemia and the commandant of Theresienstadt had to be informed.

Holm could wait no longer. After a major air raid on Berlin and a night's much-needed sleep, he and Dr Rennau started off the next day for Dresden and Theresienstadt. They managed to get into the camp with no difficulties and met the commandant, who said he required permission from the governor in Prague. Holm and Rennau then had to drive to Prague which had, for the most part, been spared the damage of war. Rennau obtained the papers he needed, even though Prague had not actually received any message from Berlin.

On the night of April 15, Captain Folke arrived at Theresienstadt, where 423 Danish Jews were ready waiting to be transported. The convoy went straight to Padborg, via Lübeck, while Holm and Rennau went back to Friedrichsruhe. There were air raids on both convoys that reached Padborg, but on April 17, Holm arrived unscathed, and the Jews continued to Sweden.

The Evacuation of Neuengamme

At the same time as the operation to rescue Jews from Theresienstadt, the Danish Assistance Corps was busy evacuating Neuengamme. Between the third and the tenth of April, 1,517 Danish police officers were sent back to Denmark, and the following week 810 civilian prisoners were sent to Sweden. The Assistance Corps came under fire a number of times.

At that time, news came from Hamburg that no more transports would be allowed. Himmler had become irate at the descriptions of conditions in the concentration camps that the Allies had broadcast after the liberation of Buchenwald and Bergen-Belsen. Bernadotte, who had arrived at Friedrichsruhe on April 19, hurried off the next day to Berlin to negotiate with Himmler. But contact had already been established on April 18 between the Danish Ambassador Yde and the Gauleiter for Hamburg, Governor Kaufmann, who took upon himself the responsibility for letting the prisoners in Neuengamme be released. However, the head of the Gestapo in the Hamburg area would not permit any transfer of prisoners without orders from the *Reichssicherheitshauptamt* in Berlin, which he was unable to contact. Despite this, Kaufmann took the responsibility for the evacuation of Neuengamme, on the proviso that the operation be concluded on April 20 at the latest.

At the Ministry of Social Affairs in Copenhagen, a swift and impressive operation was set in motion. By way of the Danish civil air defense force a total of 114 buses were requisitioned from various owners, eight to ten

ambulances, ten trucks, five or six private motor cars and five or six mo-
torcycles, which all reached Neuengamme on April 20 painted white and
with a red cross on the roof. Before the day was out, 4,224 Scandinavian
prisoners had been rescued. This was an extraordinary effort. But it was
also the day after the last executions of eight Danish Resistance fighters
had taken place in Ryvangen in Copenhagen.

I wrote as follows about my own experiences connected with this last
transport from Neuengamme:[86]

On April 20 the infirmary was emptied and Flemming and I could
join the last transport home to Denmark. We were not on the same
bus, because I had duties to perform right to the end. But we were
in the same convoy. I do not remember very much of the journey up
through Holstein. We had suffered several air attacks in Neuengamme
and our driver told us that he had been shot at several times. But the
journey was without complications. We put mile after mile of Germany behind us. I never wanted to see that country again. As we drove
through Schleswig, I wondered whether this historically disputed ter-
ritory would once again become part of Denmark. I would have voted
for that to happen.

Fever, coughing, and the pains in my chest had taken my last
strength from me. I was exhausted, but my mood became more buoy-
ant when we passed the border at Padborg. The inconceivable had happened: I was seeing Denmark again. I had a window seat and could
see a throng of people who had come to welcome us home with great
enthusiasm. The bus slowed down and finally stopped. Among the
crowd, I could see a woman looking around for someone she knew. I
recognized her immediately. It was my mother. I rushed off the bus. As
I stepped onto the ground, I heard one nurse say to the other: "Did you
see Mrs. Kieler from Horsens? She's looking for her sons. She doesn't
yet know that both of them are dead."

I walked as fast as I could to hug her, and whispered in her ear,
"Happy Birthday, Mother." It was her fifty-fifth. We were both speech-
less. When we had recovered a little, she asked, anxiously, "And Flemming?" I told her that he should be on one of the other buses in the
convoy. Then we parted. I had to get back into the bus, which would
take us to quarantine, where I would be deloused. It was crawling with

nurses, doctors and other people who were very kind to us. I was embarrassed about my nakedness. Modesty had not been lost in Porta.

After we had been deloused, our journey took us to the Frøslev camp where I met Flemming again. My mother had also managed to find him. She told me later what difficulties she had encountered finding some means of transport to get from Horsens to Padborg and how long she had had to wait at the border, with her firm belief intact that we were still alive. But on that day, April 20, she forgot all her troubles. That was her best birthday ever and I cannot remember it without being deeply moved at her boundless love for us. How much had she not suffered on our account?

Seeing Frøslev again was marked by the uncertainty of the situation. The negotiations between Bernadotte and Himmler were not yet at an end and Bernadotte wanted us all, while Himmler was setting the price high. Bernadotte drew the longest straw, but right until the end there were doubts about a small group of prisoners that the Germans did not want to release. Flemming and I belonged to that group. We were isolated from the rest, so I did not see Bernadotte when he visited the camp on April 22, before going to negotiate the final terms with Himmler. Rumors about his impending visit spread among the prisoners and they streamed out from the sick bays in order to see their savior. When Bernadotte stepped outside, the prisoners began to hum or sing the Swedish national anthem. Bernadotte removed his uniform cap, and the Germans were obliged to do likewise. He wrote in his memoirs:[87]

> This was a greeting that went right to the heart. These people were still prisoners, but felt they were within reach of freedom. They knew better than anyone else what could happen if the German camp discipline was turned on them at that moment. They took the risk in order to show their gratitude. They could not have done so in a more appropriate manner.

Bernadotte won his battle with Himmler. The Russians and the British arrived at the River Elbe on April 25, 1945, giving Bernadotte a trump card. So by the twenty-ninth, the prisoners in isolation were also released and sent by train to Sweden. It was brilliant spring weather. As we drove across the island of Sjælland, the train lost speed and some prisoners began to jump off. Flemming and I discussed whether we should do so ourselves. But we were rather reluctant as any escapes could derail the whole rescue operation. So we decided to stay put. We arrived in Sweden, where we were put in quarantine at Löderup, near the city of Ystad. It was a whole fortnight before we were allowed to go home.

We were given excellent treatment by Dr. Emil Berg from Borrby and his assistants. We enjoyed the pleasant landscape and the fine weather. But once the news of the German capitulation had reached us, we felt terribly homesick. We wanted to celebrate Liberation Day on May 4 home in Denmark. But we had to wait two weeks before the quarantine would release us. On the way home, we stopped off for a short while in Copenhagen, where we were met by Bente. Then the journey continued to Horsens, where we arrived on May 17. There were other former concentration camp prisoners on the same train, so the arrival back home was not a quiet one. There were many people standing on the platform and the joy of seeing their loved ones was great. But it was not until I was alone with my family on Torvet, the town square in Horsens, that I really felt that the war was over. The miracle had occurred. The whole family had survived.

But joy was mixed with sorrow and worry. We had already heard at Neuengamme that Klaus, Chief Constable Simony, Dr. Nordentoft and the mechanic Koch had all died in the camp at Husum. And there was no news about Koch's landlady and Margrethe Møller. But by some miracle they also turned up some weeks after the end of the war. I was, of course, interested in hearing what had happened to Flammen, whom the Gestapo had been so keen to find. It came as no surprise when I heard that when surrounded by a group of Gestapo, he had taken a cyanide capsule on October 18, 1944.

But it did come as an unpleasant surprise to hear that Mix too was dead. After our arrest, he had fled to Sweden and joined the Danish Brigade there, which was to be sent over to take part in the final Resistance struggle for Denmark, should the Germans not capitulate. But the role of a passive observer was not for Mix, and on account of some disappointments in his private life he decided on January 3 to row back to Denmark where he started working illegally for the navy. But he was caught by the Gestapo and wounded in the leg. The Gestapo gave him a speedy trial. Four days later, on March 3, he was condemned to death along with another man.

During the journey to the place of execution, the two of them tried to escape. Mix's colleague succeeded, but Mix could not run fast on account of his wounded leg and was shot dead while fleeing.

We were, of course, glad to again meet all our friends who had fled to Sweden. Nan mourned the death of Klaus, but her family soon had other worries. Her brother Tellus had kept a secret cache of explosives, which he no longer needed, and this was to be rendered harmless. This occurred during celebrations in which I did not take part. But the party came to an abrupt end when a bomb went off and blew away Tellus's right hand.

We also worried about the non-Scandinavian prisoners we had left behind at Porta and Neuengamme. We received a sign of life from them in the form of a letter from the Polish doctor, Eugen Szust, and the Danish-oriented Hans Magnussen from Flensborg, just over the German border (he was a German citizen belonging to the Danish minority in Slesvig, which became German after the war between Denmark and Prussia in 1864). The reports from Szust and Magnussen were sent to my fellow prisoner Helge Juul, who was the first chairman of our little union of ex-prisoners from Porta. I succeeded him as chairman, and before his death he handed over to me copies of his own report and the letters from Magnussen and Szust. These two letters, plus later information we received, give a grim picture of the catastrophe that we had miraculously escaped at the eleventh hour.

Ragnarok

Dr. Eugen Szust wrote about Porta, once we had left:[88]

> Our work in the Stollen continued. Every day, hundreds of vehicles arrived and took a great deal of military equipment to be stored in the bombproof Stollen. The number of prisoners increased, as two camps to the west of us were being evacuated and were grouped together with us. Those who were unable to march were taken to Neuengamme.
>
> In early April, we were taken, along with female prisoners from camps nearby, in a special train consisting of eighty wagons to Wöbbelin at Ludwigslust, not far from Brunswick. This stretch, normally covered in four to five hours, took twenty-five days to complete. During the journey, other transports were added to ours. Each wagon had between 120 and 160 prisoners and two ss guards. Every third day, we received seven ounces (200 g) of bread per person, this being the only

food. The wagon doors were kept locked the whole way all day or simply nailed shut. The prisoners went to the toilet on the bare floor and the stench was unbearable. People lost consciousness in the wagons, and each day there were between two and five deaths. We often kept quiet about the dead, so as to be able to sit on something dry – a corpse in this case. And so we finally arrived in Wöbbelin, termed the Death Camp by the Allies. On their arrival, they discovered stacks of corpses, sixty-five feet in length and ten feet high (20 × 3 m). People died by the hundreds every day of typhus and dysentery. There were some fifteen to twenty bodies every day that were cut up for food. Human flesh soup was most popular with the Russian prisoners. Several executions for cannibalism did nothing to improve the situation and there were a lot of corpses that lacked buttocks, as this was the only place on the body where you could still find a little fat.

Hans Magnussen has written about how, when the Danish prisoners had been transferred to Neuengamme, a contingent of Dutch prisoners arrived at Porta on March 19. The Americans were by now not very far away, but hopes of liberation faded when on April 1 the order was given to evacuate. There was a great tumult and prisoners began to plunder the camp depots. In the end, some thousand women prisoners were brought by train to Fallersleben, where the transport was split up. Dr. Szust ended up on the death transport as described above, while Magnussen stayed at the camp in Fallersleben, where the living conditions and comradeship were good and the food plentiful. On April 15 they were, however, put on a transport. Hans Magnussen describes this:[89]

The train journey that now followed was the most horrible thing I have ever experienced. There were 150 men per wagon with partly locked hatches, so the lack of air already made itself felt within half an hour. The people inside became half crazy, and so things remained for one long night I will never forget. We had to use our bare fists all night, simply to avoid being crushed. The next day, the German prisoners were put in a wagon of their own, so things got somewhat better. The ss couldn't care less what happened to the foreigners.

So we arrived at Salzwebel, a crowd of sick, half-starved people. It was here that we would have fallen into the hands of the Americans –

something we dearly wished – were it not for the fact that a lieutenant engineer from the Wehrmacht started the locomotive off again. We could already see the American tanks.

On April 17 we arrived at the Ludwigslust camp in Wöbbelin, where later on, Kapo Schorsch also ended up. Nor was this camp something I could ever forget… The last days at Ludwigslust were horrible. Each day, we received a piece of bread, a little marmalade and three-quarters of a liter of watery soup. That was all. People were dying like flies. It was quite normal for some fifty to sixty prisoners to die per day. On the last day, they were lying around in the yard. The corpses had to be guarded well, otherwise cannibalism would set in. I saw many skeletons – such could only be described as skeletons – with liver and heart removed. This meat was cooked and offered other prisoners to buy. But if anyone was caught defiling a body in this way, that would be the end of him.

On May 2 the hour of liberation finally came. The camp was locked up and we Germans marched along with the ss in the direction of Schwerin. People would disappear at every opportunity. I remained in a village along with three others, and we spent the night there. The next morning the Americans arrived. They greeted us in a friendly manner, but otherwise did not bother with us. So I walked to Hagenow and on to Hamburg, where I stayed for a few days, then started off for Flensborg…. I arrived late in the day at a village, where some of our Polish fellow inmates of Porta discovered me. There was great rejoicing. "Stay the night with us," they said, "otherwise you'll never get any further." We went along with them and met about twenty of our Polish comrades. They also welcomed our arrival. They served us all the food they could find and we were having a party with the Americans, long into the night. When I wanted to move on the next morning, they put a large pack of foodstuffs at my disposal.

Dr. Szust and Hans Magnussen survived their ordeal, as did my fellow prisoner Dr. Robert Naudin from Beaune. How many prisoners actually perished is hard to say. But there can be no doubt that the majority of prisoners died. The Scandinavians escaped this fate thanks to the rescue efforts, but the rest?

What happened to the two thousand prisoners of other nationalities whom the Germans forced the Red Cross to move from Neuengamme to Waldstädte in Hanover, I do not know. I have no information about them, but their fate cannot have been any more tragic than the seven thousand non-Scandinavian prisoners who were left at Neuengamme. Here is part of a report drawn up by the memorial committee for the concentration camp at Neuengamme after the war:[90]

> The evacuation of the Neuengamme camp began on April 20. The prisoners were transported to Lübeck. A commando who was left behind destroyed all the documents. An ss detachment murdered all the children, plus those prisoners who had been used for tuberculosis experiments, along with their nurses. Between April 21 and 23, the Gestapo murdered seventy-one Gestapo prisoners, men and women from the Resistance in Hamburg. In this way, all traces were to be wiped out. On May 3, 150 prisoners who had been evacuated from Stutthof in a number of barges were murdered by ss soldiers and the Hitler Jugend as they landed in the bay at Neustadt.
>
> In Lübeck, the 7,300 prisoners were put on board three ships (the *Cap Arcona*, the *Thielbeck* and the *Athen*), the plan being to sink them out at sea. In the afternoon, a British fighter attacked the three vessels as they lay off Neustadt (thinking they were being used to transport troops). The *Cap Arcona* was set on fire and the *Thielbeck* was sunk. In this way, some seven thousand prisoners died. The history of the Neuengamme concentration camp ends with an inferno. In all, some 55,000 of a total of 106,000 prisoners from that camp were killed.

This horror, which Flemming and I were spared, has been described by one of the few survivors from the *Cap Arcona*:[91]

> …The hatch through which I had manage to escape was now propped full of people, as the flames from the lower corridor crept upwards. In the panic that arose, no one was able to get out as the one stood in the way of the other…. But soon the flames had reached the hatch and hundreds – maybe more – of our companions were swallowed up in the flames. The wild cries merged to form one huge cry, which could be heard up on deck. People were burning in front of the eyes of their companions above, but nothing could be done for them.

So the end of our stay in the concentration camp became a miracle for us, but a catastrophe for many others. Nevertheless, we were not the only ones to be rescued. After Neuengamme had been evacuated, the joint Swedish and Danish efforts to help the inmates of the women's camp at Ravensbrück and the other camps around Hamburg continued, without regard for the nationality of the prisoners. Transports suffered attack from the air. Everything that moved was shot at, and both prisoners and their rescuers died. But some seventeen thousand starving prisoners were nonetheless saved, including Tulle Fiil, who had been bought out of her misery with a bottle of schnapps.

The rescue of the Danish Jews in October 1943, and the rescue of the concentration camp prisoners at the end of the war were thanks to the Danish and Swedish humanitarian help. I will leave it to the Norwegian Arne Moi to give a brief account of this:[92]

Let there be no doubt about the debt that we owe Sweden. But equally well, much gratitude should be added to that paid to Denmark, about which we did not know much at the time. It should all be seen in context; without the status that the Bernadotte expedition enjoyed, the Danes could not have done as much as they did, and without the Danes, the Bernadotte expedition would not have achieved as much. We have our lives to thank to this mixture of high-level diplomacy and clandestine actions – not to mention great efforts made under hopeless circumstances, at risk to life and limb – and to mercy and humanity.

The Kieler family reunited in Horsens, May 1945

CHAPTER 12

Peace

Seeing my family again was a joyful occasion and overshadowed everything else, once we had all finally arrived home. It was incredible that we had all survived, but that was not to say that we could simply pick up life where we had left off, as if nothing had happened. We had both physical and mental wounds, and the future for us was a very unsure one. There were still large political problems to be solved and our personal ones did not always come to the surface before we had resumed our normal lives.

In our family, it was the health of our mother that gave most concern. When I saw her again at the border on April 20, she looked rather poorly. I was in no position to find out more at the time, and it was only once we had gotten home that I found out that during a night visit to a sick person, my parents had been in a road accident in a snowstorm, where my mother had broken her arm and her kneecap, while my father had broken three ribs. This meant hospital treatment, and while my father was discharged within three days, my mother was obliged to stay in the hospital for some six weeks. During that period, Lida had to take over the household at the same time as having to take exams that were the preliminaries for her ma- triculation exam. She was very busy and had therefore not been able to accompany our mother on her journey to the German border to find her two sons.

Over and above her other misfortunes, she had contracted typhus after the trip to the border to meet us. Typhus was rife among the prisoners who had been sent to the Møgelkjær camp, and the disease spread to Horsens. So there was good reason for her, rather than we, to look like a "Mussulman" when we saw her again in mid-May.

Flemming and I were the subject of care and friendship, once we had arrived home, and this extended far beyond the walls of our flat. We had been marked by our experiences in Porta, but in other ways than expected. We did not look like emaciated "Mussulmans," but like reasonably well-nourished ex-prisoners, but differed from the rest with our shaved heads. Our problems with urination (polyuria) and diarrhea caused by starvation ceased rapidly and the weakness of our muscles seemed to disappear during our spell in Swedish quarantine. We did not take up our old sporting activities again, and our physical condition was not put under any great strain; but in the course of the summer, I felt in such good shape that I could continue my studies where I had broken off, which I subsequently did in September.

There was, however, one thing that worried me. I noticed that both Flemming's and my heads had become increasingly lopsided. It took some while for the reason to become apparent. As we consumed more salt, our edema caused by previous hunger increased. This edema spread to our saliva glands and tended to collect on one side of our head, depending on which side we would normally sleep. We really looked strange.

I shall not go into details about how we ultimately overcame the various symptoms of starvation. Things got better within the year, but it took several more for me to realize that subsequent to immediate recovery would ultimately be aftereffects, which are termed the concentration camp syndrome, to which I will return later. We never again became completely well. But the biggest challenge to face now immediately after repatriation was tuberculosis. During the first two years after repatriation, five of our companions died of TB. For Flemming the disease meant a whole year in a sanatorium before he could resume his studies and even after he did, the disease returned, resulting in a further year in the hospital. This became almost unbearable.

I was let off more lightly. The X-ray clearly showed that I had also been infected at some stage, but there were no bacteria present as such. But these were present some twelve years later, when I returned from a particularly tough one-year scholarship to New York. There was a pocket of previously dormant bacilli and so I had to undergo a year of chemotherapy with all the nausea that belonged to the cure. It was a hard time.

One cheering episode occurred when, in 1945, there was a ring at the door. There stood my good friend from Cambridge, Frank Glassow. He had just become a surgeon when he was called up for military service. He had taken part in the Normandy invasion, then followed Montgomery through Belgium and the Netherlands and was now stationed on the Lüneburger Heath, where his main task was to look after victims of Bergen-Belsen. It was a happy reunion. Once he had arrived at British headquarters in Lüneburg, he one day asked the sergeant to requisition him a jeep so that he could drive to Horsens to find out whether his Danish friends were still alive. And we were, and Frank had to take the brunt of our admiration for Britain and all our gratitude for our liberation. The friendship had survived five years of absence, and now became a lifelong one. This was a good start to our new life.

Back to My Studies

After three months of recuperation in Horsens, I went back to Copenhagen to study. We had by then lost our flat on Raadhusstræde, but the nuns of the Saint Kjeldgade Convent kindly accommodated my sisters, while Professor Carsten Høeg took us in at the residence halls called Hassagers Kollegium, of which he was the warden.

I have to admit that on account of my many experiences and my age, I felt I had grown too old for a student environment. But I look back on the two years I spent at Hassagers with gratitude and they gave me the opportunity to take part in the International Students Union (DIS) of which Carsten Høeg was also president.

What the students had in common was that they were eager to cross frontiers. All of them had, in one way or another, been locked up for five long years. This had now come to an end. The DIS played a role in this new connection, but the Medical Students' Council likewise. It was this connection that allowed me to get to know the sister and brother Eva and Johannes Mosbech, and this link was to remain with me for the rest of my life. They were both students of medicine. Johannes was a member of the Medical Students' Council and in that capacity he organized a trip to London in 1946. I registered for the trip with enthusiasm and without going into further details of this successful trip, I would like to mention that many

Danish-British contacts and friendships were established, which continue to this day. I also became engaged, then married, to Eva, a marriage that still continues to this day as well.

Contacts abroad expanded and through our work with the DIS, many students from Britain, France, Czechoslovakia, Poland and India visited Copenhagen. Our continual efforts to establish contacts with foreign countries came to a head in July 1947, when Eva and I went on our honeymoon to Paris for a couple of weeks, after we had taken our final exams. Four days after our return, we went on another trip, this time a DIS trip to the Balkans. This trip lasted forty days and gave us a lot of insights into the restoration that was occurring in that part of the world, but also an impression of the Cold War, which had already started before the last German cannon had fallen silent.

The deepest impression was made on me by Budapest, which lay half in ruins. Political tensions in that country were in evidence when we talked to Hungarian students. The highlight of our visit was the celebration of Saint Stephen's Day, with Cardinal Mindszenty giving a sermon at the Saint István basilica, and the procession with the relic – Saint Stephen's hand – being carried through the city. This was as much a political as a religious ceremony. That evening, the Communist Students' Union treated us to a counterdemonstration, a large event in one of the city's pleasure parks. A few years later, I had a chance to again visit Budapest and see how the rebuilding of that beautiful city was getting on. By that time, the cardinal had long been arrested and tortured, then in the end set free to seek sanctuary in the US Embassy.

Our long trip ended in Venice and on account of a lack of currency, we were once again obliged to travel through Germany, which had been badly bombed. I have to admit that I did not feel sorry for the Germans.

Once back home in Denmark, Eva and I began our respective careers as doctors. We hoped this would be the beginning of a normal existence and that now that peace had returned, we could start a small family and supplement our university education with a few years of practical clinical experience by working in various hospitals. Normal life ensued, but it was still marked in various ways by my past in the Resistance.

"Justice, Not Revenge"

One of the trickiest problems we had to face during the occupation was the liquidation of informers. I was of the opinion that this was a necessary evil, carried out in self-defense in a situation that could at any time prove deadly. Once the Germans had capitulated, the situation changed dramatically. I was in complete agreement with the Freedom Council in their efforts to avoid people taking the law into their own hands, and agreed that collaborators should be judged via the courts. This may seem a straightforward way of thinking, but it was not, as liberation was not accompanied by any clear resolution with regard to the events of April 9, 1940, and the subsequent collaboration with all the anti-constitutional acts that this entailed.

You could be executed after the war for having informed on a saboteur, but Buhl, who had encouraged such activity, was beyond the reach of the courts. There were also a number of cases where sentences were reduced, which meant severe punishments were meted out only in cases that could be brought swiftly to a conclusion, as opposed to more complex ones that would drag on. Many collaborators got away with their deeds on account of this.

I can well understand the later reactions to this "unbalanced justice"; but what irritated me more was the way that there were such mild sentences given top German war criminals, as opposed to the severe ones given to Danish traitors.

My attitude about all this was closely linked with my duty to appear as a witness in a series of court cases that were linked to the fate of my group. These were cases against betrayals by Germanized Danes, cell informers, Gestapo agents and the butchers of Porta.

We were familiar with the problem of Germanized Danes (Danish citizens belonging to the German minority in South Jutland) from our time in Aabenraa, when a schoolteacher had reported our arrival to the German security forces. A Germanized Dane had then proceeded to inform on Jens Jørgensen and the landlady of the Sølyst Kro pub in Styrtom, who had informed on Flemming and on Georg Jansen as they walked from Koch's house to receive fresh instructions. These were all brought to trial after the war and given prison sentences of several years apiece.

What occupied my mind most in this context was the idea that many people agreed with, whereby their Germanness was in some way a mitigating circumstance for their actions. I drew the opposite conclusion. For me, their treachery vis-à-vis Denmark was not so much determined by their loyalty to Germany, but to Hitler and they therefore became double traitors, both to Denmark as well as to Germany. The Germanized Danes could be regarded as sharing some of the collective responsibility held by their generation of Germans for the atrocities of the war. Recognition of this was a prerequisite for any later reconciliation, which at the time was still a long way off.

With regard to informers in the prison cells, I was involved in two court cases – the case against "Jan Møller" (aka Snogen) and the one against Henry. These were former members of the Resistance, both of whom tried to save their skins by working for the Gestapo. Henry therefore told the court about the mock execution that he had suffered, which he had also told me about when we were sharing a cell. The court believed his story and he only received a light sentence. As I was unable to dismiss the possibility that his story could have been true, I felt that justice had been done. Later, friends of his in Aarhus told me that his story was not true.

Jan Møller was responsible for the arrest of my sisters and of Margrethe Møller and her family. The part he played in the detention of the Staffeldt brothers is more obscure. But he tried to explain away having shot at Kelvin Lindemann by saying he was shooting a warning shot that had been ignored. This was not taken into account by the court and he was, in any case, guilty of giving information leading to the arrest of other members of the Resistance in Jutland, and their subsequent deaths, and so he was condemned to death. Jan Møller regretted his actions and tried to find solace in religion. He converted to Roman Catholicism and refused to seek a pardon, and was consequently executed. In this case too, I felt that justice had been done, until I heard about the sentences passed on three Gestapo criminals, of whom I had had personal experience.

The head of the German police force in occupied Denmark, Günther Pancke, and the head of the security police, Otto Bovensiepen, were both put on trial for their joint responsibility for what was termed "counter-sabotage," which included reprisal murders and sabotage of popular buildings, as well as their responsibility for torture and the deportation of Danish police officers and of 421 "asocial elements" and "recidivist criminals." Bovensiepen was also charged with having given the order to shoot eleven members of the Resistance on the road to Roskilde near Rorup.

Their principal defense centered around the fact that they were acting under orders from Berlin, and that some of the operations carried out by the Resistance were taken into account by the court as mitigating circumstances. On September 20 they received sentences of twenty years imprisonment and the death sentence, respectively, at the Copenhagen City Court. On July 21, 1949, Pancke's sentence was upheld by the High Court, while that of Bovensiepen was commuted to life imprisonment. On March 17, 1950, the Court of Appeal upheld these two sentences, although two judges did vote for the death penalty to be given to Bovensiepen.

The head of the Gestapo, Karl Heinz Hoffmann, was also arrested and put on trial, along with several terrorists belonging to the Peter Group. As in many other cases, Hoffmann was sentenced to twenty years imprisonment. The Danish High Court was less hard on German war criminals than the city courts. Kaj Munk's murderer, Otto Schwerdt, and Walter Söhnlein, received twenty-four and twenty years imprisonment, respectively.

Kriminalrat Bunke was never found, and Neuhaus had already died before the end of the war – as far as I am aware, this occurred during an air raid on Hamburg. But Walther Billum Falkenberg was found and interned by the Allies on March 22, 1946. He was extradited to Denmark and put on trial on August 17, 1948. I was summoned as a witness. Falkenberg had to admit to several killings and many cases of mistreatment, but denied the mistreatment of John. He shuffled off the responsibility onto Neuhaus who was by now beyond the reach of any court. I described to the court my last meeting with John, and this description ended with how I left him at the cell door where Falkenberg was waiting to take him to the ss court at the Dagmarhus. As I have already written, John pointed out to me at the time that it was Falkenberg who had mistreated him.

Two other witnesses confirmed my testimony of the torture that John had been subjected to; John had told them too that Falkenberg and Neuhaus had been responsible for his torture. But during the actual torture, only John, Neuhaus and Falkenberg were present, and Neuhaus was now dead, which meant that Falkenberg was now the only eyewitness still alive. His story was therefore accepted, and to my indescribable disgust he was acquitted on that charge. I felt myself to be John's spokesman in this matter. He himself had told me who the butchers had been, and yet this indirect testimony was not accepted by the court.

Falkenberg received a sentence of twenty years from the Copenhagen City Court. At the High Court, this was reduced to twelve years on February 24, 1949, and on September 1, 1951, he was pardoned and deported. So, like all the other German war criminals, he only had to serve a small portion of his sentence. On December 1, 1953, the first four German war criminals were released from Danish jails and deported. Among these were Bovensiepen and Kaj Munk's murderer. Against this background, Jan Møller's sentence was too harsh and my respect for the Danish system of justice took quite a knock.

Things were different when on March 14, 1948, a Franco-Belgian court tried a number of war criminals from Porta Westphalica at Rastatt in Baden-Baden. Again I was summoned as a witness, partly because by that time I was doing my in-depth analysis of the nutritional problems in the concentration camps and was thus well up on the situation that had arisen in the concentration camps, and partly because I could speak reasonable French; I ended up as some kind of chief witness. As for the trial itself, Chief Constable Knud Wiese, in his official capacity as the Danish observer, submitted a testimony that shows that there were a total of eight accused, including two ss soldiers and three Kapos. The main accused were the head of the work teams, Nau, and the Lagerältester (i.e., head of the camp) Kapo Schorsch. There were four French judges and one Belgian judge, and three Germans acting as counsel for the defense. Seven of a total of thirty-five witnesses came from Denmark. Hans Magnussen from Flensborg was also a witness. The others were Frenchmen and Germans. Wiese wrote:[93]

> The accused quite obviously behaved in an exemplary manner in court. But it has to be said that they were also treated in an exemplary manner. It was a completely fair and decent trial. The German defendants and their counsel were given the opportunity to cross-examine witnesses and no limitations were put on the counsel for the defense. Nau made a pathetic impression. The balloon had been deflated. The former stormy and impressive camp commandant had been reduced to a dispirited little figure with sunken cheeks and his head cocked to one side. By contrast, Schorsch looked his former self, but when he was questioned by the prosecutor, he started to cry as if he had been whipped.

I was questioned as to the nutritional side of things in the camp. This elicited an ironic remark from one of the German lawyers who pointed out that the civilian population of Germany, anno 1948, were hardly in a better situation. He didn't look much like a "Mussulman" himself nor, for that matter, did any of the defendants. I was then asked to detail the mistreatment that I had been subjected to and had witnessed. My testimony included hangings, arms tied behind the victim's back, being held fast with a throttle around the neck, beatings that resulted in death, stoning in the mine, being locked up naked in the unheated mortuary, plus whippings and the eternal punches and slaps. Neither Nau nor Schorsch made any attempt to deny any of this.

I was also questioned about the hygiene and the most prevalent illnesses, about the cold, dampness, the exhausting work, the eternal weariness, etc., etc. This became a pretty good repetition of the experiences I had undergone in Porta and made a deep impression on the court. Nau and Schorsch were sentenced to death. The French had brought along a guillotine for the purpose. The two other Kapos received sentences of two and eight years prison, respectively, while the guards and civilian workers who had been cruel enough to hit us received ten years imprisonment. I cannot say that I felt sorry in any way for those who were sentenced. Nor, however, did I feel anything approaching revenge. The truth of the matter was that the crimes were of such huge dimensions that no hate or feelings of revenge could be mustered to equal the enormity of the crimes involved. I was satisfied that justice had been done.

Kapo Schorsch in the court in Rastatt, 1948

Political Aftershocks

Once home, we were confronted with an unexpected and shocking problem: the politicians who had collaborated with the invader were back in the government. We also began to slowly realize that the war might have been over, but we had not been recognized as one of the Allies. We were nevertheless duly able to join the United Nations.

The appointment of Buhl at the head of the new liberation government felt like treachery. Buhl was, after all, the politician who had not only condemned the acts of sabotage, but had encouraged informers. We felt cheated by the Freedom Council who had, on September 16, 1943, promised to deal with the collaborators – the very same people they were now themselves collaborating with. The last straw was the appointment of a parliamentary commission, so that the onus was not placed on national law when the responsibility was assessed for what had happened on April 9, for the collaboration and the many breaches of constitutional law.

We were very disappointed, and things got no better when I later received the opportunity to discuss the matter with good friends who had been lucky enough to spend the last part of the war in London. Why had they not intervened? The inevitable answer was that people wanted decisions to be made in Denmark, and they had gradually lost faith in Christmas Møller, who was becoming a more and more isolated figure. I had no cause to doubt their motives, but I could not help thinking that the key decisions were being made by the Foreign Office in London. The Cold War was at hand.

This does not, however, explain why the Communists accepted the formation of the liberation government under Buhl. This may have been on account of orders from Moscow, and in my opinion this is the most likely explanation. But the only explanation I ever received from people who were close to the Danish Communist Party (DKP) was that they reckoned that the DKP would be strengthened now that the war was over and that the Social Democrats would have to accept a merger, so creating a Socialist Unity Party, as in several places in Eastern and Central Europe. This is certainly not incompatible with the idea that they had received orders from Moscow. Bent Jensen, a historian who is an expert on the Soviet Union and has had access to the archives in Moscow, has subsequently confirmed my suspicions.

The Social Democrat Frode Jakobsen, the man who had set up the Freedom Council in the first place, had become the de facto leader of this faction after the war and wanted both the old guard and representatives of the Freedom Council in the new liberation government. One of the questions I myself, and many others, asked Frode Jakobsen was: "Why did the

Freedom Council itself not form a government on its own, keeping out all the older generation of politicians?"

There are three answers to this:

1) In its proclamation of September 16, 1943, the Freedom Council had promised to resign at the end of the war.

2) The members of the Freedom Council were, for the most part, politically inexperienced.

3) The Freedom Council was already accepted by the Soviet Union as the future government, and Frode Jakobsen was afraid that if the council took over political power at the end of the war, this could lead to a change in the political system. He betrayed his promise to punish the collaborators in order to prevent a Communist coup d'état from taking place.

Amidst the jubilation at the liberation of their country, Danes had ended up in a situation similar to that of Greece, where a civil war was raging. Could this happen in Denmark, too? In theory, it certainly could. If such a civil war broke out, the collaborationist politicians could count on support from the armed forces, the police and the Danish Brigade in Sweden, while a Communist takeover would receive support from members of the illegal underground army, which totaled some forty thousand men, of which Communists were in the minority. This historical outcome is a very theoretical scenario, but nevertheless it was feared by many politicians, and by Frode Jakobsen, which is why he took on board former collaborators when forming the liberation government.

Although these political suspicions were understandable, they were not based on solid fact. Denmark's fate was determined by the military deployment in northern Germany at the time. By April 21, Eisenhower had informed the Russians that his forces were going to invade Lübeck and Kiel, triggering a race between the Russians and Montgomery. But historians differ on this matter. The Russian forces deployed along the Baltic littoral had the task of covering the Russian flank when Berlin was being attacked. But this does not rule out the possibility that they could quite well have taken Lübeck, if they had gotten there first. But they did not do so, and apart from the island of Bornholm, Denmark was in fact liberated by the British, not by the Russians. What would have happened had the Russians arrived there first is anyone's guess. Both liberating powers wanted a Danish government they could rely on. The British had their way, because while they were not tremendously impressed by the former collaborators, these were nonetheless preferable to a Communist takeover. These facts were accepted by Moscow, partly because Russia had no choice, and partly because they knew they would win the battle for Eastern Europe and even maybe for Denmark, whose strategic importance was recognized by more people than Hitler alone.

New Times

The occupation of Denmark on April 9, 1940, had led to a total collapse of the Danish foreign and defense policy from between the two wars. The return of the old politicians to power gave little hope of change in that respect. But the promise of the later prime minister, Hans Hedtoft, that Denmark would never again have to experience an April 9 did presage new times. Even if Denmark had not been recognized as one of the Allies, we were allowed membership in the United Nations. Dreams of a Nordic defense force had to be given up when we joined NATO, which gave us a greater measure of security. Here too the result was better than expected, and when we joined the EU in 1973 I had to admit that we had achieved more with our foreign and defense policies than I could have hoped for in my wildest dreams in 1945. This is all very encouraging.

Changes in domestic policy are perhaps not as obvious. But they were there too. The Denmark of between the wars was, in my experience, a divided society; it was right in the middle of an explosive process of social development at the same time as it had to fight against clashes of interests that called into question the idea of national unity. I am convinced that the fight the Resistance put up helped to end this situation, but I have to admit that the raising of living standards also helped put an end to the hateful class struggle, which plays a major part in the program that dogmatic Marxists wish to follow. There is no doubt that friendships that came about during the occupation helped promote the social and cultural truce which holds today. This has been a good thing for Denmark.

A third factor is the ideological purification that took place after the war, but the consequences of this are harder to assess. Within one year of the end of hostilities, it became clear to most people that there simply was no acceptable alternative to parliamentary democracy. April 9 played its role in this realization, when unemployment was enormous at the same time as Denmark had lost its sovereignty. Things could not have been worse at the time, so it was hardly surprising that people began to speculate about other forms of democracy apart from the parliamentary one where the people were represented by members of parliament. After the war, all such speculations came to an end and with the exception of the Communists, we all rejected any change in our system of government; in 1953, parliamentary democracy was indeed made part of our constitution.

I welcome this development, but cannot avoid a little sigh concerning the many dreamers among us. The goals of Liberty, Equality and Fraternity were inspiring, even during the occupation, but there was no doubt about the fact that liberty came first. It was therefore shocking, after the war, to experience the rise of a new generation who regarded liberty as something to take for granted, which needed no thought or duties to perform, and fraternity as a question of political solidarity that could be maintained by a plethora of trade unions; these today form perhaps the greatest threat to our parliamentary democracy. There was little understanding by then that the Resistance movement had been, first and foremost, an ethical revolt and helped to create a different kind of solidarity than that which is given expression during political debate.

I had mixed feelings about seeing my fellow students once more. I soon saw who had been in the Resistance and we had something in common. But several of my fellow students had lived a quiet life during the occupation, and we were often far from united on political questions. They were also glad about the liberation. But their joy was mixed with a desire to go back to "old times." For them, the repatriated former concentration camp victims and refugees were a disruptive and annoying element, and they did not share our desire to see conditions change. I remember especially the disaffection that was aroused when there was a question of obtaining places for those who had been in Sweden and Germany on a number of courses in practical bacteriology and other laboratory courses. The enthusiasm for taking on such people dampened over the space of several months and I soon learned to keep my personal experiences to myself and to focus on my studies, which ended in 1947 when I became a doctor.

Meeting the students who had used the previous five accursed years to study hard, as opposed to joining the Resistance, gave food for thought. This is what I would have been doing, if I had not stopped being "neutral" after having taken the first part of my doctor's exam. I now had the opportunity to see where I would have found myself, if I had not acted as I had done. The "neutral" students followed me through life, right up to when I retired. I was never able to see eye to eye with them. God knows whether they ever suffered from a bad conscience, or whether they realized how far apart we were. But I somehow doubt it.

The κz (Concentration Camp) Syndrome

When Eva and I were newlyweds in 1947, and also new as doctors, we fully realized that we could not predict the future ahead of us. We did agree that we needed some more training with regard to hospital work. However, I could not entirely dismiss the problems I had been confronted with at Porta or get them out of my mind. So, as I have mentioned above, six colleagues and I began to do medical research among surviving concentration camp inmates and also to obtain more detailed descriptions of their time in various camps. The resulting publication was 460 pages in length and was entitled "Famine Disease in German Concentration Camps: Complications and Sequels."[94] This report had great significance when the butchers of Porta were being judged by the Franco-Belgian court in Rastatt, and was also of importance for legislation in Denmark, and in other countries, with regard to compensation for harm done during the occupation.

Our research into the health of repatriated concentration camp victims took place between 1947 and 1951. Several deaths were recorded during this period and tuberculosis was still a problem for many former prisoners, including Flemming and myself. But the majority of the former inmates had been able to work again in their former jobs or continue their studies and were, by all appearances, healthy again. Many of them had received financial support from the *Frihedsfonden* – the Freedom Fund – which was set up on May 31, 1945, in order to lend support to former members of the Resistance and their families. The founders had reckoned that the fund would be necessary for five years. But afterwards, many long-term effects began to emerge, and this is what has been described as the "κz Syndrome."[95] The Freedom Fund therefore continued in operation until 1991. I joined the board in 1970 and was chairman between 1975 and 1988.

The κz Syndrome is a stress-related disorder, which is not identical to the famine syndrome. Patients suffer more from mental and neurological symptoms. These include anxiety, nightmares, nightly bouts of sweating, a lack of the ability to concentrate, memory loss, excessive oversensitivity to noise, tiredness, palpitations and periodic diarrhea. In many cases, this meant that former concentration camp prisoners were obliged to give up their careers. Other consequences included alcoholism, divorce and suicide. There was a clearly demonstrable link between the KZ Syndrome and the degree of suffering undergone during deportation, when assessing these deaths.

As was to be expected, the ex-prisoners from Porta were the worst hit and for a long time we thought this was on account of the lack of nutrition. However, later research done by the Freedom Fund has shown that the KZ Syndrome was also widespread among sailors who had been working for the Allies and had undergone a serious risk of being torpedoed. These people were not the victims of hunger and had not been mistreated. It was the fear. They never slept properly and drank heavily when ashore. The KZ Syndrome can therefore be regarded as a stress-related illness, rather than one directly linked to starvation. This is also the case regarding one symptom that it took many years for me to recognize and that was *reticence.*

My own memories from the Porta infirmary were extremely traumatic ones and I was unable to share them with anyone when I returned to Denmark after the war. I very much wanted to return to a normal existence so, like many surviving prisoners from concentration camps, I wanted to forget the unforgettable and like my fellow ex-prisoners, I had one weapon in this struggle: *reticence.* The silent ex-prisoner was as often as not surrounded by his immediate family and group of friends who wanted very much to help him forget. The answer to reticence was therefore: *no questions.*

This is how it was for thousands of former prisoners at concentration camps in many countries and also, as it turned out, for thousands of sailors who sailed in convoys carrying weapons and foodstuffs to and from Britain and the Soviet Union. There were some who were worse off, i.e., the Jews, whose families had often been murdered. One of them was the author Elie Wiesel, who received the Nobel Peace Prize in 1986. On his way back from the prize-giving ceremony in Oslo, he was honored in Copenhagen, where I gave the following speech:

Dear Comrade:

You have crossed the sea of cruelty. You have seen your faith in God and in man disappear in the waves of bestiality. You have survived a constant risk of death just to be washed ashore on a foreign coast with nothing left but a minimum of physical strength barely sufficient to keep your body alive. You were deprived of your past, and saw no future. You were deprived of your feelings, your love and even your hatred against those who had committed this incredible act of unnatural, savage destruction, because it seemed impossible for a normal human being to produce feelings of hatred of such dimensions that they would match the crime.

Several survivors from the German concentration camps have been in the same situation and all of them were in great need of help. They turned to politicians, they turned to philosophers and to artists, and they turned to their relatives and friends, if they had any: "Please help me, for heaven's sake help me to make some sense out of this madness."

They were received with compassion and generosity. "We will take care of you, we shall help you to forget." However, it proved impossible to forget the unforgettable and thousands of war victims had to start a new life in constant futile and unsuccessful attempts to escape memories from which they were unable to draw any meaningful conclusion. Quite a few found out that life as a constant refugee who is trying to run away from his own shadow is unbearable, and they put an end to it.

But you, our guest of honor, you decided to do the opposite – to turn round and walk back to the shores where you were reborn much against your will at the end of the Second World War. You protested against the loving advice to forget, and you had the courage to face the sea of cruelty once more, to face your own memories and to proclaim:

"Nobody has the right to forget the sufferings of all those who disappeared out there in the waves of bestiality. And we, who were the witnesses, we have the duty to remind the world of their fate, and to warn against those forces which can turn human beings with warm hearts into ice-cold monsters who only find satisfaction in the destruction of others. This may be a compensation for their inferiority complex, but it may also be the end of human civilization."

Your protest was a painful personal effort for which you deserve the greatest admiration. But you did not only have the courage to return to your memories, you also had the wisdom to show the way we have to go. The torturers have lost all rights to ask for forgiveness and mercy. But we lose our strength if we allow our hearts to be filled with bitterness and hatred, and we lose our moral rights if revenge becomes our ultimate goal. You realized this, and your advice was to turn the history of our past, our memories, into a strong weapon to be used in the continuous fight for human rights. This indeed is an accomplishment which deserves the highest reward.

Now, sixty years after the liberation, I still suffer from KZ Syndrome, but to a lesser extent. I think that my service to the Freedom Fund has helped me take an interest in the problems of my companions and to forget my own. I think this has had a therapeutic effect. It has also been a help that in spite of my poor hearing and eyesight I have written books and several papers, and given numerous lectures well assisted by my younger assistant, Julie Grandjean.

I received confirmation of my insights when I once again saw the Kaisershof Hotel at Porta in February 2005. The landlady was the great-granddaughter of the original owner. She was born after the war but was not unaware of the fact that her hotel had been taken over by the ss and had cost the lives of many. But she was clearly unaware of the details. Even though I had not spoken German since 1945, I was capable of having a conversation with her on one occasion which helped me to realize how difficult it must be to be a German, born after the war, and with no guilt for any of Hitler's crimes, and yet still responsible for Germany's active contribution to reconciliation for our mutual future. It was a good conversation. And that is where, for me, the Second World War finally came to an end, on February 6, 2005 – sixty-one years after my arrest in Aabenraa – without hatred.

It had been a long war.

Members of the author's resistance group killed in Denmark

Peer Borup
2.8.1921–6.2.1944
Shot by the Gestapo
at Åbenrå

Mix-Erik Koch Michelsen
21.3.1923–3.3.1945
Shot down on the way
to the execution grounds
in Copenhagen in a final
attempt to escape

Cato Bakman
15.3.1918–10.12.1943
Shot by the Gestapo
at Bispebjerg Hospital

Flammen (The Flame) Bent
Faurschou-Hviid
7.1.1921–18.10.1944
Suicide when surrounded
by Gestapo at Ordrup,
Copenhagen

John-Svend Otto Nielsen
29.8.1908–27.4.1944
Tortured and executed by
Gestapo in Copenhagen

Concentration camp victims

Jørgen Salling-Porta
24.4.1923–24.10.1959
Suicide after repatriation

Klaus Rønholt-Husum
10.4.1923–22.11.1944

Jørgen Staffeldt-Porta
30.12.1912–25.12.1944

Operations Carried out by HD2

No.[1]	Date	Target	Police Report[2]	Success[3]
I	28.10.43	Børge Hansen's punching workshop Amerikavej, Copenhagen	AS 18–732	(+)
II	31.10.43	Bryld's office – seizure of Nazi documents Amaliegade, Copenhagen	AS 18–774	+
III	4.11.43	Disarming of German officer Østerport, Copenhagen	–	+
IV*	7.11.43	American Apparate Company – radio jammers Søgårdsvej, Gentofte	AS 2–510	-

1. Operations marked * are described in greater detail in the text. All operations are described in detail in Kieler et al., *En modstandsgruppes historie* and Kieler, *Hvorfor gjorde I det?* [Why did you do it?].
2. Police reports are located in the Statsadvokaturen for særlige Anliggender (Special Department of the Public Prosecutor) collection in the Rigsarkivet (National Archives), Copenhagen.
3. Operations marked + were successes, (+) partial successes, and – not successful.

V	8.11.43	Deutsche Wurst – German butcher York's Passage, Copenhagen	AS 19–016	+
VI*	9.11.43	American Apparate Company – second attempt	AS 2–509	+
VII	12.11.43	Torvehallen – Nazi-sympathizing greengrocer Strandvejen, Hellerup	AS 2–518	(+)
VIII	13.11.43	National Civil Air Defense – seizure of Danish military radio to be handed over to the Germans Sct. Annæ Plads, Copenhagen	AS 19–167	(+)
IX	15.11.43	E.E. Kahlmann – Nazi-sympathizing leather dealer Vimmelskaftet, Copenhagen	AS 19–173	-
X	16.11.43	Scheuer & Mørch – tailors working for Germany Nørregade, Copenhagen	AS 19–175	-
XI*	17.11.43	Reinhardt's truck repair shop Lyngbyvej, Copenhagen	–	-
XII	23.11.43	Transmotor – collaborationist producing electric transformers Finsensvej, Frederiksberg	AS 1–336	+
XIII*	25.11.43	Grauballe – factory producing German uniforms Allegade, Frederiksberg	AS 1–340	+
XIV*	26.11.43	Dansk Industrisyndikat – collaborationist producing sound detectors for Germany Havnevej, Hellerup	AS 2–547	+
XV	30.11.43	Garage at Vesterport – seizure of car taken by the Germans from the Danish Navy Vesterport, Copenhagen	–	+
XVI	3.12.43	Hartmann's engineering works Vermundsgade, Copenhagen	AS 19–530	+

XVII*	10.12.43 9.4.44	Mrs. Delbo – liquidation of informer Faxegade and Sankelmarks-gade, Copenhagen	AS 19–062 AS 19–618	- +
XVIII*	12.12.43	Varde Steel Works Varde	–	+
XIX	18–20.12.43	Liquidation of four informers Copenhagen	–	+
XX	29.12.43	Møller & Jochumsen's engineering works Horsens	AS 36–321	+
XXI	29.12.43	Horsens Condensed Milk Factory Horsens	AS 36–323	+
XXII	2.1.44	Horsens Acetylene Generator Horsens	AS 20–479	+
XXIII*	15.1.44	Burmeister & Wain engineering works Strandgade, Copenhagen	AS 20–479	+
XXIV	27.1.44	Copenhagen Freight Depot – seizure of explosives Copenhagen	–	+
XXV*	5.2.44	Hamag engineering works Åbenrå	AS 68–223	+
XXVI*	5.2.44	Callesen's engineering works Åbenrå	AS 68–224	-

SOURCES AND LITERATURE

A few months after my return from German concentration camps in 1945 I started to write a report on my experiences in the Resistance movement and in German prisons and concentration camps. On two occasions half of this report was lent to the previous sabotage leader, Jens Lillelund, and the other half to the historian Leif Rasmussen, who both wanted to collect material concerning the sabotage organization Holger Danske. Fortunately I never got my reports back. In my attempts to reestablish the stability of normal life after the war my handwritten reports would probably have been lost. However, about thirty-five years later I found these reports in the National Archives in Copenhagen (the Rigsarkivet), in the material collected by Jens Lillelund and Leif Rasmussen.

This happened when around 1980 I started to contact surviving members of my Free Denmark and Holger Danske groups in order to write a collective report, which was printed in a two volume book, *En modstands-gruppes historie* (The history of a resistance group). In 1982 three hundred copies were printed. They were sent to our relatives and to a number of libraries including the Rigsarkivet, Det Kongelige Bibliotek (the Royal Danish Library) and Frihedsmuseet (the Museum of Danish Resistance), all in Copenhagen, and the local libraries in all towns where we had been active.

On the basis of this collective report and extensive additional historical studies, and in answer to the question I was asked by the historian Jørgen Hæstrup – "Why did you do it?" – I wrote my personal memoirs, which were published in 2001 under the title *Hvorfor gjorde I det?* (Why did you do it?). A complete list of 430 references is presented in that book. References related to the present publication appear below, following the lists of sources.

ARCHIVES

Frihedsmuseet (Museum of Danish Resistance), Copenhagen. The sabotage file, selected personal statements, illegal papers, part of the author's private archives and personal letters and a large collection of photos.

Rigsarkivet (National Archives), Copenhagen, including:

Statsadvokaturen for særlige Anliggender (Special Department of the Public Prosecutor), through which the collaboration between German and Danish police was organized. The archives contain all numbered AS police reports on sabotage and other resistance activities.

Rigsarkivets Håndskriftssamling IV. T. Manuscript collection including:

Personal statements collected by Jørgen Hæstrup, 1947–1949, IV. T. 38A.

Records collected by Leif Rasmussen including original statements by the author, IV. T. 54.

"Beretning vedrørende Sabotageorganisationen Holger Danske," statement by Jens Lillelund and Hans Edvard Teglers.

Jens Lillelunds privatarkiv (Jens Lillelund's private archives), RA no. 5884. Records collected by Jens Lillelund, including original statements by the author.

Jørgen Kielers privatarkiv (Jørgen Kieler's private archives) – to be submitted to Rigsarkivet and Frihedsmuseet. Includes statements by Erik Koch Michelsens (sent to me after the war by his girlfriend Henny) and Helge Juul as well as the diary of Hanne Møller.

Det kongelige Bibliotek (Royal Danish Library), Copenhagen. All printed material, illegal papers, collection of tape-recorded interviews and photos.

Landsarkivet for Sjælland (The Provincial Archives of the Island of Sealand and the City of Copenhagen), Frederiksberg. Police reports concerning the German persecution of Jews. Includes:

Woldiderich, Bjarne, and Tommy Hansen. *Københavns Politis Dagsberetninger*, 1975. No. 159 A.

Historisk Samling fra Besættelsestiden 1940–45 (Historical collection of records from the time of occupation), Esbjerg Municipal Library, Esbjerg. A large collection of statements and comments on resistance activities in South Jutland in particular and in Denmark as a whole. Includes statements by Viggo Hansen and Henning Schlanbusch.

Horsens Byarkiv (Archives of the Town of Horsens), Horsens.

BOOKS AND ARTICLES

English

Berenbaum, Michael. *The World Must Know: The History of the Holocaust as Told in the United States Holocaust Memorial Museum*. New York: Little, Brown and Co., 1993.

Dean, Robert Berridge. *Ebba Lund: The Girl with the Red Hat*. Copenhagen: Lundean and Co., 2006.

Feingold, Henry F. *Roosevelt and the Resettlement Question: Rescue Attempts during the Holocaust*. Vol. 2, Yad Vashem International Conference, April 1974. Jerusalem: Ahva Cooperative Press, 1977.

Flender, Harold. *Rescue in Denmark*. New York: Holocaust Library, 1963.

Gill, Anton. *The Journey Back from Hell: Conversations with Concentration Camp Survivors*. London: Grafton Books, 1988.

Goldberger, Leo, ed. *The Rescue of the Danish Jews: Moral Courage under Stress*. New York: New York University Press, 1987.

Goldhagen, Daniel Jonah. *Hitler's Willing Executioners: Ordinary Germans and the Holocaust*. New York: Knopf, 1996.

Hæstrup, Jørgen. *Europe Ablaze: An Analysis of the History of the European Resistance Movements 1939–45*. Odense: Odense University Press, 1978.

———. *European Resistance Movements, 1939–1945: A Complete History*. Westport, Connecticut and London: Meckler Publishing, 1981.

————. *Secret Alliance: A Study of the Danish Resistance Movement 1940–45.* 3 vols. Translated by Alison Borch-Johansen. Odense: Odense University Press, 1976–77.

Helweg-Larsen, P., H. Hoffmeyer, J. Kieler, E.H. Thaysen, J.H. Thaysen, P. Thygesen and M.H. Wulff. "Famine Disease in German Concentration Camps: Complications and Sequels; with special reference to tuberculosis, mental disorders and social consequences." *Acta Medica Scandinavica*, Suppl. 274, vol. 144 (1952).

Jespersen, Knud J.V. *No Small Achievement: Special Operations Executive and the Danish Resistance 1940–1945.* Translated by Christopher Wade. Odense: University Press of Southern Denmark, 2002.

Levine, Ellen. *Darkness over Denmark: The Danish Resistance and the Rescue of the Jews.* New York: Holiday House, 2000.

Liddell Hart, B.H. *History of the Second World War.* London and Sidney: Pan Books, 1973.

Loeffler, Martha. *Boats in the Night: Knud Dyby's Story of Resistance and Rescue.* Blair, Nebraska: Lur Publications, 2000.

Lord, Walter. *The Miracle of Dunkirk.* Ware, Hertfordshire: Wordsworth Editions, 1998.

Pais, Abraham. *Niels Bohr's Times in Physics, Philosophy and Polity.* Oxford: Clarendon Press, 1991.

Pundik, Herbert. *In Denmark It Could Not Happen: The Flight of the Jews to Sweden in 1943* [English translation of *Det kan ikke ske i Danmark: Jodernes flugt til Sverige 1943* (Copenhagen: Munksgaard, 1993)]. Jerusalem: Gefen Publishing House, 1998.

Rittner, Carol, RSM, and Sondra Myers, eds. *The courage to care: Rescuers of Jews during the Holocaust.* New York: New York University Press, 1986.

Thomas, John Oram. *The Giant Killers: The Danish Resistance Movement 1940–45.* London: Corgi, 1976.

Yahil, Leni. *The Rescue of Danish Jewry: Test of a Democracy.* Philadelphia: The Jewish Publication Society of America, 1969.

Danish, Swedish and German

Årsskrift for 4. Maj Kollegiet i Åbenrå, 1968–69. This annual report is generated by an organization of the nine *kollegier*, i.e., students' homes commemorating resistance fighters killed during the war. They are called 4. Maj kollegier, commemorating the liberation of Denmark 4 May 1945. The annual reports from these institutions are booklets containing information about the economy of the colleges, the students, celebrations, special lectures and historical papers dealing with the time of occupation.

Bauche, Ulrich, Heinz Brüdigam, Ludwig Eiber and Wolfgang Wiedey. *Arbeit und Vernichtung: Das Konzentrationslager Neuengamme 1938–1945*. Hamburg: VSA-Verlag, 1991.

Beretning til Folketinget afgivet af den af Tinget under 15. juni 1945 nedsatte Kommission i henhold til Grundlovens §45 [The Parliamentary Commission Report (with attachments)]. 16 vols. Copenhagen: J.H. Schulz, 1945–1958, 1950. This report, based on investigations and interrogations, contains detailed information about the correspondence between the German embassy in Copenhagen and the German Foreign Ministry in Berlin, as well as the German description of the fights between German troops and the Danish army and navy August 29, 1943. In many cases copies of original documents often written in German are added. These are noted as "added entries."

Bernadotte, Folke. *Sidste Akt: Mine humanitære Forhandlinger i Tyskland Foråret 1945 og deres politiske Følger*. Copenhagen: Gyldendal, 1945.

Bjerg, Hans Christian. *Ligaen: Den danske militære efterretningstjeneste 1940–45*. 2 vols. Copenhagen: Gyldendal, 1985.

Bramsen, Bo. *Blandt 100 gidsler i Horserød 1943 med forspil, efterspil og historisk tillæg*. Copenhagen: Aschehoug, 1996.

Christensen, Claus Bundgård, Niels Bo Poulsen and Peter Scharff Smith. *Under Hagekors og Dannebrog: Danskere i Waffen SS 1940–45*. Copenhagen: Aschehoug, 1998.

Drostrup, Ole, with Walter Kienitz. *Den hæmmede kriger: Et portræt af general von Hanneken*. Odense: Odense University Press, 1997.

Frit Danmarks Hvidbog: Besættelsestidens i dokumenter og kommentarer. [White book edited by *Free Denmark* with documents and comments on the time of occupation in Denmark]. 2 vols. Copenhagen: Thaning and Appels Forlag, 1945.

Friediger, Moses. *Theresienstadt*. Copenhagen: J.Fr. Clausens Forlag, 1946.

Hæstrup, Jørgen. *Kontakt med England 1940–43*. Copenhagen: Thaning og Appels Forlag, 1959.

———. *Til Landets bedste*. Vol. 1. Copenhagen: Gyldendal, 1966.

Herbert, Ulrich. *Best: Biographische Studien über Radikalismus, Weltan-schauung und Vernunft 1903–1989*. Bonn: Dietz, 1996.

Hermann, K., and P. Thygesen. "ΚΖ-syndromet." *Ugeskrift for Læger*, no. 116 (1954).

Holm, Johannes. *Sandheden om de hvide busser*. Copenhagen: Samleren, 1984.

Kieler, Jørgen. *Det cellulære aminosyrestofskifte under mitosen*. Copenhagen: Nyt Nordisk Forlag Arnold Busck, 1954.

———. *Hvorfor gjorde I det?* [Why did you do it?]. 2 vols. Copenhagen: Gyldendal, 2001.

———. *Nordens Lænkehunde: Den første Holger Danske-gruppe*. 2 vols. Copenhagen: Gyldendal, 1993.

———. "Die Zelluläre Wirkung des Eiweissmangels, Durch In-Vitro-Studien Beleuchtet." *Medizinische Konferenzen der Internationalen Föderation der Widerstandskämpfer: Spätfolgen auf dem Gebiete der Ernährung, Verdauung und endokrinen Drüsen*. Unpublished paper presented at medical conference of the Fédération Internationale des Résistants (International Federation of Resistance Fighters).

———, et al. *En modstandsgruppes historie*. 2 vols. Rungsted Kyst: privately published, 1982. Available at a number of libraries including Det kongelige Bibliotek (Royal Danish Library) and Frihedsmuseet (Museum of Danish Resistance).

Kirchhoff, Hans. "Antikominterndemonstrationerne i november 1941." In Povl Bagge et al., *Hilsen til Hæstrup, 9 August 1969*. Odense: Odense University Press, 1969.

———. *Augustoprøret 1943*. 3 vols. Copenhagen: Gyldendal, 1979.

———. *Samarbejde og modstand under besættelsen: En politisk historie*. Odense: Odense University Press, 2001.

———. and Aage Trommer, eds. *Vor Kamp vil vokse og styrkes: Dokumenter til belysning af Danmarks Kommunistiske Partis og Frit Danmarks virksomhed 1939–1943/44*. Copenhagen: Selskabet for Udgivelse af Kilder til Danmarks Historie, 2001.

Kjeldbæk, Esben. *Sabotageorganisationen BOPA 1942–1945*. Copenhagen: Frihedsmuseets Venners Forlag, 1997.

Klein, Georg. *"...i stället för hemland" – Memoarer*. Stockholm: Bonniers, 1984.

Kreth, Rasmus, and Michael Mogensen. *Flugten til Sverige: Aktionen imod de danske jøder oktober 1943*. Copenhagen: Gyldendal, 1995.

Lidegaard, Bo. *I Kongens Navn, Henrik Kauffmann i dansk diplomati 1919–58*. Copenhagen: Samleren, 1996.

Matlok, Siegfried. *Danmark i Hitlers hånd*. Copenhagen: Holkenfeldts Forlag, 1989.

Meynert, Joachim. *Verdrängte Geschichte: Verfolgung und Vernichtrung in Ostwestfalen 1933–1945*. Edited by Arno Klönne. Bielefeld: AJZ-Verlag, 1986.

Moi, Arne. "De hvite bussene." *Pigtråd-Gestapofangen* (Copenhagen) no. 7 (1981):168–170.

Nolde, Emil. *Mit liv*. Copenhagen: Gyldendal, 1996.

Outze, Børge. *Danmark under den anden verdenskrig*. Vol. 3. Copenhagen: Steen Hasselbalchs Forlag, 1968.

Snitker, Hans. *Det illegale Frit Danmark – bladet og organisationen*. Odense: Odense University Press, 1977.

Stevnsborg, Henrik. *Politiet 1938–47: Bekæmpelse af spionage, sabotage og nedbrydende virksomhed*. Copenhagen: Gads Forlag, 1992.

Stræde, Therkel. "Deutschlandsarbeiter: Dänen in der deutschen Kriegswirtschaft." In *Europa und der "Reichseinsatz": Ausländische Zivilarbeiter, Kriegsgefangene und KZ-Häftlinge in Deutschland 1938–1945*. Edited by Ulrich Herbert. Essen: Klartext Verlag, 1991.

Tortzen, Christian. *Søfolk og skibe 1939–1945. Den danske handelsflådes historie under anden verdenskrig*. 4 vols. Copenhagen: Grafisk Forlag, 1981–85.

NOTES

1. Nolde, *Mit liv*.
2. Liddell Hart, *History of the Second World War*; Lord, *The Miracle of Dunkirk*.
3. Stræde, "Deutschlandsarbeiter: Dänen in der deutschen Kriegswirtschaft."
4. Stevnsborg, *Politiet 1938–47*.
5. *Beretning til Folketinget afgivet af den af Tinget under 15. juni 1945 nedsatte Kommission i henhold til Grundlovens* §45 [The Parliamentary Commission Report], vol. 13.
6. Bjerg, *Ligaen*.
7. See Hæstrup, *Secret Alliance*, vol. 1, chapter 3; and Jespersen, *No Small Achievement*, chapter 2.
8. Kirchhoff, *Samarbejde og modstand under besættelsen*; Kirchhoff and Trommer, *Vor Kamp vil vokse og styrkes*; *Frit Danmarks Hvidbog*, vol. 1.
9. Kirchhoff, *Antikominterndemonstrationerne i november 1941*.
10. Ibid.
11. Snitker, *Det illegale Frit Danmark*.
12. *Beretning til Folketinget afgivet af den af Tinget under 15. juni 1945 nedsatte Kommission i henhold til Grundlovens* §45 [The Parliamentary Commission Report].
13. This appeared in all the newspapers. We read it in *Natonaltidende*, February 12, 1942.
14. Hæstrup, *Kontakt med England 1940–43*; Hæstrup, *Secret Alliance*; Kieler, *Nordens Lænkehunde*.
15. Kjeldbæk, *Sabotageorganisationen* BOPA *1942–1945*.
16. *Frit Danmarks Hvidbog*, vol. 2.
17. *Beretning til Folketinget afgivet af den af Tinget under 15. juni 1945 nedsatte Kommission i henhold til Grundlovens* §45 [The Parliamentary Commission Report], vols. 4 and 13. See also Kirchhoff, *Augustoprøret 1943*, vols. 1 and 3; and Outze, *Danmark under den anden verdenskrig*, vol. 3.

18. Kirchhoff, *Augustoprøret*, vol, 1, chapter 1; Outze, *Danmark under den anden Verden-skrig*, vol, 3, p. 300 ff.

19. *Frit Danmark* no. 7, October 1942.

20. *Nationaltidende*, October 7, 1942.

21. Drostrup and Kienitz, *Den hæmmede kriger.*

22. *Frit Danmarks Hvidbog*, vol. 1.

23. Kjeldbæk, *Sabotageorganisationen* BOPA.

24. Kieler, *Nordens Lænkehunde.*

25. Police report 36–263, *Statsadvokaturen for særlige Anliggender* (Special Department of the Public Prosecutor) archives, Copenhagen.

26. This was posted in numerous places all over the country and at all railway stations including the Central Station in Copenhagen, where I arrived late in the day of August 29, 1943.

27. *Frit Danmarks Hvidbog*, vol. 1.

28. Kieler, *Nordens Lænkehunde.*

29. *Frit Danmarks Hvidbog*, vol. 1.

30. *Beretning til Folketinget afgivet af den af Tinget under 15. juni 1945 nedsatte Kommission i henhold til Grundlovens* §45 [The Parliamentary Commission Report], vols. 2, 5 and 13a, added entry no. 416b.

31. Ibid., vol. 7.

32. Kirchhoff, *Augustoprøret*, vol. 2, p.485.

33. *Beretning til Folketinget afgivet af den af Tinget under 15. juni 1945 nedsatte Kommission i henhold til Grundlovens* §45 [The Parliamentary Commission Report], vol. 13a, added entry no. 667.

34. *Beretning til Folketinget afgivet af den af Tinget under 15. juni 1945 nedsatte Kommission i henhold til Grundlovens* §45 [The Parliamentary Commission Report], vol. 13a.

35. The telegrams sent from the German embassy in Copenhagen to Auswärtiges Amt in Berlin were all numbered. The numbering is just a consecutive numbering of the telegrams sent from Best to Ribbentrop and the foreign ministry in Berlin (he did not send telegrams directly to Hitler). These were found by the Allies in Berlin at the end of the war and were used as evidence during the trial in Nüremberg from where copies were sent to the Danish government. They are quoted in the Parliamentary Commission Report, which is a result of the investigation carried out by the Parliamentary Commission of all Danish ministries. In a number of cases Danish or German copies of original material, such as Goes's report and several telegrams sent by Best to the German foreign ministry, are presented in additional entries called "*bilag.*" Telegram No. 1001, for example, may be seen in the Parliamentary Commission Report, vol. 13, additional entry No. 734. The original material was sent to the German foreign ministry in Bonn after the Nüremberg trial.

36. *Frit Danmarks Hvidbog*, vol. 2.

37. Friediger, *Theresienstadt.*

38. *Beretning til Folketinget afgivet af den af Tinget under 15. juni 1945 nedsatte Kommission i henhold til Grundlovens* §45 [The Parliamentary Commission Report], vol. 3a, added entry no. 735.

39. Kieler et al., *En modstandsgruppes historie.*

40. Woldiderich and Hansen, *Københavns Politis Dagsberetninger* 159A.

41. Kieler et al., *En modstandsgruppes historie.*

42. Ibid.

43. Ibid.

44. Ibid.

45. *Beretning til Folketinget afgivet af den af Tinget under 15. juni 1945 nedsatte Kommission i henhold til Grundlovens §45* [The Parliamentary Commission Report], vol. 13a, added entry no. 418.

46. Yahil, *The Rescue of Danish Jewry,* p. 142.

47. Herbert, *Best* (in German), p. 364.

48. *Beretning til Folketinget afgivet af den af Tinget under 15. juni 1945 nedsatte Kommission i henhold til Grundlovens §45* [The Parliamentary Commission Report], vol. 13a, added entry no. 756.

49. Helweg et al., "Famine Disease in German Concentration Camps."

50. Kreth and Mogensen, *Flugten til Sverige.*

51. Friediger, *Theresienstadt.*

52. Ibid.

53. Kieler, *Nordens Lænkehunde.*

54. Kieler et al., *En modstandsgruppes historie*; J. Kieler's statements in Jens Lillelunds privatarkiv (Jens Lillelund's archives), no. 5884, Rigsarkivet (National Archives), Copenhagen.

55. Kieler et al., *En modstandsgruppes historie.*

56. Police report 2–509, *Statsadvokaturen for særlige Anliggender* (Special Department of the Public Prosecutor) archives, Copenhagen.

57. Ibid., 1–340.

58. Ibid., 2–547.

59. Kieler et al., *En modstandsgruppes historie.*

60. Jens Lillelunds privatarkiv (Jens Lillelund's archives), no. 5884, Rigsarkivet (National Archives), Copenhagen.

61. The letter is in Det kongelige Bibliotek (the Royal Danish Library), Copenhagen, in John Fellow Larsen's private archives.

62. Transcript of broadcast taken from Erik Koch Michelsen's (Mix's) report, which he wrote as a refugee in Sweden. Published in Kieler, et al., *En modstandsgruppes historie.*

63. Viggo Hansen's statement in *Historisk Samling fra Besættelsestiden 1940–45* (Historical collection of records from the time of occupation), Esbjerg; Henning Schlanbusch's statement in *Historisk Samling fra Besættelsestiden 1940–45* and no. IV.T.38 A, Rigsarkivet (National Archives), Copenhagen.

64. Police report 20,479, *Statsadvokaturen for særlige Anliggender* (Special Department of the Public Prosecutor) archives, Copenhagen.

65. Erik Koch Michelsen's statement in Jørgen Kielers privatarkiv (Jørgen Kieler's private archives); Kieler et al., *En modstandsgruppes historie.*

66. Ibid.

67. Ibid.

68. Henning Schlanbusch's statement in *Historisk Samling fra Besættelsestiden 1940–45* and no. IV.T.38 A, Rigsarkivet (National Archives), Copenhagen.

69. *Årsskrift for 4. Maj Kollegiet i Åbenrå,* 1968–69.

70. Kieler et al., *En modstandsgruppes historie.*
71. Hanne Møllers diary, Jørgen Kielers privatarkiv (Jørgen Kieler's private archives).
72. Henning Schlanbusch's statement in *Historisk Samling fra Besættelsestiden 1940–45* and no. IV.T.38 A, Rigsarkivet (National Archives), Copenhagen.
73. Viggo Hansen's statement in *Historisk Samling fra Besættelsestiden 1940–45* (Historical collection of records from the time of occupation), Esbjerg.
74. Kieler et al., *En modstandsgruppes historie.*
75. Ibid.
76. Ibid.
77. Ibid.
78. *Beretning til Folketinget afgivet af den af Tinget under 15. juni 1945 nedsatte Kommission i henhold til Grundlovens §45* [The Parliamentary Commission Report], vol. 12.
79. Kieler et al., *En modstandsgruppes historie.*
80. Jørgen Kielers privatarkiv (Jørgen Kieler's private archives); Kieler et al., *En modstandsgruppes historie.*
81. Helweg et al., "Famine Disease in German Concentration Camps."
82. Kieler, "Die Zelluläre Wirkung des Eiweissmangels."
83. Kieler, *Det cellulære aminosyrestofskifte under mitosen.*
84. Kieler, *Hvorfor gjorde I det?* [Why did you do it?]. Original manuscript written shortly after the war located in Jens Lillelund's private archives, Rigsarkivet (National Archives), Copenhagen.
85. Kieler, *Hvorfor gjorde I det?* [Why did you do it?]. The speech was reported in the press; original manuscript in Jørgen Kielers privatarkiv (Jørgen Kieler's private archives).
86. Kieler et al., *En modstandsgruppes historie*; Kieler, *Hvorfor gjorde I det?* [Why did you do it?].
87. Bernadotte, *Sidste Akt.*
88. Helge Juul's statement. Jørgen Kielers privatarkiv (Jørgen Kieler's private archives).
89. Ibid.
90. Bauche et al., *Arbeit und Vernichtung.*
91. Ibid.; Kieler et al., *En modstandsgruppes historie*; Jørgen Kielers privatarkiv (Jørgen Kieler's private archives); Meynert, *Verdrängte Geschichte*; Jørgen Kieler's statements in Jens Lillelunds privatarkiv (Jens Lillelund's archives), no. 5884, Rigsarkivet (National Archives), Copenhagen; Leif Rasmussen's collection of statements, *Rigsarkivets Håndskriftssamling* (Collection of manuscripts), IV.T.54, Rigsarkivet (National Archives), Copenhagen.
92. Moi, *De hvite bussene.*
93. Jørgen Kielers privatarkiv (Jørgen Kieler's private archives).
94. Helweg et al., "Famine Disease in German Concentration Camps."
95. Hermann and Thygesen, "KZ-syndromet."

DENMARK UNDER GERMAN OCCUPATION: 1940–1945

-------- German-Danish Border 1940

■ Concentration Camp
FROSLEV

Kattegat

ALBORG

SWEDEN

JUTLAND

ARHUS

HORSENS

VARDE

DENMARK

ESBJERG

KOLDING   ODENSE   ZEALAND   BARSEBACK

ABENRA   FYN   COPENHAGEN   MALMO

North Sea

SCHLESWIG

PADBORG
■ *FROSLEV*

Belt

Sound

Baltic Sea

Bay of Lübeck

HAMBURG   LÜBECK
■ *NEUENGAMME*

BREMEN   *WESER*   *ELBE*   STETTIN

MINDEN

■ *PORTA WESTPHALICA*   G E R M A N Y   *ODER*

BERLIN

STUDIO GIDEON DAN 02-6520464

0   100   200 Km.